# GCSE

# BRITISH AND EUROPEAN
# HISTORY

Ed Rayner and Ron Stapley

GUIDES

Longman

# LONGMAN REVISE GUIDES

Series editors: Geoff Black and Stuart Wall

TITLES AVAILABLE:
Art and Design
Biology
British and European History
Business Studies
C. D. T. – Design and Realisation
Chemistry
Computer Studies
Economics
English
English Literature
French
Geography
German
Mathematics
Mathematics: Higher Level and Extension
Physics
Religious Studies
Science
Social and Economic History
World History

FORTHCOMING:
C. D. T. – Technology
Commerce
Home Economics
Human Biology
Integrated Humanities
Music
Office Studies and Information Technology

**Longman Group UK Limited,**
*Longman House, Burnt Mill, Harlow,*
*Essex CM20 2JE, England*
*and Associated Companies throughout the world.*

First published 1989

British Library Cataloguing in Publication Data

Rayner, E.G. (Edgar Geoffrey), *1927–*
    GCSE British and European history. –
    (Longman revise guides)
    1. England. Secondary schools. Curriculum subjects: History.
    GCSE examinations.
    Techniques
    I. Title    II. Stapley, R.F. (Ronald Frank), *1927–*
    907'.6

    ISBN 0–582–02504–4

Produced by The Pen and Ink Book Company,
Huntingdon, Cambridgeshire

Set in 10/12pt Century Old Style

Printed and bound in Great Britain by
Wm. Clowes Limited, Beccles, Suffolk

# CONTENTS

# EDITORS' PREFACE

Longman Revise Guides are written by experienced examiners and teachers, and aim to give you the best possible foundation of success in examinations and other modes of assessment. Examiners are well aware that the performance of many candidates falls well short of their true potential, and this series of books aims to remedy this, by encouraging thorough study and a full understanding of the concepts involved. The Revise Guides should be seen as course companions and study aids to be used throughout the year, not just for last minute revision.

Examiners are in no doubt that a structured approach in preparing for examinations and in presenting coursework can, together with hard work and diligent application, substantially improve performance.

The largely self-contained nature of each chapter gives the book a useful degree of flexibility. After starting with the opening general chapters on the background to the GCSE, and the syllabus coverage, all other chapters can be read selectively, in any order appropriate to the stage you have reached in your course.

We believe that this book, and the series as a whole, will help you establish a solid platform of basic knowledge and examination techniques on which to build.

*Geoff Black and Stuart Wall*

# ACKNOWLEDGEMENTS

The authors are indebted to the following Examination Groups for permission to reproduce past examination questions. Whilst permission has been granted to reproduce their questions, the answers, or hints on answers are solely the responsibility of the authors and have not been provided or approved by the Groups. The Groups accept no responsibility whatsoever for the accuracy or method of working in the answers given.

London and East Anglian Group (LEAG)
Southern Examining Group (SEG)
Welsh Joint Examination Committee (WJEC)

# THE GCSE IN HISTORY

# GETTING STARTED

The aim of this book is to help all those studying nineteenth-century British and European history for the General Certificate of Secondary Education. No book can provide instant success. For this it will be essential for all students to devote several hours a week to concentrated study throughout the course. This book will help you to study to the best advantage, but it cannot engage in discussion with you; therefore it is important to follow the guidance of your teacher and to exchange ideas with your fellow students.

If on the other hand you are a private candidate studying for an examination without the benefit of contact with fellow students – even without a teacher – you will find things even more difficult. You will have no one to measure yourself against; you will have to set your own pace, and you will have only books to turn to for guidance. We have therefore written this book in the hope that it will also help you in your task.

## 1 ⟩ GCSE AIMS AND REQUIREMENTS

The introduction of the GCSE in 1988 marked a major change in the examination system. For History there are nationally-agreed aims to which all syllabuses must conform. These aims require History syllabuses to:

- stimulate interest in, and enthusiasm for, the past;
- promote knowledge and understanding of the past and its links with the present;
- link this knowledge to the historical evidence upon which it is based;
- develop skill in locating, handling and understanding historical evidence and its limitations;
- develop understanding of cause and consequence, continuity and change, similarity and difference;
- appreciate the development through time of social and cultural values;
- provide a sound basis for further study and the pursuit of personal interest.

These aims in fact embody what has been the practice of the best History teachers for many years. To achieve these aims you, the student, will need to be able to develop a number of *historical skills* deriving from the aims. Thus all GCSE candidates in History will be required:

a) to *recall* a substantial amount of historical knowledge and to *write it clearly*;
b) to *understand and make use of* the ideas of cause and consequence, continuity and change, similarity and difference;
c) to look at events and problems from the past *in the way that those living at the time* would have looked at them;
d) to show skill in studying historical evidence by *understanding and extracting information* from it; by *interpreting and assessing* it, distinguishing between fact, opinion and judgment, pointing out deficiencies in it as evidence e.g. gaps and inconsistencies, and detecting bias; and by *comparing* various types of evidence, forming conclusions based upon this comparison.

Fig 1.1  Table of GCSE Syllabuses

| | |
|---|---|
| LEAG | A  Modern World History |
| | B  British and European History from the mid-18th century |
| | C  British Economic and Social History |
| | D  Schools Council History Project |
| | Mature:  In course of preparation |
| MEG | Modern World (1914 to the Present) |
| | British & European History (Syll. E: 1789–1914) |
| | British & European History (Syll. F: 1867 to the Present) |
| | British Social and Economic History |
| | Schools Council History Project |
| | Mature:  In course of preparation |
| † NEA | A  Schools Council History Project |
| | B  Modern World History |
| | C  British Social and Economic History since 1750 |
| | Mature:  Chiefly local history and fieldwork |
| SEG | 1  British Social and Economic History since 1750 |
| | 2  World Powers from 1917 |
| | 3  British History, 1485–1714 |
| | 4  British History, 1815–1983 |
| | 5  Britain, Europe and the World, 1848–1980 |
| | Mature:  In course of preparation |
| † NISEC | Modular* |
| † WJEC | Modular* |

\* A modular syllabus arrangement is one that is composed of 'modules' (i.e. components), selections from which have to be studied for the GCSE examination. In the case of the WJEC, one of these modules contains subjects based on British History (Reaction and Reform, 1815–46 and on the Edwardian Age, 1901–12) and another module contains subjects based chiefly on Welsh History and relating to People, Protest and Politics, one in the nineteenth century and one in the twentieth.

† No *specific* syllabus on British and/or European History in the 19th century.

How candidates can develop these skills effectively will be discussed later in this chapter, and, in relation to specified topics, in subsequent chapters. But before you can develop skills a syllabus has to be chosen, and this is likely to be done by your teacher or your school rather than by you. Most of the Boards have syllabuses relating to British, or British and European, History in the nineteenth century, as shown on the list below (Fig 1.1). It should be noted that the parallel Social and Economic History syllabuses deal with rather different subject-matter from that of this book, which is chiefly political.

Two papers are normally required, in which you will be tested in ways that vary between the Boards; but all Boards use *essay questions*, in which extended writing of several paragraphs is required. Essay questions are usually *structured* i.e. divided up into two or more sub-sections. All Boards require you to answer *evidence-based questions*, and all Boards require *coursework*, although the percentage of the total marks allocated to coursework varies between the Boards. Some Boards accept a Paper 3 instead of coursework from external candidates, i.e. those studying on their own and not attending any kind of educational institution. All Boards have special topics with candidate choice, and do not expect you to have covered the whole of the syllabus. These special topics are variously called *Sections* (LEAG), *Themes* or *Topics* (MEG and SEG). MEG has a compulsory core section, and SEG has compulsory themes. Fig 1.2 gives a useful overview of important events under different Sovereigns and Prime Ministers between 1812 and 1916. Many of these 'events' are considered within the various chapters of this book and feature in the syllabuses of the Exam Groups.

Fig 1.2 A Chronology of important events.

| SOVE-REIGN | PRIME MINISTER. | GREAT BRITAIN. | DATES | OTHER POWERS. | DATES |
|---|---|---|---|---|---|
| George III (1760–1820) | 1812–27 LIVERPOOL. | Battle of Waterloo; Lord Hastings in India, 1814–23. | 1815 | Treaty of Paris; Louis XVIII King of France. | 1815 |
| | | | | Congress of Aix-la-Chapelle. | 1818 |
| | | "Six Acts"; "Peterloo"; first steamship crosses Atlantic. | 1819 | Revolution in Spain and Naples; Congress of Troppau. | 1820 |
| George IV (1820–1830) | | Liverpool's Ministry re-constructed; Death of Castlereagh | 1822 | Death of Napoleon I; Congress of Laibach. Congress of Verona. | 1821 1822 |
| | | Stockton-Darlington Railway opened. | 1825 | Charles X becomes King of France. Nicholas becomes Czar. | 1824 1825 |
| | CANNING. GODERICH. WELLINGTON. | Battle of Navarino; Death of Canning. | 1827 | WAR OF GREEK INDEPENDENCE. | |
| | | Test and Corporation Acts repealed. | 1828 | | |
| | | Catholic Emancipation Act; Metropolitan Police Force founded. | 1829 | Treaty of Adrianople. | 1829 |
| | | Manchester and Liverpool Railway opened. | 1830 | Revolutions in France and Belgium; Louis Philippe King of the French. | 1830 |
| William IV (1830–1837) | GREY. | First Reform Bill | 1832 | * | |
| | | Abolition of Slavery in British dominions; Factory Act. | 1833 | | |
| | | Reform of Poor Law. | 1834 | | |
| | MELBOURNE. PEEL. | Municipal Reform Act. | 1835 | | |
| | | South Australia Colonized; the "Great Trek". | 1836 | | |
| | | Rebellion in Canada. | 1837 | | |
| Queen Victoria (1837–1901) | MELBOURNE. | Lord Durham sent to Canada; *Great Western* crosses Atlantic. | 1838 | | |
| | | "Bedchamber" question. | 1839 | Belgian Neutrality guaranteed. | 1839 |
| | | New Zealand annexed; Penny Postage introduced. | 1840 | Alliance against Mehemet Ali. | 1840 |
| | | Chinese cede Hong-Kong. | 1841 | | |
| | 1841–46 PEEL. | Mines Act. | 1842 | | |
| | | Second Factory Act. | 1843 | | |
| | | Irish Famine. | 1844 | | |
| | | Repeal of Corn Laws. | 1845 | | |
| | | | 1846 | Spanish Marriage Question. | 1846 |
| | 1846–52 LORD JOHN RUSSELL. | Chartist Riots; Dalhousie Gov.-Gen. of India (till 1856); Anaesthetics introduced. | 1848 | The Year of Revolutions. | 1848 |
| | | The Great Exhibition. | 1851 | Louis Napoleon's *coup d'état*. | 1851 |
| | DERBY | Sand River Convention. | 1852 | Louis Napoleon becomes Emperor Napoleon III. | 1852 |
| | ABERDEEN. | Battles of Alma, Balaclava, Inkerman. | CRIMEAN 1854 | WAR. | |
| | | Fall of Sebastopol. | 1855 | Alexander II becomes Czar. | 1855 |
| | | Peace of Paris | 1856 | | |
| | PALMERSTON. | Second Chinese War. | INDIAN 1857 | | |
| | | East India Company abolished. | MUTINY. 1858 | | |
| | DERBY. | | | War of Italian Unity (1859–61); Battles of Magenta and Solferino. | |
| | | Darwin's *Origin of Species*. | 1859 | | 1859 |
| | | Maori War. | 1860 | | |
| | PALMERSTON. | Death of Prince Consort; the *Alabama* incident. | 1861 | | |
| | | | | AMERICAN CIVIL WAR. Bismarck becomes Chief Minister in Prussia. | 1862 |
| | | | | War between Prussia and Denmark. | 1864 |

| Monarch | PM | British Events | Year | Foreign Events | Year |
|---|---|---|---|---|---|
| Queen Victoria (1837–1901) | RUSSELL. DERBY. DISRAELI. | | 1865 | | |
| | | | | Austro-Prussian War. | 1866 |
| | 1868–74 GLADSTONE. | Dominion of Canada formed; Second reform Bill. | 1867 | | |
| | | Irish Church Disestablished. | 1868 | | |
| | | First Irish Land Act; Education Act. | 1869 | Opening of Suez Canal. | 1869 |
| | | Universities opened to Non-conformists; Trade Union Act. | 1870 | Franco-Prussian War (1870–71); Republic in France; | 1870 |
| | | Ballot Act. | 1871 | Formation of Empire of Germany. | 1871 |
| | | | 1872 | | |
| | 1874–80 DISRAELI. | Suez Canal shares purchased. | 1876 | The Bulgarian Atrocities. | 1876 |
| | | Queen becomes Empress of India. | 1877 | Russo-Turkish War. | 1877 |
| | | Zulu War; Dual Control in Egypt. | 1878 | Treaty of San Stefano; Treaty of Berlin. | 1878 |
| | | | 1879 | | |
| | 1880–5 GLADSTONE. | First Boer War; Battle of Majuba. | 1881 | Alexander III becomes Czar. | 1881 |
| | | Bombardment of Alexandria; Battle of Tel-el-Kebir. | 1882 | | |
| | | Third Reform Bill. | 1884 | The "Grab for Africa" begins. | 1884 |
| | | Fall of Khartoum. | 1885 | | |
| | SALISBURY. GLADSTONE. | First Home Rule Bill. | 1886 | | |
| | | Local Government Act. | 1887 | | |
| | | | 1888 | William II German Emperor. | 1888 |
| | 1886–92 SALISBURY. | | | Fall of Bismarck. | 1890 |
| | 1892–94 GLADSTONE. | 2nd Home Rule Bill. | 1893 | | |
| | | | | Nicholas II becomes Czar. | 1894 |
| | 1894–95 ROSEBERRY. | Jameson Raid. | 1895 | | |
| | 1895–1902 SALISBURY. | | | War between Turkey and Greece. | 1897 |
| | | Re-conquest of Sudan; Battle of Omdurman. | 1898 | | |
| | | | 1899 | Peace Conference at the Hague. | 1899 |
| | | | 1900 | | |
| | | Federation of Australia. | 1901 | SOUTH AFRICAN WAR. | |
| | | Treaty of Vereeniging. | 1902 | | |
| Edward VII (1901–1910) | 1902–05 BALFOUR. | Anglo-French Agreement. | 1904 | Russo-Japanese War, 1904–05. | 1904 |
| | | Anglo-Japanese Treaty. | 1905 | | |
| | 1905–08 CAMPBELL-BANNERMAN. | Anglo-Russian Convention. | 1907 | | |
| | | South Africa Act; Indian Councils Act; Union of South Africa. | 1909 | | |
| George V (1910–1936) | 1908–16 ASQUITH. | | | Portugal becomes Republic. | 1910 |
| | | Parliament Act: National Health Insurance Act. | 1911 | War between Turkey and Italy. | 1911 |
| | | 3rd Home Rule Bill. | 1912 | First Balkan War. | 1912 |
| | | | | Second Balkan War. | 1913 |
| | | | | Assassination of Archduke Francis Ferdinand. | |
| | | Britain declares War on Germany. | 1914 | Germany declares War on Russia and France. | 1914 |

## 2 ▶ PREPARING FOR THE EXAMINATION

Good preparation is absolutely essential to examination technique. As the examination is skills-based, the emphasis will be on analysis and judgment. But it would be a mistake to think that you can discuss and analyse History without knowing any. First you must *learn what happened*, and only then can you begin to tackle the basic questions of *how* and *why* it happened. No actor or musician would dare perform in public without adequate rehearsal; similarly no student can perform well in a public examination without adequate preparation. The commonest cause of examination nerves is going into the examination room knowing that you are ill-equipped to tackle the examination paper.

To help your preparation, each of the requirements demanded of GCSE History candidates, as listed earlier in this chapter, will now be dealt with in turn.

## 3 ▶ ACQUIRING HISTORICAL KNOWLEDGE

*"Note-taking and knowledge."*

When you embark upon your course, you will need a good textbook, a strong file for your notes, access to a good library and a firm commitment to study. If your teacher gives you class notes, try to learn them as soon as possible afterwards whilst the teacher's explanation is fresh in your mind. Supplement the teacher's notes with additional material from your reading. If, as is more probable, you make your own notes under guidance, develop a good **note-making technique**: use headings, sub-headings, abbreviations. Make sure that you list all the main points, rather than developing only one or two of them in unnecessary detail. Memorable events should be listed rather than described. If, when you revise, a note makes no sense, then you should refresh your memory of it by looking it up in the textbook. But if you have developed a good note-taking technique the incomprehensible note should be comparatively rare. Your notes will be the main source-base for the factual knowledge required in the examination. Only a genius can afford to dispense with note-making and note-learning.

You should also take care not to generate too much in the way of note-material, especially not multiple accounts of the same event as presented by a number of textbooks. Remember that the more care you take in the making of your notes, the more time and trouble you will save yourself when you come to use them. If pencilled in an illegible scrawl they will be a distraction and an annoyance. Likewise it is no good supposing that by carrying your notes about tucked under your arm, you will somehow absorb them. You will have to try to learn them. Each time you go through them, you make subsequent revisions quicker and easier, until at your final revision you can get through them very rapidly indeed.

When you have mastered a considerable body of factual historical information you will be able to develop all the historical skills required. Without historical knowledge, it will be like trying to make bricks without straw.

## 4 HISTORICAL SOURCES

> You use historical materials.

All the GCSE History syllabuses require the study of historical sources, and set questions based upon **source material**. The sources used are most often written ones: newspapers, letters, reports, diaries etc. But there are also maps and cartoons, and from the late nineteenth century onwards an increasingly plentiful supply of photographs. Sources that originate from the time of the event or issue with which they are linked are referred to as **primary sources**: often the writer will have been an eye-witness of the events he describes. Sources written at a significantly later date – and this is true of all History textbooks – are based upon these primary sources, but because they are at one remove from reality are referred to as **secondary sources**. Sometimes the classification is not quite so clear-cut. For example, newspapers are contemporary secondary sources, since they are based upon reports by those who may not have been eye-witnesses. All the same, they are often regarded as primary sources, since they give the contemporary view of the event as it happened, and do not have the benefit of hindsight.

In all source work careful study of the source is essential. The basic skill required is to select evidence from sources, and this usually means finding the *relevant* evidence and expressing it accurately in your own words. Examples of this are to be found in worked evidence questions in this book.

Students will also have to compare evidence sources for *reliability*: remember that what a source *omits* can be as important for judging reliability as what a source *includes*. For example, if two sources deal with a riot, it will be very significant if one source states that the police were provoked by taunts and stone-throwing, whilst the other refers to the taunts and omits the stone-throwing. If indeed there was stone-throwing, it looks by the omission as if the second source is trying to show the police action in a bad light by deliberately playing down the provocation. Or perhaps the first source invented the stone-throwing in order to bolster the excuse for police intervention.

You will also be required to recognize and identify *bias* or *prejudice* in sources: this requires practice, and can often lead to any expression of opinion being denounced as bias; but real bias arises from the deliberate or unconscious expression of some view of the author without any attempt to justify its use in the extract by reasoned argument. In the following extract from a nineteenth-century autobiography, the author, William Lovett, makes a mention of Peterloo:

> When Henry Hunt first stood forward as the champion of reform, it needed a man of his nerve and moral daring to face the formidable phalanx of corruption everywhere allied against everyone who presumed to talk of the rights of man. But he went nobly onward with his works appealing to the good sense and sound feeling of the people, being deterred not by the sabres of Peterloo, nor by threats, sneers, nor imprisonment, till he finally obtained the verdict of his country against the corruptions he assailed.

Historians should note the use of sweeping generalizations ('corruption *everywhere* allied against *everyone*'), of emotive terms (with *plus* terms such as 'nerve and moral daring', and with *minus* terms such as 'formidable phalanx of corruption'), and the use of phrases which prejudge the moral issues involved ('nobly onward' and 'good sense and sound feeling'). There is no doubt what the author feels; but, however admirable his sentiments may be, it has to be said that he makes no effort to justify his opinion, but assumes that his truths are self-evident.

You may be asked in this examination to distinguish between fact and opinion in passages like these, or to look for bias in them. When documents have a bias, or show bias, they are said *to be biased*. To be biased is the equivalent verb. Students often get this wrong. The same is true of the word *prejudice*: things show prejudice or are said *to be prejudiced*. Once you are able to detect bias or prejudice, you will be able to point out how it is achieved: by the choice of words, by exaggeration, by over-simplification, by the use of insinuation, or by statements that go only part of the way to the truth.

Evidence questions usually require the studying of more than one source. Single sources do not provide opportunities for comparative work. In cases where single sources are used, they may be used as a trigger for factual recall. Where sources are to be used as *evidence* rather than *stimulus*, they are usually followed by a series of sub-questions which begin by identifying the evidence contained in the sources, and then continue with more searching sub-questions dealing with comparison of the content, the value of the sources and their reliability, and possibly leading on to an assessment of bias where it occurs.

## 5 ▷ HISTORICAL INTERPRETATION

❝❝ GCSE requires you to demonstrate your skills. ❞❞

Once you have acquired a basic mastery of what happened (i.e. the facts) you should be in a position to consider causes and consequences. Here you begin to move away from the facts pure and simple into an area where ideas and arguments differ; and although you may well have lists of causes in your notes, the best way to develop the analytical skills required is through the prepared essay, where arguments based on evidence can be brought together and presented in as convincing a manner as possible. Effective essay writing will lead naturally to effective coursework, which for most Boards takes the form of extended prepared essays.

### CAUSE AND CONSEQUENCE

Essay writing gives scope not only for differing opinions but also for different emphases. In a question, for example, on the **causes** of the First World War, some students will lay great stress on the colonial and naval rivalries between Britain and Germany, holding this to be the primary cause, whilst others will lay the main blame on conflicting nationalisms, especially in the Balkans. Excellent answers, of course, should refer to both sets of causes, attempting to strike a balance between them; but answers of similar merit may well be different in emphasis and approach. The thing to remember is that in a matter of judgment of this sort, and unlike Mathematics, there can be no categorically correct answer universally preferred to all other 'wrong' answers.

If you do make a list of causes to learn like facts, you should make sure that you understand them sufficiently to handle them flexibly in reply to an examination question. If you were asked to

> Discuss the view that the Chartist movement was prompted as much by economic grievances as it was by political grievances.

you would find a list of memorized causes no more than a starting-point for developing an effective answer to the question, in which you would need to analyse the *relative* importance of the various causes of the movement if you were to produce a directly relevant answer. What you should not do is to trot out your list of causes, and leave the examiner to answer the question for himself.

In the respect that *causes* are not clearly-identifiable objects like chemical compounds, History is not a science. Scientific causes conform to stated and proven physical laws, but historians' causes do not. They represent instead an analysis and an evaluation based on experience. Even at GCSE level it is absurd to claim that there were twelve main causes of the First World War; someone else, by grouping them under different headings, might say there were only two, but these nevertheless might be more convincing.

**Consequences**, too, can be very much a matter of dispute. Some consequences may well be more important than others, and, as with causes, it is important to distinguish between those that were short-term and those that were long-term. A short-term consequence of the passing of the 1832 Reform Act was a series of Whig governments in the course of the 1830s; but the long-term consequences might well be taken to include a decisive shift in the balance of political power in the country in favour of the House of Commons. Those who date the decline in the power of the landed aristocracy from 1832 are taking the 'long' view, whilst those who point to the replacement of Grey by Melbourne are taking the 'short' view. The perception of these consequences depends on the historian's point of view, according to his time and place; they change as his perception changes. Remember, therefore, that no historical verdict is ever final, and that many of those you presently accept will be revised before you are much older. In the same way, in GCSE, the answer to the question

> How do you explain the deterioration in Anglo-Irish relations in the twenty years before 1914?

must vary according to the viewpoint of the historian, and would certainly be answered differently by an Englishman and an Irishman.

## CHANGE AND CONTINUITY

Historians are always interested in the ideas of change and continuity. Revolutions, such as that of 1830 in France, are episodes of concentrated **change** and are easy to identify; but change is often slower and less noticeable. Thus, social change is generally undramatic, but fairly continuous. The same may even be true of political change. It could even be argued that the political revolutions which took place in France in 1830, 1848, 1852 and 1870, though apparently spectacular, were less important than the steady advance that took place in Britain during the same years in the direction of parliamentary democracy, without any revolution at all. These differing views about revolution show that the idea of revolution to a historian is not capable of a single, clear-cut definition. Like causation, it is all a matter of opinion and argument.

While there is change, there is also **continuity**, and a historian will want to trace this continuity. Most modern problems have their origins in the past, and as a student you ought to be very much aware of this in your work. The problems, attitudes and even vocabulary of the trade unions are very much related to their recent history, which in turn reflects the history of the movement in the nineteenth century; just as the problems of Northern Ireland are rooted in the past history of the Irish Question. You will be able to name many more. Moreover, continuity is not merely a characteristic of problem areas and trouble spots. The steady and undramatic continuity, for instance, of social stability in Britain in the first ten years of the twentieth century was a background feature very easy to overlook, and one that only became obvious when it was violently disrupted by factors such as the militant suffragettes.

## SIMILARITY AND DIFFERENCE

You will notice that the last sentence contains a contrast, and that contrasts involve a comparison between one set of circumstances and another. In GCSE, you will be frequently expected to make such *comparisons* – to show, for example, the **similarities** in attitudes towards political issues of Gladstone and Disraeli, and the **differences** in their achievements in their various periods of office. Or to compare the different attitudes of the republicans, the monarchists and the supporters of Papal leadership towards the problem of Italian unification.

## BALANCED JUDGMENTS

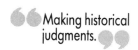

*Making historical judgments.*

The ability to deal with all these aspects of historical interpretation is a skill which will be tested in the examination. It is important, therefore, not to see History as a sequence of isolated facts without rhyme or reason, which have to be memorized parrot-fashion. Once you move from the facts to discussion it is important to make qualified and **balanced judgments**, and not sweeping generalizations. Choose your words with care. A statement such as 'successive governments by the Conservatives during the twenty years before 1906 brought nothing but stagnation to Britain' is as superficial and one-sided as any of the biased evidence given earlier in this chapter. You ought undoubtedly to find things to say in the Conservatives' favour, even if your final verdict is one of qualified disapproval. The words 'always', 'never', 'nothing' are words you ought to be wary of. Things are seldom as clear as they seem, and simple unqualified statements such as 'Cecil Rhodes was a great hero and President Kruger a great villain' show some shallowness in historical thinking. You must train yourself to make more informed judgments than these.

## 6 ▶ EMPATHY

It has already been explained that one historical skill required of you is to see past events and problems as they appeared to people living at the time. You will be tested in the examination by being asked to put yourself into a specific historical situation, and to write about it. The form of your answer will be specified, e.g. an extract from a diary, a

❝❝Empathy means a feeling for the past.❞❞

newspaper report, a letter, or whatever seems appropriate to the circumstances. To answer such a question properly, you are going to require two chief ingredients: *information* and *colour*. An answer that is imaginative and creative, painting a vivid picture of the scene it is intended to portray, but which lacks adequate supporting information, will score little or nothing for its historical strengths. An answer that is no more than a recital of the relevant historical facts, but which has clearly no feel for atmosphere, personality or circumstantial detail, will get some credit for its historical accuracy but score little for its empathy. When you provide this colour, beware of *anachronisms*, i.e. of pushing modern developments too far back in time; e.g. 'Detailed aerial photographs of the terrain enabled me to put forward to Graf von Schlieffen the main essentials of his famous Plan.' Errors such as these destroy the credibility of the rest of the answer.

The examiners will be looking for a real understanding of the past, and a skill in thinking yourself into the situation required. This is what is meant by **empathy**. At the lowest level you will be expected to recognize that people in the past had views of their own, as do those of the present. Further you should be able to see how the views of the people of the past related to the historical problems of their day. But the highest achievement will be by those who see that opinions differed amongst those of previous generations, and these differing opinions should be reflected in the empathetic answers that you write. Practice in this type of answer is essential. The following example should give you an idea of what you need to do:

Write a letter which you hope to smuggle out of Khartoum to your friends in England, describing your feelings now that General Gordon has been cut off from the outside world by the Mahdi and besieged in the city with his army.

The first answer tries to conjure up some empathy.

Dear Wayne,
I don't know how much longer I can stand it here. Living conditions have become very bad. We have been surrounded by savage cannibals who are attacking us from every side. The heat is stifling and we are all short of food and water. Now that the natives have broken through the last of our defences, I regret to have to inform you that Gordon and the whole of the garrison has been ruthlessly put to the sword.
Yours affectionately,
Harry

There is a little merit here: the letter-writer obviously has some idea of the climatic conditions in the Sudan, and knows that a garrison under siege is likely to be short of food and water. But his letter is undated, and in 1885 in fact he is unlikely to have been writing to anyone by the name of Wayne. He would also have known that the native forces supporting the Mahdi were fanatical Moslems, but certainly not cannibals. Finally, of course, if he had been put to death along with the rest of the garrison, he would not have been in a position to report General Gordon's death.

Now consider another effort.

British Military Headquarters,
Khartoum,
October 3rd, 1884.

Dear Ernest,
I am writing this to you in the hope that a fast rider may get it through to Graham and his troops on the Red Sea coast at Suakim, though after the fall of Berber at the end of May our communications down the Nile and eastwards to the sea have been cripplingly curtailed.

If you do get my letter I hope you will send it to the newspapers, especially those critical of the Prime Minister, and use it also with Harcourt and Lord Selborne so as to influence discussions in cabinet. We all know that Gladstone can be very stubborn, but surely our critical situation here in the Sudan must take precedence over the trivial details of the forthcoming Reform Bill?

I have heard that British opinion has been upset by General Gordon's recent recommendation of Zobeir Pasha as Governor-General because at one time he was a slave-dealer, but you must understand that he has long put that behind him. How absurd it is that Parliament and the Government should be so keen to send the General here, and then refuse his requests and deny him the support that could be our salvation!

We are already desperately short of supplies, and though morale is high amongst

British troops, the Egyptian gendarmerie are looking to save their own skins. It is ironic that though they have most to gain by the re-establishment of legal rule, some of them are openly critical of the General for refusing to evacuate. I'd cut off their rations altogether if I were him. We are down to iron rations now, and limited to three slimy wells inside the compound unless we take the risk of drinking river water. Even powder and shot are low. It's a good job we have some of the Lancers with us!

For Heaven's sake, make haste and send to us! If you leave things further into the autumn, we may well be finished by then. God bless you all! Long live the Queen!
Yours in haste,
Harry.

At least this answer is longer, and it has a number of points of historical reference: the name of the Prime Minister, Gladstone, and various members of his cabinet, such as Sir William Harcourt and Lord Selborne; various geographical references such as those to Suakim and Berber; mentions of Sir Gerald Graham and Zobeir Pasha; an indication that Gladstone was preoccupied with other matters and reluctant to send out reinforcements to the Sudan as his critics said he ought to have done, and so on. These facts, and the address and date at the head of the letter leave no doubt that this is about the disastrous siege at Khartoum of 1884–85. The letter bears some traces (British morale and Egyptian cowardice) of racism, a not untypical sign of the times. Of particular value is the indication that people in authority both in Britain and in the Sudan had very *different* views of what ought to be done about the problem. To refer near the end of the letter to 'powder and shot' so late in the nineteenth century when both rifles and artillery were of a more advanced design is perhaps a weakness; but even here the phrase is one that had entered into the language and might well have been used even though technically inappropriate. The note of suppressed hysteria in the last paragraph of the letter nicely indicates the anxieties of the writer.

Note also that both answers are offered in *letter* form, as requested; marks can be lost, for example, if a speech is asked for and the offering you make sounds more like a newspaper report. A newspaper article or editorial should be recognizable as such, and a diary should be in diary form and have dated entries. A cabinet memorandum needs appropriate language; it ought to avoid the mistake of one candidate whose memorandum from civil servant to minister began: 'Well, you certainly made a muck of it this time, Arthur.'

In the answers given above, you will see that the letters were both written as required in the *first person*. The use of the first person (I, we) does not necessarily strengthen the empathy, nor does its absence weaken it; but of course it has to be used in a letter. As a general guide, use the first person if the question invites you to do so, or if it seems the natural thing to do. But *third-person* empathy (he, she, they) is perfectly acceptable.

In nineteenth-century work you could be given a picture or a cartoon, or even an early photograph, and asked to think yourself into the situation of those shown in it. For example, a photograph showing soldiers in battle, or a picture portraying the denizens of the London slums, may be accompanied with the request to describe these people's feelings and their experiences, and here *information* and *colour* will be required. Whether or not you use the first person will depend on whether the question says 'Imagine you are . . .' or 'What would have been the feelings or the experiences of such a group of . . .'. A request like this should not be hard to follow if you are well-informed, understand the circumstances of the illustration, and can bring to your answer a combination of *historical knowledge* and *historical imagination*, the two key requirements in all empathetic work. But to use any illustration profitably you have to study it carefully, and to make use of the details in it. A quick glance is not enough.

## 7 > COURSEWORK

All worthwhile History courses involve **coursework**: the writing of notes and essays, the preparation of projects, and so on. But for the GCSE certain items of coursework will be required *as part of the examination*, and will carry a minimum of 20% of the mark allocation for the whole examination. In practice, 30% of the marks are allocated to coursework by the majority of Boards.

As your teacher will have chosen the syllabus and will be monitoring and assessing your coursework, you will need to rely heavily on their guidance in choosing and planning the work that you are going to do. (For external candidates who have no teacher, there is at least one Board [LEAG] which puts forward a Paper 3 [for External Candidates] instead of the coursework requirement – this paper tests the same things as would have been tested in coursework). The coursework required will normally be in written form, but may be supplemented with drawings, maps, photographs or even tape recordings. Maps, diaries, letters, extracts from imaginary newspapers could be asked for; even ordinary essay work might be acceptable. Most written work will need to be at least 1200 words long, and in some cases 2000 words or even more, so that it will normally take the form of an extended essay or project for investigating some historical issue or problem. It is not intended to offer you the opportunity to write a rather lengthy narrative.

> **Coursework is an important feature of this examination.**

At least two pieces of coursework are asked for by most Boards – sometimes three or four. The problems to be looked at in the coursework may be chosen from a specific list, but for some Boards the teacher or the student selects their own coursework titles from a broad subject area. In such a case, you should have a specific problem to investigate e.g. 'Was it a mistake for Britain to embark on the Crimean War, 1854–56?', rather than just 'The Crimean War, 1854–56' which could well lead to narrative rather than to problem analysis. Your choice will in part be determined by what interests you, and what material you have available. Be particularly careful if you have a local history option not to become involved in the over-specialized and not to descend to the trivial. 'The History of Bloggsville Football Club, 1887–1987' may well end up with more football in it than history, and candidates may be disappointed to realize that several pages of photographs of successive Bloggsville teams will *not* impress the examiners. It may well be that a study of the origins and growth of the footwear industry in Bloggsville in the nineteenth century would be a better subject to choose, or the development of the town's schools. It should be noted at the same time that it is not so much the subject-matter of a project which makes it unsuitable as the manner in which it is investigated. In other words, the development of a local football club is a legitimate area of study, provided that it is studied in a historical way, and is not simply a scrapbook put together by a local fan. Certainly local issues will give you a variety of primary sources to choose from, whilst major national and international issues will necessarily be researched from secondary sources.

Remember to discuss your choice of topic with your teacher, together with the sources you propose to consult. But do not expect precise guidance on *what* to write or *how* to write it, because the coursework will have to be certified as *your own* work and not that of anyone else – particularly your teacher. It follows too that coursework should not be lifted in chunks straight from your sources. There is little value in copying out paragraphs from a variety of books, stitching them together with a few phrases of introduction and then pretending that the work is all your own. You will be expected to show skills of arrangement, analysis, assessment and argument, and you cannot do this if you simply copy out what others have written. So your various pieces of coursework will need to be well planned in advance. They will need to be of approximately the length asked for (too wide a variation could cost you a proportion of the marks). Above all, they will need to identify and investigate a clear historical problem and offer conclusions.

Depending on the nature of the coursework set, a useful *coursework method* would be:

1   Choose and discuss the title.
2   Make a list of, and collect, the available resources.
3   Unless the theme is too specialized, read up the subject-matter in your textbook(s) and make notes, so that you have a general idea of the topic.
4   In the light of the material studied, refine and modify your title so that you can be sure that your information will enable you to deal adequately with it.
5   Start tracking your selected subject in the sources; make notes and cross-references. Be sure that you note the place where you found your material: nothing is more annoying than being unable to retrace the origin of information at a later date. Select a limited number of useful short extracts for quotation in your work (if this is appropriate).
6   Select suitable visual and statistical material, if available and if relevant.
7   Read through the collected material, plan its arrangement (including visual etc.) in a way that will help you develop your argument. Check that your conclusions are sensible.
8   Prepare a synopsis; write your first rough draft and develop your final polished version from it.

>  **Don't neglect or postpone your coursework.**

Remember that the work should be **neatly presented**, with a table of contents, and that it should be written in as effective a style as you can manage. As your coursework carries a considerable proportion of the marks, you must expect to spend a lot of time on it. Do not postpone starting the work until the closing date has almost arrived. Remember that inadequately-prepared or hastily-written coursework could well cost you a grade or even two grades in the final assessment.

## 8 > ASSESSMENT

As your grade will depend on what the examiners think of your examination work and what your teacher thinks of your coursework, it is useful for you to have an idea of what these people expect of you.

Any written answer developed beyond a word or so will be rewarded at different levels according to the skills content of the answer. Let us take an example. It is from a specimen paper issued by the Southern Examining Group (SEG).

a) Why was Disraeli interested in the Eastern Question?
b) What actions did Disraeli take over the Eastern Question between 1876 and 1879?
c) How successful was Disraeli in attempting to solve the Eastern Question?

This is a three-part essay marked out of 30. Let us take the final part. Here you are obviously being asked to exercise the skills of historical analysis and assessment, and not merely give a narrative account of what Disraeli did (you should have dealt with his actions already under part b). It will be of little extra value to select a few judgments about Disraeli at random from what you know, or to give the details of developments in the Eastern Question after 1879 in the hope that something of relevance will emerge by accident. If all you can do is to trace developments later than 1879, then the Mark Scheme will assess you at *Level one*.

**Level 1: Narrative.** Candidates relate a number of events connected with Disraeli's policy, but make no explicit judgment of him. For example: Disraeli sent Indian troops to Malta, and he took control of Cyprus at the Congress of Berlin. He tried to protect Turkey from Russia.

Such an answer will earn you from 1 mark to 3 marks, because your answer is chiefly factual and unfocused. If you can manage to include some kind of **assessment**, however, you rise to *Level two*.

**Level 2: Answers supported by generalized recall.** Candidates make a judgment about Disraeli and support it with a general account of his Eastern policy. For example: Disraeli succeeded in limiting Turkish problems. At the Congress of Berlin he used Austrian support and threats of force to reduce Russian advances.

This will earn you from 4 to 7 marks, but for *Level three* you need to provide an answer which reveals 'great familiarity with the material' and which 'supports the answer with precise detail.' You will also need to say that though he stressed British power e.g. by sending Indian troops to Malta, serious problems still remained for solution in later years, so that overall his achievement was a limited one. Such an answer will score from 8 to 10 marks.

All marking, including coursework, is to be done using these *levels of achievement*, within which marks will vary according to the amount of historical content. Your grade will be determined by the level you have reached in:

a) acquiring historical knowledge and being able to communicate it;
b) finding and making use of historical evidence, and
c) developing and making use of powers of historical reasoning i.e. using knowledge and evidence to analyse and make judgments about historical problems.

Demonstrated ability in all these will earn you a high grade.

But even if you are well-equipped with historical skills, marks can be lost through carelessness. If your skills are not as strong as they might be marks could be saved by careful attention during the examination to the following points:

*Don't forget these important points in your work.*

1 Make sure that you know what you have to do. That is, how many questions you have to answer, which parts are compulsory, and which questions cover the sections for which you have been specifically prepared.

2 Read the questions, and the source material, carefully. Make sure that you have properly understood the question *before* attempting it, that you know how many parts it contains if it is structured, and what is required in each part.

3 If the marks for a part-question are given on the examination paper, use this as a guide for how much you should write. If only 1 mark is on offer, a one-word, or one-phrase,

answer will be adequate. Anything more would be a waste of time. If 8 marks are offered, you will need to make a number of points and to develop the answer into a useful paragraph to gain maximum marks.

4  Plan your time carefully. Do not waste time on one question so that you run out of time on another. Make sure that you answer all the required questions within the examination time limit.

5  If you need to make plans for the longer answers, make them brief, just listing the points you intend to develop in your answer. If a plan is as long as the answer it is prepared for, you will find that either your answers are too brief or that you have been repeating yourself and may run out of time before you have finished the paper.

6  Remember that it is unlikely that questions will call for a lengthy narrative. Skills other than merely recalling and recounting historical information are almost certain to be required, and the more skills you demonstrate, the higher your grade is likely to be.

One final word of warning. Do not be hoodwinked by such phrases as 'merely recalling and recounting historical information' into thinking that this is the least important attribute for a student of GCSE History. No one should attempt to dismiss 'historical information' too lightly. It is the essential material on which all historical skills are practised.

## 9 > HOW TO USE THIS GUIDE

**❝Historical Developments.❞**

This guide is not intended as a substitute for a textbook. You should use it to supplement the work done, either in class under teacher guidance, or from your own reading of books. It will help you develop your skill in writing by practising the questions – of whatever type – and will provide you with a useful basis for revising for the GCSE examination itself.

Each chapter is arranged in a similar way. The sections 'Getting Started' and 'Historical Developments' give you a brief summary of the main narrative points of the topic to be studied, and also tackle issues of cause and consequence. You should explore and develop the points given here in conjunction with your notes and textbooks. The section 'Ideas and Principles' will deal with ideas, problems and vocabulary associated with the topic. 'Applied Materials' will list useful sources from which you should be able to make a selection according to what is available in your school or public library.

'Examination Questions' gives a selection of questions of different types, the answers to some of which are discussed in outline, whilst another is given in some cases in full as a 'Tutor's Answer' to serve as a model. In most cases a 'Student's Answer' indicates some of the strengths and weaknesses of answers given by typical candidates.

The chapters include brief suggestions for 'Further Work', if you feel that you need more practice in mastering the material and further developing the necessary skills.

# ADDRESSES OF THE EXAMINING BOARDS

## London and East Anglian Group (LEAG)

*London*  University of London School Examinations Board
Stewart House, 32 Russell Square, London WC1B 5DN

*LREB*  London Regional Examining Board
Lyon House, 104 Wandsworth High Street, London SW18 4LF

*EAEB*  East Anglian Examinations Board
'The Lindens', Lexden Road, Colchester, Essex CO3 3RL

## Midland Examining Group (MEG)

*Cambridge*  University of Cambridge Local Examinations Syndicate
Syndicate Buildings, 1 Hills Road, Cambridge CB1 2EU

*O and C*  Oxford and Cambridge School Examinations Board
10 Trumpington Street, Cambridge, and Elsfield Way, Oxford OX2 8EP

*SUJB*  Southern Universities' Joint Board for School Examinations
Cotham Road, Bristol BS6 6DD

*WMEB*  The West Midlands Examinations Board
Norfolk House, Smallbrook Queensway, Birmingham B5 4NJ

*EMREB*  East Midland Regional Examining Board
Robins Wood House, Robins Wood Road, Aspley, Nottingham NG8 3NH

## Northern Examination Association (NEA)

*JMB*  Joint Matriculation Board
Devas Street, Manchester M15 6EU

*ALSEB*  Associated Lancashire Schools Examining Board
12 Harter Street, Manchester M1 6HL

*NREB*  North Regional Examinations Board
Wheatfield Road, Westerhope, Newcastle upon Tyne NE5 5JZ

*NWREB*  North West Regional Examinations Board
Orbit House, Albert Street, Eccles, Manchester M30 0WL

*YHREB*  Yorkshire and Humberside Regional Examinations Boards
Harrogate: 31–33 Springfield Avenue, Harrogate HG1 2HW
Sheffield: Scarsdale House, 136 Derbyshire Lane, Sheffield S8 8SE

## Northern Ireland

*NISEC*  Northern Ireland School Examinations Council
Beechill House, 42 Beechill Road, Belfast BT8 4RS

## Scotland

*SEB*  Scottish Examinations Board
Ironmills Road, Dalkeith, Midlothian EH22 1BR

## Southern Examining Group (SEG)

*AEB*  The Associated Examining Board
Stag Hill House, Guildford, Surrey GU2 5XJ

*OLE*  The Oxford Delegacy of Local Examinations
Ewert Place, Summertown, Oxford OX2 7BZ

*SREB*  The Southern Regional Examinations Board
Avondale House, 33 Carlton Crescent, Southampton SO9 4YL

*SEREB*  The South-East Regional Examinations Board
Beloe House, 2–10 Mount Ephraim Road, Royal Tunbridge Wells TN1 1EU

*SWEB*  The South Western Examinations Board
23–29 Marsh Street, Bristol BS1 4BP

## Wales

*WJEC*  Welsh Joint Education Committee
245 Western Avenue, Cardiff CF5 2YX

# PARLIAMENTARY REFORM

# GETTING STARTED

In the course of the nineteenth century Britain took steps towards becoming a *parliamentary democracy*. A series of measures, the most important of which were enacted in 1832, 1867, 1872, 1883, 1884–85 and 1911, brought the country nearer to this ideal which many people cherished – but not always those in power. In fact governments often had *tactical* reasons for introducing reform proposals. But whether or not the reform effort was part of a conscious desire to place power in the hands of the people, the *effect* was to introduce those democratic institutions which were to be widely copied by other countries later as the most desirable system of government.

The most decisive, though not the biggest, step was the *Reform Act of 1832*. Before this time power had been exercised chiefly by aristocrats and landowners. The right to vote was linked with the ownership of property; indeed, the view that *all* men should have the vote, irrespective of how big a stake they had in society, would have been considered very dangerous and revolutionary. There had been few changes in the parliamentary system since the days of Cromwell. A few attacks had been made in the later eighteenth century on the most glaring abuses of the system, but there were many people like Edmund Burke who made a virtue of leaving things as they were for fear of producing something worse. He pointed to the frightful results when a revolution got out of hand, as it had in France in the 1790s, thus giving the Prime Minister Pitt wide popular backing for the repressive measures he directed against political agitation. Demand for reform, however, revived after 1815, when political radicals stirred the working classes to agitate for a reform of parliament which they hoped would lead to a fairer system and end the miseries the working classes were forced to endure.

# HISTORICAL DEVELOPMENTS

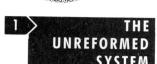
**1 > THE UNREFORMED SYSTEM**

The pre-1832 system was open to two sorts of criticism. First, the injustice arising out of the unequal distribution of parliamentary seats, and second, the lack of uniformity in the franchise.

The *distribution of parliamentary seats* heavily favoured the south and west of the country. Out of the total of 658 members of parliament, 100 of whom represented Ireland, the vast majority were English M.P.s: Wales returned only 24, and Scotland only 45, about the same number as was returned by Cornwall alone. The counties each sent two members to Parliament, the same number as was sent by each of the historic boroughs. Population changes since the middle ages meant that many boroughs, like the smaller Cornish boroughs, had decayed and were now little bigger than hamlets. On the other hand many towns, especially the northern industrial towns like Manchester and Sheffield, were

> **England before parliamentary reform.**

totally unrepresented. The effect of this over-representation of the south was that 70% of the membership of the House of Commons came from constituencies south of a line drawn from Bristol to the Wash. Boroughs, especially small rural boroughs, were often much influenced by neighbouring landed families, and many were corrupt. Some were the private property of a landlord, like Gatton Park or Boroughbridge, and as such were said to be *pocket* boroughs. Others, like Old Sarum, had so few voters that all of them could be influenced or bribed, and were known as *rotten* boroughs. East Dunwich in Suffolk had disappeared under the sea, yet was still represented in parliament! Some county voters, like those in Yorkshire, acted independently, but many borough voters allowed landed proprietors great sway. For example, the Earl of Lonsdale controlled no fewer than nine boroughs, and the M.P.s he 'set up and knocked down' at will were known as *Lord Lonsdale's ninepins*.

*Uniformity in the franchise* was also lacking. In the counties, only the forty-shilling freeholders (i.e. the men who owned enough land to be rented out an annual rental of £2) were allowed to vote. Farmers who were only tenants, i.e. worked on land belonging to someone else, could not vote even if they paid £40 a year in rent. On the other hand in the boroughs, there was a wide variety of franchises. There were *potwalloper boroughs*, where every occupier of a house with a fireplace big enough to boil a pot was enfranchized. There were *scot-and-lot boroughs*, where those who paid local rates or taxes could vote, or *corporation boroughs,* where the vote attached only to members of the corporation. Some gave the vote to *burgage tenants* i.e. those who owned some particular building or piece of land. A few, like Nottingham, which had 2000 voters, were *freemen boroughs*, and enfranchized often the largest and most independent group.

The system was also one of *open voting*, so that intimidation and disorderly scenes occurred frequently. There were often complicated local customs governing polling at election times. Some two-seat boroughs created additional difficulties by permitting *plumping* by voters i.e. a voter casting both his votes for the same candidate. Further, there was no proper electoral register, and only about 435,000 men out of a total of 14 million in England and Wales could vote.

**2 > THE DEMAND FOR REFORM**

Although there had been sporadic demands for reform in the 1820s, the changes made in 1821 and 1829 were only small, and pressure for reform was steadily mounting. A wealthy middle class of manufacturers and merchants was demanding a share of political power, and a widening of the franchise enough to give them, but not their social inferiors, the vote. In France, a revolution in 1830 had produced a more democratic system, and this was regarded as a hopeful sign. The new King of England, William IV, who succeeded George IV in 1830, was also more ready to accept reform than his predecessor. At the same time,

> **The growth of the reform movement.**

members of the poor working class had been led to believe by the radicals that if they supported the reform movement they would get the vote and so be able to improve their lives. In fact, the Whig Party was largely aristocratic, and although it hoped to secure support for its reform programme from the middle and the lower classes, it loved neither. It was simply hungry for office and aimed to break the stranglehold on power held by the Tories. In practice, most Whigs were reactionaries: they had behaved savagely in crushing the Captain Swing riots earlier in 1830, and were clearly no friends of democracy. The majority of Whigs wanted to see how *little*, rather than how much, they could change.

The Tories, on the other hand, were the main beneficiaries of the unreformed system and were strongly opposed to change. Many approved of pocket boroughs for having made possible the early emergence of leaders such as Canning and Peel. Many subscribed to the doctrine of *virtual representation* – the view that although some towns, such as Manchester, were not actually represented in parliament, they were as good as represented by other voters of similar outlook elsewhere. There were some, like Peel, who defended the varieties of the existing system on the grounds that it permitted the representation of *all* classes – such as the pot-wallopers – whilst a middle-class franchise would not. All argued that reform would weaken the habit of obedience to authority, and of respect for property.

It was the Duke of Wellington's refusal to consider reform that forced Earl Grey to take up the cause. He entrusted the drafting of the bill to a small committee of four, which included the two leading reformers in the cabinet, Lord John Russell and the Earl of Durham.

## 3 > THE PASSING OF THE REFORM BILL

The first Bill, introduced by Russell in March 1831, was greeted with derisive laughter. It passed its first reading, but was thrown out in Committee. Grey resigned, and a general election was held which increased his majority and persuaded him to continue. A second, modified, Bill was introduced in June. This passed the House of Commons, but was thrown out by the House of Lords in October.

All over the country reform riots broke out. In Nottingham, the castle was captured; in Bristol the bishop's palace was burnt by the mob, who also broke into the prisons and set free the prisoners. For some months the country smouldered on the verge of revolution.

**The troubles of the Reform Bill.**

The third reform Bill, containing a few concessions to appease its opponents, was introduced in December 1831. Behind the scenes the King and the ministers were trying to persuade members of the Upper House to change their minds. At the same time William IV was threatening to create a small number of new peers to make certain that the Bill would pass. Once again the Bill went through all its stages in the Commons, and in April 1832 also passed its second reading in the House of Lords, but by the perilously narrow margin of nine votes. After Easter, when the Lords voted to postpone reform, the Whigs took this as a challenge and treated the postponement as a matter of confidence. Grey went to the King and asked him to create fifty peers. The King demurred, whereupon Grey resigned, and Wellington was summoned to form a government. Within a week, Grey was back in office, but Peel and other Tories, fearing that Wellington might consider it his duty to bring in a modified reform proposal, refused to serve under him. There was widespread protest in the country at large, and even a threatened run on the banks. Grey now forced the King to agree to the creation of peers, but even the threat of it was enough to persuade the Upper House to withdraw its opposition and pass the Bill. So in June 1832 the Bill passed the Lords and with the royal assent became law as the First Reform Act.

## 4 > THE TERMS OF THE 1832 REFORM ACT

The *redistribution* proposals of the Act were slightly less sweeping than they had been at first. Fifty-six boroughs, returning 111 members, were disfranchized entirely, and 30 lost one of their two members. Of the 143 seats surrendered, 44 went to new boroughs big enough to receive two M.P.s each, and 21 to single-member boroughs. To balance this number, a further 65 seats went to English and Welsh counties, some of which received a third seat, whilst others went up from 2 to 4 seats and were split into two divisions. A further 8 seats were given to Scotland and 5 to Ireland. The total size of the House of Commons remained unchanged at 658 members.

**Changes made by the Reform Act.**

The *franchise* was also standardized. In the boroughs a uniform franchise was set up in favour of those occupying property with an annual rental value of £10 or more, most of whom were middle-class. Under the new arrangements nobody lost his vote, since the old qualifications continued for the lifetimes of the existing voters and then were to die out. In the counties, the forty-shilling freeholder was retained but the vote was extended to include copyholders, long-leaseholders with land of an annual rental value of £10 or more, and tenant farmers paying £50 a year in rent. The Act also standardized the holding of elections. There was to be an official register of voters, and voting was normally limited to two successive days.

**5  THE IMPORTANCE OF THE 1832 REFORM ACT**

And lack of change.

The Act is almost as important for what it did *not do* as for what it did. It did not create a democracy; indeed in many ways it can be said to have been designed to stave it off. Though it is true that the Tories were weakened by the abolition of pocket and rotten boroughs, many smaller boroughs still survived, and were as corrupt as before. Toryism if anything was strengthened by the extra seats given to the counties, and by the continuance of the increasingly out-of-date assumption that the rural interest should still dominate politics. Furthermore, much of the old system remained unchanged. The life of Parliament remained at a maximum of seven years, and the powers of the House of Lords, the traditional stronghold of the aristocratic interest, were unaltered. There was no effort to modernize the procedures of the Lower House, which continued to programme short sessions largely devoted to private business. Though the basis of political power was somewhat widened by giving the middle class the vote, the total electorate even now was little more than 650,000 in a population in England and Wales of over 16 millions. It was clear that there was little concern to entrust power to the hands of the lower orders of society.

Manipulation of the system was almost as blatant as before. Without secret ballots and proper checks on spending at election times, corrupt activities continued unabated. Indeed, it was thought perfectly proper that those with wealth and influence within the system should use them to the full. For some years there were a lot of voters who did not take the trouble to get their names on to the register. Others doubted whether it was worthwhile to pay the shilling registration fee. On the other hand the 'fixers' generated as many votes for their nominees as they could. In the counties, Tories multiplied leaseholders for their own supporters, so that it was reckoned that £1000-worth of land could be made to produce as many as 500 voters. The Whigs did much the same with what remained of the old system within the boroughs, trying to influence elections with fictitious rent-certificates to show that their supporters were £10 householders, and disfranchizing their opponents by alleging that they were behind in paying their rates. *Compound householders*, i.e. those who paid their rates along with their £10 rent to the landlord, were in a particularly difficult position. They had to apply specially to go on to the register, and until 1851 had to renew their applications annually. The result was that in practice many did not get the vote.

After the election of 1832 – the first under the new system – the new House of Commons looked very much like the unreformed Chamber. Over 150 M.P.s were related to members of the House of Lords; over 200 were lawyers, or were serving officers of the Army or Navy, or were connected with the Established Church. Only 50 merchants or manufacturers were elected. Radicals, conscious of having been cheated, were not slow to grasp the realities, and almost immediately began to clamour for further change. They did not, as might have been imagined, abandon parliamentary methods and turn instead to direct revolution in face of the hostility of the ruling classes. Oddly, their failure merely confirmed their strategy of agitating for power through the traditional channels. *Chartism* was the natural outcome of this thinking.

Consequently, after the Reform Act, political power began to shift. The Whig Party strengthened its power, especially in the newly-enfranchised industrial towns, and over the next decade it enjoyed a spell of almost uninterrupted power. The struggle that followed, however, in the next thirty years was not one between aristocrats and people, but one between two different types of property and wealth – landed proprietors and middle-class manufacturers or merchants. The working classes were deeply disappointed. They felt they had been betrayed by their social betters, and this feeling was reinforced by the middle-class character of many of the reforms of the next decade. Political power in the towns was handed over to the middle classes, and little was done, even in the Factory Act, for the ordinary working man. Indeed, the reform of the Poor Law in 1834, in the name of financial economy, made things even tougher for the poor and the unemployed.

**6  THE REFORM ACT OF 1867**

In the middle years of the century there was a lull in the campaign for further parliamentary reform. This was partly due to the fears aroused by the Chartist agitators, most of whom failed to secure middle-class support, and partly to the robust opposition of Lord Palmerston, who, though at any time he might have been overwhelmingly elected on a more popular franchise, nevertheless regarded it with an aristocratic disdain which betrayed his true conservatism. Thus Disraeli's reform effort in 1859 came to nothing in spite of the parliamentary support of his rival Gladstone, foundering on the instinctive conservatism of public opinion and the unwillingness of the middle classes to share political power.

The 1860s, however, brought signs of movement. To some extent this was due to the revival of radicalism as memories of Chartism faded, and also to the greater affluence brought to the middle classes by the mid-Victorian prosperity. A new, moderate trade unionism was coming into being, no longer seeming to threaten employers with chaos and revolution. Its leaders, like Robert Applegarth, were articulate and sensible men who wanted to work with the bosses rather than against them.

Abroad, too, it was a time of change. In 1864 the popular hero of the Italian national movement, Garibaldi, visited Britain and addressed a great rally at the Crystal Palace. In the U.S.A. Lincoln led the forces of northern democracy against the slave-owning southern states during the American Civil War.

A few public figures in Britain were bold enough to express their misgivings about democracy. Liberal Robert Lowe had visited Australia and had a poor impression of the workings of popular government. He saw in the U.S. Civil War the kind of extremism to which it led, and counselled caution in spreading the vote more widely. He was vigorously supported by the writer Thomas Carlyle who roundly asserted that parliamentary democracy meant:

> the calling in of new supplies of blockheadism, gullibility, bribeability, amenability to beer and balderdash by way of amending the woes we have had from our previous supplies of that bad article.

and went on to ask the sarcastic question:

> If Manhood, why not Horsehood, Doghood ditto?

**The renewal of the reform movement.**

In 1865, Palmerston died and one of the obstacles to further reform disappeared. Russell, the Prime Minister, and Gladstone brought in another Bill, lowering the franchise to £7 in the boroughs and to a rating qualification of £14 in the counties. The total electorate had grown by natural increase since 1832 from 650,000 voters to about a million, but there were still five million other adult males who were denied the vote. This reform, it was estimated, would swell the total number of voters by half a million. An effort was made to weight the franchise in favour of the respectable classes, for example, by giving an additional vote to anyone with more than £50 in savings banks, but nonetheless it was a step towards popular democracy. As such, the measure was bitterly resisted by Robert Lowe and his supporters. It was also opposed by Disraeli, for the Conservatives, but on the rather curious ground that it was not democratic enough – though many of his fellow-Tories would have said exactly the opposite. As a result, Russell's government was defeated and resigned, and Lord Derby, the Conservative leader, became Prime Minister in a minority government in June. Both parties seemed to agree that a general election on the issue would reveal the divisions within both parties, and do them both more harm than good.

Public indignation was reflected in the following month in a large demonstration to be held in Hyde Park. Influential people were dismayed at the prospect of disorder, and on the day of the rally the cabinet decided to close the Park altogether. The result was that the crowd's anger was vented outside rather than inside the Park. Nearly a mile of the iron railings surrounding it were pushed down, and many Conservatives, including Disraeli, drew the conclusion that further delay would be dangerous. Derby, the Prime Minister, was reluctantly persuaded that Disraeli was right.

**The Conservative Party moves towards reform.**

Strangely, the Tories gave the matter as little thought after the Hyde Park demonstration as they had done before, and the cabinet were not agreed about the details of the Bill before the meeting of Parliament in February 1867. There were two chief viewpoints. One group, led by Disraeli, believed that there ought to be a franchise extending to all ratepayers, suggesting that the radical effects of this could be offset by a number of 'fancy franchises' such as had been included in Russell's bill. The other group, led by more right-wing figures such as Lord Cranborne (the future Marquess of Salisbury), doubted whether these safeguards would be sufficient, and preferred the traditional limits on voting. The cabinet was still arguing about the matter on the day when Disraeli was due to announce the reform proposals to the House. A meeting just before the session opened gave the cabinet's decision against Disraeli, and the 'Ten Minutes Bill' (so-called because of the brevity of the discussion on it) announced later that afternoon that the less adventurous solution had been adopted. The borough franchise was to be reduced to a £6 limit, the county franchise to a £20 rating limit.

The Bill pleased no one. Disraeli felt that his party had missed the chance to get ahead of the Whigs in the race for reform (a process known as 'dishing the Whigs'); while Russell and his colleagues on the other side of the House pointed out that having rejected the Liberal bill on the supposed grounds that it was not democratic enough, the Tories were now bringing in one that was even less democratic. Hence the Bill was allowed to go into limbo, and in March Disraeli brought forward the proposal he had first thought of.

His Bill embodied the idea of a ratepayer franchise in the boroughs, safeguarded by 'fancy franchises'. This enabled a man who was a university graduate, a clergyman, who paid at least £1 per year in direct taxation, and had money in the 'Funds' (i.e. in government securities) to accumulate five or six votes perfectly legally. He intended to reduce the county rating limit to £15 – still higher, incidentally, than the Liberals' £14. If it was Disraeli who suggested this measure, it was Gladstone who now set to work on it in order to make it genuinely more democratic. He forced Disraeli to agree to bring down the county limit to £12, and pointing out the complexity and the likely corrupt manipulation of multiple franchises, eventually persuaded him to abandon them altogether. Disraeli also surrendered on the question of the compound householder, adding nearly half a million new voters at a stroke by agreeing that those who paid their rent and rates together should not be disqualified from voting. In this form, the Second Reform Act became law in August 1867.

## 7 ▸ EFFECTS OF THE 1867 ACT

The 1867 Act added a million new voters to the electoral register and just about doubled the electorate. In the counties, those rated at £12 a year received the vote, as did all copyholders and all lease-holders holding land worth £5 a year. Many of these, like the existing voters, were middle-class and relatively better-off. In the towns, however, working-class voters were in a majority. All householders who paid rates – either personally or through their landlord – got the vote, as did lodgers who paid £10 a year in rent for unfurnished rooms.

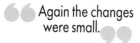 The 1867 changes.

At the same time, the redistribution clauses further reformed the constituencies. Boroughs with fewer than 10,000 inhabitants lost one of their two M.P.s, and the 45 seats thus released were redistributed according to much the same principles as in 1832: 25 were given to the counties, 15 to newly-represented towns, 4 as 'third members' for Leeds, Manchester, Liverpool and Birmingham, and 1 given to the University of London. In this way, the 'balance' between town and country was maintained.

Some of the results of the Act were unexpected. Though more seats were given to country than to town, in practice the power of the landlord was weakened, for much of this influence had previously been exercised through the smaller boroughs, and these were now far more democratic. Another odd result followed from an amendment carried in the House of Lords, whereby voters still retained two votes even in three-member constituencies. This meant that by careful management, party leaders in the larger cities could still be fairly sure that all three seats could be won – a discovery which greatly accelerated the growth of constituency organizations at the grassroots. The Conservative Constitutional Association, moreover, was first founded in 1867, and further developed by Lord Randolph Churchill. He later (as a tribute to Disraeli) launched the Primrose League, whose membership was also Conservative. Shortly afterwards, Joseph Chamberlain, a radical republican industrialist who became Mayor of Birmingham and one of its Liberal M.P.s, formed the National Liberal Federation in 1877.

However, as in 1832, the immediate changes brought about by the Act were less than anticipated. Separate acts were passed for Scotland and Ireland, although the effects were less radical than in England and Wales. In Irish boroughs, for instance, voting was limited to £4 ratepayers. Though many had feared that the act, as Lord Derby put it, would be a 'leap in the dark', the new Parliament looked much like the old one. There were still 155 M.P.s who were related to the aristocracy, and about the same number of lawyers, clergymen and army and navy officers as before. M.P.s representing the industrial interest increased only from 90 to 112 between 1867 and 1880. After 1867 there were still over 70 boroughs with populations of fewer than 10,000 represented in Parliament, so that small towns were still heavily over-represented. Many of the old political habits survived e.g. large numbers of seats still went uncontested at election times, thus denying the voter the opportunity to express his preference. Corruption still took place during elections, and there was still no secret ballot.

Again the changes were small.

One of the long-term political consequences of the Act soon began to emerge. The Liberal Party, linked to the manufacturing and merchant classes, had previously been the middle-class party, but now the Conservative Party began to replace it, as Disraeli had hoped it would. A far-sighted political periodical, the *Fortnightly Review* said in 1874

> The Conservative Party has become as much the middle-class party as the Liberals used to be. The sleek citizens who pour forth daily from their snug villas round London, Manchester and Liverpool and believe that the country will do very well as it is . . . Conservatism has opened its arms to the middle classes and has reaped its just reward.

Long years associating Toryism with the aristocracy, the High Church and the landed interest were steadily being replaced by something more contemporary.

## 8 ▷ THE SECRET BALLOT ACT

> **Doing away with corruption.**

'Vote by Ballot' formed part of the programme of a number of political movements in the 18th century, and had made several appearances in the 19th century. The most recent was as one of the Six Demands of the Chartist petitions. Support for the ballot had already been expressed by leading political figures, and Gladstone himself took up the cause in his First Ministry. One of his aristocratic supporters, Lord Hartington, introduced in the Lords a proposal in 1870 to establish *secret voting*, and in 1871 the House of Commons introduced a Bill to the same effect – but the Lords cared little for either proposal and threw them both out.

There was a good deal of prejudice against the ballot. Some complained of the big changes that its adoption would bring about. Others, who meant much the same thing, said simply that such a reform would be 'pandering to the lower classes.' Perhaps the most serious criticism was that to allow a voter to creep into a polling booth and put a cross on a ballot-paper was to encourage him to vote without thinking, or at least without having any proper discussion about it. Some cynics said that Gladstone had an ulterior motive in making his proposal, since it was generally the poorer and lower-class voters who were the victims of anti-Liberal pressure. The secret ballot would help to solve the problem, and incidentally strengthen Gladstone's grip on the House of Commons. Perhaps this view was not without truth. It may have been a combination of high moral values and basic political self-interest which brought Gladstone out in favour of it.

When the Bill was brought in again in 1872, and once more passed by the Commons, Gladstone said rather threateningly

> The people's Bill has been passed by the people's House, and when it is next presented at the door of the Lords it will be with an authoritative knock.

Fig 2.1 Gladstone's ballot act helped to stop election scenes like this.

The Lords took the hint and gave way, and the secret ballot came into being. The Act, however, was only to last until 1880, when it expired. It had to be renewed annually thereafter until 1918, when it became permanent. The Act had the effect of discouraging interference with the impartial holding of elections. It checked threats and intimidation from another candidate's supporters, and it stopped bribery, since no candidate was likely to bribe a voter when he could not be certain that the voter would vote as he had promised.

The main beneficiaries of the new secrecy were Irish voters. In the past they had been the victims of the most blatant manipulation by their landlords, as a result of which their true wishes were seldom expressed at the polls. Now the leader of the Irish Nationalist Party, Parnell, grasped the opportunity which the Act offered to the Irish Nationalist Party, and Nationalist representation in the House of Commons soon began to advance by leaps and bounds.

## 9 ▷ THE CORRUPT PRACTICES ACT

Secret voting, however, performed disappointingly in reducing political corruption at election times; this was tackled by the *Corrupt Practices Act* of 1883. Corruption was defined as bribery, treating, undue influence, assault, abduction, impersonation or perjury, and was made punishable by heavy fines. There were lesser penalties for 'illegal practices', including paying voters, providing conveyances, wearing party favours or excessive spending. Up to this time, richer candidates had the advantage over poorer ones in that there were no effective limitations on what they could spend. This system on the whole benefited Conservative candidates more than Liberal ones, and once again, morality and self-interest combined to persuade Gladstone to step in to check it. As a result of the Act, a ceiling was laid down for the sum of money that could be spent on an election campaign. The total depended on the number of electors the constituency contained, and had to cover all election expenses – hire of halls, printing bills, etc. Almost overnight, the Act brought corruption at the polls to an end.

## 10 ❯ THE THIRD REFORM ACT, 1884–85

**The changes of 1884–85.**

Gladstone, strongly supported by the more radical Chamberlain, went on in 1884 to introduce further franchise reform. Since 1867 there had been a basic unfairness in the system. The towns operated on the democratic basis of a ratepayer franchise, but the rural areas were still under a class-based system favouring land and wealth. In the face of resistance from the Upper House, the Liberals brought in this third measure. The Lords dared not oppose it outright, for fear of revealing their mistrust of democracy. The point was not lost on Joseph Chamberlain, who launched a fierce popular campaign to end class privilege – a struggle of 'Peers against the People.' In the Lords, Salisbury was as hostile to reform as he had been in 1867, but sought to delay rather than defeat it, by refusing to accept it until a redistribution act had been put on the statute book. He seemed to hope that its terms would be so difficult to arrange that the whole enterprise would perish. In the end it did not, and both acts went through on agreed terms in 1884 and 1885.

As far as the franchise went, the rural voter could now vote on the same basis as the urban voter. Ratepayers in all areas could now vote, and in addition the Act provided a new occupational franchise for those with lands or tenements worth £10 per year, the equivalent of the £10 lodger franchise invented in 1867. As had been foreseen, this Act ended in county politics the familiar influence on government enjoyed by the great families and the younger sons of the aristocracy. Now, only sentiment could keep the upper classes in power, and the customary respect of the rural areas was at last beginning to wear thin. In Ireland, where arrangements were now the same as in England, there was an even bigger step towards democracy. The large number of ordinary people who enfranchized there – largely poor peasants – produced an ever more rapid growth of the Irish Nationalist Party.

The effect of the Act in terms of votes was to increase the electorate from about 3 million to about 5 million. In practice, this was far from the manhood suffrage that the Chartists had demanded. It is true that the Act included the so-called *service franchise* which entitled domestic servants such as butlers to vote. But about half the adult male population were still without voting rights – men who for one reason or another were not ratepayers, such as grown-up sons living with their families, lodgers in cheaper accommodation, many members of the armed forces, and so on. As yet no woman was entitled to vote. The country had still some way to go before it could call itself a genuine democracy.

The redistribution involved was massive. Seventy-nine towns with fewer than 15,000 inhabitants ceased to be represented, and a further 36 towns of 15–50,000 people lost one of their two members. Only the universities and the very large towns (50–165,000) remained as two-member constituencies, and the rest of the country was chopped up into single-member constituencies as at present. This break with historical tradition turned out to be very significant. There were many towns where a middle-class businessman and a working-class radical had run in double harness as Liberals, and where both had habitually got in, at the expense of Conservative fortunes. But unless, like Leicester, they still remained plural constituencies, these places were now forced to abandon this cosy habit, and the Liberals were the chief sufferers.

## 11 ❯ THE PARLIAMENT ACT, 1911

**Clipping the claws of the Lords.**

This Act arose out of the bitter quarrel between the Commons and the Lords over the issue of heavier taxation for the upper classes (see Chapter 9). The so-called People's Budget was eventually enacted after a constitutional crisis which seemed to threaten the stability of the whole country. However, having won one victory the Lower House were not inclined to leave things like that. They were determined to 'clip the claws' of the Lords. This they did in the Parliament Act of 1911.

The Act contained three main requirements. Firstly, all bills which the Speaker of the House of Commons declared to be 'money bills' (and this of course included all budgets) were to become law within one month whether the Lords approved of them or not. This established beyond all future doubt that the Lower House controlled the purse strings. Secondly, all other bills, if passed by the Commons in three successive sessions, were to become law with the royal signature, even if the Lords had rejected them, provided that two years had elapsed between the bill's introduction and its final passage. Thirdly, the maximum life of any Parliament was reduced from seven years to five, thus making it more clearly dependent on the wishes of the electorate than previously.

As in 1832, the Bill was debated long and furiously in the House of Lords. Attendances were larger than they had been for many years. Even the so-called 'backwoodsmen', who had never put in an appearance before, hired their ermines to join in the fray. Opinion was divided; some wished to let the measure through, hedging their bets against a later measure turning out even worse for them; others wished to resist the proposal to the last ditch. These groups jokingly became known to observers, presumably because of the agricultural pursuits of the upper classes, as 'hedgers' and 'ditchers'. The new King, George V, renewed the threat of his predecessor to create up to 250 peers, much to the resentment of the traditionalists of the House of Lords. But even the Liberals seemed disinclined to pursue the matter, though there is no doubt that such a step would have given them lasting control over that Chamber. Eventually, moderate counsels prevailed and the Parliament Act was passed by a slender majority in August 1911.

**❝Salaries for M.P.s.❞**

Payment of M.P.s was brought in at almost exactly the same time. This was thought necessary by the Liberal Party, for the lack of parliamentary salaries favoured those who had private means and could afford to be an M.P. It also meant that working-class people were mainly excluded from membership, and the handful who were M.P.s had to live in cheap lodgings and do various part-time jobs such as writing for the newspapers in order to make both ends meet. Some persuaded the trade unions that sponsored them to provide a small stipend and perhaps offer them a job when their period in the Chamber was over. But after the Osborne Judgment in 1909, the 'political levy' which the unions had started to collect from their members for this purpose was declared illegal, except on a public and voluntary basis. The political funds of the union shrank dramatically as a result, and some Liberals as well as Labour members began to feel the pinch.

The proposal for salaries was carried out, not by statute, but merely by a standing order of the House of Commons. In future, M.P.s were to be awarded a parliamentary salary of £400 per year, which was about twice as much as they could be expected to earn as a working man. Some annoyance was expressed by the House of Lords that the procedure adopted prevented them from debating the proposal. However, even if there had been a statutory proposal to that effect, they would not have been able, under the new Parliament Act, to block it, since it would have been certified by the Speaker as a money bill. In any case there were good historical precedents for doing this sort of thing by parliamentary resolution instead of by statute, so the Lords' protest was of little avail.

If, in the long run, these measures weakened the constitutional position of the House of Lords and gave increasing power to the Commons, the Lords had really no one to blame for their misfortunes other than themselves. They had consistently opposed the advance of democracy for over a century, and had accepted it with poor grace only when it was forced upon them. In a democratic age, their position as an unelected chamber with an absolute veto over an elected House of Commons was impossible to justify. It was only to be expected that they should lose their stranglehold, and that Britain should, especially at the time of the First World War, take more rapid strides towards political democracy.

Fig 2.2 Parliamentary reforms in the nineteenth century: Summary of changes

| Date | ELECTORAL AREA | | FRANCHISE QUALIFICATION | | No. of voters | Population (Great Britain) million |
|---|---|---|---|---|---|---|
| | *County* | *Borough* | *County* | *Borough* | | |
| Before 1832 | Every county had two members, but Yorkshire had four. | Boroughs sent two members mainly in south and west. | Freeholders of land worth 40s. a year. | Widely different franchises e.g. scot-and-lot payers. | 435,000 | 16.4 |
| 1832 | Larger counties sent more members. | 56 rotten boroughs disfranchised. Industrial towns represented. | Long-lease holders & £50 tenants as well as 40s. free-holders. | Householders with premises worth £1,000 a year in rent. Old franchises to die out. | 657,000 | 16.5 |
| 1867 | Larger counties sent more members. | More small boroughs disfranchised. Seats given to larger towns. | Ratepayers rated at £12 & smaller leaseholders. | All ratepaying householders & £10 lodgers. | 1,057,000 | 25.0 |
| 1872 | Secret Ballot | | | | | |
| 1883 | Corrupt Practices Acts | | | | | |
| 1884–5 | Counties divided into single-member constituencies. | Smaller towns have fewer members, larger towns have more. | All ratepaying householders and £10 lodgers. | | 4,391,000 | 30.4 |
| 1911 | Parliament Act | | | | | |
| 1911 | Payment of M.P.s | | | | | |

# IDEAS AND PRINCIPLES

**Constitutional Government**

Britain is governed under the limitations imposed by a constitution, much of which is unwritten. At its head there is a constitutional monarch (Queen Victoria from 1837 to 1901), exercising customary powers.

**Parliamentary Monarchy**

Government is by *Crown in Parliament*; the Crown does not normally act independently of Parliament, and Parliament acts only with Royal consent. The relations between the two are fairly closely defined, though in unusual situations it would not be illegal for one to act without the other.

**Popular Sovereignty**

Authority stems from the people, symbolically headed by the Monarchy, which is supposed to act on their behalf. Parliament also represents the various groups (or 'estates') in the Realm, including the ordinary people. It is they who elect the House of Commons. In theory, therefore, there should be no conflict between the various institutions which together make up the system.

**Parliament and Government**

M.P.s who agree tend to form themselves into groups or 'parties', each under its own leader. Groupings which can control the majority of the votes in the House of Commons form the *Government*, e.g. the Conservatives from 1841 to 1846, and their leader, Peel, becomes the *Prime Minister*. They sit on the government benches on the Speaker's right hand in the Commons, with the ministers sitting on the front bench. If, as often happened in the 19th century, the Prime Minister, e.g. Lord Salisbury, sits in the House of Lords, there is a *Leader* of the House of Commons. Similarly there is a Leader in the House of Lords when the Prime Minister, e.g. Disraeli, sits in the Commons.

**Cabinet Government**

The Prime Minister is assisted by a number of other *ministers*, chosen and removed by the Prime Minister at will, each usually the Head of a particular Department, such as the Foreign Office or the Treasury. These ministers meet regularly as a *cabinet*, and smaller groupings meet on other occasions as the Prime Minister thinks fit. They are answerable to the House of Commons for their actions, and have to answer their questions. If M.P.s do not like the way the Government is behaving, they can defeat it by voting against it, or they can pass a vote of no confidence in it to force it to resign. Ministers act together on the principle of cabinet unanimity. If they disagree with the Prime Minister or their colleagues, they are supposed to resign, as Chamberlain did over the Irish Question in 1886, and retire to the back benches.

**Parliamentary Business**

One of the cabinet's main jobs is to lay down the programme of the Government and to guide it through the House of Commons. Government business now takes up nearly all the week, with only one day set aside for private members' bills. In the 19th century, the proportion of time was far smaller, and parliamentary sessions much shorter. As a result, the powers of the ruling party and of the Prime Minister have enormously increased.

**Political Parties**

Formerly these were very fluid and informal groupings with very little control over their members, though nowadays they are more tightly organized, and the threat of expulsion from them is more significant. In the 19th century the two main parties were the Tories (later called Conservatives) and the Whigs (later called Liberals). Later still in the century there was the Labour Party. Another important 19th-century party was the Irish Party.

## 13 > ENACTING LEGISLATION

Parliamentary proposals are known as *bills*, and have to pass through the same procedures in both Houses before they become *acts* of Parliament. They become part of the statute book, i.e. laws, when they receive the Royal Assent. They become law as follows:

| | |
|---|---|
| **First Reading** | This is something of a formality. The bill is laid before the House so that they can become acquainted with the text, and it is then introduced by the minister responsible and a day fixed for the second reading. |
| **Second Reading** | This is the first full discussion on the subject. The minister in charge of the bill speaks to the motion 'That the Bill be read a second time', and a full debate ensues. The debate deals with broad principles rather than with details, but if the bill is defeated it fails for that session. If passed, it goes to Committee. |
| **Committee Stage** | When the bill is in committee it is examined in detail clause by clause, and amended where necessary. Money bills go to a Committee of the whole House, but there are usually about five or six Standing Committees, drawn from the different parties in the same proportion as in the House, to consider details of bills. Committee procedure is more relaxed than in a formal session on the floor of the House. After 1887, when Irish Nationalist M.P.s deliberately wasted a lot of time in obstructing bills, efforts were made to curtail discussion by the *Guillotine closure*, which placed a time-limit on the discussion, and the *Kangaroo closure*, which enabled the Committee Chairman to select certain amendments for discussion, thus leaping over others. |
| **Report Stage** | The amended bill is then brought back before the full House and further amended if necessary. |
| **Third Reading** | This is the final full debate, usually shorter than the second reading, after which the bill receives the Commons' approval and goes to the Lords, or is sent by the Lords for the Royal Assent. Bills amended by the House of Lords have to go back to the Commons for these amendments to be approved. |

## 14 > OTHER VOCABULARY

| | |
|---|---|
| Constituency | An area electing an M.P., and which the M.P. elected represents. *All* the people of this area, and not simply his supporters, are said to be his *constituents*. |
| Electorate | The total number of people entitled to vote. Each member of the electorate is called an *elector*. |
| Franchise | The legal holding of a particular right, such as the right to vote. |
| Land tenure | *Freeholders* own their land completely, and hold the title-deeds to it. *Copyholders* are not so secure in their tenure, but hold a copy of the title-deeds. *Leaseholders* do not own their land, but hold it at an agreed figure for the number of years specified in their lease; leases may be renewed if both parties are agreeable. *Tenants* have less secure rights in their holdings; they pay rent and hold a rent-book, and the length of notice required to terminate a tenancy is the same as the interval between payments of rent. |
| Left-wing; right-wing | Names given to two sides in politics, arising from the fact that the House of Commons is constructed on the *adversarial principle*, i.e. the two sides confront each other. |

The government sits on the right-hand side of the Speaker, the opposition on the left. Since the party resisting change has often been in power, 'right-wing' has come to mean Conservative, and since the party advocating it has often been in opposition, 'left-wing' has come to mean 'reforming'. Of course, when the reformers are in office, they sit on the right-hand side, though they are still said to be left-wing.

**Polling** — The period of, or the process of, counting up the parliamentary electors' votes; the counting of heads (from the old word *poll* for head). After the adoption of the ballot, the process is nowadays known as *balloting*.

**Radical** — Basic or fundamental. The word derives from a Latin word meaning a root, and is the same word as radish. Radicals wish to get down to the roots of a problem in order to reform it, and are not interested in making cosmetic changes. In Britain, Radicals have not formed a separate party; indeed there are radicals in both major parties. In the 19th century, radicalism tended to be associated with extremism, and often still is.

**Reactionary** — Deeply, and often foolishly, opposed to change; often excessively attached to things as they used to be. If a Radical is an extreme reformer, a Reactionary is an extreme conservative.

# APPLIED MATERIALS

## BOOKS

CASE, S. L. & HALL, D. J., (1967). *World History from 1783 to the Present Day.* Arnold. Chapters 5 & 6.

HILL, C. P. & WRIGHT, J. C., (1981). *British History 1815–1914.* Oxford. Chapters 2, 8, 10 & 15.

NASH, E. N. & NEWTH, A. M., (1967). *Britain and the World 1789–1901.* Penguin, SH 4.

NASH, E. N. & NEWTH, A. M., (1967). *Britain in the Modern World: the Twentieth Century.* Penguin, SH 5. Chapter 1.

RICHARDS, D. & HUNT, J. W., (1987). *Illustrated History of Modern Britain 1783–1980.* Third Edition, Longman. Chapters 9, 15 & 18.

STEER, C., (1986). *Radicals and Protest 1815–50.* Macmillan.

TUCKER, E. M. M., (1981). *British History 1760–1914.* Arnold.

## MORE DETAILED BOOKS

ABBOTT, B. H., (1972). *Gladstone and Disraeli.* Collins, Britain in Modern Times series. Chapters 2 & 3.

ADELMAN, Paul. *The Second Parliamentary Reform Act of 1867.* History Today, May 1967.

MAEHL, W. H. (Ed.), (1967). *The Reform Bill of 1832.* Holt, Rinehart & Winston, European Problems Studies.

## DOCUMENTARY SOURCES

NICOL, Jon, (1987). *Government and People 1700–1900.* Blackwell, Evidence in History series.

PEARCE, Malcolm, (1987). *The Nineteenth Century.* Bell & Hyman, Sources in History series.

## AUDIO-VISUAL

The Early Victorian Era 1837–60   A.V.P. 509

# EXAMINATION QUESTIONS

**1**  a) Why was there a strong feeling in favour of parliamentary reform in 1830?
   b) How was a Reform Act passed in 1832?
   c) What changes did the Act make in the distribution of parliamentary seats and the qualifications for voting?
                                                                                    (LEAG)

**2**  Study the table below and then answer all the questions which follow

| GROWTH OF THE ELECTORATE IN ENGLAND & WALES, 1830–86 | |
| --- | --- |
| *Year* | *Number possessing the vote* |
| 1830 | 435,000 |
| 1832 | 652,000 |
| 1866 | 1,056,659 |
| 1868 | 1,991,180 |
| 1883 | 2,618,453 |
| 1886 | 4,391,260 |

   a) What difference did the Reform Act of 1832 make to the number of people who could vote?
   b) The increase in voters between 1866 and 1868 was due to the Reform Act of 1867. Why was it decided that Britain needed a reform of Parliament?
   c) How would you expect a Conservative, who had voted against the Reform Bill in 1866, to feel about the Reform Bill of 1867? Explain your answer.
   d) What effect did the growth of the electorate have on political parties by the end of the nineteenth century?
                                                                        (*25 marks*; SEG)

**3**  a) Why did a reform of the parliamentary system in England and Wales come about in 1832?
   b) To what extent did the Great Reform Act change the system?
                                                                                    (WJEC)

# OUTLINE ANSWERS

**1**  This is a three-part question where approximately equal weight will be given to the various parts of your answer. If the whole answer is marked out of 30 marks, there will be approximately 10 marks for each part, allowing a small margin for flexibility. It is thus important to give sufficient attention to all parts of the question.

   a)  The first part of the question asks 'Why?' It is not enough merely to give an account of the unreformed parliamentary system. Any facts you have should be used to explain the strong feelings in 1830 on the subject of parliamentary reform. You should remember, too, that different people held different views. What the Radicals thought about it, for example, was quite different from Whig views. The opinions of the Tories, who opposed parliamentary reform, are not of primary relevance in this answer.
   b)  This part of the question calls for an outline account of the *steps* by which the Bill was passed into law. Material on this will be found in the text under the subheading of 'The Passing of the Reform Bill'. It is perhaps worth noting that narrative answers of this sort are relatively unusual in this examination.
   c)  This part of the question also calls for a descriptive answer. Note that there should be two parts to it. The first concerns the distribution of parliamentary seats, and the second the qualifications for the franchise. The examiner will give approximately equal weight to each section. The longer-term consequences of the Act are not asked for.

**2**  Though there are four parts to this question it seems unlikely that they are given equal weight in the assessment. The answer to the first part can be given very briefly, possibly in a single sentence, and so is not likely to carry more than 2 or 3 marks. However, there is an *incline of difficulty* in the other parts of the question, up to about 8–10 marks, which you should take into account carefully in the amount you write. Note also that the skills of *explanation* and *assessment* called for in the answers are of a higher order than the more factual first part.

a) The figures given in the table provide the answer, and would score at least 1 mark. If you see more than 1 mark on offer, you should consider elaborating your answer a little, for example, by showing that smaller towns lost their representation, whilst large towns, previously not included, now returned members to Parliament.

b) An answer such as 'Palmerston had opposed parliamentary reform, but in 1865 he died' would go some way towards an answer, but the full answer is not as simple as that. Within Parliament, opinion remained divided on the subject, and the decision-taking took place at least as much outside it as inside. The effects of foreign and domestic developments at this time should be taken into account in your answer (See the section of the text under the heading 'The Reform Act of 1867' for some ideas on the answer).

c) There should be an element of empathy in this answer, since the question is asking *how a Conservative would have felt.* Note that you are required not only to state your feelings, but also to provide reasons for them. It is worth observing that not all Conservatives thought alike on this question. Right-wingers thought it was wrong and opposed it on the grounds that it was irresponsibly surrendering power to the ignorant masses. The followers of Disraeli not only thought that it would 'dish the Whigs', but that it would win the Conservative Party a good deal of support amongst the newly-enfranchised.

d) The assessment called for here is the most difficult part. The increasing number of voters, of course, meant that the parties were now more clearly obliged to respond to popular control. The Act also meant, indirectly, that the parties started to develop national and local organizations, and that they began to issue manifestos and to market their ideas more clearly and palatably. The fact that the working man in the town could now vote also led to the emergence of a new Party that claimed to speak for him – the Labour Party. The Act also aided the development of the Irish Nationalist Party.

# A STUDENT'S ANSWER WITH EXAMINER'S COMMENTS

**QUESTION**

a) Why did a reform of the parliamentary system in England and Wales come about in 1832?

b) To what extent did the Great Reform Act (1832) change the system?

> Largely descriptive. The answer says more about why parliamentary reform was *resisted* than about why it came about.

a) The political system before 1832 was unjust and unfair and only a small number of people in the country had the vote. Small towns, especially those in the south of England were over-represented, but the northern industrial towns had no members. Many of the methods used in the towns for the election of members were corrupt, and such burroughs were called 'rotten' boroughs. Some rich landlords were able to control seats because of the land they owned. The Tories were well-satisfied with this arrangement which kept them in power for many years, and they were not willing to see it changed.

> **❝** This account of the passing of the Bill shows that the student prefers to write down what he has *memorized* rather than try to answer the question. **❞**

> **❝** More detail should be offered, and the new arrangements in the borough and in the county could profitably be briefly summarized. **❞**

> **❝** Indicating the effects of the Act on the character and actions of the new Parliament is a good idea, but this answer exaggerates the benefits of the reform for the working classes. **❞**

> **❝** A mention of the ways in which the effects of the Act turned out to be limited is also a good 'balancing' point. Unfortunately the whole of this answer is under-developed and historically rather thin. **❞**

b) The first Reform Bill was brought in by Lord Russell in 1831 but it failed to pass the House of Commons and there was another election and it returned Grey to power. He brought in a second Bill, which passed the Commons but was defeated in the Lords. There were riots all over the country, so the Whigs brought in a third Bill, but the Lords threw it out again. Wellington tried to form a government, but people said 'To stop the Duke, go for gold' and so he gave up his efforts. The King, William IV, said he would create peers and so the Lords eventually let the Bill pass in 1832.

The Act abolished rotten boroughs and gave the vote to the middle classes. In the counties, however, the influence of the old county families was almost as great as ever. All the same, over the next ten or twenty years, a lot of new reforms were brought in by the reformed parliament which improved the conditions of the factory worker and helped to raise living standards everywhere.

The Act left a lot of things untouched. It did not bring in secret ballot, and there was still a lot of intimidation went on. Parliaments still lasted for seven years, and the powers of the House of Lords were undiminished.

# SUGGESTIONS FOR FURTHER WORK

1  Find out what *Punch* thought about parliamentary reform in the course of the 19th century. Take *two* of his cartoons on the subject and explain them, suggesting how present-day cartoons might take a different line.

2  Look out for some contemporary accounts of what happened in 1831–32, and show how political attitudes have changed over the past century and a half. (Tip: Try *Portraits and Documents: Earlier 19th century,* ed. Dennis Holman [Hutchinson Educational, 1965], pp. 87–93.)

3  You are a comfortable city lady or gentleman living opposite Hyde Park with your family and servants. Write a letter to a friend in Cheltenham explaining your feelings at the time of the Hyde Park Demonstration, July 1866, and saying what you would have done in the circumstances if you had been a member of the cabinet.

# THE POOR LAW AMENDMENT ACT AND CHARTISM

## GETTING STARTED

No civilized society deliberately leaves its poor to starve to death, but governments are not always keen to accept the responsibility for the relief of the poor if they can foist this duty upon others. During the Middle Ages the Church dealt with the poor, and it was only with the Reformation and the dissolution of the monasteries that the medieval system of poor relief broke down. The government was now forced to play a direct role, and after a great deal of experimentation a system was devised whereby the genuinely unemployed were to be found work or be put into workhouses, and the lazy and idle were to be punished and to be confined in the harsh conditions of houses of correction. As the financing of the new system was to be local, out of the newly devised system of rates on property, the details of the application of the Elizabethan Poor Law were left in the hands of the local Justices of the Peace who constituted the local authority. It is not surprising that local magistrates soon discovered what local authorities have constantly found since: that the cost of looking after the poor in institutions is much greater than giving them meagre financial assistance so that they can support themselves. Thus by the eighteenth century houses of correction had virtually disappeared, although idle poor were still occasionally flogged before being sent on their way, and most parishes were too small to be able to maintain a workhouse. The eighteenth century poor who could not be made to work, or could not be found work, were almost invariably supported by money provided by local magistrates out of the local rates. In order to prevent one district being swamped by poor from other areas, strict settlement laws prevented movement of the poor from parish to parish. Although the rich grumbled about the rates, until the latter part of the century the system seemed to work well enough.

# HISTORICAL DEVELOPMENTS

Two major problems arose for relief of the poor: first, the breakdown of the parish system in areas of rapidly growing population, and second, the impact of war-time inflation. It might be thought that a huge population increase, brought about by the growth of factories and work opportunities, would not give rise to a corresponding growth in the number of poor and destitute. But there was a world of difference between one overseer of the poor looking after a handful of destitute in a small village, and looking after much larger numbers in a heavily populated urban sprawl. Moreover, fluctuations in employment, temporary lay-offs, and war-time trade dislocation could increase unemployment to the point where those dependent on the overseer ran into several hundreds. As the industrial revolution got under way, all attempts to maintain the settlement laws were doomed to failure. Small parishes on the fringe of urban areas found themselves in danger of being swamped by poverty-stricken migrants on their way to seek a new and more prosperous life in the factories and workshops of the new towns. The administrative machinery could, in times of crisis, be stretched to breaking point. The crisis came with the war with France which began in 1793. The war forced up the price of bread, while wage increases lagged well behind price increases and more and more agricultural labourers were forced to apply to the parish overseers for financial help.

**❝❝Paupers on the move.❞❞**

It was not intended that money paid to the poor should *supplement* wages. Yet such was the desperate need and so great were the price fluctuations, that overseers found not only that the normal allowances for the poor were inadequate and needed constant revision, but also that *employed* labourers were frequently requiring assistance. Normally the sum paid to the poor in each parish or in the group of parishes covered by the Quarter Sessions district was a fixed sum which could only be changed by a full meeting of the magistrates. These were too infrequent to cope with the situation, and in 1797 the magistrates of Berkshire devised their own solution. In order to make frequent meetings of magistrates unnecessary and to deal with rapid rises in the price of bread, they met in the Pelican Inn at Newbury and there drew up a scale of payments to the poor based on the price of bread and number in the family.

> . . . The magistrates very earnestly recommend to the farmers and others throughout the county, to increase the pay of the labourers in proportion to the present price of provisions; and agreeable thereto, the magistrates now present, have unanimously resolved that they will, in their various divisions, (i.e. the areas covered by each of the Quarter Sessions), make the following calculations and allowances for relief of all poor and industrious men and their families, who to the satisfaction of the Justices of their parish, shall endeavour (as far as they can) for their own support and maintenance.

The magistrates' intention was kindly enough. If the employers could not be persuaded to increase wages, then the scales would have to provide an alternative. In effect they were to become a means of supplementing wages. On the original 1795 scales a man with a wife and three children would receive nine shillings a week if the price of a gallon (8lb. 11oz.) loaf was a shilling (5p), and twelve shillings and threepence if the price of a gallon loaf was one shilling and sixpence. In effect if a man earned less than the amount to which the scales entitled him, then the difference would be made up out of the poor rate. The action of the Berkshire magistrates was so successful and beneficial that it was not long before magistrates in other parts of the country drew up their own scales of relief and began applying them. The scales were frequently changed and varied considerably from district to district. Parliament had nothing to do with the Speenhamland scales and their imitators. They were drawn up locally, for local use. Indeed, although scales were soon operating throughout the South and much of the Midlands, much of Northern England was not covered by it. Rapid industrial growth and continuous labour migration made the scales unworkable in most of the northern areas where they were tried. Here the Poor Law was not used to subsidise the wages of those in regular work, but provided financial relief for those without work of any kind. It was a financial cushion for those on piecework, such as handloom-weavers, whose earnings had become too meagre and intermittent for subsistence.

**❝❝It is very important to remember that parliament was not involved here.❞❞**

In 1815, the Napoleonic War ended, and the landowners in parliament protected their interests with the Corn Law, which prevented the importation of cheap foreign corn. High bread prices naturally coincided with years of bad harvests and the amounts paid out in poor relief continued to rise. It seemed that the whole agricultural community was helping to subsidise the wages of the labourers from the rates, and that the landowners no longer found it necessary to relate wage rates to the amount needed to maintain a family. Labourers knew that not only would their wages never rise, but also that they would always be dependent upon poor relief to supplement their meagre income, despite working long hours. They felt resentful, degraded and humiliated that they received as charity from the parish what they ought to have been receiving as wages from their employers. The ratepayers, too, were resentful. In 1818 poor law expenditure reached a peak of almost £7,900,000. In 1831, when bread prices were a third lower, poor law expenditure was at its highest since 1820, reaching just over £7,000,000. It is not surprising that ratepayers feared the return of famine bread prices, and believed that the poor rate would go on rising and was out of control. A poor rate of ten shillings per acre was not uncommon, meaning that a landowner with a small holding of about thirty acres would have to pay a poor rate of £15. It is understandable that, bearing in mind the money values of those days, the poor rate seemed an intolerable burden.

## 2 > THE POOR LAW REPORT 1834

> Try to get to grips with this account of Bentham's ideas.

In 1830 the Whigs came to power after a long period of Tory rule. By the Reform Act of 1832 they curbed the power of the landowners in parliament and prepared the way for further change. They felt themselves to be enlightened, and concerned with the well-being of their fellow-citizens. They also felt themselves to be efficient, and concerned with achieving maximum progress at minimum cost. They owed much to the ideas of Jeremy Bentham, the philosopher who had helped to found London University, and who had died in the year of the Reform Act. He had none of the traditional loyalty to existing institutions which so obstructed progress and reform. He subjected every aspect of law and society to searching questioning; his purpose was to discover how far it made a contribution to human happiness. He aimed at the 'greatest happiness of the greatest number' and measured all laws and institutions by the extent to which they promoted such happiness. His doctrine of 'utility', the degree of its usefulness in promoting the greatest happiness of the greatest number, was the yardstick by which everything in society was measured. Although he was known as a Radical, he had admirers within the Whig party who were prepared to adopt his methods without fully accepting all his ideas, and Utilitarian influence was strong out of all proportion to the limited number of direct Utilitarian followers of Bentham. It was not surprising that the Utilitarians focused their attention on the poor law, the relief of poverty which had generated uncontrollable expenditure, yet made such little impact on poverty itself. The Whigs had good reason to be concerned about the countryside. The 'Swing' riots of 1830–31 had alarmed the government and led to a punitive series of Assizes in which nine were hanged and hundreds transported. It was against this background that the government established the Poor Law Commission to investigate

> . . . into the practical operation of the laws for the relief of the poor in England and Wales, and into the manner in which these laws were administered, and to report our opinion whether any and what alterations, amendments, or improvements may be beneficially made in the said laws, or in the manner of administering them, and how the same may be best carried into effect . . .

Note that the Commissioners were not asked to investigate the *causes* of poverty, but merely the *ways* in which poverty was relieved. It is not really surprising that under the circumstances the Poor Law Commissioners, who did their best under difficult conditions, came out with an all-round condemnation of Speenhamland. They pointed out the heavy burden on the rates, the way in which the rates paid by the poor subsidised the wages paid by the rich, how the wages were kept artificially low, and how dependence on poor relief discouraged independence and enterprise among the labourers. They noted how a scale system of relief encouraged labourers to increase the size of their families, thus adding to the rate burden, and how nothing was done to discourage fraud and laziness. These criticisms were to be expected; what was unexpected was the far-reaching nature of the changes the Commissioners proposed. The most revolutionary was that to abolish outdoor relief:

> First, that except as to medical attendance, and subject to the exception respecting apprenticeship herein-after stated, all relief whatever to able-bodied persons or to their

families, otherwise than in well-regulated workhouses . . . shall be declared unlawful, and shall cease, in manner and at periods hereafter specified . . .

In effect this would mean that able-bodied persons requiring relief would, together with their children, have to enter a workhouse. The only exceptions were for those who were sick or aged, or in some way incapacitated. This proposal, together with virtually all the others recommended by the Commissioners, was adopted in the Act which followed.

**❝❝ Don't forget the exceptions here. ❞❞**

**3 ⟩ THE POOR LAW AMENDMENT ACT, 1834**

The Act
1   Abolished all outdoor relief, except to the sick and aged.
2   Required all able-bodied people seeking relief to enter a workhouse. This 'workhouse test' was imposed to discourage people from seeking relief unless they were really destitute. Those entering workhouses faced harsh conditions, separation from wives/ husbands and from their children, so it was hoped that labourers would make every effort to seek employment, and use the workhouse only in the last resort.
3   In order to reduce the burden of workhouses on parishes which were small or poor, parishes were grouped in 'Unions', with several parishes sharing a workhouse between them.
4   All male ratepayers were to elect for each Union a Board of Guardians responsible for fixing the poor rate and administering the poor law. The elected guardians would employ suitable persons full-time to run the workhouses and to administer the other forms of relief.
5   To make sure that the new poor law was uniformly administered throughout the country – it caused chaos if some workhouses were more welcoming than others – a Commission of three men, working from London, supervised the working of the system, and determined exactly how 'outdoor relief' was phased out. The secretary to the three Commissioners was Edwin Chadwick, a keen utilitarian and follower of Bentham, who had played a major part in drawing up the report.

How this was to promote the greatest happiness of the greatest number it is not easy to see. The ratepayers might welcome the fact that for the first time they were to have direct control of the rates they paid, also that they would pay less rates because money would only be spent on matters of absolute priority, and that the pauper's true happiness and welfare would be encouraged by trying to make him independent. The labourers were far more alarmed at the prospect of the workhouse test than they were excited by the prospect of their employers having at last to give them a living wage. And the landowners with a large labour force would not appreciate having their substantial wage subsidy withdrawn. For two years the work of the Commissioners went smoothly. By the summer of 1837, 90% of all the parishes of England had been provided with Boards of Guardians, and apart from isolated protests, the Act met with little opposition. The new workhouses separated families and were spartan in comforts, but the diets recommended by the Commissioners suggested that the workhouse inmates, though fed on rather stodgy diets, at least usually had enough to eat. Dickens's example in Oliver Twist is rather an exaggerated one, and what is supposed to have happened at Andover, where the inmates fought over the gristle from the bones they were preparing for glue, was the exception rather than the rule. But adequate food was little compensation for lack of comfort and separation of families. In the North particularly, the workhouses soon came to be regarded as prisons and acquired the nickname 'Bastille' after the notorious pre-1789 Paris prison of that name. Insofar as some workhouses ill-treated their inmates, failed to provide them with the recommended diet, and put them to stone-breaking and oakum picking, these abuses were soon eliminated under pressure from public opinion and propagandists like Dickens. But the workhouse test continued and workhouses remained fearful places where families were torn apart in case they should breed more paupers; fear of ending up in the workhouse accompanied the working-classes throughout their drab and hard lives. The replacement of the Poor Law Commission by a Poor Law Board in 1847, headed by a minister directly responsible to parliament, delighted public opinion in that it took away the almost independent power of the three Commissioners ('the three Bashaws of Somerset House'). Yet the new system survived several parliamentary investigations and committees of enquiry before it was eventually swept away in 1929.

'OLIVER ASKING FOR MORE'

Fig 3.1 Charles Dickens's exposure of poor-law administration in *Oliver Twist* illustrated by George Cruikshank.

Fig 3.2 The Andover Scandal – Evidence of Charles Lewis, Labourer.
From *British Social & Economic History from 1760 to the Present Day*, Peter Lane (Oxford, 1979) p. 73.

*What work were you employed about when you were in the workhouse?* – I was employed breaking bones.
*Were other men engaged in the same work?* – Yes.
*Was that the only employment you had?* – That was the only employment I had at the time I was there.
*Was the smell very bad?* – Very bad.
*How did you break them?* – We had a large bar to break them with.
*During the time you were so employed, did you ever see any men gnaw anything or eat anything from those bones?* – I have seen them eat marrow out of the bones.
*Have you often seen them eat the marrow?* – I have.
*Did they state why they did it?* – I really believe they were hungry.
*Did you see any of the men gnaw the meat from the bones?* – Yes.
*Did they used to steal the bones and hide them away?* – Yes.
*And when a fresh set of bones came in, did they keep a sharp look-out for the best?* – Yes.
*Was that a regular thing?* – While I was there.
*(Report from the Select Committee on the Andover Union 1846)*

## 4 ▶ THE NEW POOR LAW AND CHARTISM

In the South of England, where the Speenhamland System had been widely used to subsidize wages, the new Poor Law, in the short-term if not immediately, forced wages to rise. In the North the efforts of Chadwick and the Commissioners to introduce the workhouse system was delayed until 1837, and they coincided with the onset of an industrial slump which led to a dramatic increase in unemployment. What the unemployed needed was temporary assistance until they found other jobs, or until trade improved. What they were threatened with was the workhouse, which offered no solution to urban unemployment, and could only arouse working-class discontent. Chadwick and the Commissioners were not quite so inflexible as was popularly believed. They had even given guarded approval to some Unions in the South who continued to provide *temporary* outdoor relief to supplement wages. But this was only in special circumstances; the Commissioners believed it to be contrary to the spirit of the Act to allow wage supplementation on a wide scale in the North. They therefore tried to insist on the establishment of Unions and the building of workhouses. They were met with dogged resistance. Surprising opposition from employers, such as John Fielden of Todmorden, was added to frequent rioting and attacks on workhouses. No workhouse was built in Todmorden during Fielden's lifetime, and some opponents of the workhouses even advocated the use of violence, as did the Methodist minister, the Revd. J. R. Stephens:

> If the musket and the pistol, the sword and the pike are of no avail, let the women take the scissors, the child, the pin or the needle. If all fails, the firebrand – ay, the firebrand, the firebrand, I repeat. The palace shall be in flames. I pause, my friends. If the cottage is not permitted to be the abode of man and wife, and if the smiling infant is to be dragged from a father's arms and a mother's bosom, it is because these hell-hounds of commissioners have set up the command of their master the devil, against our God.

The link between the Poor Law and Chartism is very important.

Despite such opposition, Unions were often formed and guardians elected, but the building of workhouses often had to wait until periods of full employment brought about an atmosphere of local calm. The wait was often long; trade did not really begin to revive until after 1842. In the meantime, fear of the workhouse, and resentment at the stopping of financial relief for the unemployed became major factors in the rise of the Chartist movement. The methods of protest and resistance which frustrated the efforts of the Poor Law Commissioners in Lancashire and Yorkshire soon became the methods by which the Chartists attempted to put pressure upon parliament itself.

## 5 > THE CAUSES OF CHARTISM

### DISAPPOINTMENT WITH THE REFORM ACT

The working-classes had supported and agitated for the Parliamentary Reform Act of 1832 with great enthusiasm. They seemed to have some idea that the Act which swept away rotten boroughs was going to give them the franchise, or at least going to lead to a marked improvement in social conditions. It did neither. Far from introducing a working-class franchise, the Reform Act abolished what working-class franchises there were (they were to disappear after the deaths of the existing holders). Also, far from gaining improved living standards, the agricultural poor were hounded in the 1833 Assizes for their outbreaks of agricultural protest, and the deserving poor were to be rewarded for a lifetime of drudgery by probably having to end their days in the bleak new workhouses.

### THE FAILURE OF TRADE UNIONISM

Disappointed by the Reform Act and realizing the futility of spasmodic rural unrest, agricultural labourers flocked to join the Friendly Society of Agricultural Labourers, an organization which was a member union of Robert Owen's Grand National Consolidated Trade Union (the G.N.C.T.U.). This union was an attempt by Owen, in the days before effective rail and telegraph communication, to give the working-class movement more muscle power by organizing one great unifying trade union on a national basis. The alarmed Whig government had not defeated the landowners over parliamentary reform in order to replace landowner influence with working-class power, so it set out to undermine Owen's union. It attacked at its weakest point, the Agricultural Labourers union, prosecuting six farm workers of Tolpuddle in Dorset for taking the illegal oaths the union thought necessary to protect its secrets and membership from informers and spies. The six were found guilty and sentenced to seven years' transportation, a savage sentence which earned for them the title of *Tolpuddle Martyrs*. Although pressure of public opinion secured the release of the six within two years, the working-classes felt bitter and betrayed. Savage treatment of the Tolpuddle labourers showed that the government meant business, and the G.N.C.T.U. collapsed in a matter of months.

### DEPRESSION AND UNEMPLOYMENT

Although political action to secure better conditions had failed in 1832, trade union activity had been shown to be ineffective in 1834; perhaps this was the time to turn again to political methods. The time was not so much opportune as necessary. In 1837, a trade depression began which brought increasing unemployment and falling living standards; the depression continued, with fluctuations, for six years. It was no coincidence that when the trade depression was at its worst in 1838–39 and in 1842, the Chartist movement attracted its greatest following and made its most determined efforts.

## THE POOR LAW AND OTHER SOCIAL CONDITIONS

Enough has already been said to link the Poor Law with Chartism. In the summer of 1838 those who attended anti-Poor Law meetings in many parts of the North found themselves listening to speeches in favour of the Six points and the Petition. Realizing that they had gone as far as they could in obstructing the spread of workhouses by illegal acts of obstruction and violence, many who listened were impressed with the idea of securing power through parliament and getting the hated Act abolished legally. The northern men carried over into the Chartist movement rather more violent methods than those of the South, whose aims were mainly political. Unemployment heightened the fear of the workhouse without removing the working-class resentment at the conditions endured by those 'lucky' enough to be in work. Middle-class philanthropists did much to draw attention to the long hours, low pay and appalling conditions in the factories, and this helped to lead people towards the political protest which took shape as Chartism.

## 6 > THE ORIGINS OF CHARTISM

It is usual to trace the origins of Chartism to the London Working Men's Association founded by William Lovett and Francis Place in 1836. This body had as its aim

> . . . to draw into one bond of unity the intelligent and influential portion of the working classes in town and country. To seek by every legal means to place all classes of society in possession of equal political and social rights . . .

So although Chartism is associated with a six-point political programme, this was to be the means whereby the social changes desired by the working-classes could be achieved. At first the movement concentrated on gathering support. Its members toured the country, promoting its ideas and aims, and by 1838 it had helped to create or had granted affiliation to 150 similar associations throughout England and Wales. The affiliated societies included the powerful Birmingham Political Union, among whose leaders was the banker Thomas Attwood, and Yorkshire where the fiery Feargus O'Connor was most influential. At Birmingham, in August 1838, representatives from all over the country met, and gave the Chartist movement its name by adopting the Charter, drawn up by the Chartist leaders.

## THE SIX POINTS OF THE CHARTER

The Birmingham meeting attracted men of wide shades of opinion. The Yorkshire and Lancashire men were mostly concerned to carry on the fight against the Poor Law – by force if necessary. The Birmingham leaders were keen on currency reform, while the Londoners wanted reform through parliament. Yet the representatives were welcomed by a Birmingham crowd of 200,000 which wanted quick and united action. Thus the representatives sank their differences and adopted the Charter with wild enthusiasm, decided to organize a country-wide Petition in its support, and present this to parliament against a background of public demand so great that parliament dare not refuse it. The Charter contained six points or demands:

1  **Universal manhood suffrage:** i.e. the right to vote for all men. Attempts to modify this to include women as voters were voted down and often ridiculed.
2  **The introduction of the secret ballot:** in this way influence by landowners on their tenants and by factory owners on their employees would be reduced to a minimum, since no-one would know how a voter had voted.
3  **The removal of property qualifications for people wishing to enter parliament:** this made it possible for working-men to become members.
4  **The payment of members of parliament:** if working-men were to give up their jobs to enter parliament they would need to be paid, otherwise parliament would remain effectively closed to them.
5  **The division of the country into equal constituencies:** this ensured that each constituency had approximately the same number of voters, rather than continue with the situation in the post-1832 parliament where constituencies with very few voters exerted influence out of all proportion to their size and importance.
6  **Parliament to be elected annually:** thus presenting the most effectual check to bribery and intimidation, since though a constituency might be bought once in seven years (even with the ballot), no purse could buy a constituency (under a system of

universal suffrage) in each ensuing twelve months; and since members, when elected for a year only, would not be able to defy and betray their constituents as now.

The representatives agreed to elect a Chartist Convention to meet in London for the purpose of presenting the Petition to parliament. In the meantime they returned home to set about the task of collecting signatures for the Petition. Public meetings were held to choose the delegates to the Convention, which met in February 1839, significantly on the very same day as the first Anti-Corn Law League Conference. The delegates showed their claim to represent the people by putting M.C. (Member of the Convention) after their names, in imitation of M.P. (Member of Parliament). When it was discovered that the number of signatures collected was little more than 600,000, feverish efforts to collect signatures were ordered by the Convention, while it discussed other matters. It unanimously declared itself to be hostile to the Anti-Corn Law League, but this was virtually where its unanimity ended. On the issue of what to do if parliament rejected the Petition there was much discussion, and it was eventually agreed to hold a General Strike, which was given the less fearsome name of 'Sacred Month'. As this would require the funds and co-operation of the trade unions (which the trade unions were most reluctant to give), its prospects of success seemed remote. When the Convention began to discuss other methods, disagreements rapidly appeared. The Northern Chartists, led by Feargus O'Connor and his powerful newspaper 'The Northern Star', argued for the use of force (although O'Connor was always careful not to commit himself to it absolutely). Most of his followers were less cautious and were known as the *Physical Force* Chartists. Lovett was brave enough personally, but he and Attwood believed in persuasion by legal methods, and not in intimidation by illegal methods; their followers were known as *Moral Force* Chartists. This division, and the attack on the Anti-Corn Law League, were grave handicaps to the Chartist cause. Talk of violence scared away many moderate Chartist delegates; it also frightened off possible middle-class supporters who were enthusiasts for the Anti-Corn Law League which the Convention had so vigorously denounced.

> **These early disagreements are very important.**

In May 1839, worried by the attentions of the Metropolitan Police, the Convention was transferred to Birmingham where there were no police. Neither, by now, were there any Birmingham delegates. In July a contingent of the Metropolitan Police was sent to Birmingham, where it used force and shed blood to arrest Chartists in the Bull Ring (Birmingham's town centre), where magistrates had forbidden meetings to be held. The Convention passed a resolution denouncing the police action as provocative:

> . . . This Convention is of opinion that a wanton, flagrant, and unjust outrage has been made upon the people of Birmingham, by a bloodthirsty and unconstitutional force from London . . .

As Lovett alone signed the resolution he took full responsibility for it and he was immediately arrested and imprisoned. During the crucial months that followed, leadership of the movement passed to others. A week after Lovett's arrest Attwood presented the Petition, of which he did not fully approve, to parliament, who rejected it by 235 votes to 46. The number of M.P.s who attended the debate on the Petition was disappointing, but so was the size of the Petition – a mere 1,200,000 – after all the expectations of four or five million. The rejection of the Petition was not unexpected, but when the Convention proceeded to declare August a National Holiday (i.e. the 'Sacred Month'), despite warnings from many delegates that it would fail, the country did not respond. The attempt to coerce the government with a nation-wide strike failed, and by November the Convention delegates had all returned home and Chartism's first major effort had ended in failure.

## VIOLENCE AND GOVERNMENT COUNTER-MEASURES

The government was certainly alarmed by the size and the violence of the Chartist activities in 1839. Its main resource was troops, who, with most of the main-line railways as yet unbuilt, could not easily be moved from place to place. The magistrates were helpless against huge crowds, and although the new police could be very effective, as the Metropolitan Police were in both London and Birmingham, very few police forces were yet in existence. The government was in part, therefore, forced to rely on divisions among the ranks of the Chartists and the unwillingness of many of them to break the law. It could also try to deploy what limited troops it had to best advantage. It did this in the North, where Sir Charles Napier concentrated his troops in major urban centres, particularly Manchester, and showed his artillery to local Chartist leaders to demonstrate the futility of armed rebellion against a properly equipped professional army. Napier's efficiency disposed of a real threat in Lancashire. Elsewhere, scattered unrest and riots were on too small a scale to be a danger. The Newport 'rebellion' of November 1839 occurred when most of the disturbances had died down. Its immediate purpose was the rescue of an imprisoned Chartist, Henry Vincent, from Monmouth prison. This was to be effected by gathering an armed force at Newport and marching to Monmouth, picking up reinforcements on the way. But the authorities had been warned. Night marches are hazardous for amateurs and many detachments got lost and marched aimlessly about. When the marchers belatedly entered Newport in broad daylight they were met with a hail of rifle fire from twenty-eight soldiers barricaded in an hotel. Fourteen Chartists were killed and fifty wounded; the rest of the Chartists fled. The authorities made 125 arrests, but this did not include Feargus O'Connor who was conveniently away in Ireland. John Frost the leader of the Newport Chartists was sentenced to death, but the government decided not to make a martyr of him and the sentence was not carried out.

## THE PETITION OF 1842

> The 1842 Petition is often dismissed too briefly by historians. Give it some close attention.

The Newport rising was the 'last gasp' of the 1839 agitation. Chartism slumbered until the release of its leaders from jail, especially Lovett, and until the trade recession of 1842, which was a setback to the very slow trade recovery which had been continuing since 1839. The coming to power of Peel's Tory ministry (the working classes were not impressed by its new name Conservative) might possibly lead to even less government enthusiasm for reform than that of the Whigs. The second Petition benefited from better Chartist organization and attracted over 3,000,000 signatures. It might have had the support of the Anti-Corn Law League when Joseph Sturge in his New Move tried to draw the two associations together. But O'Connor was suspicious of the middle-class, quarrelled with Lovett who supported Sturge, and the opportunity was lost. Lovett's enthusiasm was weakened by the quarrel and he allowed O'Connor to be the main Chartist spokesman. But the House of Commons was even less willing to consider the Petition than it had been in 1839 and rejected it by 287 votes to 49. The speech against it in the House of Commons by Macaulay, the essayist and historian, was typical:

> I believe that universal suffrage would be fatal to all purposes for which the government exists, and for which aristocracies and all other things exist, and that it is utterly incompatible with the very existence of civilisation. I conceive that civilisation rests upon the security of property . . . I will assert that while property is insecure, it is not in the power of the finest soil, or of the moral or intellectual constitution of any country, to prevent the country sinking into barbarism.

O'Connor had tried moral force again and failed. Should he now try physical force? Strikes and disturbances broke out, but now there were organized police forces and the authorities knew, from 1839, the likely trouble spots: 2,000 troops were brought into Manchester. Threats of wage cuts caused workers in the Lancashire mills to rake out the fires and draw the boiler plugs from the boilers providing steam power for the mills – the so-called 'Plug Plot'. The Chartists tried to make capital out of the Plug Plot, and accused manufacturers supporting the Anti-Corn Law League of trying to worsen working-class poverty in order to blame Protectionist policies for it. Order was forcibly restored by the government, however, and as the disturbances fizzled out, so too did Chartist hopes.

## THE PETITION OF 1848

It is not easy to see why there was a Chartist revival in 1848. O'Connor's reputation had been tarnished by a land scheme which was as pathetically fanciful as it was unintentionally fraudulent. Yet he was popular enough to secure election to parliament in 1847. Even so, Lovett remained in the background, and the usual recession was not so marked or so severe as it had been in 1839 and 1842. But O'Connor could not resist the excitement brought about by the downfall of Louis Philippe of France and other lesser European monarchies in the spring of 1848. Republicanism was in the air.

A National Assembly of Chartists was summoned to prepare and present a new charter. It resembled those of 1839 and 1842 except that O'Connor persuaded delegates to drop the ballot from it. Perhaps he thought that dropping the ballot would give the Petition an easier reception in parliament. Millions of signatures were collected – O'Connor boasted of six million (there were actually less than two million) – and plans were made to gather a huge crowd on Kennington Oval. The crowd would march on parliament with the Petition and, imitating recent Continental crowds, coerce the ruling classes into making the demanded political concessions. In reply, the government enrolled 100,000 special constables to defend London (including the future Emperor of France, Louis Napoleon) and banned the Chartist procession from crossing Westminster Bridge. O'Connor had flirted with physical force and made many inflammatory speeches, but he shrank from direct confrontation. The meeting at Kennington took place during heavy rain, which reduced the size of the crowd. O'Connor met the chief of the Metropolitan Police and promised to obey the law. The Petition was carried to parliament in three horse-drawn cabs, where the House of Commons took pleasure in counting the number of signatures rather than debating its political demands. There were probably as many false and ridiculous signatures in the First and Second Petitions as the House of Commons was able gleefully to report were contained in the Third. In 1839 and 1842 Chartism had seemed a dangerous threat and not something to laugh at. In 1848, the House of Commons felt it could bury the Chartist threat under a mountain of ridicule.

Chartism never recovered after 1848. O'Connor died in an asylum, and other leaders grew old and uninterested. The growing Victorian prosperity rubbed off even on the working classes, giving them hope for the future and making them less willing to commit themselves to so risky a cause. Those still with a burning desire to serve their fellow-men turned to trade unionism or socialism, and some less politically committed entered local government, now opened up by the Municipal Corporations Act of 1835. In 1867 and 1872 the first major steps towards implementing the Chartist programme were achieved without a major political or social upheaval. But by then the Chartists had long since passed into History.

<table>
<tr><td>

**7** > **REASONS FOR THE FAILURE OF CHARTISM**

</td><td>

It has often been argued that the Chartists had little chance of success. Unless they were prepared to become a fully organized revolutionary movement and take up arms to enforce their demands, or were prepared to confine themselves to political demands and try to win support from other classes, they could achieve little. In fact, they had the worst of both worlds. The split between the Moral Force Chartists and the Physical Force Chartists prevented any resort to force, and caused confusion. This was made worse by O'Connor's fiery speeches, in which he roused his followers to action, but qualified his words then or later, or disappeared when trouble threatened. If the Chartists were to rely on moral persuasion they went about it the wrong way. It was bad enough that they had a radical political programme of Six Points which were far too advanced for their time, but many of them abused the Anti-Corn Law League when they might have sought its alliance, and harboured fiery demagogues who frightened the life out of the middle classes with their

</td></tr>
</table>

"Use this section to develop your own analysis of the failure."

talk of socialism and the class struggle, or bemused them with their talk of currency reform. It was no wonder that Chartism was denied the funds and the representation in parliament which only the middle classes, whom many Chartists strove so hard to alienate, could provide. Moreover if the Chartists scorned to woo the middle-classes they could at least have learned from their methods. The Anti-Corn Law League exploited the new railways and the Penny Post; it is remarkable what little use the Chartists made of these innovations.

The incompetence of the Chartists can be contrasted with the resolution shown by the governments of the day. They saw it as their duty to maintain order, and they did it to the best of their ability. Napier was the government hero in 1839. The Duke of Wellington, put in command of the defence of London, was the hero of 1848. By imprisoning the leaders the government showed they meant business, and bought themselves time during which, as in 1840, the Chartist movement drifted leaderless with little sense of direction. It may also have influenced O'Connor to his half-hearted abandonment of his challenge to the government at Kennington Oval in 1848. Of course, O'Connor's weakness at that moment may have been influenced also by the heavy rain which both dampened Chartist spirits and reduced the Chartist crowds. Rain had played a part in the 1839 Newport fiasco also, but neither rain nor ridicule are serious reasons for failure. The House of Commons could only resort to ridicule and laugh uproariously over such signatures as *Victoria Rex, Mr. Punch, No cheese* and *the Duke of Wellington*, once they knew that Chartism had had its day. There was no such laughter in 1839 and 1842. By 1848 the country was beginning to pull itself out of the long depression that had helped to launch Chartism in 1838. Confidence was beginning to return to industry and hope replaced despair on the factory floor. Factory Acts were beginning to improve working conditions, the Repeal of the Corn Laws was confidently expected to bring cheaper bread. In 1839 the working class believed that social improvement could only come as a consequence of political reform, but improvement had come nevertheless, while political reform had proved elusive. Northern Chartists also noted how little impact Chartism had had upon the introduction and implementation of the New Poor Law in their areas. The New Unions of the 1840s and 1850s seemed the proper channels through which to pursue social advance; and Chartism faded into oblivion.

# IDEAS AND PRINCIPLES

| | |
|---|---|
| **Assizes** | Criminal courts conducted by judges usually sent from London. The judges moved from one country town to another according to need, and they were able to try cases which were of too serious a nature to be tried by the local magistrates even when sitting jointly in Quarter Sessions. |
| **Handloom weavers** | These were weavers who continued to make a living working in their own homes on looms which normally had no power source, in contrast to the looms powered by steam which were being concentrated in large numbers in the new factories. The handloom-weavers generally did well during the war period (1793–1815) when there was not enough cheap factory-produced cloth to satisfy demand. After 1815 industrialization and therefore factory competition caused widespread hardship among handloom weavers whose numbers fell from about 100,000 in 1815 to less than 30,000 within fifteen years. |
| **Moral force** | The means by which peaceful Chartists hoped to achieve their aims. The belief that parliament and the nation could be *persuaded by argument* of the justice of the Chartist demands. |
| **Overseers of the poor** | These were the paid officials appointed by the local magistrates before 1834 to administer the relief of the poor. |
| **Parish** | The smallest unit of local government, normally coinciding with the smallest administrative area of the Church, and most often consisting of a village and the land belonging to the village. Because it was usually too small to sustain a workhouse from its own resources, parishes were often grouped into unions as a result of the 1834 Poor Law Amendment Act. |
| **Physical force** | The means by which more violent Chartists, particularly those with experience of the anti-Poor Law agitation, hoped to achieve their aims. Such Chartists felt that only by the taking up of arms and using intimidation through strikes and massive demonstrations could parliament be frightened into granting the Chartist demands. |
| **Rates** | All land and property was charged a poor rate, which was supposed to be based on land and property values, but varied widely from parish to parish. The rates were not necessarily proportional, so a man with property worth £1,000 did not necessarily pay ten times more than a man with property worth £100. Before 1834 the rich man's rates helped to subsidize the wages of his labourers. It was a source of grievance to poorer rate-payers that they might be paying a substantial rate to subsidize their richer neighbours when they themselves could not afford to employ any labourers. |
| **Union** | The 1834 Poor Law Amendment Act provided for the grouping of parishes in 'Unions', so that they could build and maintain a workhouse jointly. 'Union' soon became one of the nicknames by which the poor came to refer to the workhouse itself. |

# APPLIED MATERIALS

### BOOKS

PEACOCK, H.L., (1968). *A History of Modern Britain, 1815–1968*. Heinemann. Chapters 6 and 8.
RICHARDS, D. & HUNT, J.W., (1987). *Illustrated History of Modern Britain. 1783–1980*. Third Edition, Longman. Chapters 8, 10 and 13.

### MORE DETAILED BOOKS

SEARBY, P., (1967). *The Chartists*. Longman, Harlow.

### FOR FURTHER READING

FRASER, D., (1973) *The Evolution of the British Welfare State*. Macmillan.

### DOCUMENTARY

*English Historical Documents, 1815–1870*. Methuen, (1964).
'*A bread and cheese question*' Longman Source.

### AUDIO-VISUAL

Chartism Audio HMO

# EXAMINATION QUESTIONS

1   For what reasons was Chartism unable to achieve its aims?

2   a)  Why did parliament consider the Poor Law Amendment Act necessary in 1834?
    b)  Why did the Act arouse such widespread opposition outside parliament?
    c)  Explain the importance of the Poor Law Amendment Act in contributing to the rise of Chartism.

# OUTLINE ANSWERS

1   This question is about the failure of Chartism, but as it is worded you would be able to display your knowledge of the Six Points. This is because in discussing the failure to achieve aims, it is sensible to state what the aims were. But the main thrust of the question is on Chartist *failure*. It would be a simple matter to list haphazardly any reasons you happen to think of, and hope for a reasonable mark. But if you were able to examine the mark scheme (it is not, of course, available to candidates) you would find that the marks for Level 1 range from 1–6, and this is offered for a few scattered points. For Level 2, 7–13 marks, a list of separate reasons is expected and the mark awarded will depend on how many reasons are offered. Level 3 (14–20 marks maximum) will demand a 'complex web of causality', or in other words the reasons should be offered in a coherent order, and effectively linked together. This is not always easy to do. But if you look at the section in this chapter headed 'Reasons for the failure of Chartism' you will notice that, unlike the causes earlier, the reasons have not been separated and each is linked to, and leads on logically from, the previous one. If you study closely how it is done you should be able to apply the technique, which is in fact an important historical skill, in other historical situations. Writing a 'complex web' in this way does not mean that you have to produce an *exhaustive* list of reasons; you can

probably think of one or two that have been omitted here. But it is unlikely that you are going to be penalised for minor omissions.

2   Both a) and b) are asking for *reasons* and not for description ('factual recall' is the phrase examiners use). Remember that in a) it is parliament's reasons you are looking for; parliament is sure to have been impressed with the findings of the Poor Law Commission and you could concentrate on the reasons given earlier in the text – rising costs, wage subsidization, unfair distribution of the burden of the Poor Law, lack of disincentive to the lazy and idle, encouragement of large families, utilitarian arguments. If you link them together in an effective order you could achieve a top Level 'web of causality'.

In b) the ending of outdoor relief *for the able-bodied* (a qualification which must not be forgotten), the workhouse test, workhouse conditions, the different conditions in the industrial North, are all relevant.

There is a danger of embarking on all the causes of Chartism in c) when it is vital to concentrate on the *importance of the Poor Law Amendment Act* as contributing to the rise of Chartism. Thus while it is one of several major sources of working-class discontent, the special significance of its major contribution in leading Northern England to Chartism needs to be emphasized.

# A  TUTOR'S  ANSWER

## WORKING-CLASS ORGANIZATION

**QUESTION**   Study sources A–C below, and then answer all parts of the questions which follow.

Make use of the information in the Sources and also any other relevant information you have.

When referring to Sources in your answers, you should identify them by letter.

### Source A

A company of the 45th Regiment was stationed at the Westgate Hotel, and the crowd marched towards it. When they arrived in front of the hotel an attack immediately started: the magistrates, police and specials were driven from the streets and fled to the hotel for refuge. The soldiers were stationed at the windows, at which a number of people began to fire. The soldiers, as a matter of course, returned the fire. The result was that in about twenty minutes ten of the Chartists were killed on the spot, and about fifty others wounded.

(from *History of the Chartist Movement (1854)* – R. G. Gammage)

### Source B

The suffrage, to be exempt from the corruption of the wealthy and the violence of the powerful, must be secret . . . The legislative and constituent powers, for correction and for instruction, ought to be brought into frequent contact . . . Therefore we demand annual parliaments. With power to choose and freedom in choosing, the range of our choice must be unrestricted. We are compelled by our existing laws to take for our representatives men who are incapable of appreciating our difficulties, or have little sympathy with them; the merchants who have retired from trade and no longer feel its harrassings, proprietors of land who are alike ignorant of its evils and its care, lawyers . . .

(from *History of the Chartist Movement (1854)* – R. G. Gammage)

**Source C**   (See drawing alongside)

a) What differences are there between the account of the riots in Newport in Sources A and C?                                                                          *(4)*

b) Why do you think these Sources disagree?                                          *(12)*

c) Do Sources A, B and C prove that all Chartists were violent revolutionaries? Explain your answer.                                                                     *(12)*

d) There was a reform of parliament in 1832, yet the Chartists wanted further changes. What more did the Chartists want?                                              *(4)*

e) Read the following list:

   1  Bad working and living conditions in the towns.
   2  The failure of trade unionism.
   3  The success of working-class agitation in favour of the Reform Bills between 1830 and 1832.
   4  Improvements in communications.

   Historians have suggested that these are all causes of Chartism.

   i) Do you agree that each of these were causes of Chartism?
      Explain your answer.                                                            *(8)*

   ii) Do you think that all these causes were equally important, or that some were more important than others? Explain your answer.                                      *(10)*
                                                                                  (SEG)

a) In Source C the Chartists appear to be firing at the police and not at the soldiers, who in Source A are said to be at the windows, but are not shown in C. Whether the two sources are similar or different depends on whether 'attack' (Source A, line 2) is by firearms or not. If it is, then the drawing shows the police at the point of being driven into the hotel, *before* the soldiers were attacked, and it does not necessarily disagree with Source A.

b) First of all it is not clear that they do, although there is some doubt as to whether the police are fleeing into the hotel (Source A) or making some sort of stand outside it (Source C). If there is a difference it could arise both from the nature of the evidence, and the purpose for which the evidence was produced. Source A is written evidence set down, admittedly 15 years after the event, but it may, while endeavouring to get at the truth, be relying on eyewitnesses who have firsthand knowledge of the events described. Gammage could have got his evidence from reports of the court proceedings which followed the Newport Rising. An artist producing a visual reconstruction expects artistic licence. He is unlikely to have been present, and if he had been he might well not have had so excellent a viewpoint. He is more likely to have been concerned with dramatic representation rather than historical accuracy, especially if he was hoping to sell his drawing to the press.

c) Sources A and C show and describe a violent incident, but it is very unsafe to generalize from one event. Source B uses powerful language and the demands of source B would certainly appear revolutionary at the time, but it would be presumptuous to assert from this text that they were violent. Similarly Sources A and C certainly show the occurrence of violence but that they were revolutionaries is not clear from Source C. The Chartists here could well have been reactionaries or honest citizens defending their homes against mutinous police and troops for all we know. The danger of relying on such limited sources is easy to demonstrate from knowledge of the Chartists. Lovett and Attwood, two of Chartism's most influential leaders, were supporters of 'Moral Force' and would certainly disapprove of the Chartist action shown here, and so, probably, did most of the Chartists.

d) The Chartists wanted the Six Points of their political programme accepted by parliament. These were to give *all* men over 21 the right to vote – the most important point and the one which would turn Britain into a democracy and pave the way for the removal of social evils. To protect the working-class voter from intimidation it would be necessary to introduce the ballot. Equal electoral districts would ensure that one man's vote was approximately as important as the next man's, and annual parliaments would keep parliament in close and frequent touch with the voters. To ensure that working-men could enter parliament the property requirement for membership was to be removed, and payment of members would remove financial anxiety from members with limited or no means.

e)  i)  Bad urban working and living conditions are always a breeding ground for discontent and Chartism gained much of its support in Northern areas where conditions were at their worst. The collapse of Owen's Grand National Consolidated Trade Union in 1834 left political activity rather than trade unionism as the best hope of improvement for the working classes, and insofar as the working classes deluded themselves that their agitation had been effective and rewarding in 1830–32, they may well have thought that a revival of the mass demonstrations of those years was the best way forward. Improvements in communications can hardly be a *cause* of Chartism: men did not take to the streets and become Chartists because of railways and post, although they might or might not make use of them to further their cause.

   ii)  These can hardly be of equal importance when communication improvement is hardly a cause at all. In fact the Chartist campaign of 1839 preceded the Penny Post, and most of the important railway lines had yet to be built. It is interesting to note that although the Chartists made some use of railways in 1839 and 1848 to concentrate large number of followers e.g. in Lancashire (1839) and in London (1848), they were remarkably neglectful, unlike the Anti-Corn Law League, of the opportunities for the spread of propaganda presented by the Penny Post. Perhaps it was lack of funds which limited their use of such facilities, but of course improved communications did help Chartists to keep in touch with each other. Memories of successful working-class agitation lack a powerful enough motive to drive men to the verge of rebellion. It would be a minor factor as set against the general working-class discontent, which incidentally focused its anger strongly against the new Poor Law – something was being done in the Factory Act to begin an improvement of working conditions, but the Poor Law represented a specific deterioration. The failure of trade unions, which drove working-class leaders to turn back to political activity to secure their social and political aims, would certainly be a powerful reason, but this list of causes is uneven in importance, and there are major omissions.

# A  STUDENT'S  ANSWER

**QUESTION**

In which of the years 1839, 1842 and 1848 did Chartism have its best chance of success? Give reasons for your answers.

> This is a useful summary of reasons for the weakness of the Chartist threat in 1839. It could do with a little more development in places, and sometimes lacks explanation. The main criticism of this approach is that the crises are being taken one at a time, so that the opportunity for point by point comparison has been missed.

Unless the chartists were united in aim and methods there was little chance that they would succeed against governments which were determined not to give in. In 1839 sheer force of numbers could have overwhelmed the Metropolitain Police at the Chartist Convention in London but the leaders were divided about how to force parliament to accept the Charter, and to move to Birmingham was a bad decision. Poor organisation and the failure to win over the trade unions doomed any hope that the Sacred Month would be successful, and the Newport Rising was a badly planned and executed fiasco. The Chartists lacked the organisation to secure enough votes for their Petition and they often delayed when instant decisions might have been useful, as for example during the brief

> ❝ This is a little misleading. Most textbooks dismiss the 1842 Petition briefly, but the government took it very seriously, and there were widespread disturbances which Peel's government was hard pressed to put down.
> The Plug Plot originated through economic discontent it is true, but it has a stronger link with Chartism than is suggested here. Although the 1842 Petition is undervalued there is some attention to the idea of comparison in the first two sentences. ❞

> ❝ This contains the very common error of O'Connell instead of O'Connor which weakens the answer. But there is some useful assessment of the 1848 episode, and an attempt to arrive at a judgment in the last sentence. ❞

change of government at the time of the Bedchamber Crisis. Government determination was as strong in 1839 as in the other crisis years. Their movement of troops, their choice of Napier for the North and their effective use of the Metropolitan Police meant that the general public had little to fear from chartism.

There was no real danger in 1842. This was a minor period of Chartist activity compared with the other two dates. The 'Plug Plot' caused problems in the North, but this was more concerned with wage cuts and the trade depression than Chartism. Even though there were more signatures on this Petition than that of 1839, parliament was less likely to take notice of it now the Conservatives were in power than it had been under the whigs.

1848 was the great propaganda effort of the Chartists. Chartism was now led by Physical Force supporters who were determined to frighten parliament into accepting the Petition. But O'Connell was an unstable and unreliable leader and his commitment to physical force was questionable. The government, by filling London with troops and special constables and appointing Wellington to command them, showed its determination to fight. But the Chartists lacked weapons and effective leadership. O'Connell backed down in the face of government determination. Neither in 1839 nor in 1842 had the Chartists threatened to take control of London, the centre of political power, so 1848 might seem the most dangerous year.

# SUGGESTIONS FOR FURTHER WORK

1   As an observer, summarize the views put forward at a Chartist meeting in 1839, where there are opposing arguments about how to secure the Charter.
2   From the early and relevant chapters of Dickens's *Oliver Twist* find and list the points Dickens is making against the new Poor Law.
3   Give the dates and circumstances when 5 of the 6 points of the Charter have been achieved. Why do you think that one point of the Charter still remains unachieved?
4   In what ways did the Poor Law and its administration change between 1834 and 1929. What were the reasons for the changes you have noted?

# LORD PALMERSTON

## GETTING STARTED

Palmerston was born in the late eighteenth century before the French Revolution, and was extremely important both in foreign and domestic politics for much of the nineteenth century. Some of his ideas were rather old-fashioned, though with the bulk of the people they were none the worse for that. He showed great talent for coming to terms with many of the new ideas of the century, and turning them to his country's benefit. Opinions about him varied remarkably. Many of his contemporaries held him in the highest regard for his judgment and his decisive action in defence of British interests: Lord Shaftesbury, for example, said of him:

> I do not hesitate to say that the two great objects of his heart – one, the institution of a true and vigorous foreign policy suited to the honour and position of the Kingdom of England; the other the extinction of the slave trade – were founded not only on his personal love of freedom but on his deep and unalterable conviction that civil liberty all over the world would be good for the human race, and especially so for the British people.

But others, like his colleague Benjamin Disraeli in 1855, called him:

> an impostor, utterly exhausted, and at best only ginger-beer and not champagne, and now an old painted pantaloon, very deaf, very blind and with false teeth which would fall out of his mouth while speaking if he did not hesitate and halt so in his talk.

Whatever truth underlay either one judgment or the other, in the country at large *adoration* would not have been too strong a word to apply to the way he was regarded: he always had a great appeal, as was said, to the 'man on the Clapham omnibus'.

# HISTORICAL DEVELOPMENTS

❝ Palmerston's political background. ❞

Originally a Tory, Palmerston became a supporter of the Whig Earl Grey in 1830, having had previous cabinet experience under Liverpool and Wellington as Secretary at War. He was renowned for his detailed and painstaking methods, and was now entrusted with the Foreign Office, where he was 'blooded' almost immediately by a revolution in France, and, shortly afterwards, by a national revolt in Belgium. He was Foreign Secretary twice, 1830–41 and 1846–51, and Prime Minister twice, 1855–58 and 1859–65, until his death. During his career he gave close attention to foreign questions, even when he was Prime Minister and the Foreign Office was under his former leader, Russell. Although his manner was brusque and even abrasive (he was sometimes called 'Lord Pumicestone'), he was as much loved by his fellow countrymen as he was hated by foreigners.

While he was handling the major issues of British overseas policy, he was also extremely influential in domestic matters, but here his conventional attitudes were more obvious. He was not very interested in some issues which concerned politicians at the time, such as Factory Acts, and always remained doubtful about the need for parliamentary reform. Because of this, many people felt that he was 'a liberal abroad, but a conservative at home', though he was, at heart, a conservative in both respects.

His career reached a climax in a great victory over Russia in the Crimean War (1854–56), when he was over seventy years old. After that his powers were declining, and though he remained fit and vigorous almost to the day he died, his later policies were clouded by serious misjudgments and repeated failures. The main issues of his foreign policies are listed in Fig. 4.1

Fig 4.1 Palmerston's Foreign Policies

| *1830–41* | *Foreign Secretary under Grey and Melbourne* |
|---|---|
| 1831–33 | Established an independent Belgium |
| 1833 | Revolt of Mehemet Ali against the Sultan. Palmerston takes no action. |
| 1834 | Civil war in Portugal. Palmerston sets up Quadruple Alliance. |
| 1835–39 | Civil war in Spain. British troops intervene against Carlists. |
| 1839 | Outbreak of First Opium War with China. Punitive expedition to Canton. |
| 1839–41 | Mehemet Ali crisis. Britain and Russia co-operate against France Treaty of London (1840) Straits Convention (1841) |
| *1846–51* | *Foreign Secretary under Russell* |
| 1846 | Spanish Marriages affair |
| 1847 | Swiss Sonderbund |
| 1848–49 | Palmerston showed sympathy for 1848 revolutions. Welcomed overthrow of Louis Philippe in France. Opposed continuance of Austrian power in Italy. Supported overthrow of Metternich. Sympathized with Hungarian Revolt. |
| 1850 | Don Pacifico affair. *'Civis Romanus Sum'* speech. Queen's Memorandum. General Haynau affair. |
| 1851 | Visit of Louis Kossuth to London. Coup d'Etat of Louis Napoleon in Paris. Palmerston dismissed from Foreign Office. |

| 1855–58 | *Prime Minister for the first time* (Foreign Office: Russell) |
| --- | --- |
| 1855–56 | Successful ending of Crimean War. Treaty of Paris. |
| 1856 | Lorcha *Arrow* seized off Canton. Second Opium War. |
| 1859–65 | *Prime Minister for the second time* (Foreign Office: Russell) |
| 1859–60 | War of Italian unification. Palmerston helps nationalists with diplomatic support and a naval expedition. |
| 1860 | Third Opium War. Burning of the Summer Palace in Pekin. Treaty of Tientsin opens further treaty ports. |
| 1861–65 | U.S. Civil War. |
| 1861 | *Trent* incident. |
| 1862 | *Alabama* affair. |
| 1863–64 | Palmerston threatened aid to Danes over Schleswig-Holstein. Failed to support Denmark over Schleswig-Holstein. |

## 2 PALMERSTON AND THE FOREIGN OFFICE

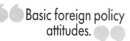

**His views.**

When Palmerston first came to the Foreign Office it had a small staff of about thirty, and a very small budget. He ruled over his Department with a rod of iron, working long hours at a stand-up desk which avoided his getting out of his chair. He even suggested improvements in the handwriting of his junior clerks! When there was an important job in hand, he stuck at it until it was finished; hence his reputation for spectacular unpunctuality. He would keep visitors waiting for hours; for days if he did not like them. He was habitually late for meals; even at state banquets he would slip into his place halfway through the meal with a perfunctory apology.

**His foreign policy.**

He saw the job of Foreign Secretary as safe-guarding Britain's overseas interests; if he failed to do this, he would not be a good Foreign Secretary. This view produced a flexibility of response that sometimes puzzled observers. In 1848, he summed up his attitude himself when he said:

> It is a narrow policy to suppose that this country or that is to be marked out as the eternal ally or the perpetual enemy of England. We have no eternal allies, and no perpetual enemies. Our interests are eternal, and these interests it is our duty to follow.

This did not mean that his thinking was confused, but that his responses were sometimes unpredictable. However, his main strategy was clear:

### THE PROTECTION OF BELGIUM

**Basic foreign policy attitudes.**

Pitt, at the time of the French Revolution, had said that 'Belgium is a pistol pointing at the heart of England.' This view was based partly on its proximity, and partly on its economic importance. Palmerston showed an active interest in Belgium, protecting it against both Dutch and French encroachment.

### COMMERCIAL SECURITY

Trade was vital to Britain. Trading contacts stretched from Latin America to the Far East. British sensitivity over trading rights could be seen at the time of the so-called Opium Wars with China in 1839 and 1856.

### IMPERIAL SECURITY

Britain's trade was largely with its empire, and secure enjoyment of these colonial benefits relied on strategic bases like Gibraltar, Mauritius and Singapore. Palmerston had this in mind in 1839 when he secured Aden. More important to him was India, where he regarded Russia as his chief foe.

### PROTECTION OF BRITISH CITIZENS ABROAD

In his famous *Civis Romanus Sum* speech in 1850 he promised 'that the watchful eye and the strong arm' of Britain would be used to protect British nationals overseas. This speech was in the case of Don Pacifico, a Portuguese Jew born in Gibraltar and only technically a British citizen, on whose behalf Palmerston intervened in Greece to demand substantial financial compensation.

## OPPOSITION TO RUSSIA

Distrust of Russian ambitions around the eastern Mediterranean could be seen in British policy from 1770 onwards, and to this extent Palmerston's policy was not new. Canning had shown the same mistrust at the time of the War of Greek Independence, and Palmerston showed it repeatedly after 1830, most notably at the time of the Crimean War. Thus he always supported Turkey, in whose cruelty and decadence he did not fully believe. Sometimes, however, he sought to achieve by subtlety what he hesitated to demand by force: this could most clearly be seen in 1839–40, over the Mehemet Ali question.

## CONSTITUTIONAL GOVERNMENT

Palmerston believed that states which were governed liberally and constitutionally were likely to be more stable and contented than those governed by a tyrant. The view was shared by Gladstone and many other Liberals. As early as 1832, Palmerston said:

> The independence of constitutional states . . . can never be a matter of indifference to the British Parliament, or, I should hope, to the British public.

Examples of the support that Palmerston gave to governments trying to govern constitutionally were Spain and Portugal in the 1830s. There was evidence of it, too, in his intervention in Switzerland in 1847, in the matter of the *Sonderbund*.

## NATIONALISM ABROAD

Palmerston accepted the wish of peoples abroad to live under governments of their own choosing – sometimes called the principle of *self-determination*. He recognized the legitimacy of such ambitions and in many cases tried to help achieve them. This was true of the Belgians, whom he helped against the Dutch, and the Italians, whom he helped against the Austrians. Sometimes, as in the case of the Poles, his support was not effective; whilst in one case, that of Schleswig-Holstein in the 1860s, he actually denied the rights of German nationals for union with their fatherland, preferring the fiction that the Duchies were really Danish. He never fully trusted nationalism, and if it conflicted with any higher priority it would be the one to be sacrificed.

**3 ▷  'A LIBERAL ABROAD'**

**❝❝ Palmerston's liberalism. ❞❞**

At first, Palmerston's attitudes and policies seemed close to Canning's, but before long his natural optimism broke through, and his statements came to have a more distinctive flavour. In August 1830 he wrote a letter after the fall of Charles X in France in which he said:

> We shall drink the cause of Liberalism all over the world . . . This event is decisive of the ascendancy of Liberal principles throughout Europe.

Years later, even after his early enthusiasm for it cooled, he still continued to think that Liberalism would be beneficial if it were introduced into other countries:

> It is always easy to say, with regard to any country where men do not wish to see constitutional government established, that such a country is not ready for it, and that it would not work there; but Her Majesty's government does not happen to recollect any country in which the constitutional system has been established that has not on the whole been better off in consequence.

In 1850, in his *Civis Romanus Sum* speech he confessed to his fear of left-wing revolution, but he still believed the reactionaries of the far right to be much more dangerous and oppressive.

His sympathy for Liberalism could be seen in a number of different ways:

## THE SLAVE TRADE

· Palmerston regarded this as a 'criminal adventure' and did his best to stamp it out, using British naval patrols to intercept slaving ships. The slave-trading lobby was especially powerful in Portugal, and Palmerston tried to bring pressure on the Portuguese government to introduce effective controls, making British support for the Portuguese government conditional on its better behaviour. His actions, and his persistent lectures to foreign governments, eventually paid off, and the slave trade was successfully eradicated.

## SPAIN AND PORTUGAL

When Ferdinand VII died in Spain in 1833, he left his daughter Isabella, a child of three, with her mother as Regent. The king's younger brother, Don Carlos, challenged the right of a female to occupy the throne, and secured the support of the upper classes in claiming it for himself. Palmerston supported the more liberal *Progressistas* who took the side of the Infanta and her mother Queen Christina.

Something similar happened in Portugal. When John VI died, his elder son Dom Pedro, who represented the Portuguese throne as Emperor of Brazil and lived in Rio de Janeiro, passed his claim to his young daughter the Infanta Maria. This action was challenged by Pedro's brother Dom Miguel, who also aimed to secure power for himself. His first attempt to seize the throne had been frustrated by Canning in 1826, but he renewed the attempt in 1834. Palmerston hoped to expel both pretenders, and produced a Quadruple Alliance with the French and with the Liberal parties in Spain and Portugal. He was proud of his achievement, which he said was 'a capital hit, and all my own doing.' The Miguelists were expelled shortly afterwards, though the struggle in Spain dragged on until 1837. French enthusiasm rapidly cooled, but Britain pressed on and the Carlists were finally defeated.

## GREECE

In the early 1830s Otto of Bavaria became king of a newly-independent Greece. Britain joined France and Russia to guarantee his position and to lend him 60 million francs to establish his government firmly. Unfortunately Tsar Nicholas was less enthusiastic about Liberal principles than Palmerston was, and it was only due to the insistence of Palmerston that a Constitution was introduced for the country. It was ironic that Palmerston should object so strenuously to external interference by autocratic powers when he indulged in it himself for liberal purposes.

## THE SWISS SONDERBUND

The lowland Protestant cantons of Switzerland, which were more heavily populated than the mountainous Catholic cantons, had been trying for some time to reform and modernize their ancient constitution. They were resisted by a group of Catholic cantons, which in 1847 formed a break-away League, or *Sonderbund*. Palmerston managed to persuade Austria, which rather approved of its sound conservative principles, and France, which rather supported the Catholic cause, *not* to intervene. As a result, the Protestants secured most of their objectives, and a united Switzerland survived.

## ITALY

Although he was no friend of Catholicism, and generally supported the nationalist claim that the Italian people had the right to govern themselves, Palmerston had no wish to see a popular republic set up in the Papal states by Mazzini and Garibaldi. He thought that the Austrians had 'no business in Italy at all' in 1848. However he did not wish the Italian nationalist cause to become either the excuse for French adventures in Italy, or the occasion of a weakening of the Austrian Empire, which he believed was the bulwark of central European security against Russian expansion. These factors, together with his deep suspicions of the political extremism of Italian popular leaders, explain why Palmerston's support for the Italian cause was more verbal than practical.

## SCHLESWIG-HOLSTEIN

Although Holstein was inhabited almost exclusively by German nationals, and there was a large German population in Schleswig, the King of Denmark, lacking an acceptable claim to the ownership of the Duchies, had made repeated attempts to incorporate them into his kingdom. The Germans resisted this, and Prussia – with Austria's support – took up their cause though neither was a great friend of popular nationalism. Palmerston was suspicious of Prussia's schemes, and tried to resist, but his efforts were in vain. His worst suspicions were confirmed when Bismarck annexed both Duchies to Prussia in 1866. His somewhat luke-warm support of Denmark has succumbed to his greater fears of Prussia.

## 4 ▷ A 'GUN-BOAT DIPLOMAT'?

In the popular mind, Palmerston personified the patriotism and the down-to-earth realism of which many Englishmen approved. A Russian émigré referred perceptively to

> the finest meteorological instrument in England, Palmerston, who indicates with the greatest fidelity the temperature of the middle classes.

Palmerston hated weakness and cowardice. He was intensely proud of his country's achievements and its status. He put the idea more bluntly when he said

> Diplomats and protocols are very good things, but there are no better peacekeepers than well-appointed three-deckers.

Palmerston upheld British rights with great conviction. The intensity of his feelings sometimes caused him to use intemperate language and to take extreme attitudes, but in a world of individualism and self-assertiveness, such convictions were widely shared by his countrymen. They were in evidence in a number of areas.

### BELGIUM

When the Belgians rebelled against the Dutch and declared their independence in 1830, the British and the French under their new 'citizen' king, Louis Philippe, accepted the situation, and warned off Russia, Prussia and Austria from interfering. A Belgian National Congress would have given the throne of their new country to a son of the French King, but Palmerston insisted on a British nominee, and Leopold of Saxe-Coburg, the uncle of the future Queen Victoria of Britain, became king instead. He refused to meet the Dutch demand that the Duchy of Luxemburg be restored to them, and this provided the Dutch with their excuse to attack Belgium. They were prevented from overrunning the country completely only by the intervention of a French army, which entered the country from the other side to support the Belgians. Palmerston was seriously displeased by this. He had not come out in favour of Belgium only to see it pass into French control. The flaws in the so-called 'cardboard' alliance became visible, and Palmerston began to threaten:

> One thing is certain – the French must go out of Belgium, or we have a general war, and war in a given number of days.

In August 1831, he expressed his opposition to any idea that the French might be rewarded by receiving Belgian territory with characteristic bluffness:

> Not a vineyard shall they have; no, not a cabbage patch!

In the end, Belgian independence owed much to the military intervention of the French, and to a naval blockade of the coast of Holland by the British Navy, but France did not gain an inch of territory as a result.

### CHINA

Shoot first, talk afterwards?

The Opium War in 1839 in China produced some characteristic sentiments from Palmerston. In Canton, the captain and crew of a British ship were arrested and a cargo of opium impounded by the local mandarin. Palmerston sent an expedition to the Far East to bombard the city as a token of British displeasure. Whilst he may have been right in insisting on the proper treatment of British nationals and on the freedom of international commerce, he appeared to overlook the more sinister aspects of the opium trade, which the Chinese government was doing its best to stamp out. The Chinese were eventually forced to sign a humiliating treaty, handing over Hong Kong to Britain and opening other ports to British trade whether they liked it or not. Palmerston crowed over his victory when he summed up the story thus:

> We said 'This won't do. This is no go, gentlemen of China. You have extorted valuable property from British subjects.' So we used force against China. We said to the Chinese: 'You have behaved very ill; we have had to teach you better manners; it has cost us something to do it, and you must pay our charges.' That was done, and they certainly profited by the lesson. They have become free traders, too.

### MEHEMET ALI OF EGYPT

Ever since he had supported the Turkish government against the Greek rebels in the 1820s, Palmerston had held the Egyptian leader in poor regard. He called him 'an Albanian tobacco-dealer' – a reference to Mehemet's earlier career. The Sultan had refused to pay off Mehemet for his help against the Greeks with the territory he demanded. Mehemet attacked his overlord and defeated him, later repeating the defeat when the Sultan tried to drive him from the lands he had occupied. Rather surprisingly, Palmerston secured Russian support against Mehemet Ali. The Tsar evidently thought that if Mehemet were successful he might strengthen Turkey, and believing that a weak Sultan is preferable to a strong one, gladly helped Palmerston to overthrow Mehemet Ali. Louis Philippe of France, on the other hand, believed it best to assist Mehemet Ali, as the best way of helping Turkey to revive its power. Palmerston would have none of this and cried defiance to both France and Turkey:

> If France throws down the gauntlet we shall not refuse to pick it up. If she begins a war, she will certainly lose her ships, colonies and commerce before she sees the end of it . . . and Mehemet Ali will just be chucked into the Nile.

Eventually Mehemet Ali was defeated, Louis Philippe climbed down, and Britain and Russia produced a treaty which settled the question of the navigation of the Straits for a while, temporarily shoring up the crumbling Turkish Empire.

## DON PACIFICO

David Pacifico, also called 'Signor', 'Mr.' and 'Don', was a Jewish money-lender who was set upon by a mob in Athens in 1847. They destroyed his books, stole his jewellery and set fire to his house. Pacifico had been born in Gibraltar, held a British passport and was technically a British citizen. Palmerston demanded over £26,000 as compensation for the victim, broke off relations with Greece and sent a squadron of ships to put ashore a party of marines and enforce a blockade of the Piraeus. Europe was outraged, and Palmerston's own cabinet colleagues were dismayed by his high-handed venture (later referred to as 'gunboat diplomacy'). In a remarkable speech in the House of Commons in June 1850, Palmerston not only defended his actions, but also justified the whole course of his foreign policy over the previous twenty years. He carried the whole House, and the whole nation, with him when he concluded:

> I therefore challenge the verdict which this House is to give on the question before it: whether the principles on which the foreign policy of Her Majesty's Government have been conducted are proper and fitting guides for those charged with the government of England, and whether, as the Roman in days of old held himself free from indignity, when he could say *Civis Romanus sum*, so also a British subject, in whatever land he may be, shall feel confident that the watchful eye and the strong arm of England will protect him against injustice and wrong.

## THE UNITED STATES

Palmerston's attempts to bully the U.S. government were less successful. Officially, Britain was neutral during the American Civil War, but Palmerston felt more affinity with the plantation owners of the south (Confederate) than he did with the brash republicans of the northern states, and did not hide his sympathies. The 'Yankees' soon showed their feelings. In November 1861 Captain Wilkes of the Federal warship *San Jacinto* intercepted the British mail steamer *Trent* bound for Southampton from Havana (Cuba). He took off two southern envoys who were on their way to Britain to plead for the Confederate cause. Seizing passengers on a neutral ship between neutral ports and in international waters was a blatant violation of the law of the sea. Palmerston could not tolerate it. He wrote a dispatch that was so abrupt that the Prince Consort used all his energy to persuade Palmerston to tone it down, and President Lincoln was able to avoid the embarrassment of a quarrel with Britain, passing off the episode as excessive zeal of Captain Wilkes.

Shortly afterwards, it was Britain's turn to give offence. The Federal Government discovered that the British were secretly building warships to fight on the Confederate side. One, the *Florida*, was already in the South, and had considerably damaged Northern shipping. In 1862, another vessel known as the *No. 290*, was under construction on Merseyside. The British government tried to arrest the ship, but it escaped, and crossed the Atlantic under the new name of the U.S.S. *Alabama*. During the next two years it attacked and captured 76 Northern vessels, before it was eventually sunk by the Federal cruiser *Kearsage* in 1864. After the war, in 1865, the U.S. government demanded $15m for the losses inflicted by Britain's negligence, but Palmerston, though in the wrong, would not hear of it.

## SCHLESWIG-HOLSTEIN

Bluff or bullying?

Palmerston's arguments were also unsuccessful in his quarrel with Bismarck over the future of the Danish duchies. In 1863 it became evident that the Prussians and the Austrians intended to step in to prevent Denmark absorbing them. Palmerston resorted to bluster:

> We are convinced – I am convinced at least – that if any violent attempt were made to overthrow (Denmark's) rights and interfere with her independence, those who made the attempt would find in the result that it would not be Denmark alone with which they would have to contend.

Bismarck was a political realist, and not taken in by Palmerston's bluff. He suggested that if British forces intervened he would 'call out the police'. The cabinet urged Palmerston to dispatch the fleet to Copenhagen, but he replied that this would do no good, and in the end climbed down. He explained rather feebly that when he said 'it would not be Denmark alone with which they had to deal', he really meant that someone else might come to their assistance. In the end, he seemed quite reconciled to defeat. Palmerston, in his last years, was only a shadow of his former self.

**5 ▷ PALMERSTON AND THE ROYAL FAMILY**

Palmerston and the Queen ...and Prince Albert.

Relations between Palmerston and the young Queen Victoria in 1837, when she came to the throne, were close and cordial. He was thoughtful and protective, she was conscientious and grateful for the support her minister was giving Uncle Leopold in Belgium. By 1840, however, her new husband Prince Albert of Saxe-Coburg was encouraging her to show more independence. Under Albert's instruction, the Queen realized that she had a duty to state her views on matters of policy and guide her ministers along the paths she thought they should follow. This did not go down well with Palmerston, who saw Albert as an interfering busybody, and wished he would leave policy matters to responsible experts. Friction between the minister and the royal household soon built up.

## PORTUGAL

The Queen, prompted by Prince Albert, suspected that Palmerston dealt with matters without discussion. Although she agreed with him, she often felt that he lacked proper respect for foreign sovereigns. Twice she reproached him for lack of consultation, but he passed off the criticism, blaming the Foreign Office clerks. His line was that 'he presents his humble duty to Your Majesty, but . . .' and then he would go on exactly as he did before.

## THE SPANISH MARRIAGES

In 1846, Louis Philippe of France caused Palmerston more problems. He had earlier promised the British government that he would allow one of his sons, the Duc de Montpensier, to marry the younger sister of Queen Isabella of Spain, but only after Queen Isabella herself was married. Now, he allowed a joint ceremony of marriage for Maria Louisa with Montpensier, and of Isabella to the eighty-year-old Duke of Cadiz. The British were outraged. Victoria was angry at the personal affront of the king going back on his word. Palmerston was more concerned at the possible future threat to Britain from a union of the French and Spanish thrones if Maria Louisa ever became Queen. Victoria again found Palmerston disrespectful towards foreign royalty, and disapproved strongly of what she considered unnecessary military interference in Spanish affairs to put down a Carlist rising. She sharply reproached Palmerston by saying to him in a letter that she

> cannot help being struck how much matters have been mismanaged.

## ITALY

Albert and Victoria deplored Palmerston's offhand treatment of the Austrian royal family as much as his irresponsible encouragement of the undermining of authority by the Italian nationalists. They could see no consistency in what their minister was doing, and she did not hesitate to say so:

> The Queen must say she is afraid that she will have no peace of mind and there will be no end of troubles as long as Lord Palmerston is at the head of the Foreign Office.

Prince Albert kept a dossier of the minister's actions, in case he should confront Palmerston at a future date with his errors.

## THE QUEEN'S MEMORANDUM

In 1850, this growing lack of confidence in Palmerston's conduct resulted in a letter to him, outlining his ministerial duties as the Queen understood them to be. She made four points:

- that he should always make clear what line of conduct he is proposing;
- that once the Queen has agreed to such a policy, he should not afterwards change it without further consultation;
- that she expects to be fully informed of what passes between him and the various foreign ministers of other countries; and
- that she expects to receive dispatches in time to be able to read them and acquaint herself with the contents before they are sent off.

In the case of any future transgression, she made it clear what she thought:

Such an act she must consider as failing in sincerity towards the Queen, and justly to be visited by the exercise of her right of dismissing that minister.

## HAYNAU AND KOSSUTH

General Haynau, an Austrian soldier was notorious for his brutal suppression of a revolt in Hungary. He came to London in October 1850, and when visiting a brewery was roughly handled by a gang of angry draymen. They jostled him, stoned him and called him the murderer of women and children. Palmerston's apology had no conviction, and was sent before the Queen had seen it. All her earlier fears were confirmed.

The following May, Louis Kossuth, the hero of the recently-defeated Hungarian Republic, also came to London. He was welcomed by the press and the public, but tactlessly, Palmerston received him at his home. The Queen objected to this lack of impartiality in a sharp note to the Prime Minister, Lord Russell. Russell protested mildly to Palmerston, and received a blistering reply:

I have just received your letter and I am told your messenger waits for an answer. My reply then is immediate and is this: There are limits to all things, and I do not choose to be dictated to as to whom I may or may not receive in my own house, and I shall use my own discretion on that matter. You will of course use yours as to the disposition of your government. I have not detained your messenger five minutes.

Russell did not dismiss Palmerston, but communications between the Queen and her Foreign Minister ceased abruptly; he was clearly at the 'end of his tether'.

## THE COUP D'ÉTAT OF LOUIS NAPOLEON

**Palmerston falls from office.**

In December 1851, Louis Napoleon, Prince-President of the Second French Republic, unexpectedly seized power in France. Palmerston preferred an empire to a republic, and did not want any relative of the former king, Louis Philippe, to recover the throne. Privately, he expressed his approval of the coup to the French ambassador. The Queen and the Prime Minister were furious at not having been consulted, and Victoria insisted that Palmerston be dismissed. This was done, but Palmerston kept the Queen and Russell waiting at Windsor Castle for two hours, when he failed to arrive to hand over the seals of his office.

### 6  PALMERSTON AND THE CRIMEAN WAR

Although Palmerston had reached agreement with Russia over the Near Eastern question in 1841, the settlement was unlikely to have been a lasting one. The existence of the Turkish Empire had been internationally guaranteed, and navigation through the Straits had been closed to warships in peacetime. However, the Tsar knew that while Turkey remained weak, he could easily get his own way in Constantinople and by keeping Mehemet Ali from the throne he had effectively stopped Turkey from recovering its strength. So when Russian encroachment on Turkey began again in the 1840s, although the treaty was only recently signed, Palmerston had no right to be surprised. Eventually he acknowledged his belief that he was 'all for making a clatter' against Russia, since 'that is the best way to save you from the necessity of making war against her'. But, whether he wanted it or not, that war came in 1854.

Tsar Nicholas had already contacted Lord Aberdeen, the British Prime Minister, about the disposal of the lands belonging to the Sultan, whom he referred to as 'the sick man of Europe'. Aberdeen thought it indecent to dispose of the estate before the invalid's death, and refused the Russian advances. Palmerston backed him to the full, stoutly declaring:

> All that we hear every day of the week about the decay of the Turkish Empire, and its being a dead body, or a sapless trunk, and so forth, is pure and unadulterated nonsense.

However, Nicholas sent a special emissary, Prince Menschikov, to Constantinople to get the Sultan to agree to two demands. Firstly, that he should reaffirm his recognition of Russia's right to protect the Christian subjects of Turkey. Secondly, that he should recognize the claims of the Orthodox Church to the guardianship of the Holy Places in Palestine, which was at this time part of the Sultan's empire. Sultan Abdul Mejid, urged on by the British Ambassador to Turkey, refused to agree with the first demand on the grounds that it was incompatible with his authority over his own subjects. As a result Russian troops occupied the Turkish provinces of Moldavia and Wallachia in the Balkans.

Efforts were made to resolve the problem by negotiation, but it proved impossible to agree on a suitable form of words, and in the autumn of 1853 Turkey declared war on Russia. Napoleon III of France had no desire to see Russia triumph over Turkey, nor to allow the claims of the Catholics in Palestine to be subordinated to those of the Orthodox Church. So, he co-operated with Britain to send a fleet to the Mediterranean, which passed through the Dardanelles en route for Constantinople. Nicholas took this as a declaration of war, and promptly sank a Turkish fleet at Sinope off the southern shore of the Black Sea. In January 1854, therefore, the allied fleets entered the Black Sea, and Britain and France declared war on Russia. The Tsar hastily ordered the evacuation of the Danubian provinces to avoid a direct clash with the allied armies in the Balkans, but the British and French governments were not to be cheated, and in September 1854 a joint force was sent to the Crimea to capture Sebastopol, Russia's main base in the area.

The war that followed was bloody and confused. The troops were put ashore some way from Sebastopol, and fought their way to the city over rugged terrain. Costly battles ensued, and it was early in the following year before they reached Sebastopol. In the meantime, the allies had suffered every misfortune. Supply ships had been destroyed in a hurricane with an enormous loss of stores. The armies in some cases had been equipped with tropical gear, and were living under canvas in spite of the harshness of the Crimean winter. The allied generals were elderly and fumbling, and the more junior officers untrained and irresponsible (the battle of Balaclava was the occasion of the disastrous Charge of the Light Brigade). Public criticism led to the resignation of the Aberdeen government and the appointment of Palmerston as Prime Minister – the 'Inevitable', as Queen Victoria grimly admitted.

**❝❝Palmerston the Inevitable. ❞❞**

Palmerston is generally credited with the victorious ending of the war. Allied troops laid siege to Sebastopol early in 1855, beat off a Russian attempt to raise the siege in August, and finally captured the city in September, forcing the Russians to look for peace. Undoubtedly some credit must go to Palmerston for his vigorous prosecution of the war, but in the interim, things had changed. First, the Italian state of Piedmont had joined the war and sent a sizeable army to the Crimea. Second, Tsar Nicholas had died and had been succeeded by his son Alexander II, who was anxious to end the war and embark on a programme of reforms at home. Finally, in the later stages of the war it was France that had won most of the victories, not Britain. Indeed after Sebastopol had finally fallen, Palmerston was actually urging the Piedmontese to continue to fight with the British to win further victories and 'bring the war to a victorious conclusion'. All the same, Palmerston was believed to have won his war and his credit in the country never stood higher.

The war ended with the Treaty of Paris (1856), when the powers did their best to put back Turkey firmly on the map. Russia gave up its claims to the protectorate of the Balkan Christians, and whatever rights it had in Moldavia-Wallachia. Russia retired from the area around the mouth of the Danube known as Lower Bessarabia and from the towns of Kars and Batum on the eastern side of the Black Sea. The Russian government agreed to demolish its naval bases along its south coast and accept the demilitarization of the Black Sea and the international control of the Danube navigation. Turkish integrity was to be guaranteed by the European powers (including Russia), and Turkey was to be admitted to full membership of the diplomatic community of Europe with the right 'to participate in the public law and concert of Europe'. Finally, the Sultan promised better treatment for his Christian subjects in future.

Overall, the treaty was not very satisfactory. Though it helped to bolster Turkey for the time being, the causes of the country's long-term decay were too serious to be easily remedied. Its territorial disintegration began again when Moldavia and Wallachia broke away to establish their union and independence as Romania in 1861. The improvement in the Sultan's treatment of his Christian subjects did not take place, and his brutality and incompetence, together with his continuing inclination to treat them as inferiors and overtax them, drove them to new outbreaks of revolt within twenty years. Russia, though temporarily checked, had by no means given up its desire to expand to the Mediterranean at Turkey's expense, and was prepared to use the excuse of any Balkan disturbance to further its aims.

## 7 > CONSISTENCY OR INCONSISTENCY?

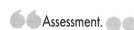

Assessment.

The policies of Lord Palmerston were not always easily understood, and even when they were, not always accepted by his contemporaries. This mistrust and uncertainty lay behind the Prince Consort's criticism that Palmerston was:

> a man of expediency, of easy temper, no very high standard of honour and not a grain of moral feeling.

Palmerston, however, was sure that he was right. Certainly he would not have been concerned at the charge of lack of principle, since it was always the pursuit of his *country's* interests rather than his own which guided him. But those of his contemporaries who ignored his errors were just as worthy of blame as those who exaggerated them.

### FRANCE

Here, Palmerston's views hovered between an inbred mistrust, and a certain respect for the country's effectiveness, a belief that it would make a better ally than an enemy. In 1830 he quickly rejected Charles X on account of his lack of liberality; and, partly because he did not like republics, he preferred the royal government of Louise Philippe instead. Later, after such episodes as the Mehemet Ali affair and the Spanish Marriages, he grew to dislike Louis Philippe, and welcomed his overthrow in 1848. The Second Republic, however, roused all his old fears:

> I grieve at the prospect of a republic in France. Large republics seem to be essentially aggressive, and the aggressions of the French will be resisted by the rest of Europe, and that is war.

So when the régime was overthrown in 1851 in a right-wing coup, Palmerston went out of his way to welcome the future Emperor Napoleon III, whose warlike name he believed concealed largely civilian ambitions. But the honeymoon was short-lived. Although Britain and France were allies during the Crimean War, Palmerston was annoyed that the French did so much better in the later stages of the campaign; at the peace conference that followed, France seemed sometimes closer to its old enemy Russia than to its ally Britain. By the 1860s, Palmerston's mistrust of Napoleon III had become an obsession, and he was pressing his Chancellor of the Exchequer, Gladstone, for bigger Treasury grants to build improved defences along the south coast to repel a French invasion.

### AUSTRIA

Palmerston mistrusted the autocratic government of Austria and never liked its Chancellor Prince Metternich. Until his overthrow in the revolutions of 1848, Palmerston regarded him as a pedantic humbug, capable of making diplomatic mountains out of very ordinary mole-hills. Yet on a number of occasions after 1848 Palmerston suggested that a strong and stable Austria was necessary for European security, largely as a line of defence against Russian expansion in the Balkans and the Near East. For this reason he was never keen on the political unification of Germany, which he feared might weaken Austria's position in Central Europe. But this policy, too, lacked some overall consistency. He was not without feeling for the subject peoples of the Austrian Empire, and felt that the Vienna settlement of 1815 had paid too little regard to their wishes. In the case of the Italians, in particular, he expressed approval and support, saying:

> North of the Alps we wish Austria all the prosperity and success in the world. Events have rendered it unavoidable that she should remain south of the Alps and as far west as the Adige; but beyond that line, depend upon it, she cannot go.

Nor, in spite of the respect that Victoria expected him to show for foreign royalty, did he moderate his intemperate language about the Austrian royal house. In 1849 he referred to them as 'odious and detestable assassins', whilst of their army he said:

> They are the greatest brutes that ever called themselves by the undeserved name of civilized men.

This condemnation referred to their work in crushing the Hungarian rising, yet he would not have wished to see the revolt succeed for fear of further encouraging the Russians to Balkan adventures.

## TURKEY

Palmerston spent much of his time attempting to preserve the Turkish Empire, yet he could scarcely disguise his contempt for the Turks. He asked:

> What energy can be expected from a nation who have no heels to their shoes and spend the whole of their life slip-shod?

Even the British Ambassador to Constantinople, who hated the Russians so much that he spent most of his career defending the Sultan against them, seemed to think that there was little chance the Sultan would ever become civilized. Though the evidence of Turkish barbarism was obvious, Palmerston chose to ignore it. His attitude towards the Balkan nations was that he was quite content to leave them saddled with a tyrannical government much more brutal than any in the rest of Europe. To him, this was necessary if British interests in the Near East were to be safeguarded.

Palmerston was often accused of being flippant and trivial in his dealings with others, as well as being offensive and a bully. However, the underlying concern he had throughout his life was that of keeping foreigners in their place and standing up for his country. This, in spite of the criticisms, is what he always thought he was doing.

# IDEAS AND PRINCIPLES

| | |
|---|---|
| **Autocracy** | A system of authority heavily concentrated on the central exercise of power by a government which pays no regard to the wishes of its subjects. *Personal autocracy* or *dictatorship* occurs when such power lies in the hands of one individual. (See also Chapter 10, *Absolutist Government*.) |
| **Coup d'état** | A French phrase to describe any sudden and illegal change of government, usually involving the seizure of power by some individual or group. |
| **Feudalism** | A traditional social and political system, based on the ownership of land and often tracing its roots back to the Middle Ages. This system continued in some parts of Central and Eastern Europe until well into the nineteenth century, and the word *feudal* is still sometimes used even today to describe something that is extremely old-fashioned. |
| **Liberalism** | The belief in a constitutional form of government, and, in a wider sense, the belief that individuals have the right to take the responsibility for government decisions by sharing in the decision-making process. In a particular sense, the word *Liberal* is used to describe one of the two major political parties in Britain in the nineteenth century. (See also Chapter 10, *liberalism*.) |
| **Lobby** | A pressure group seeking to persuade members of a government to support certain policies, by using personal contacts with them, especially in the *lobbies* i.e. those parts of the government legislature to which the public are admitted. |

| | |
|---|---|
| **Nationalism** | The belief in an independent form of government for any nation group free from the control of any foreign power. *Nationalist parties*, such as the Irish Nationalist Party, come to be set up in order to further this aim of national political independence. (See also Chapter 10, *nationalism*.) |
| **Régime** | Any system of ordering, especially any political system of government or administration. The French phrase *ancien régime* = 'old order' is often used to describe the form of government previously existing. |
| **Republic** | A system of government without a monarch or emperor, and usually under an elected president. Popular movements such as those in the Italian states in the nineteenth century often aimed to overthrow traditional régimes under the various princes, and set up republics instead. |
| **Self-determination** | The right to choose, especially the right of a people or a nation group to choose its own form of government without foreign interference. |

# APPLIED MATERIALS

## BOOKS

HILL, C. P. & WRIGHT, J. C., (1981). *British History 1815–1914.* Chapters 3 & 7.

BEN JONES, R., (1987). *History of Britain: 1760–1914. The Challenge of Greatness.* Hodder & Stoughton. Chapter 9.

LINDSAY, D. & WASHINGTON, E. S., (1966). *Portrait of Britain: Between the Exhibitions. 1851–1951.* Oxford. Chapter 11.

RICHARDS, D. & HUNT, J. W., (1987). *Illustrated History of Modern Britain 1783–1980.* Third Edition, Longman. Chapters 12 & 14.

WHITTLE, John, (1966). *Great Prime Ministers.* A. & C. Black. Chapter on Lord Palmerston.

## MORE DETAILED BOOKS

WARD, D. R., (1972). *Foreign Affairs 1815–65.* Collins, Britain in Modern Times series. Chapter 5.

## DOCUMENTARY SOURCES

HOLMAN, D. (Ed.) *Portraits and Documents: Earlier Nineteenth Century.* Hutchinson Educational. pps. 134–157

## AUDIO-VISUAL

| | |
|---|---|
| Palmerston | Audio Learning  HM 0020 |
| Palmerston | Audio Learning  HEAO 13 (more advanced) |
| The Early Victorian Era 1837–60 | AVP 509 |

# E X A M I N A T I O N   Q U E S T I O N S

**1**   Study sources A and B and then answer questions a) to d) which follow.

**Source A**   (A cartoon of the early 1860s showing Palmerston and Cobden)

THE OLD SENTINEL.

(PAM: "DON'T YOU MEDDLE WITH THINGS YOU DON'T UNDERSTAND, YOUNG FELLER")

**Source B**   (taken from *The Times*, published on Palmerston's death)

It is impossible not to feel that Lord Palmerston's death marks the end of an era in English politics. 'The old order changeth, yielding place to the new.' Other ministers . . . may introduce a new spirit into foreign relations, and abandon the style of secret diplomacy which he never failed to support. Others may well advise her Majesty with great gifts of persuasion; but his place in the hearts of people will not be filled so easily. The name of Lord Palmerston, once the terror of the Continent, will long be connected in the minds of Englishmen with an era of unbroken peace and great prosperity, and cherished together with the brightest memories of the reign of Queen Victoria.

a) i)   How is Palmerston dressed in the cartoon?

*(1)*

ii)   What is the most likely reason for his being shown dressed like this?

*(1)*

iii)   Against which European country was this cannon most likely to have been pointed at this time?

*(1)*

iv)   What does the picture of Cobden pouring water into Palmerston's cannon indicate about the differing attitudes of the two men towards this European country?

*(2)*

b) i)   In what year did Source B appear?

*(1)*

ii)   Give two examples of incidents which seem to support *The Times*'s belief that Palmerston had an affectionate *place in the hearts of the people*.

*(2)*

iii) Comment on the truth of *The Times*'s view that the era of Palmerston was one of *unbroken peace and great prosperity*.

*(3)*

c)  Describe two incidents in his foreign policy which seemed to support the newspaper's claim that Palmerston was *once the terror of the Continent*.

*(6)*

d)  Referring to both Sources A and B, explain what attitudes towards Palmerston they have in common.

*(3)*

(LEAG)

**2**  a)  Why was Palmerston so interested in the Belgian Revolt?
  b)  How did Palmerston safeguard British interests in relation to Belgium between 1830 and 1839?
  c)  How successful was Palmerston as a foreign minister?

(SEAG) *(30 marks)*

**3**  Describe Palmerston's handling of *four* of the following in foreign affairs: the Don Pacifico affair )1850); the coup d'état of Louis Napoleon (1851); the wars with China (1856–58 and 1859–60); the wars of Italian unity (1859–60); the *Alabama* affair (1862–64); the Schleswig-Holstein affair (1864). To what extent does Palmerston's handling of the episodes you have selected illustrate his concern to protect Britain's interests abroad?

(London)

**4**  Draft a memorandum from the Prince Consort, Albert, to Lord Palmerston in 1850 showing how and why you support the points set out by Queen Victoria in the Queen's Memorandum to her Foreign Minister.

# OUTLINE ANSWERS

**1**  a)  i) He is dressed as a soldier, in uniform.
  ii) Because of his warlike attitudes and actions.
  iii) France. N.B. brief answers will suffice when the mark allocation is only 1.
  iv) It shows that Palmerston was very hostile towards the French but that Cobden took a much more friendly attitude. There will be one mark for a mention of either man. It would be acceptable to say that Cobden was responsible for a free trade treaty with the French in 1859.

  b)  i) It must have been 1865, since Source B is an obituary notice, and Palmerston died in 1865. The answer '1865' would score the mark.
  ii) There is a wide choice of answers here. His actions towards China in the First Opium War, or his attitudes in the Don Pacifico case would score 1 each. N.B. a full description of neither incident is required, since only 2 marks are on offer.
  iii) A mention of Britain's manufacturing and trading position would score 1 mark here, with a second mark for the observation that the Great Exhibition (1851) occurred in the course of his career. The third mark might be earned, for example, by saying that this *great prosperity* was not always evenly spread, or for saying that the *unbroken peace* was interrupted by events such as those of the Crimean War.

  c)  His dispatch of a blockading fleet to the coast of Holland in 1832, or his sending of an expeditionary force to fight the Carlists in Spain later in the 1830s, could be two examples of ways in which Palmerston's actions intimidated the Continent. There will be about 3 marks for each episode, so a little detail would be appropriate in each case, with an indication of the reason why Palmerston's actions gave rise to *terror*. It is desirable not to repeat the same episodes as have been used in your answer to b) ii) – the sending of a fleet to blockade the Piraeus in 1850, for instance, would overlap with Don Pacifico.

  d)  Three points of similarity here would suffice to score the full 3 marks. The figure of Palmerston in soldier's uniform illustrates his popular image 'in the hearts of the people'; his willingness to use direct action (e.g. the cannon) shows that he was 'once the terror of the Continent'; and the caption 'The Old Sentinel' matches the sentiment of the obituary with its phrase 'an era of unbroken peace.' There may be other similarities between the two sources which you would prefer to use.

**2** a) The question here ('Why?') calls for an explanation of Palmerston's interest, and should not focus on the narrative detail of the revolt, nor on its causes. Answers should relate to the proximity of Belgium to the British coast, its strategical importance for Britain, the unwillingness of the British government to allow the country to fall victim to Holy Alliance repression or to pass into powerful foreign hands (e.g. the French). Palmerston also had some sympathy for liberal principles and for the rights of smaller nations 'struggling to be free.'

b) Specific examples of this safeguarding need to be provided. His major effort was *diplomatic*, and examples of his co-operation with France in the interests of Belgian independence, or of the diplomatic checks he imposed on France when he grew suspicious of their motives, will need to be provided. The Treaty of London, establishing Belgian independence and neutrality, is relevant here. Part of his effort was *naval*, and the British blockade of the Dutch coast is also relevant.

c) This is a wider question, relating to the whole conduct of Palmerston's foreign policy. It should therefore not be confined to the Belgian question, nor to the period 1830–41. Narrative detail may occur in the course of your answer, but the question is designed to be one of *assessment*, and instances of his success or lack of success will help you arrive at a verdict. The criterion of success is whether Palmerston furthered British interests, rather than whether he was popular or whether he had the support of the Queen; so the examples you choose should relate to this.

N.B. You must assume for the purposes of this question, and for all other cases where there is no specific tariff of marks printed, that the total of 30 marks is divided approximately equally between the three parts.

# A STUDENT'S ANSWER TO Q.3

> There are a number of careless spelling errors here which detract from the appearance of examination work. You should check the proper spelling of 'quarrel', 'suppress' and 'parties'. There is also some inconsistency in spelling 'oponents' with one 'p' but 'opposition' with two.

> Some useful narrative detail here, but no mention at all of Palmerston.

> This is the 1839 China episode, and is outside the dates in the question. There is also factual confusion in placing the 'Arrow' episode at the wrong date.

3 Louis Napolean had been elected as President of the Second Republic under its constitution of 1848, but there had been a number of quarells between him and the Assembly over the next three years. He had been slow to send troops to Italy on the side of the nationalists, and he had often used his powers to lock up his oponents and supress opposition partys. His chance came in December 1851 when he resisted the efforts of the Assembly to limit the franchise. He was able to pose as a suporter of democracy and arrest 70 leading political figures, plastering Paris with posters proclaiming himself Emperor.

In the first of his wars with China, Palmerston sent troops to Canton to take reprisals for the action of a local official, Lin, in ceasing a confinement of opium and putting the crew of the lorcha 'Arrow' in jail. This shows that Palmerston would not be messed about by foreigners, and so he took control of Hong Kong and opened up five other treaty ports to European trade. This made him very popular.

During the wars in Italy in 1858-59 Palmerston helped Cavour in his quest to unite together all the Italian states. It was the intervention of the British navy which

66 Factually shaky. It is doubtful whether Garibaldi was Cavour's *ally* in these years. (See further Chapter 12). 99

66 Again stronger on historical mythology than on evaluation of Palmerston's role in Italy. Note that only *three* episodes are discussed here. 99

66 An attempt at assessment here, but it is not very informative and relates to episodes *outside* the four that are referred to in the terms of the question. 99

enabled Garibaldi, Cavour's ally, to land in Cisily, and he also helped while his troops crossed the straits and landed in Naples. The muskets his troops had were army surplus and came from Woolwich Arsenal with Palmerston's blessing.

Palmerston handled these episodes because he was concerned to protect British interests abroad. These interests were very important to him and to Parliament and the nation at large because Britain was a trading Nation that depended heavily upon its fleet and its colonies. Palmerston was also anxious to protect British citizens abroad, as he did in the Don Pacifico case. The Spanish Marriages also showed he would not allow himself to be outsmarted by Foreigners.

# A TUTOR'S ANSWER TO Q.4

4   The Queen is distressed at the often unpredictable behaviour of Her Foreign Minister in matters vital to this country, and at his unprecedented interpretation of the British Constitution.

Nowhere does the Constitution demand an indifference on the part of the sovereign to political matters, and nowhere would such indifference be more condemned than in England. There was no interest of the Royal House involved in any of the questions with which we quarrelled with the Foreign Minister, neither in Greece nor Italy, Sicily, Holstein, Hungary etc.

Why are Princes alone to be denied the credit of having political opinions based upon an anxiety for national interests and honour of their country and the welfare of mankind? Are they not more independently placed than any other politician in the state? Are their interests not most intimately bound up with those of the country? Is the sovereign not the natural guardian of the honour of his country, is he not *necessarily* a politician? Has he no duties to perform towards his country?

# SUGGESTIONS FOR FURTHER WORK

1   Draw up a table to outline the foreign policy of Canning (1822–27), and make a list of the arguments which could be used to show that Palmerston was a 'disciple of Canning.'

2   Find out what you can in detail about the Treaty of London (1839). You may wish to refer to the text of the treaty, pp. 88–98 in *The Concert of Europe, 1815–1914*, ed. R. Albrecht-Carrié (Harper Torchbooks, 1968). What was the importance of this treaty down to 1914?

3   Write entries for Palmerston's personal diary and for the diary of the Queen for June 27th 1850, the day after the *Civis Romanus Sum* speech in the House of Commons, illustrating how they would have viewed the Don Pacifico episode differently.

## GETTING STARTED

Gladstone and Disraeli were the two rival political leaders when Britain made her first real step to becoming a male democracy in 1867. The age of Palmerston was dead, and the public, through the rapidly expanding press, was keen to put the spotlight on the new politicians and their policies. Their period of rivalry was comparatively short, dating from 1867 until Disraeli's death in 1881. Before 1867 the political stage was dominated by others including Palmerston, and after 1881 by the Conservative leader Lord Salisbury, who seemed to lag behind Gladstone in popular appeal, if not in electoral appeal.

Gladstone and Disraeli started political life on the same side, and entered parliament as Conservatives. W. E. Gladstone (1809–98) had to live down the fact that his father was not only a Liverpool merchant, but was also a slave-owner. He had a distinguished career at Oxford and had no difficulty in entering parliament in 1832 when he was only 23 years old. The Duke of Newcastle was so impressed with Gladstone's relentless opposition to the 1832 Reform Bill that he provided Gladstone with a safe seat at Newark.

B. Disraeli (1804–81) did not find entering politics so easy. His father, Isaac d'Israeli had converted from the Jewish to the Christian faith after his son Benjamin was born. He did not send his son to university and, despite several years of trying, Benjamin was unable to secure a seat in parliament until 1837, by which time his marriage to a rich widow had provided him with the necessary funds. He was now 33, and starting his political career ten years later in life than Gladstone.

Both men were skilful with the pen: Gladstone wrote serious essays, especially on religious and political subjects. Disraeli wrote novels, but few took him as seriously as he took himself, for his novels often had a deeply felt social message. Disraeli's difficulty in being taken seriously was not helped by his eccentric appearance; long black ringlets curled over his neck when it was fashionable for men to wear their hair short, his brightly-coloured waistcoats and his habit of wearing his rings over his gloves, marked him out as an oddity. When he gave his maiden speech (i.e. his first speech) in parliament the Irish M.P.s decided against all precedent to refuse him a courteous hearing because of his known hostility to O'Connell. Unable to continue amid the House of Commons clamour, Disraeli was heard to shout

> I am not at all surprised at the reception I have experienced. I have begun several things many times, and I have often succeeded at the last – though many predicted that I must fail, as they had done before me. I sit down now, but the time will come when you will hear me.

# HISTORICAL DEVELOPMENTS

**1** **COLLEAGUES AND RIVALS**

66 Their early lives compared. 99

Gladstone had the unenviable task in his first speech of replying to an attack on his father's slave-holding record. All agreed that he had achieved a successful defence of his father with a combination of humility and a commitment to slave emancipation. Both men in later years were listened to with respect, Gladstone for his sincerity and Disraeli for his wit. Both looked to the time when the Conservatives would be in power and they would be able to join Sir Robert Peel's government. This was formed when the General Election of 1841 gave the Conservatives a majority of over eighty. Gladstone by now had been in parliament for nine years, had been a member of Peel's first ministry in 1834–35 and was widely expected to be included in the new one. He became Vice-President of the Board of Trade, an important but not senior post, and one in which he became a convinced free-trader in a government which was committed to maintaining Protection. Disraeli, too, expected to be offered a post in the government, but he had been in parliament only four years. Although regarded as a leading Conservative – he had been included by Peel at a meeting of sixteen leading Conservatives in 1840 – he had already made enemies within the party. Lord Stanley declared that if 'that scoundrel' Disraeli were offered a place he would not remain in the government himself. Later, as Lord Derby, Stanley was only too happy to have Disraeli serve in his own ministries, but in the meantime Disraeli waited in vain for Peel's summons. He even wrote a grovelling letter to Peel, virtually begging for a government post, to which Peel replied with a dignified refusal. There is no doubt that Peel's treatment of him rankled with Disraeli, but it was not the main reason for the clash that was to come in 1846.

Gladstone was by no means subservient to Peel and disagreed with him on a number of occasions, but his work on the tariff revisions of 1842 was invaluable and in 1843 Gladstone became President of the Board of Trade, with a seat in the Cabinet. Disraeli quarrelled with his leaders more often. He was becoming suspicious of the government's lack of commitment to Protection, and defended the landowner interest with his new constituents at Shrewsbury by insisting that any moves towards Free Trade should be reciprocal, i.e. that we should only reduce or remove duties if governments of other countries would act similarly. He surrounded himself with a group of M.P.s, popularly known as 'Young England', who sniped at the government from the back benches and whose activities seemed to make Disraeli's inclusion in the government an impossibility for the foreseeable future.

In 1846 came the great political crisis caused by the Irish famine and Peel's determination to give in to the demands of the Anti-Corn Law League by abolishing the Corn Laws. At this crucial time neither Disraeli nor Gladstone were in the Cabinet which took this momentous decision. Disraeli would no doubt have fought it tooth and nail as did his old enemy Stanley. Gladstone might well have made a valuable contribution in defence of Peel's policy but in January 1846 Gladstone was appointed to the Colonial Office in Peel's reconstructed government, and Gladstone was required by the custom of those days to seek the approval of his constituents for this promotion. Newark, under landowner influence, refused to re-elect him. Gladstone failed to find a new seat until Oxford University elected him in August 1847. Thus during the crucial Corn Law debates Gladstone was not in the House of Commons to defend his leader Peel from the bitter charges of betraying his party levelled at him by Disraeli. With the help of the Whigs, Peel secured a majority for the repeal of the Corn Laws, but it took five months to get the Repeal through parliament, and the Conservative Party was split in two. The crisis placed Disraeli and Gladstone on opposite sides. Disraeli was now undisputedly the effective, if not the nominal, leader of the Protectionist wing of the party. Gladstone was Peel's most devoted lieutenant in the Free Trade or Peelite wing of the party. Gladstone never forgave Disraeli for his treatment of Peel in 1846: from then on the two men can certainly be regarded as rivals.

66 They become political enemies. 99

**2** **PARTY UNCERTAINTIES**

The issue of Protection v. Free Trade which split the Conservative Party in 1846 did not remain a live issue for long. Peel died in 1850 and in 1852 Disraeli virtually abandoned any notion of a return to Protection. Personalities rather than party issues now kept both men apart, and while Disraeli believed the Protectionists to be the true Conservatives,

Gladstone hovered between Peelites and Whigs after 1850, uncertain about which group was most in sympathy with his ideas. Disraeli was briefly Chancellor of the Exchequer in the Derby (formerly Lord Stanley) ministry in 1852. Gladstone became Chancellor of the Exchequer in Lord Aberdeen's Peelite ministry in 1852. He continued the work towards Free Trade by abolishing over 120 duties and talked of reducing the income tax which he always disliked. However, his plans were frustrated by the Crimean War (1854–56) and income tax had to be doubled. Disraeli made great efforts to persuade Gladstone to join Derby's second ministry in 1858, even offering to stand down as Chancellor of the Exchequer to make way for him. Gladstone wisely declined. It may be that memories of 1846 made it impossible for him to join a government of which Disraeli was a member. It may be that Gladstone was well aware that if he did so he would eventually have to contest the leadership of the Conservative Party with Disraeli, while the Whig leaders were elderly men and the succession to the leadership there was wide open. Yet it was not some principle of British politics which lured Gladstone into the Whig camp in 1859 to join Palmerston whom he had so often criticized and denounced. It was his sympathy for Palmerston's views on the Italian question (see Chapter 4) that convinced him.

Gladstone had become Chancellor of the Exchequer in 1859 and in his Budgets of 1860 and 1861 completed Britain's adoption of Free Trade, retaining only 48 duties for revenue purposes. Thwarted by the House of Lords in his attempt to get the paper duties abolished in 1860, he succeeded in 1861 by putting all his Budget proposals in one Bill instead of presenting them in a series of separate Bills, so that the House of Lords had either to accept the budget as a whole or take on the political risks of rejecting it as a whole. Gladstone gained a great reputation as Chancellor of the Exchequer during the 1850s and 1860s, enough to make him indispensable to the Whig party he had joined in 1859, even if it did not make him popular. Disraeli, on the other hand, was Chancellor of the Exchequer twice, in 1852 and 1858, but was in office so briefly that he made little impression, especially as in 1859 he was busy with a parliamentary reform bill (see Chapter 2) which neither pleased his own side nor satisfied the opposition.

## 3 LEADERSHIP AND PARLIAMENTARY REFORM

Gladstone's wisdom in rejecting Disraeli's overtures to join the Derby government of 1858 seemed justified when he became leader of his party in 1867. Disraeli had to wait for the Conservative leadership until 1868 when Lord Derby resigned. The revival of the parliamentary reform question in the year after Palmerston died gave both politicians the chance to show their mettle. Gladstone proposed in 1866 a very cautious extension of the franchise; in a way typical of him he aroused great hopes only to dash them down.

> I venture to say that every man who is not presumably incapacitated by some consideration of personal unfitness or of political danger is morally entitled to come within the pale of the Constitution. Of course, in giving utterance to such a proposition, I do not recede from the protest I have previously made against sudden, or violent, or excessive, or intoxicating change.

He was opposed by Disraeli on the grounds that the reform did not go far enough, and when the defeat of the Whig Bill brought Derby and Disraeli back to power, Disraeli, after a pale imitation of the Whig Bill had been abandoned, proposed a ratepayer borough franchise safeguarded by extra votes contemptuously called 'fancy franchises'. Gladstone threw his previously declared caution to the winds, forced Disraeli to abandon his 'fancy franchises' and pushed Disraeli into a Reform Act that enfranchised a million new voters (see Chapter 2). For this Act the voters gave Gladstone, rather than Disraeli, the credit in the General Election of 1868. Perhaps this is why subsequent parliamentary reform legislation was Gladstone's rather than Disraeli's, but the main revival of demand for such reform did not come until after Disraeli's death in 1881. The Ballot Act of 1872 was necessitated by the enormous increase in the number of borough voters who could not be accommodated on an open hustings, rather than arising as a party issue. Even so the 1872 Ballot Act removed the fear of intimidation from the working-class voters, most of whom were expected to support Gladstone and the Liberals. The Corrupt Practices Act of 1883 struck the most effective blow at corruption at election times. The Reform Act and Redistribution Act of 1884–85 placed the county franchise on the same qualifications as the borough one, and carried out a major and necessary redistribution of seats.

## 4 ▷ DOMESTIC REFORM 1868–80

❝❝ Follow the argument of this comparison carefully. ❞❞

Both Gladstone and Disraeli followed their respective election victories of 1868 and 1874 by a spate of domestic reforms. Those who argue that Gladstone's reforms were administrative and were aimed at removing corruption and inefficiency from government, thus pleasing the middle-class, while Disraeli aimed at social reform to please the working-class, are guilty of over-simplification. Of course politicians at the time pointed up a contrast for electoral reasons. Disraeli regarded Gladstone's reforms as a threat to all the British time-honoured institutions the Conservatives had pledged themselves to defend, while the Liberals tried to belittle Conservative reform by calling it a 'policy of sewage'. Yet there is a strong social element in Gladstone's reforms, and Disraeli's were more wide-ranging than merely cleaning up towns.

Gladstone's *Ballot Act* (1872) may have been administratively necessary to cope with the large increase in the number of voters, but it also had important social significance in freeing the poorer voters from the influence of landlord or employer. The Forster *Education Act* (1870) set up the machinery whereby ratepayers were to build elementary schools in areas where the number of voluntary schools was insufficient. School Boards, elected by ratepayers, were to be responsible for the running and financing of these schools, and were given power to make attendance compulsory if they so wished. The system of payment by results, established in 1861, by which state aid was given to voluntary schools in accordance with the results of examinations held by government inspectors, was to apply to the new Board schools. Disraeli did not oppose the Act as a whole, but focused attention on the unsatisfactory nature of the compulsory non-denominational religious education that the Board schools were required to provide. The Act generated much passionate religious rather than political opposition, but the social achievement in placing basic education (at least elementary reading, writing and arithmetic) within the reach of all, singles out this Act as one of the most important pieces of progressive legislation in the nineteenth century.

When Disraeli came to power he made no attempt to undermine it, rather to consolidate Gladstone's work: Lord *Sandon's Act* in 1876 penalised parents who kept their children from school unless officially exempted by the inspectors, thus depriving the School Boards of the discretionary power on attendance, and *Mundella's Act* in 1880 in effect made attendance compulsory up to the age of 13. Gladstone's *Universities Test Act* of 1871 removed the social injustice which until then had confined scholarships, teaching and administrative posts at Oxford and Cambridge Universities to members of the Church of England. From 1871 they were to be open to all, regardless of class or religion.

Gladstone's government had widened opportunity both at the bottom and at the top in education. It hoped to do similarly in the civil service and the army. In 1870, examinations were introduced for all but the very highest ranks in the civil service, thus making ability rather than connection the key factor in entry and promotion. *Cardwell's army reforms* were certainly designed to make the army more efficient: the War Office was reorganized and the Commander-in-Chief made subordinate to the Secretary for War. Recruitment was encouraged by reducing the period of service to six years on active service and six years with the reserves. Regiments were to be divided into two battalions – one for service at home, the other for service abroad. Local patriotism was to be encouraged by associating the old numbered regiments with individual counties and giving them county names. The abolition of flogging in peace-time made army service less barbarous, and the abolition of the purchase of commissions, which encountered much opposition in the House of Lords, opened the middle and higher officer ranks to men of ability, making them less of a preserve for the sons of the aristocracy. These changes certainly led to an improved quality of recruit from a wider social base and to better officers, even though for the present the War Office obstinately refused to introduce breech-loading artillery, despite its proved success in the Franco-Prussian War. In general, the army was much more efficient and able to take on whatever was demanded of it for the rest of the century. Disraeli confined his criticism to attacking the constitutional device by which Gladstone avoided opposition in the House of Lords to the abolition of the purchase of commissions by getting the Queen to abolish them by royal Warrant.

The *Judicature Act*, passed by parliament in 1873, was Gladstone's effort to simplify the chaotic complexity of the Law courts. The eight courts, with their separate staff of judges, but overlapping responsibilities, were replaced by a High Court divided into three separate sections, and a Court of Appeal. Gladstone's removal of the final right of appeal from the House of Lords was the main point of attack by Disraeli, and when Disraeli came back into power this right was restored in 1876. The administration of justice became smoother and cheaper. The losers were the lawyers who made money out of the old incomprehensible system, and the gainers were those of the general public who found it necessary to go to law. The Act was hardly likely to touch the lower classes unless the poor were brought before the law as criminals, but the Trade Union legislation very much affected them. During the 1850s trade union growth had been largely confined to skilled workers, but during the 1860s the unskilled began to be organized. The new unions found it difficult to enforce a strike without intimidation and even violence, and impossible in consequence of a court decision of 1867 to protect their funds against dishonest officials. A Royal Commission was set up to investigate all matters relating to trade unions, and the legislation of Gladstone's government was based on its findings. Perhaps with the 'Sheffield outrages' fresh in their minds the members of the Commission were rather unsympathetic to trade unions, and the legislation reflected this. The *Trade Union Act* of 1871 gave trade unions the right to go to law and thus to protect their property and funds, but the *Criminal Law Amendment Act* of the same year banned intimidation in such sweeping terms as to make even peaceful picketing impossible, thus effectively depriving trade unions of the power to strike. Trade union anger and agitation against Gladstone's legislation led Disraeli's government in 1875 to introduce the *Conspiracy and Protection of Property Act* which permitted peaceful picketing and which allowed strikers in a body to undertake any act which would be legal if committed by an individual. Thus if it was lawful for one person to absent himself from work, then it was lawful for more than one to absent themselves in a strike. The *Employers and Workmen Act* of the same year made breach of contract by workmen or employer a civil offence. Thus a worker on strike need no longer fear criminal prosecution and possible imprisonment. The Gladstone Acts of 1871 had given the trade unions legal status, but it was the Disraeli legislation, for which Home Secretary Cross was responsible, which appeared to give the trade unions a legal power and immunity unchallenged until 1900.

Whatever their consequences, Gladstone's reforms were certainly administrative rather than social in intent, but he was responsible for a *Public Health Act*, an *Adulteration Act* and a *Mines Act*, all in 1872. These paved the way for Disraeli's later legislation, as did Gladstone's *Licensing Act* of 1872. Drunkenness was undoubtedly a major social evil, but Gladstone's proposal in 1871 to cut the number of liquor licences and put the rest up for auction aroused intense opposition from the liquor trade. It did not go far enough for the temperance reformers, who wanted to close all the public houses. The 1872 Act limited public-house opening hours and made some provision to improve the quality of the beer and spirits sold. The liquor trade remembered Gladstone for his 1871 proposals rather than the weaker Act of 1872, and it was not well pleased when in 1874 Disraeli's government cut opening hours still further by the *Cross Licensing Act*.

Some of the legislation of the Disraeli ministry was in response to, or as amendments to, legislation passed by the Gladstone ministry. But some of it was specifically social and directed to improving the condition of the working classes whose votes Disraeli was trying to wean away from the Liberals. Some modern historians have been highly critical of Disraeli's work, pointing out its limitations, and Disraeli's lack of interest in it. The words of his Home Secretary, Richard Cross, who was responsible for much of the domestic legislation have often been quoted:

> When the cabinet came to discuss the Queen's Speech (1874), I was, I confess, disappointed at the want of originality shown by the Prime Minister. From all his speeches, I had quite expected that his mind was full of legislative schemes, but such did not prove to be the case; on the contrary, he had to rely on the various suggestions of his colleagues, and as they themselves had only just come into office, and that suddenly, there was some difficulty in framing the Queen's speech.

This view is given added weight by the fact that the famous Plimsoll line introduced under the *Merchant Shipping Act* of 1876 to prevent the overloading of merchant ships, had to be forced from a complacent government by the angry words of Samuel Plimsoll in the House of Commons. There is also the charge that much of the social legislation was permissive rather than compulsory, and that Rowntree's investigations showed how little impact it had had on poverty and social conditions by the end of the century. But it should be remembered that Peel and Gladstone had brought about the triumph of *laisser-faire* economics during the 1840s and 1850s, that most state regulation was regarded as unwarranted interference, and that by the standards of the day, and in comparison with what Gladstone had done in 1868–74, the social reform of Disraeli's government was bold and innovative.

Apart from the Merchant Shipping Act, Disraeli's social reform is contained in three

**66** Was Disraeli a committed reformer?

major legislative measures. The *Artisans Dwellings Act* of 1875 gave local authorities power to purchase and demolish slums, and although the Act did not give the power to purchase compulsorily, some authorities like that of Birmingham made effective use of the Act's provisions. The *Public Health Act* of 1875 consolidated previous Health Acts: it did employ compulsion in making local authorities appoint Medical Officers of Health; and infectious diseases were to be compulsorily notified; the provision of drainage, sewage, water supply and refuse collection also became a statutory responsibility of the authorities. Factory legislation which had always been compulsory was amended in 1874 to give the Ten Hour Day for which humanitarians had been campaigning for so long, and in 1878 a consolidating *Factory Act* drew together all existing legislation and brought all factories and workshops within the scope of the factory inspectors. In addition to these three, useful work was achieved by the *Sale of Food and Drugs Act*, 1875, which extended the scope of previous Acts to prevent unwholesome additives in food and drink. The *Climbing Boys Act*, 1875, put an end once and for all to the social evil of child chimney sweeps, and the *Enclosure of Commons Act*, 1876, placed limits on enclosure and helped to preserve Epping Forest from enclosure in 1878. The *Rivers Pollution Act* for the first time imposed some control on what was discharged into British rivers.

## SUMMARY OF THE DOMESTIC LEGISLATION OF 1868–80

| Gladstone | Disraeli |
|---|---|
| 1870 Civil Service reform | 1874 Licensing Act |
| 1870 Education Act | 1875 Factory Act |
| 1871 Trade Union Act | 1875 Climbing Boys Act |
| 1871 Criminal Law Amendment Act | 1875 Sale of Food and Drugs Act |
| 1871 Universities Test Act | 1875 Public Health Act |
| 1872 Ballot Act | 1875 Conspiracy and Protection of Property Act |
| 1872 Licensing Act | 1876 Merchant Shipping Act |
| 1872 Mines Act | 1876 Enclosure of Commons Act |
| 1872 Public Health Act | 1876 Sandon's Act |
| 1872 Adulteration Act | 1876 Rivers Pollution Act |
| 1871–3 Army reforms | 1880 Mundella's Act |
| 1873 Judicature Act | |

**5 ▷ FOREIGN POLICY 1868–80**

Although in the last year of his life Palmerston seemed to lose his grip on a changing world, critics were quick to contrast Gladstone's foreign policy with that of Palmerston in his heyday. It was sensible of Gladstone, with a small and unreformed army, to avoid continental commitments which could lead to war. Britain kept out of the Franco-Prussian War in which British sympathies, at first with Prussia, soon veered round to the underdog, France. Gladstone persuaded Prussia and France to respect the neutrality of Belgium, but he could not prevent Russia using the opportunity of the war to destroy the Black Sea clauses of the Treaty of Paris. All he could do was to solemnly protest that international treaties should not be changed without the consent of all the original signatories. In 1872 Gladstone agreed to submit the longstanding dispute with the U.S.A. over the '*Alabama*' to international arbitration. It was greatly to Gladstone's credit that this was one of the first disputes between great powers to be dealt with by such arbitration. A hostile verdict seemed inevitable as Britain was so clearly in the wrong to allow the Confederacy to build armed merchant ships in Britain during the American Civil War. There were bitter protests about the £3,250,000 damages awarded, one third of the American claim, and much was made of the American difficulty in finding rightful claimants to the money. But it was a small price to pay to settle such a dispute with little rancour and no conflict, although it cost Gladstone dearly at the 1874 General Election.

Gladstone's desire for peace and the avoidance of unnecessary commitments help to explain why in 1870 he failed to take the opportunity to buy the Suez Canal outright for Britain. Disraeli did not let the same opportunity slip by in 1875. The Khedive of Egypt was bankrupt and desperate to sell his Suez Canal shares to the highest bidder as quickly as possible. Rather than see the shares be bought by the French, Disraeli borrowed from a private banker rather than risk delay through the cumbersome procedures of raising a loan from the Bank of England. Gladstone criticized the purchase as unconstitutional in method and commercially and financially unsound, but eighty per cent of the ships using the Canal were British, and Gladstone himself during his second Ministry (1880–85) was to take

**❝❝ The high point of Disraeli's career. ❞❞**

steps to make the British position in Egypt more permanent.

Disraeli's handling of the Eastern Question (see Chapter 14) seemed to present an even greater contrast with the conciliatory policies of Gladstone. The ending of the Black Sea clauses of the Treaty of Paris in 1870 had brought Gladstone's ineffective protest, but had enabled Russia to undertake the refortification of Sebastopol and the revival of a Black Sea fleet. Thus when the Balkan crisis began in 1875, Disraeli was reluctant to push the Turks into concessions for fear of weakening Turkey to the advantage of Russia. Turkish atrocities in 1876 were an embarrassment to the British government, but a great opportunity to Gladstone who emerged from his retirement to denounce both the atrocities and British efforts to preserve the Turkish Empire. His pamphlet, *The Bulgarian Horrors and the Question of the East*, had a profound effect upon public opinion, and Gladstone used his most colourful language to denounce the Turks:

> Let the Turks now carry away their abuses in the only possible manner, namely by carrying off themselves. Their Zaptiehs and their Mudins, their Bimbashis and their Yuzhashis, their Kaimakams and their Pashas, one and all, bag and baggage, shall I hope clear out from the province they have desolated and profaned.

He seemed out of character here in advocating a policy which could only result in war. Disraeli regarded Gladstone's intervention as unhelpful, and described the pamphlet as the greatest of all the Bulgarian horrors. Even so Gladstone's coupling of the cause of liberty with the cause of Russia alarmed some of his colleagues, and Disraeli's majorities during the crisis were swollen by the votes of dissident Liberals. The Russian war against Turkey caused the British fleet to be sent to the Dardanelles, and Britain's long-standing suspicion of Russia seemed to be well-founded when Russia enforced the treaty of San Stefano upon Turkey, creating a huge Bulgaria obviously dependent upon Russia. Neither Britain nor the major Continental powers were prepared to tolerate a revival of Russian power. Disraeli took the credit in Britain for the Congress of Berlin, which revised the San Stefano Treaty and allowed Disraeli to claim that he had brought back peace with honour. He certainly had brought back peace with Cyprus, but Gladstone claimed that Cyprus had been gained by placing millions of Macedonians and Bulgarians back under Turkish rule, and that the struggle to free them would have to be fought all over again. The British public was not yet convinced that Britain had 'backed the wrong horse' as Lord Salisbury was to admit later. For Disraeli, 1878 was a year of triumph, and the shops were flooded with trinkets and mementoes of his achievement, and the papers filled with tributes to his diplomacy. For Gladstone, 1878 was a frustrating year, and it is necessary to look elsewhere than his campaign for the oppressed peoples of the Balkans to explain his electoral victory in 1880.

## 6 > IMPERIALISM

In 1872, Disraeli made a speech at Crystal Palace, London, attacking Gladstonian Liberalism and setting out the policy of the Conservative Party on issues such as social reform. He reserved a special part of his speech to support the idea of the British Empire. After attacking the record of the Liberals in breaking up the British Empire during the preceding forty years, he went on:

> But self-government, in my opinion, when it was conceded, ought to have been conceded as part of a great policy of Imperial consolidation. It ought to have been accompanied by an Imperial tariff, by securities for the people of England for the enjoyment of the unappropriated lands which belonged to the Sovereign as their trustee, and by a military code which should have precisely defined the means and responsibilities by which the colonies should be defended, and by which, if necessary, this country should call for aid from the colonies themselves. It ought, further, to have been accompanied by the institution of some representative council in the metropolis, which would have brought the colonies into constant and continuous relation with the Home Government.

All this was very idealistic. Gladstone's government of 1868–74 had been lacking in Imperialist ventures. Disraeli's government of 1874–80 had plenty of Imperialist expansion, but those who hoped for an Imperial tariff, an Imperial defence policy and an Imperial parliament as suggested in the speech were to be disappointed. *Imperialism* was put forward by its advocates as a high ideal, but in practice it often degenerated into the mere acquisition of territory. The purchase of the Suez Canal shares in 1875 and the annexation of Cyprus in 1878 were justified to the public because of Britain's economic and trading interests in the eastern Mediterranean. The proclamation of Queen Victoria as Empress of

India on January 1st, 1877 was perhaps intended to give India some political cohesion, but this was backed by a forward policy in Afghanistan which was intended to curb Russian influence there. General Roberts marched into Afghanistan with a large force and overthrew the pro-Russian Emir, but the massacre of the small garrison he left behind in Kabul led to a full-scale military campaign against the Afghans. The heroism of Roberts' march from Kabul to Kandahar offset some British defeats, and enabled Afghanistan to be held down by force. Gladstone showed how unnecessary it all was. He had criticized the intervention in Afghanistan as an unwarranted interference in the affairs of an independent state. When he came to power in 1880, the British forces were withdrawn, and Afghanistan remained friendly to Britain anyway.

Gladstone did not extricate himself so easily from Disraeli's entanglement in South Africa (see Chapter 7). In 1878, the bankrupt Boer republic of the Transvaal was threatened by the Zulus. Many, but by no means all, of the Boer leaders agreed that annexation by Britain was the only solution. The Zulus overwhelmed Lord Chelmsford's small force at Isandhlwana in January 1879, but six months later the Zulu power was utterly broken at the battle of Ulundi and the Zulu chief Cetewayo captured. The Boers of the Transvaal were disappointed to find themselves a crown colony when they had expected self-government, and they found an able supporter in Gladstone, who attacked Disraeli's policy in parliament. But when Gladstone came to power in 1880 he refused to restore the independence of the Transvaal. The Boers rose in rebellion and in 1881 defeated a British force at Majuba Hill. Gladstone responded by withdrawing British forces from the Transvaal and giving British recognition to the South African Republic in 1884, although the question of ultimate sovereignty was to be a source of dispute in the future.

By now the notion of expanding the Empire, and with it the lofty ideals of christianising and civilizing the natives, had begun to take hold even within the Liberal Party. In 1882 a nationalist rebellion in Egypt seemed to threaten British interests in the Suez Canal. France was unwilling to intervene to protect her own interests there, and Gladstone took on the responsibility of suppressing the rebellion; Arabi Pasha's army was defeated at Tel-el-Kebir (1882). Although Egypt was not annexed outright, enough British forces were kept in Egypt to guarantee stable government, and in 1883 Sir Evelyn Baring (later Lord Cromer) began his long stint as British agent and Consul-General in Egypt. For the next twenty years he was in fact, if not in name, ruler of Egypt. Although Gladstone felt obliged to become involved in Egypt there were no British interests at stake in the Sudan. Egyptian garrisons in the Sudan had been penned back in their fortresses by the Sudanese religious leader, the Mahdi, and his growing armies. In November 1883, General Hicks and his Egyptian troops were annihilated by the Mahdi, and in consequence Sir Evelyn Baring advised the evacuation of all Egyptian forces and their British advisers from the Sudan. Others advised differently, and Lord Hartington had much support in Cabinet for his view that to evacuate the Sudan would leave the Egyptian garrisons already isolated and cut off there to the mercy of the Mahdi. The Cabinet appointed General Gordon, a former governor of the Sudan, to investigate the Sudanese situation. As soon as he reached Egypt, the Khedive made him Governor-General of the Sudan. Gordon's previous record had not shown him to be a man of caution. He regarded his duty to the Khedive as taking priority over any duty to the British government. He moved to Khartoum, announced that he was going to remain there, and soon found himself besieged by the Mahdi's forces. Gladstone had no intention of changing his policy of withdrawal into a campaign for the conquest of the Sudan, especially if such a change of policy was being forced on him by a disobedient general. He resisted all urgings to send military assistance to Gordon. The Queen herself sent a telegram to Lord Hartington, who she thought was sympathetic to Gordon and would use his influence to bring Gladstone to his senses:

> It is alarming; General Gordon is in danger; you are bound to try to save him. Surely Indian troops might go from Aden and could bear the climate though British cannot. You have incurred fearful responsibility.

Gladstone declared that an expedition to the Sudan would be 'a war of conquest against a people rightly struggling to be free'. Not surprisingly, when Gladstone at last decided to send an expedition to rescue Gordon, it was too late. At the end of January the Mahdi's warriors stormed into Khartoum and Gordon was killed; the relieving force arrived two days later. Gladstone brushed aside censure from the House of Lords and from the Queen and took the opportunity of Gordon's death to announce what he had always intended in the first place – the complete evacuation of the Sudan.

In the Sudan affair Gladstone had chosen the wrong man to go to the Sudan and had then

**Was Gladstone merely being obstinate?**

encountered Imperialist opposition in his own Cabinet. He had more success when he called up the reserves and alarmed the Russians into accepting arbitration over the town of Penjdeh which they had occupied near the Afghan frontier. But the arbitrators' award in 1885 was favourable to Russia, and public opinion was almost as hostile to Gladstone over Penjdeh as it was over the death of General Gordon. Disraeli had been dead for four years but he had left Gladstone the legacy of a country where public opinion was increasingly Imperialist and a Cabinet whose Imperialist wing was soon to find Gladstone's Irish policy unacceptable (see chapter 6).

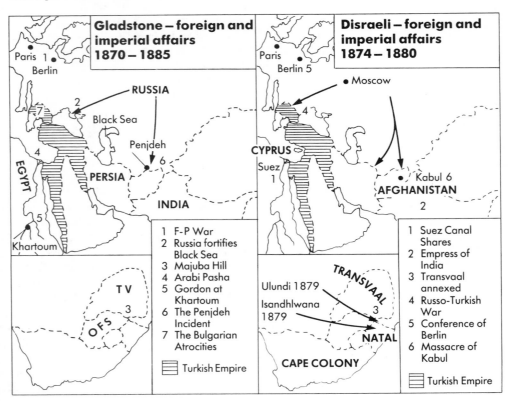

Fig 5.1  Comparing the foreign and imperial affairs of Gladstone and Disraeli.

## 7  CHANGING ELECTORAL FORTUNES

The General Election result of 1868 appeared to give Gladstone, rather than Disraeli, the credit for the 1867 Reform Act. But it was a different story in 1874. The Conservatives achieved power with an absolute majority of over 50 in the House of Commons. In a bitter reference to the unpopularity of his licensing legislation which had turned every public-house into a Conservative committee room, Gladstone complained that he had been 'borne down in a torrent of gin and beer'. Yet there were other reasons for the Liberal defeat. Gladstone's reforms had offended many interests; the deeply religious objected to his undenominational schools, civil servants did not take kindly to the new competitive examinations, nor army officers to Cardwell's drastic army reforms. Trade unionists voted Conservative in their thousands in protest at the Criminal Law Amendment Act. Gladstone's pacific foreign policy was considered by many to be not vigorous enough, and the *Alabama* arbitration was widely criticized as favouring the Americans. In 1872, at Crystal Palace, Disraeli had put forward what was in effect a Conservative Manifesto. In parliament, he had attacked the Gladstone government which had got itself into some minor domestic scandals and began regularly to lose by-elections. He refused to take office in 1873, compelling Gladstone to return at the head of an increasingly troubled government. Disraeli contemptuously described Gladstone's ministers as 'a range of exhausted volcanoes'. The superior Conservative party organization, the result of the efforts of John Gorst, provided a model the Liberals were glad to copy during their forthcoming six years' spell in opposition.

They got their revenge in the General Election of 1880, which reversed the 1874 result by giving the Liberals a majority of more than 50 over all other parties. Oddly enough, Disraeli's trade union legislation had removed the obstacle to working-class voters supporting the Liberal Party, and Disraeli's social reforms had petered out after 1876. The onset of depression in the late 1870s, particularly in the rural areas hit by cheap corn imports from North America, lost the Conservative Party much support. The phenomenon known as the 'swing of the pendulum' was made much of at the time – the idea that voters preferred to change governments on a regular basis, and that Liberal and Conservative governments should alternate. Gladstone's government of 1880–85 was beset by Irish problems (see Chapter 6) and seemed unable to make up its mind about Imperialism. It lacked domestic reform, apart from the Reform Act of 1884, and the unimpressed voters reduced the size of Liberal representation in the General Election of 1885 to approximately that of the Conservatives. Not until Gladstone's conversion to Home Rule was announced did the Irish Nationalists line up in support of Gladstone, but Home Rule shattered the Liberal Party, and in the 1886 General Election the voters swept the Conservatives back into power. In 1892 the Liberals gained a small majority dependent on the support of the Irish Nationalists, but Gladstone was not prepared to take on the House of Lords in the battle over Home Rule, and finally retired from public life in 1894.

## 8 > ASSESSMENT

> *Be prepared to point out similarities and differences in your assessment of these two leaders.*

Gladstone and Disraeli were the political giants of the late nineteenth century. Gladstone joined the backward-looking aristocratic Whig Party in 1859 and by 1868 had transformed it into the modern forward-looking Liberal Party. Disraeli had led a Tory faction and turned it into the modern Conservative Party. He had shown that Conservatism did not mean opposition to change and had committed his party to a policy of social reform, while Gladstone had committed his party to progress and reform. Both welcomed the advent of democracy. Disraeli caught, or created, the public mood with his advocacy of Imperialism and it was his legacy to Gladstone that growing Imperialism made a solution to the Irish Question virtually unattainable. Although Disraeli was accused of being a charlatan, and Gladstone was accused of deviousness and pomposity, both men were strong in principle and honest in their belief that they were working for the good of the country. Their rivalry was healthy for the democracy they both had helped to create, and both made major contributions to the improving social conditions of Victorian Britain.

# IDEAS AND PRINCIPLES

| | |
|---|---|
| **Arbitration** | The consideration of a dispute by independent assessors who are not party to, or involved in, the dispute. In international affairs arbitration avoids confrontation and the possibility of armed conflict, and requires the willingness of both sides to accept the decision of the arbitrators. |
| **Denominational schools** | Denominational schools in Gladstone's day were those schools run by, and financed by, a particular Christian sect (e.g. Anglican, Methodist, Roman Catholic). In such schools the religious teaching was specific to its particular denomination. The 1870 Education Act required religious instruction in Board Schools, but it was to be undenominational, i.e. it was to be simple Bible reading, unrelated to any specific Christian sect. This aroused the anger of the churches, who seemed to regard undenominational religion as worse than no religion at all. |
| **Imperialism** | The idea of expansion of empire. It attracted those with noble motives who believed that such expansion civilized and christianised native peoples. It also attracted politicians for whom it often meant no more than territorial expansion, and business men for whom it meant sources of raw material and markets for manufactured goods. |
| **Picketing** | The practice of representative strikers (pickets) standing outside the entrances to establishments whose work-force was on strike, in order to persuade employees not to break the strike by returning to work. Peaceful picketing was legalised by Disraeli, but intimidation and violence remained illegal. |

**Protection**

The opposite to Free Trade. The maintenance of tariffs (customs duties) for the specific purpose of raising the import prices of foreign goods and thus reducing their power to compete with home-produced goods. In the 1830s and 1840s British manufacturers did not need protection from foreign competition, so most manufacturers supported Free Trade. Farmers and landowners, backed, until Peel's conversion, by the Tory Party, were strongly Protectionist, believing that farming prosperity was threatened by cheap corn imports.

**The Whig Party**

The Whig Party had a strong aristocratic tradition. Despite its part in the Reform Act of 1832 and the reforming legislation that followed, it was suspicious of democracy, and was content in the 1850s and 1860s with policies of consolidation rather than reform. Lord Palmerston typified this attitude. It was Gladstone who absorbed Whigs and Peelites into the party that under his leadership came to be called Liberal. It was progressive, forward-looking and democratic in outlook, even though the Whig element continued to regard Gladstone as something of a wild revolutionary, and continued to exert its influence within the Liberal party throughout most of Gladstone's leadership of it.

**Young England**

A group of Conservative M.P.s which first became prominent in 1843 under Disraeli's leadership, and embarrassed the Conservative leadership from time to time by attacking government policies. At that time Young England was much concerned with the 'condition of England' and wanted the Conservative Party to concern itself with improving the lot of the poorer classes. Disraeli's democratic Conservatism had its origins in Young England.

# A P P L I E D   M A T E R I A L S

## BOOKS

PEACOCK, H. L., (1968) *A History of Modern Britain, 1815–1968*. Heinemann. Chapters 13, 14, 15 and 16.
RICHARDS, D. & HUNT, J. W., (1987) *Illustrated History of Modern Britain, 1783–1980*. Third edition, Longman. Chapter 15 and 16.
ROBERTS, M., (1986). *Britain and Europe, 1848–1980*. Longman. Chapter 2.
STOKES, J. and G., (1973). *Europe and the Modern World, 1870–1970*. Longman. Chapter 8.

## FURTHER READING

HAMMOND, J. L. & FOOT, M. R. D., (1952). *Gladstone and Liberalism*. EUP.

## FILM STRIPS

| | |
|---|---|
| Late Victorian Era | AVP 511 |
| Gladstone | AVP 591 |
| Disraeli | AVP 792 |

# EXAMINATION QUESTIONS

1 a) Describe the achievements of Gladstone in reforming each of the following in his First Ministry:
   (i) the army,
   (ii) the civil service,
   (iii) education,
   (iv) the method of voting.
   b) Explain why Gladstone lost the General Election of 1874.

(LEAG)

2 a) What improvements were made by the domestic reforms of Gladstone's ministry of 1868–74?
   b) In what ways were Disraeli's domestic reforms of 1874–80 of a different kind to those of Gladstone?
   c) Which of the two sets of reforms, Gladstone's of 1868–74 or Disraeli's of 1874–80, had the greater effect on life in Britain? Give reasons for your answer.

(SEG)

# OUTLINE ANSWERS

1 a) This asks for straightforward description, which is not a method of approach favoured by all the GCSE boards. The description, however, hinges on achievement and some attempt should be made to assess each reform in terms of achievement. The *army* reform necessitated by the Crimean War was thorough and produced a small but skilled and well-equipped force ready to undertake any reasonable demands made upon it. Remember to include the various facets of the reform: length of service, linked battalions, abolition of purchase of commissions, reduced authority of Commander-in-Chief, county regiments, better equipment, no peace-time flogging. The main *civil service* reform was the introduction of competitive examinations; as an achievement it led to higher quality of personnel and improved administration. The *education* reform includes both elementary provision and universities, although the School Boards will be the major feature and the social importance of the reform should be commented upon. The *method of voting* refers to the Ballot Act only – do not include material from other ministries. As an achievement it went a long way towards removing influence at elections and was a major step towards democracy. For b) there is a useful section on the 1874 election earlier in the chapter, and this could be used as a model.

2 a) The main domestic reforms of Gladstone's ministry of 1868–74 are listed earlier in the chapter and covered in the text. The emphasis is on improvements, so it is important to stress why the reforms were necessary and particularly to show how far they effected an improvement. In b) you are invited to *contrast* Disraeli's reforms with those of Gladstone, and to show how they differed. You can do this in part by relating the reforms and showing that for the most part they tackled different problems, but some treatment of Gladstone's laisser-faire commitment and Disraeli's concern for social improvement would heighten the contrast. The contrast asked for in b) does not have to be continued in c); you may, of course, follow the traditional administrative/social division, but an argument which, as in the text of the chapter, warns against undervaluing the social effects of Gladstone's reforms without diminishing the social importance of Disraeli's, would be highly rewarded if argued from the evidence.

# A TUTOR'S ANSWER

**QUESTION** Gladstone's Cabinet is discussing in the summer of 1884 whether to send an expeditionary force to the Sudan. Give an account of the arguments put forward at the meeting.

Gladstone opened the discussion by pointing out that General Gordon had been sent to the Sudan specifically to evacuate it, that there were several weeks during which he might easily have withdrawn from the place, and that his persistence in remaining was a deliberate defiance of the government which had sent him. Was the government to be forced into a policy of which it disapproved by the action of one of its disobedient servants? When Lord Hartington commented that having chosen Gordon for the task the least the Cabinet should do would be to listen to his advice, Gladstone reminded him that Gordon had not been the unanimous choice of the Cabinet and that Sir Evelyn Baring had advised against his appointment – he was now proving to be right.

One of Hartington's supporters raised the question of the scattered Egyptian garrisons in the Sudan. Were they to be left to their fate? Everyone knew what would happen to them at the hands of the Mahdi, whereas a show of force in the Sudan might destroy the Mahdi's threat before it could be a danger to Egypt. When someone protested that Britain had no interests in the Sudan, several voices raised the question of Egypt and the Canal. We had found it necessary to deal with Arabi Pasha in 1882, and if the Mahdi was able to establish himself in Egypt untold damage would be done to British interests. But Gladstone reminded the Cabinet that the Mahdi posed no threat to Egypt: his was a nation struggling to be free from Egyptian rule, it was hardly likely that he would receive a welcome in Egypt.

Lord Hartington agreed; but he was concerned about the blow to British prestige if Britain gave in to the threat from the Mahdi and abandoned the garrisons to their fate. Britain's potential enemies abroad would take comfort from Britain's lack of resolution, and it could make Britain's task harder in South Africa and India and encourage the Russians to make further moves towards Afghanistan. To leave Gordon to his fate would seem heartless and would appear to the public to be placing a doubtful principle – that of Cabinet responsibility – above a matter of national honour. He had personal knowledge of the Queen's concern, and he had no doubt that in this instance the Queen was more in tune with public opinion than the Prime Minister. Here Gladstone was heard to mutter that the Queen would undoubtedly like to see Britain take over the Sudan and was using Gordon as the means to blackmail the Cabinet into agreeing to do so. Gordon was well-stocked with ammunition, he had food supplies for six months and could probably hold out for longer, and he had several armed river-boats which could keep open local communications. There was no need to take any decision which would lead to rash action. In the end the Cabinet agreed to postpone a decision and no preparations were put in hand for a relief force to rescue General Gordon despite the insistent demands of Lord Hartington.

# A STUDENT'S ANSWER WITH EXAMINER'S COMMENTS

**QUESTION** Why did Gladstone and the Liberals win the General Election of 1880, but lose that of 1886?

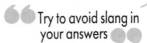
Try to avoid slang in your answers

In 1880 everyone was fed up with Disraeli. He had been Prime Minister for six years and people felt that now it was time to give the Liberals a turn. Many people had been won over by Gladstone's Midlothian Campaign in which he had denounced Disraeli for leaving the people of the Balkans to be massacred by the Turks, and Disraeli had run out of reforms by 1876 and the people of Britain were desperately anxious for more reforms. The trade unionists were no

> This is a mixed answer. It makes a number of useful points, but exaggerates on the question of reforms and the influence on the election of Disraeli's rudeness.

> This is a reference to the 1874 election, not that of 1880, and is a little unkind to the motives of the voters.

> This is a very valid and useful point.

> It is right to look at Gladstone's record during the years 1880–85, and indeed the passing references here could have been developed a little further.

> The essay ends strongly and has a good analysis of the situation in 1886.

longer angry with Gladstone for his harsh trade union laws, because Disraeli had changed them and the working classes were suspicious of Conservative claims to represent their interests, and felt it safer to support Gladstone. Besides, Disraeli had been very rude about Gladstone and had accused him of using too many big and incomprehensible words so that no-one ever knew what Gladstone meant. He said that Gladstone was 'inebriated by the exuberance of his own verbosity' and many people thought this was very unkind.

Also in 1880 Gladstone had promised to abolish the income tax, and as British voters are usually very selfish they hoped to gain money out of Gladstone's election. The radical Lord Mayor of Birmingham, Joseph Chamberlain had organised a National Liberal Federation which copied the organising techniques of the Conservative Central Office, and this organisation helped to turn Disraeli's unpopularity into votes for the Liberals.

In the 1885 General Election the Liberals lost seats and were only able to regain power with the help of the Irish Nationalist Party. Those who turned away from the Liberals in 1885 had done so because of the lack of reform, because of the disaster to General Gordon, and because the 'swing of the pendulum' dictated that now was the time to let the other side back into office again. Many of the new voters to whom Gladstone gave the vote in 1884 appeared to have voted for their landlords' Conservative candidates, despite the ballot allowing them to vote freely without fear of intimidation. There was no reason to suppose that the voters had changed their minds between 1885 and 1886. But in 1886 there was a powerful additional reason why the voters turned away from Gladstone: Ireland. Gladstone in 1886 tried to rush his party and the country into Home Rule for Ireland. Within his own party was a strong Imperialist wing led by Lord Hartington, and he and the country appeared to believe that a self-governing Ireland was inconsistent with the expansionist aims of a great Empire. The Conservatives under Randolph Churchill had alarmed protestant England with the prospect of Northern Ireland Protestants at the mercy of a Roman Catholic government in Dublin, so imperialism and religious prejudice helped in Gladstone's defeat.

# S U G G E S T I O N S   F O R   F U R T H E R   W O R K

1   Use encyclopedias to help you write briefly about the achievements and importance of Gladstone's Cabinet colleagues H. A. Bruce and W. E. Forster, and Disraeli's Cabinet colleague R. Cross. Write a brief biographical note also about Samuel Plimsoll.

2   Explain the ways in which the British people *benefited* from the reforms of Gladstone and Disraeli.

3   List the main issues on which Gladstone and Disraeli disagreed and explain why they disagreed on those issues. On what issues were they generally agreed?

4   Write three letters to the Times in 1870, one arguing the case for the Education Bill, one expressing reservations, and the other opposing it.

# IRELAND

## GETTING STARTED

Poverty and exhaustion, together with bitter memories of the savage treatment they had received at English hands, kept the Irish relatively quiet during most of the eighteenth century. Yet this was the period when Irish Catholics were denied all political rights, were regarded as unreliable witnesses in the courts, could not serve on a jury and could not acquire substantial property. Irish grievances were thus four-fold: *conquest* – they had been conquered by an alien nation; *religion* – they had had an alien religion thrust upon them while their own was virtually outlawed; *land* – they had become tenants of an alien aristocracy, without a fixed rent or a long-term lease; *politics* – they possessed very few of the basic political rights.

For a while, Catholics and Protestants combined to agitate against Ireland's injustices, and to seek a better Ireland for Catholic and Protestant alike. Property rights, and even the right to vote, had been secured for Roman Catholics by 1793. There was even talk of Roman Catholic Emancipation, the right of Roman Catholics to enter parliament and become M.P.s. But this talk was premature. When Catholic Irishmen found that they were not to get further political concessions they turned to France for help. Since Britain was at war with France, most Protestant Irishmen regarded any contact with France as treasonable, and Protestant and Catholic extremists reverted to their old practice of killing each other instead of working together. The unity of the two main religions behind a united Irish cause was shattered. The Irish rebellion of 1798 was largely, but not entirely, Catholic; it was resisted by the Protestant gentry and speedily smothered by British troops. A measure of order was restored.

One last opportunity might have saved the situation. In 1800 the Protestant Irish parliament was bribed into voting itself out of existence and Ireland became joined to England, Wales and Scotland by the Act of Union. It had been the intention of the Prime Minister, William Pitt, to follow the Act of Union by the granting of Roman Catholic Emancipation. But Pitt had neglected to secure in advance George III's consent for this, and George III regarded the entry of Roman Catholics into parliament as a breach of his coronation oath to preserve the Protestant religion. The Irish felt they had been betrayed. When Catholic Emancipation did come in 1829 it was too late to reconcile the Irish to the Union.

# HISTORICAL DEVELOPMENTS

**1**  **THE IRISH
PROBLEM IN
THE 1820s**

## LAND

When the English nobility had taken over control of the land from Irish clan chiefs, the Irish peasants found their status considerably changed. Their right to the land disappeared with the confiscation, and the new owners were careful not to restrict their own management of the land by granting lengthy leases or agreeing to fixed rents. So the typical Irish peasant would find himself a tenant of an absentee landlord – a lord who left the management of his estates to an agent and possibly never visited his Irish estates at all. A tenant would be lucky to have a lease for a period longer than three months. More likely it would be for one month, or he could be a tenant-at-will, liable to eviction at a moment's notice. Fixed rents were rare, so he would have to renegotiate his rent at frequent intervals. The agent's task was to raise as much income as possible for his lord, so he drove a hard bargain with the tenant. If the tenant repaired a barn, or drained a soggy field, this increased the value of his farm, and he would be faced with a demand for increased rent. If he could not pay, he would be evicted and the farm rented to someone who could pay. The only defence against this was to avoid farm improvements, to neglect the buildings and the fences and drainage, and to cultivate the *minimum* area needed for the family's subsistence. Corn growing had been very profitable in the eighteenth century, but a huge surge in population caused land hunger and helped to push the rents even higher. Many tenant farmers gave up the constant struggle to grow enough corn for them to satisfy the landlord's monetary demands. They turned instead to the growing of potatoes, which produced a large crop from a small acreage. An acre of potatoes could feed twice as many as an acre of corn, and by the early nineteenth century potato cultivation was widespread. Boiled potatoes became the staple of the Irish diet. Even so, as the tenant and his large family huddled in their leaking farmhouse which they often shared with one or two farm animals, and as they allowed all but the potato patch to revert to the wild, the threat of eviction still hung over them.

Ireland's population had doubled in little more than a century, reaching its peak of over 8,000,000 by the mid-1840s. For every squalid tenancy there were often at least two would-be tenants. Tenancies were often illegally sub-divided and sub-let. Landlords who tried to prevent these practices could find themselves, their steward or their property subjected to violence.

So it was not so much the growth of population as agricultural neglect and decay which turned Ireland from being a net *exporter* of food to a net *importer* by the 1830s. One radical solution suggested was to eliminate landlordism altogether, and turn the peasants into small farmers with their own plots of land. Another idea was fixed rents, long leases, compensation for improvements and transferable tenancies. In the 1820s, however, the land problem remained in the background as the political and religious problems seemed more immediate.

## RELIGION

Although actual religious persecution had long since disappeared from Ireland, religious grievances and religious prejudices remained into the 1820s. The Protestant community was small in number except in Ulster and Dublin and some of the larger towns. Yet all the country's ancient churches, together with their very considerable wealth, were in the hands of the minority Protestant Church of Ireland. Even Ulster with its Protestant majority was of a different brand of Protestantism – Presbyterianism – and the national Church of Ireland was in a minority there, too. The Irish Catholics were forced to see their large, ancient churches devoted to Protestant worship, while they crammed into modest Catholic chapels, where they maintained their priest out of voluntary offerings they could ill afford. Worse still, the Protestant clergy were maintained from the compulsory tithe – the biblical tenth part of the produce of the land. The Protestant priest's tithe-barn bulged after harvest with the offerings of the faithful, while the faithful owed their allegiance to another church. Devout Catholics regarded the Protestant priest and his flock at best as heretics, at worst as agents of the devil, and believed that their tithe was helping to do the devil's work. The village church and the tithe were continual reminders to the Catholic population of British injustice. If the £20,000,000 endowments of the Church of Ireland were not immediately noticeable, there were always the well-informed to draw attention to them.

> Protestant against Catholic.

> The Irish Protestant Church was rich in cash and property but poor in membership.

## POLITICAL GRIEVANCES

The long subordination of Ireland to England caused much Irish bitterness. Reminders of English domination were part of Irish everyday life: the churches in Protestant hands, the absentee landlords, the historic organizations such as the Orangemen, and the Steelboys and the Whiteboys. Ireland, more so than most nations, kept alive its past, and in doing so helped to perpetuate its divisions.

In the 1820s the major political grievance was the exclusion of Roman Catholics from parliament. If the Roman Catholics had a voice in parliament, then parliament would have to take note of Irish grievances and take steps to remedy them. But some people felt that the Act of Union itself had been a betrayal, and that nothing short of the Repeal of the Union would satisfy Irish hopes.

## 2 > THE CATHOLIC ASSOCIATION

In 1822 the so-called 'Enlightened Tories' came to power in Britain. They were prepared to undertake a programme of modest reform, but most, except Canning and his followers, were not prepared to grant Roman Catholic Emancipation, which they felt would be the first step towards undermining British control in Ireland. In 1823 a Roman Catholic lawyer, Daniel O'Connell, founded the *Catholic Association*. Its purpose was to campaign for Roman Catholic Emancipation as the first step towards the Repeal of the Union. Funds poured in from the 'Catholic Rent', the penny a month that even the poorest Catholics were asked to pay. The Catholic priesthood gave its powerful support and organization to the Catholic Association, thus giving it respectability and divine approval. Its success amazed its supporters and alarmed the government. In 1826 the Catholic voters of Waterford, despite the absence of a secret ballot, defied their landlord, Lord George Beresford, and voted for a liberal Protestant in his place. It seemed that enthusiasm for the Catholic Association had overcome the tenants' traditional fear of their landlord.

## 3 > ROMAN CATHOLIC EMANCIPATION

O'Connell was now eager to test the real strength of his Association. The opportunity came in 1828, when government changes had removed most of O'Connell's Tory sympathisers from office, and new appointments, according to the customs of those days, made by-elections necessary. One of these was in County Clare, where Vesey Fitzgerald, a popular Protestant, was seeking re-election to parliament on his appointment as President of the Board of Trade. O'Connell had hoped that he could obtain *Catholic Emancipation* through growing support in parliament. But the death of Canning and the resignation of Huskisson and his supporters meant that the government was united behind Peel and Wellington in its opposition to Emancipation. Without malice to the unfortunate Fitzgerald, O'Connell decided that he could wait no longer for Emancipation as a gift from parliament. He would have to force the government to give way, and made his position clear in a letter written in 1826:

> One may as well endeavour to coax a pound of flesh from a hungry wolf as to conciliate the Established Church. From our numbers, our combination, and the continued expression of our discontent . . . there would appear such a union of physical force with moral sentiment that Mr. Peel would be insane if he continued with his opposition. We *never never never* got anything by conciliation.

Although ineligible as a Roman Catholic, O'Connell offered himself as a candidate in the by-election. A few days before the election the government removed the last political restrictions from the Non-Conformists by repealing the *Test and Corporation Acts*. Although these restrictions were technical and had long since ceased to be enforced, their removal added to the excitement in Ireland, because now Roman Catholicism was the only Christian sect to be discriminated against by law. Thirty thousand O'Connell supporters flooded into County Clare. Fitzgerald did not stand a chance; all his local influence counted for nothing. Priests led the voters to the hustings, and on the fourth day of the election with a majority of more than 2 to 1 against him, Fitzgerald conceded defeat. The remarkable organization and self-discipline of O'Connell's supporters (there was not one recorded incident of serious violence during the election) was a credit to the Association and a demonstration of its unity and strength. If the Catholic Association could topple the most popular Protestant in Southern Ireland, there would not be a safe government seat anywhere in Catholic Ireland. But O'Connell's victory did not make him an M.P. – if he was to take his seat in parliament the law would have to be changed.

Both Wellington as Prime Minister, and Peel as Home Secretary, were greatly surprised by Fitzgerald's defeat. What they had thought of as the activity of a noisy minority seemed to have the approval of the whole Irish nation. Peel realized that Ireland was on the verge of rebellion and that refusing to grant Roman Catholic Emancipation would precipitate it. He was convinced that the government would cope with such a rebellion, but what would be the point if a government victory merely suppressed dissent and provided no acceptable solution to the problem? Wellington declared that he would lay down his life to prevent one month of civil war; Peel stated that after a government victory

the question would remain precisely what it was, but with all animosities . . . doubly infuriated, and with all the relations of society, and all the connections between man and man, poisoned to an infinitely greater extent than they were before that collision took place.

Peel and Wellington both gave way. They persuaded George IV, who was not as obstinate and principled as his father George III had been on this issue, although it cost several threatened and one actual resignation of the government to get him to agree. Then they had to persuade their own party. Here, they were less successful, and had to rely on Whig support for passing the *Act of Emancipation* through parliament. By the Act only the monarchy, and the offices of Regent, Lord Lieutenant of Ireland and Lord Chancellor were barred to Roman Catholics. At last, Roman Catholics could become members of parliament. The freehold qualification for the Irish franchise was raised from land of £2 annual value to £10, which probably disfranchised 100,000 voters and was a concession to Tory die-hards, although Peel defended it on the ground that it would make the sub-division of free-holdings for political purposes more difficult.

The Catholic Association was also to be disbanded. As the Act was not made retrospective, O'Connell had to fight another by-election after the passing of the Act before he could take his seat in the House of Commons. Ireland now had an able spokesman at Westminster, recognised by his countrymen as the 'Liberator', who was soon to gain the admiration and respect of both the major political parties. But for Ireland the concession had come too late. Whigs and Tories alike hoped that the Act marked the end of the struggle – in fact, a new phase of the struggle was now to begin.

## 4 ▶ TITHE, FAMINE AND REPEAL OF THE UNION

The issues of Roman Catholic Emancipation had split the Tory party and helped to bring the Whigs to power in 1830. O'Connell had been joined in parliament by a growing group of Catholic Irish M.P.s, who supported the Reform Act of 1832, although they were bitterly disappointed that the Whigs had not restored the £2 free-holder franchise in the Irish Reform Act. Even so, they looked to the Whigs to legislate to remove Irish grievances. O'Connell's first aim was to stop the payment of tithe by the Catholic Irish peasantry to the Protestant Church of Ireland. Peasants withheld their tithe and were also advised by O'Connell to withhold their rents from extortionate landlords. It was impossible under such circumstances to prevent violence. In 1831, eighteen policemen were killed in one skirmish in County Kilkenny when trying to enforce payment of tithe. However much O'Connell deplored it, murder and deliberate burnings of tithe-barns and landowners houses spread across Catholic Ireland during the early and mid-1830s. The government replied with a *Coercion Act* in 1834, which followed the pattern of previous coercion acts in suspending trial by jury in 'disturbed areas', and in suspending the Habeas Corpus Act in order to detain suspects indefinitely without trial. In 1835, despite his detestation of coercion, O'Connell allied himself more closely to the Whigs by the Lichfield House Compact. In return for his parliamentary support they agreed to do something for Ireland, but in fact could offer him very little. The *Tithe Commutation Act* of 1838 reduced the tithe by a quarter and converted it into a payment to be added to the rent. The direct payment of tithe by Catholic peasant to Protestant priest was thus ended, but the grievance remained that peasants, through their rent, were helping to maintain an alien church. Those who withheld their rent now had a religious reason for doing so.

O'Connell may have been disappointed with the Whigs but he remained loyal to them. His advice to the Irish people was to 'keep quiet and trust in the law', and this, together with the improvement in the Irish administration brought about by Lord Mulgrave and his Under-Secretary Thomas Drummond, gave Ireland some comparatively quiet years. But O'Connell had never given up his ultimate aim of the Repeal of the Union. He knew that he would lose Whig support if he campaigned for that, but when Peel came to power in 1841 it released him from his obligation to the Whigs, and there was always the prospect that a repeat of the tactics of 1828–29 might force the Conservatives to make further concessions. O'Connell organized huge meetings to demand Repeal, and was enthusiastically supported by all but the most cautious of the Catholic clergy. The government doubted whether O'Connell could control his followers and banned a Repeal meeting he had arranged at Clontarf in October 1843. O'Connell obeyed the government, much to the anger of the newly formed (1842) Young Ireland Movement. Despite his compliance, O'Connell was arrested and convicted of conspiracy by a Protestant jury, but was released on appeal to the House of Lords. He returned to Dublin in triumph, but his influence was in a decline. He had given in to the government, and the future lay with men who had less respect for law and order. O'Connell died in 1847.

Peel had been tough with O'Connell, but was prepared to do something for Ireland. He trebled the meagre grant to the Maynooth College for training Catholic priests. Queen's colleges were founded at Dublin, Cork and Galway, but since they were undenominational, they were regarded by both Catholics and Protestants as 'Godless'. Peel proposed a measure of compensation for improvements made by tenants, but this met with strenuous parliamentary opposition. The situation in Ireland now demanded something more immediate, because 1845 was the year of the great famine.

Half of the population of Ireland depended almost entirely upon potatoes; the other half on corn and potatoes. In 1845 both crops failed, and the potato crop failed in 1846 as well. Politically, the effect brought about the Repeal of the Corn Laws in 1846 and a split in the Tory Party. Economically, it brought disaster on an unprecedented scale to Ireland. Desperate attempts were made to prevent deaths from starvation. Soup kitchens were opened; maize was imported from the U.S.A. and sold at a penny a pound, although corn exports from Ireland continued, often under armed guard. Relief works began, and the destitute were employed on local projects with enough pay to buy the maize. The relief scheme was badly administered, and by 1847 direct outdoor relief was necessary, with at least three million Irish depending on relief in one form or another. Over two years, Ireland's population fell by more than one and a half million. Few died by direct starvation, but a million died from fevers and wasting diseases such as tuberculosis brought about by severe and long-term malnutrition. Many people emigrated, mainly to the U.S.A. They took with them nostalgia for their homeland and a hatred of England, whom they blamed for all their suffering. The fall in population reduced the pressure on the land, but the *Encumbered Estates Act*, which facilitated the sale of over-mortgaged estates, led to the appearance of new ruthless landlords who were even more ready to 'rack-rent' (push the rents up unjustifiably) and evict tenants than were the previous landlords.

'Young Ireland', so-called in admiration of Mazzini's 'Young Italy', had taken over O'Connell's leadership of Ireland. In some ways it reverted to the principles of a United Ireland in that many of its leaders were Protestant and out of sympathy with O'Connell's sectarianism. But they were dreamers and visionaries rather than men of action, although their talk was of revolution and resistance. The movement could do little during the height of the famine, but the beginning of recovery from the famine coincided in 1848 with revolution in Europe and Chartism in England. Some leaders contacted European revolutionary leaders, and were arrested and brought to trial on dubious charges. Others, led by Smith O'Brien, made the call to arms, and a body of half-armed peasants were routed by 46 policemen and a railway guard in 'Widow McCormack's cabbage patch' in Ballingary in July 1848. O'Brien was arrested, tried, and sentenced to be hanged, drawn and quartered. He protested bitterly when he found that the sentence was not to be carried out and he was to be transported instead. 'Young Ireland' did not revive, and although the next ten years were comparatively peaceful for Ireland, violence continued on both sides. Agrarian outrage by peasants against landlords and the authorities needs to be balanced by the fact that during these years evictions of peasants were running at an annual rate of nearly 10,000.

> The end to the 1848 revolution was ridiculous rather than tragic.

## 5 › THE FENIAN SOCIETY

Attempts by the Irish to organize secret societies during the 1850s were broken up by the government. However, the government had no power in the U.S.A., where in 1858 the *Fenian Brotherhood*, so-called after the Fianna or armed force which was supposed to have defended Ireland long ago, was founded with a mixed membership of Irish emigrants and American well-wishers. The American Civil War gave the Brotherhood's members immediate and local problems to worry about, and the society did not take root in Ireland until 1865. It aimed at an Irish republic, and planned armed rebellion in Ireland, funded by American money. The government suppressed the movement and imprisoned the leaders, but in May 1866 the movement was strong enough to spread into Canada from the U.S.A. In February 1867, 1,200 Fenians gathered in Chester to attack Manchester. The leaders were arrested and an attempted rescue led to the death of a police constable in September 1867. In December, an attempt to release Fenian prisoners from Clerkenwell prison resulted in the death of twelve people, and the execution of Fenians involved gave ready martyrs to the Irish cause. Fenian terrorism roused little support in Ireland, where the peasants could see little connection between blowing up an English prison and burning down an Irish mansion. But the Irish problem had been brought to the English mainland, and although Fenianism died away after 1867, it confirmed Gladstone's opinion that the Irish question must be tackled.

## 6 ▷ GLADSTONE'S MISSION TO PACIFY IRELAND

Gladstone was widely known as a man of principle. In 1845, he resigned from Peel's ministry because the increased Maynooth grant conflicted with his earlier public views, even though he now approved of the increase. Those who accused him of making capital out of the Irish Question for political reasons in 1868 when he declared his 'mission was to pacify Ireland' should have noted his brave words in 1867 at the height of the Fenian outrages when he claimed that if Irish grievances were removed:

> instead of hearing in every corner of Europe the most painful commentaries upon the policy of England towards Ireland – we may be able to look our fellow Europeans of every nation in the face.

Gladstone was a devout member of the Protestant Church of England, yet he began by depriving its sister church, the Protestant Church of Ireland, of its privileged position. In 1869 it was disestablished, and ceased to be Ireland's official church. It became self-governing and chose its own bishops, who no longer sat in the House of Lords. It also kept two thirds of its property and endowments, the other third was used for public purposes as determined by parliament. The tithe charge, part of the rent since 1838, was to be gradually reduced and eventually abolished. The *Act of Disestablishment* did not entirely remove the religious grievances. The Church of Ireland retained the ancient churches and in many areas continued to use them for public worship. The end of the tithe removed a religious grievance, but reductions in rent to reflect the end of the tithe were often not granted.

Gladstone hoped to remedy these grievances in his next measure – the *Land Act* of 1870. This granted compensation to those evicted for any reason other than non-payment of rent, and provided compensation to evicted tenants for any improvements made during their tenancy, thereby hoping to discourage eviction. The Act also contained provisions for tenants to purchase their land from landlords, but the purchase clauses were too complicated and unworkable. Landlords got round the eviction clauses by rack-renting and then evicting for non-payment of rent. Gladstone hoped that these measures would help to eliminate Irish grievances, but within a year agrarian disturbance forced him to revert to coercion. It is a sad judgment on Gladstone's work that the first General Election (1874) after these two Acts was the first to produce a majority of Irish M.P.s who were committed to the Repeal of the Union and Home Rule.

## 7 ▷ THE HOME RULE MOVEMENT

The Home Government Association of Ireland was formed in Dublin in 1870. Isaac Butt soon emerged as leader, and in 1873 the Home Government Association was renamed as the Home Rule League. Its aims were:

> To obtain for our country the right and privilege of managing our own affairs, by a Parliament assembled in Ireland, composed of Her Majesty the Sovereign, and her successors and the Lords and Commons of Ireland; to secure for that Parliament, under a federal arrangement, the right of legislating for and regulating all matters relating to the internal affairs of Ireland, and control over Irish resources and revenues, subject to the obligation of contributing our just proportion of Imperial expenditure; to leave to an Imperial parliament the power of dealing with all questions affecting the Imperial Crown and Government, legislation regarding the Colonies and other dependencies of the Crown, the relations of the United Empire with Foreign States, and all matters appertaining to the defence and stability of the Empire at large . . .

These demands might seem remarkably moderate today, but in their day they seemed revolutionary and threatening. All British politicians, including Gladstone, combined to

It is important to consider Disraeli's attitude towards the Irish Question.

pour scorn on them. It was Gladstone who had pushed through the *Ballot Act* in 1872. The Irish voter, who since 1852 had enjoyed a similar franchise to that operating in the rest of the British Isles, was now freed from the influence of his landowner. In 1874, 57 Home Rulers were returned to parliament. Disraeli, who came to power by that same General Election, had no real Irish policy. Butt annually presented a parliamentary motion for the Repeal of the Union; it was always overwhelmingly defeated. In Ireland, a brief period of comparative prosperity preceded the onset of the agricultural depression in 1878 and agrarian violence subsided a little. Nevertheless, Disraeli maintained various coercive measures, and 1879 saw both the full vigour of the agricultural depression and the death of Butt. Butt's place was taken by Charles Stewart Parnell, a very different character. In that same year Michael Davitt helped bring about the Irish Land League, and persuaded Parnell to become its President. The two organizations planned complementary campaigns. The Home Rule League began a programme of parliamentary obstruction, its first success being the continuous debate in which the Irish members held up the Act to annexe Transvaal for twenty-six hours in 1877. The Land League organized the tenants to decide for themselves what was a fair rent. If the landlord refused it and evicted any of his tenants, no one was to take over the vacant tenancy. If they did, they would be treated like an outcast, 'as a leper of old'. (Captain Boycott, agent for a landowner who evicted his tenants and then tried to find new ones, was an early victim of this treatment, and gave his name to it.) The Land League had Parnell's approval for boycotting; he was less enthusiastic about

Make sure that you understand Parnell's attitude towards Irish violence.

'moonlighting' in which intimidation and physical violence sometimes led to murder, and in which hay ricks were burned down and cattle maimed. The 1880 General Election was fought as violence raged in Ireland, but English voters were more concerned about violence in the Balkans. It was the Bulgarian atrocities rather than the Irish ones which persuaded the voters to defeat Disraeli and bring Gladstone back to power. Ireland was to dominate not only Gladstone's new ministry, but also the rest of his political career.

## 8 ▶ GLADSTONE'S SECOND MINISTRY, 1880–85

Gladstone hoped that further legislation could deal with the grievances and solve the problem, but first he had to tackle the violence. A Coercion Bill, in 1881, suspended the Habeas Corpus Act, making possible indefinite detainment of suspects. The Home Rule Association had helped to elect 65 M.P.s to parliament in 1880, and these, led by Parnell, called themselves Nationalists and responded angrily to the Coercion Bill by obstructive tactics in the House of Commons. Interminable speeches prolonged one debate for forty-one hours, until the Speaker broke the deadlock by calling for a vote on his own initiative. The *Coercion Act* became law, and Gladstone felt that it should buy him enough time to tackle the agrarian problem once again. He knew that for some time Irish agrarian reformers and the Land League had been asking for the three Fs – fair rents, fixed tenures and free sale. 'Fair rents' is self-explanatory and if they were fair they would almost inevitably be lower. 'Fixed tenures' meant freedom from eviction, and 'free sale' meant the right of the tenant to sell his tenancy to whomsoever he chose, at whatever price he could get.

Gladstone believed if these were granted, agrarian unrest would cease. So the *Second Land Act*, 1881, granted the peasants a right to the land without taking away that of the landlord, but denying the landlord the right of eviction. It gave the peasants the right to sell their tenancy, and it set up Land courts to fix fair rents. Parnell had not been consulted by Gladstone about the terms of the Act. The Nationalist Party feared that the Land courts would not be drastic enough in reducing rents. Alternatively, if the courts successfully eliminated agrarian grievances, demand for Home Rule, to which the Nationalists were committed, would lie down. Parnell therefore refused to recognize the Land courts, and advised his followers to refuse to co-operate with them; agrarian violence continued. After all, if violence could force Gladstone to propose the Land Act, what further concessions would more unrest bring?

Gladstone did in fact urge his Cabinet to agree to further measures, including local self-government, but the Cabinet was divided and several members demanded that Gladstone denounce Parnell and the Land League. Parnell was perhaps unaware of the pressure Gladstone was being subjected to, and he publicly defied and insulted Gladstone in a speech at Wexford, referring to him as:

> this masquerading knight-errant, this pretending champion of the rights of every other nation except those of the Irish nation.

Gladstone had tried conciliation and had failed. He now turned to coercion. The Cabinet agreed to the arrest of Parnell and other Irish leaders, and they were sent to Kilmainham jail in Dublin, in October 1881. Parnell stayed there for seven months, universally regarded in Ireland as a martyr to the Irish cause. The violence got worse: there were fourteen murders and sixty-one attempted murders in rural Ireland during the first six months of Parnell's imprisonment. Parnell felt that extremism would wreck Ireland's hopes in a blood-bath of which he disapproved. He informed Galdstone that he was prepared to denounce violence, and to urge co-operation with the Land Act, in return for Gladstone's promise to deal with rent arrears. The arrears had arisen out of the Land League's advice to tenants to withhold their rent, and they provided landlords with the legal justification for further evictions. Negotiations between Parnell and Gladstone were conducted by Parnell's friend, Captain O'Shea, and not through the Viceroy of Ireland. The agreement was popularly known as the Kilmainham Treaty, an ironic comment on a negotiation furtively conducted, and concluded in a prison. When Parnell was released from prison, the Viceroy and the Irish Secretary, Forster, resigned in disapproval. Within a week of Parnell's release the new Secretary, Lord Frederick Cavendish and the senior Irish civil servant, Burke, were stabbed to death in the presence of the new Viceroy in Dublin's Phoenix Park. The extremists who committed the murder called themselves the 'Invincibles', and their act wrecked the prospects of an agreed settlement. Gladstone, it is true, secured the passage through parliament of the promised *Arrears Act* which eliminated arrears by sharing their cost between government and landlord. But this was accompanied by a *Crimes Act* and another *Coercion Act* which extended arbitrary arrest and imprisonment and drastically curtailed trial by jury. Despite Parnell's dislike of violence he got much of the public blame for it, especially when Irish extremists carried out violent acts in Britain. Parnell gained few friends when he refused to answer accusations of inciting violence by claiming that he was answerable only to the Irish people. The Land Act and Arrears Act reduced, but did not end, rural unrest in the remaining years of Gladstone's second ministry. Many landlords despaired of improving their estates in the existing climate of opinion and increasingly looked for an opportunity to sell to their tenants. Severe government repression maintained an outward appearance of order, but Parnell got his political revenge on Gladstone when the Irish Nationalists helped the Conservatives to defeat Gladstone's Budget in 1885 and bring Lord Salisbury to power.

## 9 ⟩ HOME RULE

> Imperialism against Home Rule.

For several months after the fall of Gladstone there was political confusion. Salisbury's government had to rely upon Irish votes, and could not hold a General Election until the new registers were ready, based on the 1884 Reform Act. Relations between Parnell and Gladstone were at a low ebb, and the Conservatives toyed with a limited form of Home Rule in order to buy Nationalist support. In the General Election of 1885 the Irish Nationalists were encouraged by their leaders to vote Conservative where there was no Nationalist standing, and this prevented an electoral landslide which Chamberlain's radical reform programme seemed at one time likely to win for the Liberals. In the event, the Liberals had a majority of 86 over the Conservatives and the 86 Irish Nationalists held the balance. As early as 1882 Gladstone had considered whether a moderate measure of Home Rule might not be the only way to settle the Irish Question once and for all. But he drew back from forcing such an unpopular and anti-Imperialist idea upon his colleagues, and hoped that Irish reform could be settled as a non-party issue by agreement. But his son Herbert let it be known rather prematurely that his father favoured Home Rule. The Conservatives rather thankfully, for the unity of their party, dropped any commitment to it they might have made, and Parnell swung his vote to the Liberal side. This brought down Salisbury's government, but when Gladstone formed his, he was faced with revolt within his own party. Lord Hartington, who had been Liberal leader during Gladstone's temporary retirement, refused to take office and Chamberlain, who had enabled the Liberals to do so well in the recent General Election, resigned when he learned the details of Gladstone's Irish proposals. Gladstone certainly did not try to educate his party to accept Home Rule, and to many of them the First Home Rule Bill came as a profound shock. It proposed to set up an Irish parliament at Dublin to control Ireland's internal affairs, and to leave trade, foreign and Imperial policy under the control of the British parliament which was to contain no Irish representatives. To many Liberals it seemed that to split the British Isles politically, while Britain was taking on new Imperialist responsibilities, was contradictory and weakening. Disraeli's Imperialist crusade had captured the Conservative Party and obtained a foothold among the Liberals. The Imperialist wing of the Liberal Party had created difficulties for Gladstone in the later years of his Second Ministry. Now it fought him tooth and nail in two months of debate, and the 93 Liberals who voted against the Bill helped to defeat it by 343 votes to 313. Rather than resign, Gladstone fought another General Election. The result was a Conservative majority of 110 seats, including rebel Liberals now calling themselves Liberal Unionists. It seemed, for the moment, that the country had given its verdict against Home Rule.

## 10 > PARNELL AT BAY

As a consequence of the Liberal defeat and split, Lord Salisbury returned to power and appointed his nephew as Irish Secretary. His policy was to suppress disorder and to try to reduce agrarian crime by tackling its causes. Accordingly, a severe *Crimes Act* in 1887 removed trial by jury from all offences against law and order and unlike previous Coercion Acts was to be permanent. At the same time an Act was passed which gave tenants government assistance to purchase their farms. The Act was not widely used, especially as the tenants were caught up in the Land League's 'Plan of Campaign', but tenant purchase was the key to solving the land problem. The 'Plan of Campaign' had begun in the autumn of 1886, when the Land League had become convinced that nothing could be gained from the Conservatives. It encouraged tenants to fix their own rents and contribute it, if the landlords refused to accept it, to the funds of the League. Few landlords, except the terrified and intimidated, would allow tenants to fix their own rent, so the landlords resorted to evictions, which led to boycotting, cattle-maiming, violence, arson and murder. Disorder reached a climax when the Crimes Act was going through parliament, and its passage was made easier by a series of articles in the *Times* newspaper which claimed to link Parnell with crime and the approval of crime. In April 1887 the *Times* published a letter in which Parnell apparently explained why he had found it necessary five years earlier to denounce the Phoenix park murders:

> Dear Sir,
>   I am not surprised at your friend's anger, but he and you should know that to denounce the murders was the only course open to us. To do that promptly was plainly our best policy. But you can tell him and all others concerned that, though I regret the accident of Lord F. Cavendish's death, I cannot refuse to admit that Burke got no more than his deserts. You are at liberty to show him this, and others whom you can trust also, but let not my address be known. He can write to the House of Commons.
>     Yours very truly,
>       Chas. S. Parnell.

Although Parnell denied all knowledge of this letter, and parliament and the politicians believed him, the country at large believed the accusations. Until parliament set up a Special Commission in 1888 to investigate the *Times* letters, public sympathy was in full support of the Crimes Act and its enforcement. But the *Times* had been fooled by Richard Pigott, a journalist who forged the Parnell letters for cash. The *Times* apologised to Parnell, who enjoyed a temporary respectability that bordered on hero worship, despite the fact that the Commission reported that the Land League's encouragement of intimidation led directly to violence. Parnell's Protestantism was an asset in his temporary popularity. But it was a disadvantage to his Irish leadership if it meant he believed he could get away with the divorce scandal which became public knowledge in 1890. Once there was no doubt that Parnell was the guilty party in the case involving the wife (Kitty) of his friend Captain O'Shea, he lost the support of the Catholic hierarchy, many of his party in the House of Commons, and the co-operation of the Liberals. Gladstone haughtily declared that if Parnell continued in his leadership of the Irish Nationalists, he, Gladstone, could not continue in his leadership of the British Liberals. There was no need for Gladstone to carry out his threat. Support for Parnell fell away and in a matter of months Parnell was dead (October 1891). He had been a great leader. His enemies believed that he hated Britain; perhaps it was simply that he loved Ireland more. His legacy was that, after him, no solution of the Irish problem short of Home Rule would ever be acceptable. His single-mindedness had helped to create a great Irish political party; it had also helped to wreck a great British one.

> " Then, a public figure's private life had to be beyond reproach. "

## 11 > HOME RULE AGAIN

In the 1892 General Election Gladstone, with the help of the Irish Nationalists, had a majority of 81. Gladstone, despite or perhaps because of his advanced age of 83, was determined to do battle again on the Irish Question, and perhaps settle it once and for all.

His Second Home Rule Bill proposed a parliament of two Houses in Dublin to run Irish domestic affairs, and the permanent presence of Irish members in the British parliament at Westminster to deal with those things forbidden to the Dublin parliament – foreign and imperial affairs, and defence – though they would not be able to vote on matters purely British. Conservatives and Unionists fought the Bill vigorously, but could not defeat it in the House of Commons. The House of Lords, however, with its permanent Conservative majority, rejected the bill overwhelmingly. Gladstone would have liked to challenge the Lords by an appeal to the voters in a General Election, but his Cabinet advised against it. They felt that in its present mood an Imperialist nation which had acquired vast territories abroad was unlikely to approve by its vote the giving away of territories at home. Feeling that he could do no more, Gladstone resigned, leaving Lord Rosebery to carry on as Liberal Prime Minister for a year until 1895, when the General Election swept the Conservatives and Unionists back into power for the next ten years.

## CONSERVATIVE REMEDIES – 'KILLING HOME RULE BY KINDNESS'

There was nothing very kind about a rigorous and permanent Crimes Act. But the Conservatives had the advantage of the weakening of the Irish Nationalists by the Parnell divorce scandal, and so could rule Ireland firmly, while using reform to weaken demand for Home Rule. In 1898 the system of County Councils created for Britain ten years earlier was extended to Ireland, to give local communities, whether Catholic or Protestant, control of local affairs. Such experience was to prove invaluable when these authorities were given control of education, and was a major step towards the Conservatives' intention to give Ireland every form of self-government short of Home Rule. The Conservatives provided the solution to the land problem. Tentative efforts to allow tenants to purchase their land had been made in the 1880s by both Liberal and Conservative governments. In 1903, the Conservative government abandoned caution and tried to replace landowners with a landowning peasantry. Wyndham's *Land Purchase Act* proposed to lend tenants the money to buy land if the landlord was willing to agree to a fair price. Loan repayments were to be spread over 68½ years at an interest rate of only 2¾%. The terms were favourable, and the landlords were very anxious to rid themselves of what had become more of a burden than a source of income. Within ten years, over a quarter of a million tenants had taken advantage of the offer, and the land problem was in effect solved. Of course it was too late to solve the political problem, because the Irish population, except in the North, was so committed to Home Rule that it would be content with nothing less.

## HOME RULE AND ULSTER

In 1905 the Liberals returned to power, and in 1906 won a large overall majority. The 83 Irish Nationalists were not enough to hold the balance in the House of Commons, and in Ireland the countryside was, by Irish standards, comparatively quiet. The Liberals did little directly for Ireland and an Act of 1909 actually slowed down the rate of land purchase. But Liberal social reform applied to Ireland as well as to Britain, and Old Age Pensions made a major contribution to keeping Irishmen out of the workhouse. In 1910, however, the political situation changed. The Liberals were in bitter dispute with the House of Lords over its rejection of the 1909 Budget, and a General Election had given Liberals and Conservatives an almost equal number of seats. Thus the Irish Nationalists and the Labour Party held the political balance, and with it the opportunity to get revenge on the House of Lords for depriving Ireland of Home Rule in 1893. The Irish Nationalists helped the Liberals to curb the House of Lords by the *Parliament Act, 1911*, which limited the Lords power to delay Bills approved by the House of Commons to two years. In return, although there was no formal agreement with the Irish Nationalist leader John Redmond to do so, the Liberal government introduced the Third Home Rule Bill in 1912.

The Third Home Rule Bill differed in minor details from the Second Home Rule Bill. Most significant was the reduction of the proposed number of Irish M.P.s at Westminster from 80 to 42, but with the right to vote at Westminster on *all* issues, irrespective of whether they concerned Ireland or not. No longer could the opponents of Home Rule rely on the Bill's rejection by the House of Lords. A growing opposition developed outside parliament. Randolph Churchill had appealed to the Ulster Protestants in 1886, but the appeal had proved unnecessary at that time. Now the appeal to Ulster was revived; unable to defeat the Bill in parliament, Conservatives stepped outside the law. The Ulster Unionists, led by the Conservative M.P. and lawyer, Sir Edward Carson, organized armed men in an Ulster Volunteer Force, signed a Solemn Covenant never to recognize the authority of a Dublin government, and held mass public meetings at which the sentiments expressed bordered on the treasonable. There were even proposals to set up an illegal provisional Ulster government in the North if the Home Rule Bill became law. Sir Edward taunted the government to arrest him and make a martyr of him. While the government hesitated, a number of British officers at Curragh camp in Dublin issued a statement in March 1914 that they would refuse to march North against Ulster, even if ordered to do so. The government gave way to this threat of virtual mutiny, promising that the officers would not be sent against Ulster. Meanwhile the Ulster Unionists imported arms from Germany, and Irish Volunteers armed themselves on the Nationalist side. Civil war seemed likely, and strenuous efforts were made to bring the parties together and effect some compromise. The efforts failed, and the Third Home Rule Bill became law in September 1914. The Irish Nationalist Party was in favour of getting down to the serious business of fighting the Germans, and was willing to agree, when the government postponed putting into effect the terms of the Bill. An immediate Irish crisis, had an attempt been made to force Home Rule on Ulster, was thus avoided. There is no certainty that the war would have made the Ulster Protestants and their political leaders any less determined. But if the government hoped that fighting side by side with Britain against a common enemy would lead the Irish to forget their differences and accept Home Rule as offered, it was soon shown to be mistaken.

Fig 6.1  Patrick Buckland, *Irish Unionism*, (The Historical Association, G 81, (Cover)). Copyright: Punch.

THE FIGHT FOR THE BANNER.

JOHN BULL. "THIS TIRES ME. WHY CAN'T YOU CARRY IT BETWEEN YOU? NEITHER OF YOU CAN CARRY IT ALONE."

Many Irish resented the postponement of Home Rule, and decided that Home Rule was not enough – they wanted complete independence. The Sinn Fein movement ('Ourselves alone') demanded complete independence, would consider no compromise on Ulster, and opposed Ireland's involvement in the war against Germany. The Easter Rising of the Republican Brotherhood in Dublin, 1916, was not popular with the Irish people, but the execution of a few of its leaders gave Ireland and the Sinn Fein their martyrs, and in the 1918 General Election Sinn Fein won 73 Irish seats and the Irish Nationalist party was almost annihilated at the polls. What emerged during the years 1918–22 – an independent free state separated from the six Northern counties – after four years of painstaking negotiation punctuated by civil war, was very different from the aims of Parnell or O'Connell. It was also beyond the worst fears of the Liberal Unionists who had fought so hard in 1886. And 100 years after Gladstone's Home Rule Bill was intended to end a century of Irish crisis, the Irish Question is still unsolved.

# IDEAS AND PRINCIPLES

**Boycotting**

The policy adopted by the Land League towards anyone in Ireland who had offended it. This usually meant refusal to speak to or deal with such a person, and to treat them like outcasts or lepers. Landlords who rack-rented, and peasants who took over a tenancy from which the previous tenant had been evicted, were likely victims. The name derives from its first victim, Captain Boycott, a notorious and unscrupulous land agent.

**Coercion**

The use of force to maintain order. Coercion Acts invariably meant a reduction of civil rights, most often by placing disturbed areas under the direct control of the military and suspending normal courts and safeguards against arbitrary (unreasonable) arrest in those areas.

**Disestablishment**

Usually used in its religious context of bringing to an end the close (established) relationship between church and state. The church regains its independence and becomes self-governing and self-reliant. It is no longer the official church and its higher clergy are no longer official appointments.

**Emancipation**

The granting of a specific right or freedom. In its Irish context it means the granting to Roman Catholics of the right to become Members of Parliament and to hold certain other offices under the crown, rights long denied to them.

**Eviction**

The act of depriving a tenant of his cottage and land, usually because of non-payment of rent. The refusal of tenants to obey eviction orders meant that police and army were often called in to carry out the evictions, forcibly if necessary. Although the Land Act of 1881 and the Arrears Act of 1882 should have stopped evictions, the withholding of rents in the 'Plan of Campaign' meant that they continued in considerable numbers until the Land Purchase Act of 1903 began to be effective in transferring land ownership from landlord to tenant.

**The Fenian Society**

This was started by Irishmen in the U.S.A. in 1858. It proposed to free Ireland from British rule by violence. It was influential only in the 1860s, but its campaign in England leading to the Manchester and Clerkenwell incidents alerted not only the British public to the need to tackle the Irish problem, but also Gladstone, who was to devote much of his political career to it.

**The Habeas Corpus Act**

The Act which required that citizens who were held in custody for more than twenty-four hours were to be charged with an offence, or, if not charged, were to be released. This Act was often suspended in Ireland in order to imprison suspected persons indefinitely without trial.

**Rack-renting**

The process of securing the highest rent for a holding by frequent raising of rent and frequent changes of tenant. Little regard was paid to the claims of an existing tenant regardless of how long he and his forbears had been tenants of the land, and rack-renting was usually accompanied by forcible evictions. Absentee landlords made the problem worse, because it was the function of the steward to maintain and increase the landlord's income regardless of the interests of the tenant. The absence of the landlord meant that he could not develop a personal interest in and concern for his tenants as he might have done had he looked after his estates personally.

**Sinn Fein**        Founded in 1899 by Arthur Griffith, this organization worked for an independent Ireland which it believed it could achieve by 'ourselves'. As it took over in popularity from the Nationalists it became more and more Republican and less hostile to the use of force. It played a key role in the events of 1918–22.

**Young Ireland**    Founded in 1842 in imitation of Mazzini's Young Italy and aimed at Irish independence. Its leaders were mostly Protestant, but their more extreme approach caused them to quarrel with O'Connell, and briefly took the centre stage of Irish political activity after O'Connell failed to defy the government at Clontarf. The influence of Young Ireland faded after its pathetically incompetent attempt at revolution in 1848.

# APPLIED MATERIALS

## BOOKS

PEACOCK, H. L., (1968). *A History of Modern Britain, 1815–1968*. Heinemann. Chapters 3, 13, 15 and 17.
RICHARDS, D. & HUNT, J. W., (1987). *Illustrated History of Modern Britain, 1783–1980*. Third edition, Longman. Chapters 15 and 16.
STOKES, J. and G., (1973). *Europe and the Modern World, 1870–1970*. Longman. Chapter 10.
School Council Syllabus Titles, (1987). *The Irish Question*. Blackwell.
*Longman's Modern World Studies (1987). Ireland 1800–1970*.

## FURTHER READING

HAMMOND, J. L. & FOOT, M. R. D., (1952). *Gladstone and Liberalism*. EUP.

## DOCUMENTARY

GIBBONS, S. R., (1986). *Ireland 1780–1914*. Blackie.

# EXAMINATION QUESTIONS

1  a)  What was the 'Irish Question' and why was Gladstone concerned about it?
   b)  Outline the attempts made by Gladstone, from 1868 to 1893, to deal with Ireland.
   c)  Why was Gladstone unable to solve the problem of the Irish Question?        (SEG)

2  a)  Write an account of the work of Charles Stewart Parnell as leader of the Irish Home Rule Movement.
   b)  Explain the circumstances in which Parnell lost control of the Irish party.
   c)  What had Parnell achieved for Ireland by the time of his death in 1891?        (LEAG)

# OUTLINE ANSWERS

1  a)  A definition should briefly explore the historical, political, religious and agrarian aspects of the Irish Question and show how and why Gladstone was likely to be concerned about them. The Fenian 'outrages' are of course relevant here. In b) a narrative of disestablishment, Land Acts, and Home Rule Bills will go only part of the way towards a maximum answer. The question asks for *attempts to deal with*,

and Gladstone's motives in putting into effect the various aspects of his Irish policy will therefore be needed. In c) a series of reasons, such as the rise of the Irish Nationalist Party, the opposition of Liberal Unionists and House of Lords, Gladstone's advancing age, agrarian violence undermining the Land Acts will go a long way towards an answer. But for the highest marks the reasons should be demonstrated as interrelated and attention drawn to the changing nature of the problem over a span of a quarter of a century.

2 a) Requests for description, or factual recall, are likely to be increasingly uncommon in GCSE. This example will require care; it asks for Parnell's *work* as leader of the Irish Home Rule Movement and not for a potted biography. So little reference will be needed to the years before Parnell entered parliament in 1875, other than his Protestantism, and that he inherited his dislike of England from his mother. The question does not make it clear whether the main part of your answer should date from his Presidency of the Home Rule Confederation of Great Britain in 1877 or of the Irish parliamentary party in 1879, so play safe and mention both. After that several main points will need to be discussed: his handling of the party leadership in the House of Commons, his Presidency of the Land League and his attitude towards its aims and method including his lukewarm attitude to the reforms of Gladstone's second ministry, his imprisonment and the Kilmainham Treaty, his relations with both major British political parties in 1885–6, and his acceptance of the Home Rule solution despite his reservations. b) requires an explanation, not so much of the *Times*/Pigott affair, as of the O'Shea divorce case and its consequences – Gladstone's virtual ultimatum, the withdrawal of the support of the Roman Catholic clergy, and his desperate and losing fight to hold his leadership and keep the Nationalist party together. In c) an assessment of Parnell is required and you should avoid merely repeating material already offered in a) and b). His achievements could include uniting all but Protestant Ireland behind his leadership, creating a strong Nationalist party in the House of Commons large enough to hold the political balance as in 1885, making the British people and the British political parties realize that the Irish problem could not be swept to one side (as it had by Disraeli in the 1870s), but must be faced and tackled. The mark allocations suggested for this question were a) 10, b) 6, and c) 4.

# A TUTOR'S ANSWER

**QUESTION**  Study extract A and picture B below and then answer **all** the questions which follow.

**Extract A**  My son drained and fenced the land and put a road on it. He made more improvements on it than his father did before him. There was a field on it, that man never worked until my son drained it, and now it is coverd with oats. In the old times water would have got on it over a man's knee boots.

*(Mother and son were evicted by an absentee landlord in 1860)*

**Picture B**

THE RIVALS

a) How did the actions of absentee landlords make the political situation in Ireland worse?

*(3 marks)*

b) Why did Gladstone decide on a policy of land reform in Ireland?

*(4 marks)*

c) How do you think an Irish Protestant would have felt about the Home Rule Movement in Ireland? Explain your answer.

*(8 marks)*

d) Why do you think Gladstone's attempts to give Home Rule to Ireland failed?

*(10 marks)*

(SEG)

a) Landlords who lived in England rather than on their estates in Ireland usually had no personal link with their tenants. They often appointed agents whose task was to extract as large an income from the land as possible; thus they increased rents frequently, often with the intention of forcing a tenant to give up his tenancy in order to make room for one willing to pay a higher rent. This rack-renting was a major Irish grievance.

b) Gladstone hoped that by tackling the religious and agrarian problems of Ireland the political problem would solve itself. He believed the main cause of Irish unrest to be agrarian, particularly after the religious question was settled by disestablishment in 1869. He had been committed to solving the Irish question from the time he first took office as Prime Minister; its successful solution would strengthen him politically, and his deep religious conviction made the land question a moral issue for him – its solution would be doing God's work.

c) There were, of course, different kinds of Irish Protestants, and the Presbyterians of the North had a long tradition of resistance to authority, and some of them might see a self-governing Ireland as preferable to an Ireland whose problems were so often ignored by Britain. But their religious fears were played upon by Randolph Churchill and others in 1886, and the vast majority of Irish protestants came to believe that Irish Home Rule would mean the Roman Catholic domination of Ireland in which the Protestants would be second-class citizens. This feeling was stronger amongst members of the Church of Ireland in areas where most of the population was Catholic. Even so the first two leaders of the Home Rule movement, Isaac Butt and Parnell himself, were both Protestants, and there is no reason to suppose that Protestants were not to be found among the rank and file of the movement.

d) Gladstone faced an uphill task. In an age when Imperialist views were taking hold in the Liberal party despite Gladstone's denunciation of them, it would be necessary for Gladstone to educate his party to accept that Home Rule was not the first step to the dissolution of the Empire, and that Home Rule was not the same as independence. But Gladstone made no such attempt, and his conversion to Home Rule was announced in such a way as to take most of his party completely by surprise. His effort to bring in Home Rule straightaway seemed to some of his party to be arrogant and badly timed. Public opinion in both Britain and Protestant Ireland needed educating as well, but the opposition were able to combine fears of the dissolution of the Empire with fears of 'Rome rule', and they had able and unscrupulous leaders like Randolph Churchill. Among the Liberals Hartington found hidden reserves of parliamentary skill in attacking Gladstone, and he was ably assisted by Chamberlain from the opposite wing of the party. It seemed that Gladstone was prepared to break up his party for the sake of Home Rule; he was taunted by the opposition as 'an old man in a hurry'. This image of Gladstone had an effect upon public opinion which had been soured by the agrarian catalogue of crime, and was unwilling to give way to violence and intimidation by granting Home Rule. When the British public *did* narrowly appear to vote for Home Rule in 1892 (without the Irish Nationalists Gladstone would have had a slender majority) Gladstone could not overcome the opposition of the Conservative-dominated House of Lords. His colleagues dissuaded him from taking on the Lords in a political fight: he was too old to do battle, and anyway if the Lords forced an election the public's uneasiness about Home Rule could well have led to another Conservative victory. It was a valiant effort: Gladstone had in 1886 come close to securing Home Rule, he had also come close to wrecking the Liberal Party.

# A STUDENT'S ANSWER WITH EXAMINER'S COMMENTS

A village on the Ulster border is considering, soon after O'Connell's death, erecting a monument to his memory. At a public meeting to make a decision discussion becomes heated. Give an account of the meeting.

> This is a useful empathetic start, but you are asked to deal with the meeting, and this occurs outside it. The touch of attempted humour is perhaps rather out of place in this context.

> It is doubtful whether the agent would have been allowed to get away with sentiments of this kind at such a meeting. Certainly they would have been challenged.

> The priest (or student?) is a little misleading. O'Connell had not, it is true, solved the tithe question, but the reduction of tithe and the transfer of responsibility for payment to the landlord had gone part way to solving the problem.

> But the first Protestant is correct in his grievance if his freehold was worth between £2 and £10, and the Republican is on the right lines.

> In an empathy answer it is likely that one side or other will overstate its case. So the priest's income will not have fallen so drastically by the Tithe Commutation Act, and surely the priest ought to know that O'Connell was a Roman Catholic and not a Protestant as he claims.

> There is the usual implied confusion between O'Connell and O'Connor, and this together with the other errors reduces the value of the answer. But it has some useful merit.

The meeting was packed. Many people could not get in and those standing outside, unable to hear what was going on, began to amuse themselves by battering each other with their placards, some of which were inscribed 'Liberator' and others carried the legend 'Remember Clontarf.' A number of broken bones resulted, but troops who were standing by made no effort to intervene. I did not want to venture into this melée, but I was fortunate in being able to squeeze into the meeting through a side-door which no-one happened to be watching.

When I eventually got inside the cost of the monument was being discussed. The figure of £500 was mentioned, and was felt to be a reasonable sum for a village of this size. But an agent for a local landowner was heard to say that if the village could afford that much he would have put up the rents years ago. As a spokesmen for the landowners he had no doubt of O'Connell's qualities as a man, and he respected O'Connell's determination to keep within the law, but he had stirred up a lot of trouble, and the landowners certainly were not going to contribute. Several Roman Catholic priests were present: those who had marched with O'Connell in County Clare wasted a lot of time reminiscing and praising his memory, but one scathingly remarked that it was all very well putting Catholics into parliament to do some good, but what good had O'Connell done? Ireland was still desperately poor and overcrowded and he had given way on the tithe question.

A lot of noise and shouting followed this, and when it subsided a local Protestant complained that O'Connell had lost him his right to vote in 1829 and he still had not got it back. The Protestant priest said that although O'Connell was a Protestant he had taken up the Catholic cause and his tithe compromise with the whig government had reduced his income by more than a half. Other Protestants claimed that O'Connell's demand for Home Rule would mean that they would be ruled by the Pope instead of Queen Victoria. At this a young man who declared himself to be a Republican said that neither Queen Victoria nor the Pope should rule Ireland, the Irish should rule themselves, but he felt that O'Connell had forfeited all claim to the gratitude of the Irish people by giving in to the government at Clontarf.

Other speakers referred to O'Connell's involvement with Chartism and his belief in physical force, and this led to such violent clashes in the hall between supporters and opponents of violence that the meeting broke up without coming to any decision.

# SUGGESTIONS FOR FURTHER WORK

1 Use encyclopedias to list the main events in the lives and careers of Daniel O'Connell, Charles Stewart Parnell and John Redmond.
2 Follow the history of Ireland beyond 1914 by
  a) explaining why Lloyd George failed to achieve by 1922 the sort of Irish settlement he had hoped for in 1918, and
  b) how far and for what reasons there has remained an Irish problem after 1922.
3 Make a comparison of the three Home Rule Bills of 1886, 1893 and 1912. Which of these would you think most likely to have solved the Irish problem had it passed into law?
4 A peasant is on trial before a jury in 1885 accused of physically assaulting his landlord's agent. The peasant admits the assault but pleads justification. Summarise the evidence of the witnesses for the prosecution and of the final speeches of the counsel (lawyers) on both sides.

# THE BRITISH EMPIRE IN THE NINETEENTH CENTURY

## GETTING STARTED

The loss of the American colonies in the late eighteenth century considerably dented the image which the British had of themselves as a colonial power. Several overseas possessions were acquired in 1815 as the result of the Congress of Vienna, but many consisted of small staging posts useful to Britain as bases for the Royal Navy and the mercantile marine rather than as fully-fledged colonies. By the 1830s the Whigs, once the champions of colonial expansion, spoke gloomily of the cost of the colonies, suggesting that whilst they were a liability they were content to remain dependent on the Mother Country; but when, like the American colonies, they were able to stand on their own feet, they began to seek their freedom. This view prevailed in South Africa in 1852–54, when, because of the continuing involvement of the British government in local wars between the Boer settlers and the Bantu natives, the Prime Minister, Aberdeen, decided to grant independence to the Boer republics of the Transvaal and the Orange Free State.

Later in the century, however, there was a swift upsurge of interest in the Empire – now significantly spelt with a capital letter. Disraeli once spoke of the colonies as 'millstones round our necks', but suddenly discovered an enthusiasm for them which Britain, in the later part of Queen Victoria's reign, willingly shared. As late as the reign of Edward VII, British people spoke sentimentally and without conscious hypocrisy of the 'White Man's Burden' – the duty which more advanced nations owed to their less fortunate brethren in far-flung heathen lands. Sir Edward Elgar's triumphantly rousing strain was matched with A. C. Benson's sentiment suggesting

> Wider still and wider, shall thy bounds be set:
> God, who made thee mighty, make thee mightier yet!

To suggest that this sense of British superiority was sheer racial intolerance, would be quite wrong. There was a clear sense of moral duty, as was shown by the many members of the Indian Civil Service who worked themselves to death in that country under the Queen-Empress. Critics saw nothing but exploitation in the way Britain handled its natives, and this view is not without truth, as could be seen when the missionaries who controlled Nyasaland first forced the natives to pay 'hut tax' in return for their supposed protection. Some of the religious fervour was however genuine, and some of the benefits for the native population were real enough.

# HISTORICAL DEVELOPMENTS

Empire-building was not only a British preoccupation. Spain and Portugal had led the way, and in the nineteenth century were followed by Germany, Italy, Belgium and others. Greed played a big part in the search for raw materials and markets for manufactured goods. Much of this expansion, and especially what came to be known as the 'Grab for Africa', took place after 1870. By the end of the century, independent Africa (and countries like Indochina and the East Indies) had almost disappeared from the map, as the colonial powers jostled for position in what felt like a rapidly shrinking world.

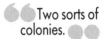**Two sorts of colonies.**

The British overseas colonies in the nineteenth century may be divided into two groups. *Colonies of settlement* were partially empty lands where white men had gone to make their homes, and where they expected to have the same rights as those who had stayed at home, moving steadily towards democratic government and independence. *Colonies of administration* were largely peopled by natives, and the white man was the ruler, or adviser to the ruler.

**1 > COLONIES OF SETTLEMENT**

British emigrants sailed to uninhabited or thinly-peopled places to establish settlements there in the seventeenth and eighteenth centuries. Such lands became the possessions of the British Crown, and were often ruled as *Crown colonies* under a Governor sent out for the purpose. A colonial governor chose his own assistants to help him govern. He appointed members of a legislative council to help him draft the laws, and an executive council to put these laws into effect. The first step towards political freedom came when Governors allowed the colonists *representative government* by permitting the election of a representative assembly to speak for the colonists. Such an assembly could not control the Governor, for he was paid by the government in London and commanded by it. During the Maori Wars in New Zealand, colonists wanted the natives completely defeated. However, the Home government was concerned over the cost of the wars, and also sympathized with the Maoris, and ordered the wars to be stopped.

**Development of colonial government.**

Pressure from the colonists gradually persuaded the British government to take the next step, and introduce *responsible government*. This not only allowed colonial citizens to elect their assembly, but also gave them at first a small, and later a bigger, say in the choice of colonial officials. Ultimately their position was similar to that of Britain itself. Elections established a majority party, which formed a government and operated through a Prime Minister and a cabinet answerable to the Governor. In the final stage the colony ceased to be subject to day-to-day interference by Britain, and acquired *dominion status*. This meant that in most domestic matters (though not yet in its external relations) these former colonies achieved independence. A Governor-General still represented the Crown, but he had no more powers in the Dominion than the Crown had in Britain, and was merely Head of State. The process of Dominion-building went on in most colonies of settlement throughout the nineteenth century.

**Colonies and Dominions.**

## CANADA

This colony had been divided by Pitt in the 1790s into English Canada and French Canada, according to the colonists' nationality, language and religion, but there had been friction between them and open rebellion broke out in 1837. The British had little difficulty in suppressing the rebellion, and sent out the radical Lord Durham to enquire into the situation in Canada and make recommendations. The *Durham Report* of 1839 caused some surprise by suggesting that the two halves of Canada be reunited and that responsible government be introduced. The Whigs as a result put through the *Reunion Act* in 1840, but it was not until Durham's son-in-law, Lord Elgin, adopted the practice of appointing ministers from the majority party that a fully-responsible government came into being. This worked well for a time, but in the 1850s trouble broke out again and there emerged a strong movement towards some form of federal union. Eventually, by the *British North America Act* of 1867 a Dominion of Canada appeared. This consisted of four provinces: Quebec, Ontario, New Brunswick and Nova Scotia, each with its own separate parliament to deal with local affairs, but all united under one Union Parliament for the whole Dominion. Provision was made for the union to grow. British Columbia joined in 1871 on being promised the construction of a Canadian Pacific Railway. In due course the prairie provinces of Manitoba, Saskatchewan and Alberta also joined the union, situated along the route of the railway.

## AUSTRALIA

Captain Cook's explorations in the late eighteenth century led to the development of settlements for convicts after 1788. The climate of the interior and the size of the continent made colonization difficult, so that separate coastal settlements were made in different areas. Some, like those at Hobart and Melbourne, were convict settlements, whilst others, such as along the Swan River in Western Australia, were free settlements. The places in the east were at first parts of New South Wales, but later, like Victoria and Queensland, became separate colonies. South Australia originated in 1834, and first attempted 'systematic colonization' as suggested by the radical Gibbon Wakefield. He believed that land should be sold to settlers instead of being given away, and the proceeds used to develop the colony. Adelaide was chosen as the capital of the colony, and the enthusiasm of the Governor, Sir George Grey, was one of the factors leading to its success.

Six colonies, including Tasmania, eventually emerged, all very jealous of their political independence. A number achieved representative government in 1851, and responsible government in 1855, though Queensland, being later, was slower. Later in the century the small populations of these separate colonies and their isolation turned their minds towards their joint defence. None of them wanted unrestricted immigration from Asian countries, and a 'white Australia' policy developed. Internal difficulties, such as separate tariff barriers, and the construction of railways on different gauges also obstructed development. Above all, the separate governments found it hard to raise adequate investment funds to develop the continent. The result was the *Commonwealth of Australia Act* in 1900. Each state retained its own government to deal with local matters, but for purposes of defence, currency, railways and immigration, there was a federal commonwealth government, consisting of a Senate and a House of Representatives with a new federal capital on its own territory at Canberra. The Governor-General was the Queen's representative and had similar powers to the British Crown.

## NEW ZEALAND

Cook also claimed the two islands of New Zealand for Britain later in the eighteenth century, and they attracted colonists who formed settlements along the coastline, making homes amongst the native Maoris in both islands. It was not until 1840 that the British government played any active role in New Zealand. Friction with the natives had led to bloodshed. Grey was brought in from New South Wales to be Governor, and Wakefield transferred his colonial experiment from Adelaide to Auckland. By the Treaty of Waitangi (1840) the Governor received the submission of the Maori chiefs but guaranteed them their lands – a promise which the white settlers failed to honour. The result was a long and bloody struggle in the Maori Wars. Grey subdued South Island between 1848 and 1853, but his successor was faced with an even harsher struggle for North Island in 1860. The struggle did not end until 1871, and then at a frightful cost to the native population. The Maoris were not fully accepted as part of the population until the twentieth century.

In 1846, Earl Grey's *Government of New Zealand Act* created the two provinces of New Ulster and New Munster for North Island and South Island, though the representative assembly suggested by it for the two colonies never in fact met. In 1852, under another constitution, there was to be an elected parliament for the whole of New Zealand, but the six smaller provinces of Auckland, Taranaki, Wellington, Nelson, Canterbury and Otago were to have local assemblies of their own. In 1857, the New Zealand Parliament, with British consent, arrogated to itself the power of responsible government, and went on in 1876 to abolish the provincial assemblies, substituting for them county local governments. The weakness and isolation of New Zealand led to the suggestion in 1900 that it be linked with Australia. New Zealanders were unwilling to be linked with a country over a thousand miles away, and pressed for Dominion status of their own. This was granted by Britain in 1907.

## SOUTH AFRICA

> Trouble brewing in South Africa.

Friction between the Dutch and the British settlers in Cape Colony was evident as early as 1836, when the Boers left the Cape in scattered groups in what became known as the *Great Trek* across the Vaal and Orange rivers. It was these republics whose independence was recognized in the early 1850s. Giving up responsibility for the actions of the Boers did not, however, solve the problem. The struggle between the white men and the Bantu broke out again, and the chief of the Basuto appealed to the British for protection against the Boers. Basutoland became a British Protectorate in 1868, as did Swaziland and Bechuanaland at later dates. The Boers resented British interference in what they regarded as their own affairs, and relations steadily soured. At about the same time, diamonds were discovered near Kimberley, and the British government, acting on the pretext of an appeal for help from the chief of the Griqua tribe, annexed Griqualand West in 1871. This annexation of territory beyond the Orange River checked the movement of the Boers westward, just as Basutoland prevented their expansion east.

Soon afterwards, serious trouble threatened in the Transvaal. Here, insensitive treatment by the Boers of the native Zulu peoples led to an explosive situation which might have produced adverse effects on the British-ruled areas if it had spilled over there. Supposedly acting in the interests of peace and security, the British government ordered the annexation of the Transvaal, and sent out Sir Bartle Frere as Governor of the Cape and High Commissioner for the whole of South Africa. A collision with the formidable Zulu armies, under their warrior king Cetewayo, followed in 1879. The Zulus defeated the British troops at the battle of Isandhlwana, and Natal threatened with invasion, but the gallant defence of Rorke's Drift by a handful of British soldiers averted the danger. Some weeks afterwards the Zulu forces were beaten at Ulundi, Cetewayto submitted and Zululand was eventually annexed by the British Crown.

Once the Zulu danger was averted, the Boers clamoured for the restoration of their independence. In Britain, Gladstone's incoming government in 1880 seemed to favour the claim, but the grant of self-government was delayed. The Boers took up arms, and British forces were again defeated, this time by the Boer settlers at Majuba Hill. Reinforcements were sent from Britain, but before they reached the country Gladstone decided to give the Boers what they wanted, and the *Convention of Pretoria* was signed with them in 1881. This decision not only left the Boers with an exaggerated idea of their own might, but also gave the impression that the British were prepared to yield to force what they would not grant to reason. This idea, that the best way to get satisfaction from the British lion was by twisting its tail, finally resulted in the outbreak of the South African War in 1899.

## 2 ▶ COLONIES OF ADMINISTRATION

The rapid development of the imperial idea after 1880 led to the British taking the responsibility for lands which were far from being empty. The initiative for the new trend in many cases was scientific, although later it became commercial. In Africa, there had for some time been respectable activity by exploring teams: Burton and Speke, in east Africa, looking for the sources of the Nile; Mungo Park, seeking the source of the Niger in west Africa, and then the explorations of the basins of the Zambesi and the Congo in the 1870s by Livingstone and Stanley.

In the 1880s came the *grab for Africa*. A Colonial Congress of Berlin, held in 1884–85, began the process. The Belgian Crown was confirmed in its possession of the Congo, and the other colonial powers distributed other African territory between them, imposing their own arbitrary frontiers on the country and leaving very little of it independent.

Soon commercial companies, chartered by the British government, were opening up the continent and negotiating concessions from native chiefs to secure control of the minerals these areas contained. The *Royal Niger Company* was set up in 1886 to trade in territory assigned to it by the Berlin Congress. The *British East Africa Company* received its charter in 1888 to work in the regions of Zanzibar, Kenya and Uganda. In the area of what later became known as Rhodesia, a *South African Company* was organized by Cecil Rhodes to exploit the resources of the region, and in particular the valuable 'yellow metal', copper, and to sell Lobengula, the Matabele king, cheap rifles for his warriors. The British government, with some justice, denied any responsibility in these areas of influence, but as imperial sentiment grew it was increasingly under pressure to take a hand in claiming areas for Britain, or 'painting the map red.'

### NORTH AFRICA

Britain had already shown an interest in Egypt soon after the purchase of the Suez Canal shares by the Disraeli government in 1875. National disturbances pushed Gladstone into occupying Egypt in 1882, and from there he went on very reluctantly to become involved in the Sudan, where troops under General Gordon were massacred in 1885. It was not until 1898 that a joint Anglo-Egyptian force under Kitchener reconquered the Sudan. Under Sir Evelyn Baring (Lord Cromer) as 'Consul-General' for Egypt and adviser to the Khedive, the country obtained 'water and justice', and some of the benefits of British supervision became apparent.

## EAST AFRICA

The British had set up trade and a steamship service in the 1870s with the offshore Sultanate of Zanzibar, and also secured mainland concessions. But it was not until the Congress of Berlin in 1884–85 that Anglo-German agreements were reached to define boundaries between the various areas of interest. Britain proclaimed a protectorate over *Somaliland* in 1884 and over *Zanzibar* in 1890, going on to establish protectorates over *Uganda* in 1894 and *Kenya* in 1896. *Nyasaland* had been taken over in 1891 by Scottish Presbyterian missionaries operating from Rhodesia. All these areas were eventually transferred from the British Foreign Office to the Colonial Office.

## WEST AFRICA

Britain had been interested in west Africa since the days of the slave trade and began to establish a foothold there in the early nineteenth century. There were wars against chieftains of local tribes, such as the Ashanti in the 1870s, and in the 1880s there was an Anglo-French agreement setting out agreed terms for colonizing the area. The *Gambia* became a British Protectorate in 1889, and *Sierra Leone* followed in 1896. Both areas had provincial commissioners appointed by Britain and answerable to the British Governor, but the authority of the native chiefs generally remained. A British Resident was appointed for the *Gold Coast* in 1896, but not until 1901 was it annexed to the Crown. *Nigeria* was taken over by the Crown in 1899, and Lord Lugard, whose name is famous for his development of the system of *indirect rule* through local tribal chiefs, became British High Commissioner. Economic development of all these areas went on rapidly, but there was no idea as yet that these possessions should aspire to democratic government.

**THE INDIAN MUTINY, 1857**

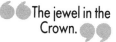

India, large, rich and heavily-populated, was often regarded as the brightest jewel in the British imperial crown. It was so important that it was under neither the Colonial Office nor the Foreign Office – it had a department of its own, the India Office. After a bitter struggle between the British and the French in the days of Clive in the eighteenth century, a British empire in India was firmly established, based on a series of ports like Bombay, Madras and Calcutta. In its early days India was a commercial concern under the *British East India Company*, but acts of Parliament in 1773 and 1784 brought the British government into the affairs of 'John Company' in the interests of the welfare of its Indian subjects. In 1813 and 1833, the commercial monopoly of the company was progressively dismantled.

Large areas of native India were controlled by independent Indian princes and nominally part of a Mohammedan Empire still governed by a Mogul resident in Delhi. As time went by, the area of British control grew, and from a number of coastal areas, the largest of which was in Bengal, Bihar and parts of the Carnatic, a series of successful governors such as Marquis Wellesley and Marquis Hastings spread British control. By about 1825, most of the sub-continent was directly or indirectly under British control. Later Governors-General, however, showed some lack of sensitivity towards Indian feelings; both Bentinck (1828–35) and Dalhousie (1848–56) brought in western reforms on a large scale, setting aside the traditions and beliefs of the Indian peoples as of no account. They regarded many of the native customs as barbarous; they abolished *suttee*, the ancient practice of burning widows on their husband's funeral pyre, and banned *thuggee*, a type of ritual assassination by priests of the goddess Khali. They showed scant respect for the Indian *caste* system, which was agreed by Hindus to be essential to the country's stability. They also revised Indian codes of law along European lines, interfered with traditional educational practices and introduced English into the sub-continent as the medium of instruction. The British also introduced the electric telegraph (which natives regarded superstitiously) and began to build railways, which were also widely feared and shunned. Dalhousie took control of large areas on the pretext that they were misgoverned, bringing the Punjab and many of the Central Provinces in the Deccan under British rule. He ignored Hindu custom, and seized those states whose ruler died without heirs, using the convenient fiction that they had 'lapsed' to the British Crown. Seven states were acquired in this way. He also deposed the King of Oudh on the dubious grounds that this lazy monarch was a tyrant. There were other causes of trouble. Many Indians feared that the British were on the point of banning their religions and forcing Christianity on them, whilst others superstitiously believed that British control over India would end in 1857, a century after the battle of Plessey had begun the country's humiliation.

The military reasons for Britain's weakness in India were even more interesting. There

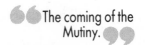
**The coming of the Mutiny.**

were generally too few Europeans in the Indian Army, and even some of these had been withdrawn during the Crimean War. There was no unified structure of command, and prestige had been lost after the rough handling which Europeans had received during the Afghan Wars in the 1840s. Furthermore, the British ignored Indian customs such as the caste system, saying it was bad for military discipline. They also ignored sepoy fears of a loss of caste if an Indian crossed the seas, and expected them to serve abroad. There was the famous affair of the 'greased cartridges', where the British thoughtlessly overlooked the fact that Hindus regarded the cow as sacred, whilst Moslems looked upon the pig as unclean. A combination of all these things led to a military revolt in 1857.

The mass of the population stayed aloof from this military rising, which was confined to the Ganges valley. Bombay and Madras took no part in the Mutiny, and the Sikhs and the Gurkhas remained loyal throughout. The first disorders took place around Calcutta, at Dumdum and Barrackpur, but the most important part of the revolt was further up the river. The garrison at Meerut revolted and murdered its officers, and the sepoys marched on Delhi where the mutineers proclaimed the restoration of the Mogul Empire. Two other important centres were Cawnpur, where a Maharatta leader carried out a savage massacre of the European population, and Lucknow, where the garrison held out for several weeks before being relieved by General Havelock. The relievers were in turn besieged, and it was not until November that Sir Colin Campbell finally rescued them. In the meantime, loyal troops had been collected from amongst the Sikhs and Delhi had been recovered, and the backbone of the Mutiny was broken. Oudh was not reconquered until 1858, and Sir Hugh Rose experienced further difficulties in his efforts to pacify the hilly country south of Gwalior. The policy of Lord Canning, the Governor-General (nicknamed 'Clemency' Canning by his critics) largely contributed to the final re-establishment of order in India.

**The aftermath of the Mutiny.**

After the Mutiny the British behaved more wisely in India. Reforms were introduced more cautiously, and more respect was shown for Indian customs. Fewer people were keen to carry out mass conversions of the natives to Christianity, and there were fewer efforts to regulate social behaviour. The doctrine of 'lapse' was abandoned. In particular, military grievances were rectified, the Indian Army was brought up to date, and the proportion of British troops to natives was increased.

The chief result, however, was the *Government of India Act* of 1858. The East India Company was abolished and the future government was placed in the hands of the Crown. The Company's army was merged with the regular army, and its navy abolished. Political responsibility in practice was taken by a Secretary of State for India, whose office was in London, and who was advised by a Council of members experienced in Indian affairs, initially representing the Company, but later the British cabinet. In India, a Viceroy represented the Queen, with an Executive Council to assist him, chosen by himself. Later, the *Royal Titles Act* of 1876 made Queen Victoria Empress of India. Lord Canning became the first Viceroy in 1858, assisted by the Secretary of State for India in London, Lord Salisbury. Over many years the two posts were filled with men of great ability, and relations were closer after 1870, when direct telegraphic communication was established with India. The posts created harmonious partnerships, such as that between Viscount Morley (Secretary of State) and Lord Minto (Viceroy) between 1906–10. Their most important reform, embodied in the *India Councils Act* of 1909, was the introduction of elected members of the Provincial Legislative Councils for advising on local affairs.

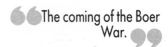
**4 ⟩  THE SOUTH AFRICAN WAR**

**The coming of the Boer War.**

Anglo-Boer relations were not much improved by the Convention of Pretoria (1881) at the end of the First Boer War of 1881. For one thing, the Convention contained a mysterious reservation that the two Boer states, the Orange Free State and the Transvaal should still be subject to the *suzerainty* of the British Crown, and this they took to detract from their independence. The offending phrase was removed by a second agreement, the Convention of London, in 1884. However, the sense of the original reservation was paraphrased in the new one, and the change was one of form, rather than of substance. Furthermore, Boers and British did not get on with each other any better. The Boers were paternalistic and distant in manner, with simple rural ways. They hated the encroachment of commercialism, in the form of gold prospecting and diamond mining. They despised the de Beers Mining Corporation and in particular the dealings of Cecil Rhodes's South Africa Company, whose activities in Bechuanaland and Rhodesia threatened to surround them. Bechuanaland lay in the path of the direct route to the North, towards the rich Zambesi Valley, which Rhodes hoped to control. He had even vaster ambitions, to create a federation for the whole of South Africa and an 'all-red line' of British territory from the north to the south of

Africa, together with a Cape-to-Cairo railway. These ambitions brought him into conflict with the Boer leader, Paul Kruger ('Uncle' Paul, as he was affectionately known to his people), who resented Rhodes's policy of expansion and the consequent threat to the Boer way of life.

In 1886, to make matters worse, gold was discovered on the Witwatersrand in the Transvaal. It was chiefly low-grade ore, requiring heavy machinery for crushing and grinding the rock and extensive smelting plants to extract the gold. The country was flooded with foreign immigrants – 'outsiders', or *Uitlanders*, as the Boers called them. Johannesburg swelled overnight from a small community of about 200 people to a town of over 20,000. Within ten years it was a city of 100,000 people. The Boers detested this onslaught of international capitalism.

By 1892 there were about 80,000 Uitlanders, many British, and some of them the scum of the earth. Without offending the British government, the Boers were determined to have as little to do with them as possible. They housed many in barrack-like 'shanty' towns without lighting, paving or sanitation, imposed strict police supervision on them, controlled their supplies of liquor and refused to grant them civil rights. Yet the Uitlanders paid heavy freight charges to transport the ore, and had to purchase dynamite from a government monopoly, which overcharged them. Furthermore, they paid about 90% of the country's taxes. It is not surprising that in 1892 they formed the *Uitlander National Union* and began to press for the vote. In this they had the support of Cecil Rhodes, who by this time was Prime Minister of the Cape.

The problem came to a head at Christmas, 1895. The Uitlanders planned a rising to take over Johannesburg and the entire country, and asked the British for military support. One of Rhodes's officers, Dr. Starr Jameson, who was an administrator in the South Africa Company and in charge of about 500 armed railway police who protected the line northwards through Bechuanaland, crossed into the Transvaal to help the rebels. The Boers, however, had no difficulty in putting down the rising. After four days they rounded up the invaders, accepted a sizeable ransom from Rhodes, and handed them over to Britain for punishment. The light sentence imposed on Jameson when he appeared at Bow Street showed the world clearly where British sympathies lay, but the unsavoury episode reflected very badly on Britain's pretensions as leader of the world's moral opinion. Rhodes was ruined and had to retire as Cape Prime Minister. Kruger appeared as the injured party, especially after the Kaiser congratulated him for dealing with the 'armed hordes' invading his country. But the matter did not rest there. In 1898, a Uitlander called Tom Edgar was murdered. A petition was presented to Queen Victoria, and the British government, taking up the authority which most Boers believed had been surrendered in 1884, sided with the Uitlanders. Sir Alfred Milner, the British High Commissioner, tried to negotiate a settlement with Kruger, but Milner's obstinacy and Kruger's wily obstruction combined to defeat the attempt. In the autumn of 1899, war resulted.

The Boers were much better prepared for war than the British. For some time they had been importing artillery and small arms from Germany and Holland, and although their population was small, they had far more men under arms than Britain. These men knew the country well, were expert riders and marksmen and had the advantage of wearing drab khaki instead of military scarlet. In the early stages of the war the Boers achieved numerous successes.

**The Boer War.**

The war fell into three phases. Initially the Boers had the advantage and seemed all-conquering. Their troops entered Bechuanaland, Natal and Cape Colony, and laid siege to the key towns of Mafeking, Kimberley and Ladysmith. In 'Black Week', just before Christmas, British forces were defeated three times, at Stormberg, Magersfontein and most seriously at Colenso. The British were shocked, but not disheartened. Victoria commented resolutely:

There is no one depressed in *this* house. We are not interested in the possibilities of defeat; they do not exist.

Phase 2 began when large reinforcements were sent under the command of Roberts and Kitchener at the end of 1899. The Boer generals, Cronje, de Wet and de la Rey were repeatedly defeated, expelled from the territory they had invaded and the besieged towns eventually relieved. In March 1900, Roberts took one of the Boer capitals, Bloemfontein, and in June the other, Pretoria. Successive Boer 'commandos' (swift-moving raiding parties disrupting British communications) were captured in Cape Colony. By October, most key positions in the two Boer states had been taken, organized resistance was at an end and President Kruger had fled to Portuguese territory. By this time, reinforced by large detachments from the Empire, Britain had half a million men in South Africa, to deal with only 30,000 Boers. Even so they found it hard to clinch victory.

In phase 3 of the war, the Boers refused to give in after the official annexation of the two states in October. They resorted to guerrilla warfare, with small bands of troops hiding amongst, and receiving support from the civilian population. The occupying armies found them hard to catch, as they somehow melted into the countryside, rather than standing to fight. The guerillas did immense damage, proving that it was easier to conquer a country than to occupy it. This guerrilla phase did not end until the Treaty of Vereeniging in May 1902. Meanwhile, Kitchener had set up a scheme to protect the railways by building concrete blockhouses to defend them, and employed large numbers of men, not only as patrols, but also to ensure the guerrillas were not supplied with their needs. Farms had been destroyed, cattle driven away and large areas laid waste. British troops had organized 'drives' to corner their elusive opponents in an ever-narrowing area, until their capture. More controversially, large numbers of civilians had been 'concentrated' in large camps, often behind barbed wire, so that they could not help the guerrillas. Conditions in these *concentration camps* were often appalling. Sanitary and medical facilities were almost non-existent, and food was short. Eventually, of the 120,000 prisoners in these camps, over 20,000 died. Humanitarian opinion in Britain was shocked at the ruthless excuses which the authorities put forward, but in the end, the Boers were beaten and had to ask for peace.

**The aftermath of the Boer War.**

Under the Treaty of Vereeniging the Boers surrendered themselves and their munitions, and the two republics were annexed to the British Crown. But the rest of the treaty was remarkably lenient; there was no punishments for the Boers, unless they had been guilty of specified acts of brutality. Guns could be retained for the future, provided they were licensed. The Dutch language could be used in schools and law courts, though English was to be the official language. No special taxes were imposed to pay for the war, and the two Boer states had their independence restored as soon as possible. Britain even made a grant of £3m to the Boers to help repair the devastation, and lent a further £40m at modest interest rates to rebuild and re-stock Boer farms – possibly the only time in history when the victor has paid reparations to the vanquished! However, there was little mention in the treaty of the situation that had caused the war. Only the clause allowing British subjects to be repatriated at British expense made any reference to the Uitlanders, and no mention at all was made of the native peoples, who had been only spectators, playing no part in the war. This omission was perhaps the most serious one, since there were no safeguards that in future the natives would be any better treated than they had been in the past. Racial problems were to recur in South Africa from the very beginning, and in the end were to prove the most difficult that the country faced.

The South African War was important for Britain in a number of ways. Not only was the War Office persuaded by the author Conan Doyle to scrap military scarlet in favour of camouflage khaki, but the war also altered Britain's concept of the overseas empire and made it less intolerant of colonial self-government.

In 1907, after the discontinuance of the 'coolie labour' that had so distressed Liberals at the 1906 election (see Chapter 9), a new constitution was granted to the Transvaal. Louis Botha was elected Prime Minister of the country, with J. C. Smuts as his chief colleague. Later in the year, similar concessions were made to the Orange Colony, which now received back its former name, and Abraham Fischer became Prime Minister with the former general Hertzog as his main lieutenant. In 1908, four delegations met in Durban to consider in more detail the federation proposals that had been periodically suggested since the days of Governor Grey in the early 1850s. These ideas were forwarded to London and in 1909 the *Union of South Africa Act* was passed by the British Parliament, coming into force in 1910.

Under the act, the four colonies of the Cape, Natal, the Transvaal and the Orange River State were to form the Union of South Africa, of which they were to be provinces. Their separate parliaments were to be abolished. In future South Africa was to be a Dominion, since its Governor-General was to be answerable to the South African parliament. Parliament consisted of a Senate and a House of Assembly, disputes between them being resolved by joint session. Parliament was to sit in Cape Town, but the administrative centre for the Union was in Pretoria. English and Dutch were the official languages. One feature of the agreement was important for the future – there was to be no uniform franchise throughout the Union, so that, notwithstanding the entrenched safeguard in the act that the Cape Coloured were to retain their voting rights, the mass of Africans were denied the vote.

The act did much to restore harmonious relations between the British and the Boers. The South African Party, led by Botha, Smuts and Hertzog, encouraged the close association of the white races to promote a South African nation. Hertzog left the party in 1912 to form a rival organization known as the Nationalist party, many of whose members favoured Boer dominance. Botha and Smuts, both of whom became Prime Minister in turn, remained loyal to the British connection and gave vigorous support to Britain during the First World War.

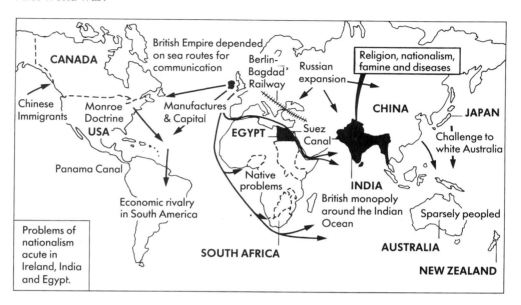

Fig 7.1 Imperial Problems

**5** ▷ **COLONIAL POLICIES AND THE FIRST WORLD WAR**

The Colonial Question before 1914.

In the forty years before 1914 the great powers, including the newly-united states of Germany and Italy developed an interest in the idea of empire. This was partly due to the supplies of raw materials and products which colonies could supply, partly to their strategic positioning and value as bases, but chiefly to the prestige which the possession of such colonies conferred. Colonial expansion in these years did much to make the world smaller and bring the great capitalist giants into conflict with each other. As these areas of the world were claimed, the great powers found themselves jostling for position. Their colonial disputes added fuel to the fires of their quarrels in Europe.

### BRITAIN v FRANCE

Britain and France both had joint interests in Egypt and the Suez Canal for some years after it opened. The British purchase of some Canal shares led to the establishment first of a Debt Commission in which the two powers were the main participants, and later to a system of *dual control* which they operated. Joint intervention was planned in Egypt when nationalist disturbances took place there in 1881, but a domestic crisis supervened in France, and Britain proceeded alone, becoming solely responsible for Egypt after 1882. The French felt annoyed at this, and were pleased when Gordon failed to establish British power in the Sudan in 1885. Meanwhile, the French had set themselves up as masters of Algeria, Tunis and much of north-west Africa, their possessions reaching down to Senegal and to the Ivory Coast and Dahomey on the Gulf of Guinea. This vast political monopoly alarmed Britain, and caused much ill-feeling in places like the Gambia, where the two sides were in confrontation.

In the mid-1890s the French saw that the lawless Sudan formed a political vacuum, and sent an expedition eastwards from French Equatorial Africa under Captain Marchand to make contact with French Djibouti in the east, creating an 'all-green (French) line' from west to east of the continent. At the same time, the British decided to reconquer the Sudan. Kitchener won a series of victories over the Dervishes at Dongola and Atbara, and eventually defeated and killed the Khalifa, the Sudanese leader, at Omdurman in September 1898. The two sides – Kitchener with about 30,000 troops, and Marchand with about 30 – met at Fashoda on the White Nile. Britain had already made it clear that:

the advance of a French expedition under secret instructions right from the other side of Africa into the Nile Valley would be an unfriendly act and would be so viewed by England.

The British government did not hide its disapproval. When the French refused to lower their flag, an English colour-sergeant willingly did so, replacing it with the British and Egyptian flags. A small British garrison was placed alongside the French, and for some time the two countries stood on the brink of war. Only after some weeks did the French instruct Marchand to leave. Eventually, in 1899, an Anglo-French Convention tidied up the problem, awarding the French a large tract of Saharan territory beyond the watershed west of the Nile – what the Prime Minister, Salisbury, contemptuously called 'sand for the Gallic cock to scratch in.' But there was no doubt that Britain came out the winner.

It was more surprising, therefore, that Britain and France should resolve their differences so speedily in their *Entente Cordiale* of 1904. For the future, France gave Britain a free hand in Egypt and the Sudan, whilst Britain gave France a free hand in Algeria and West Africa, proving its sincerity by three times coming to the aid of its entente partner in 1905, 1909 and 1911. The Entente showed that whilst colonial problems were serious, they were certainly not insoluble.

## BRITAIN v GERMANY

There were numerous clashes between Britain and Germany in various parts of the world before 1914, aggravating their serious commercial and naval rivalry. In 1905, in Tangier, Germany championed the right of the Sultan of Morocco to be free from foreign interference, testing the strength of the newly-signed Entente Cordiale. In 1911, the Germans sent gunboats to Agadir and appeared to make a bid for neutralizing Gibraltar as a strategic base. In 1908, France and Germany clashed more directly when the French broke into the German consulate at Casablanca to arrest three deserters from the Foreign Legion, and with British support took the affair to the International Court for a settlement in which the Germans accepted French predominance in West Africa. All these episodes had the effect of driving Britain and France closer together, and deepening the gulf between them and Germany.

However, there were other areas of friction between Britain and Germany. The most important was the Near East, where for some time Germany had been gaining the sympathies of Turkey, by sending economic and technical advisers and offering military expertise to reorganize the Turkish Army. About 1890, Germany proposed the idea of the *Berlin-Baghdad railway*, to connect Germany with the Persian Gulf. Such a scheme would short-circuit the Suez Canal and provide an even quicker route to the East. Permission to construct the railway was given by the Turkish authorities in 1899, but people originally in favour of it, like Rhodes, now opposed the scheme, since it threatened Britain's whole middle eastern position. Suspicion continued for the next decade, and it was only in 1913 that an arrangement was reached whereby Britain agreed to the railway, provided that the last stretch of line, from Basra down to the Gulf, was owned by a separate company most of whose shares should be in British hands. This helped to relieve some of the tension in Anglo-German colonial relations on the eve of the First World War.

# IDEAS AND PRINCIPLES

| | |
|---|---|
| **Dominion Status** | A Dominion is a former colony or protectorate within the British Empire which has achieved self-government and in the twentieth century complete independence within the Commonwealth. It acknowledges the Crown as the symbolic Head of the Commonwealth. Its status is said to be Dominion status. The word *dominion* carries the meaning of *rule* or *control*, but in fact the Crown does not exercise this over a dominion. |
| **Entrenchment** | If, for example, a particular provision of a constitution, say guaranteeing the voting rights of natives, is more difficult to alter than the rest of the constitution, such a provision is said to be *entrenched*. |

| Federalism | A *Federation* or *Confederation* is a form of government where the various units are linked together in a central (*federal*) government for a number of purposes, but where each unit still retains rights of self-government for other, usually local, purposes. The Dominion of Australia is one such federation. *Federalism* is that type of political thinking which puts forward the idea of federations as a means of strengthening or developing units which would otherwise be too weak. |
| --- | --- |
| **Imperialism** | Favouring the rule of an empire. A process by which a strong or dominant nation imposes its rule on a weaker nation or people. In the nineteenth century the word refers to a political doctrine enabling countries like Britain and France to build up vast overseas territorial possessions in Africa, India etc. In the thinking of later figures such as Marx, the word comes to be used in a more general sense for other forms of exploitation of the weak by the strong. Thus *economic imperialism* and *cultural imperialism* mean exploitation of a specific type instead of by the direct exercise of the power of government. |
| **Indirect rule** | Lord Lugard suggested the wide use of the principle that 'the chiefs should govern their people, not as independent, but as dependent rulers.' British advisers should take care not to interfere too much, but should support the chief's authority and teach the ruler to develop a sense of responsibility. Critics said that in practice such a system merely propped up forms of African 'feudalism'; even at best it was no more than a policy of 'wait and see.' |
| **Suzerainty** | A political/legal concept to be distinguished from *sovereignty*. A sovereign exercises power *directly* over those who are governed; a *suzerain* reserves these powers, and exercises them only when asked. A useful parallel might be this: a football referee exercises his powers directly by blowing his whistle; a cricket umpire gives his decision only when appealed to by the players – 'Howzat?' |

# A P P L I E D   M A T E R I A L S

## BOOKS

CASE, S. J. & HALL, D. J., (1967). *World History from 1783 to the Present Day*. Arnold. Chapter 11.

HILL, C. P. & WRIGHT, J. C., (1981). *British History, 1815–1914*. Oxford. Chapters 17, 18 & 19.

LINDSAY, D. & WASHINGTON, E. S., (1960). *Portrait of Britain Between the Exhibitions, 1851–1951*. Oxford. Chapter 12.

RAWDING, F. W., (1986). *The Rebellion in India. 1857*. Cambridge.

RICHARDS, D. & HUNT, J. W., (1987). *Illustrated History of Modern Britain 1783–1980*. Longman. Chapter 17.

## MORE DETAILED BOOKS

SOUTHGATE, G. W., (1957). *British Empire and Commonwealth*. Dent.

WILLIAMSON, J. A., (1965). *A Short History of British Expansion*. Macmillan.

## DOCUMENTARY SOURCES

TEED, P. & CLARK, M., (Eds.), (1969). *Portraits and Documents: Later Nineteenth Century 1868–1919*. Hutchinson. pp. 117–41, 156–61.

## AUDIO-VISUAL

The British Empire in the Nineteenth Century     Audio Learning HM0022
The Indian Empire/English-speaking Africa     Audio Learning HEA010
The New Imperialism     Audio Learning HUA029
European Partition of Black Africa     Audio Learning HUA056
Shipping, Trade and Empire     A.V.P. 1099
The Rise and Fall of the British Empire     E.A.V. N3850
The Scramble for Africa     Longman (History Games)

# EXAMINATION QUESTIONS

**1**   a) From the following choose **two** important factors which caused the Second Boer War. Explain them and say why they were important.
    i)    The discovery of gold on the Witwatersrand
    ii)   The formation of the British South Africa Company
    iii) The opening of the railway line from Pretoria to Delagoa Bay
    iv) The Jameson Raid
  b) From your own knowledge, explain why the Boers were at first successful, but finally unsuccessful in the war.       (LEAG)

**2**   What do you understand by the term *dominion status*? Explain how *each* of the following British possessions became dominions in the years before 1914: a) Canada; b) Australia; c) New Zealand and d) South Africa.       (London)

**3**   BRITAIN AND AFRICA, 1870–1913

### Source A

Cecil Rhodes in 1877:
I contend that we are the first race in the world, and that the more of the world that we inhabit, the better it is for the human race. I contend that every acre added to our territory provides for the birth of more of the English race . . . added to which the absorption of the greater portion of the world under our rule simply means the end of all wars.

### Source B

Paul Kruger in an interview to *The Times*, 1891:
You are afraid to give us a seaport. Can our two or three ships upset the balance of the first navy of the world? . . . You think that if I had a port I might give preference to foreigners. It is nonsense. England, if she will treat me fairly, will have the preference always . . . I ask nothing better than to work with England as a younger brother might work with his elder, but I will not work with her as a slave.

### Source C

Joseph Chamberlain in the House of Commons, May 1896:
A war in South Africa would be one of the most serious wars that could possibly be waged. It would be in the nature of a civil war. It would be a long war, a bitter war and a costly war . . . it would leave behind it the embers of a strife which I believe generations would be hardly long enough to extinguish.

### Source D

Wilfrid Blunt, English poet and traveller, writing after the victory of Omdurman in 1898:
The whole country, if one may judge by the press, has gone mad with the lust of fighting glory, and there is not a moral sense left in England to which to appeal.

**Source E**

A cartoon published in the
*Manchester Evening Mail*,
30 August 1899:

"WON'T BE HAPPY TILL HE GETS IT."

1  a) What official positions were held by Kruger and Chamberlain, when they made the remarks in Sources B and C?

*(2)*

   b) Explain the meaning of the words on the paper held by 'John Bull' in Source E.

*(3)*

2  Did Chamberlain's speech in Source C prove to be an accurate prophecy?

*(5)*

3  Using Sources A, B and E, explain why Rhodes and Kruger were such rivals.

*(5)*

4  a) On the evidence of these sources, what can be learned about British aims in Africa in the last quarter of the nineteenth century?

*(5)*

   b) How reliable would you consider these sources to be as evidence of British aims in Africa?

*(5)*

5  In Source C, Chamberlain seems reluctant to go to war, yet in Source D, Blunt says England 'has gone mad with the lust of fighting glory.' This shows that most English people did not agree with Chamberlain's ideas on war in Africa. Do you agree? Explain your answer carefully.

*(5)*
(MEG)

**4**  BRITISH EMPIRE TO COMMONWEALTH, 1867–1980.
   Read this extract and then answer questions a) to e) which follow.

The discovery of diamonds near Kimberley and gold near Johannesburg led to trouble between the Boers and the British. The First Boer War settled nothing but the Second Boer War (1899–1902) ended in British victory and the two Boer states were taken over. In 1910 the Union of South Africa was formed from the Boer states and the two other British territories of Natal and Cape Colony.

   Since then the Boers have had the greater influence and have provided all the Prime Ministers. The first of these were moderate men but in 1948 the Afrikaaner Nationalist Party won power. Their racial policies have led to South Africa's increasing isolation from other nations.

a) Explain the meaning of the term 'Boers' used in the extract above.
b) Why was Britain more successful in the Second Boer War than in the First?
c) Why since 1910 have the Boers 'had greater influence and have provided all the Prime Ministers'?
d) Why is it unlikely that the Party which won power in 1948 would have many supporters of British descent?
e) i) Explain the ways in which its racial policies have led to South Africa's increasing isolation from other nations.
   ii) Why did this racial policy become more of an issue after the 1950s than when it was first introduced?                              *(25 marks)* (SEG)

# OUTLINE ANSWERS

**1** The wording of a) entitles you to select *two* factors which helped to cause the South African War, and asks you to explain them and to say why they were important. The emphasis therefore should be on *causes*, and the explanation called for should have a focus on cause. The *importance* called for should have a similar focus. Pure description, whilst admissible to some extent, will not score so highly as material focused in the required fashion.

*Explanation* is also required in b). The first focus requires you to say *why* the Boers were at first successful, and should develop in more detail the brief points dealt with in paragraph 5 of the Section on the South African War in this chapter; then for the second you should explain *why* the Boers were eventually defeated. These points could include: the overwhelming numerical and technical superiority of the British and Empire forces; the diplomatic and geographical isolation of the Boers and their difficulties in obtaining foreign supplies; their limited financial means; their tactical errors on the battlefield and the dispersal of their limited resources on small-scale and fruitless efforts. Factual knowledge of the campaigns of the war is not specifically called for, but if you can refer in your answer knowledgeably to what actually happened it will make your answer more convincing.

**2** This is a five-part question, and therefore will be marked out of 4/4/4/4/4, perhaps varying this in appropriate cases by a small margin (say 4/3/5/5/3). The first part requires an attempted *definition*, and here you could build your answer on what this chapter provides in the 'Ideas and Principles' Section; whilst the other four parts call for an outline of the process whereby each of the countries mentioned moved towards that status in the years before 1914. An outline of the material needed here is given in the Section of this chapter on Colonies of Settlement. It is worth noting that there may be some temptation to go into too much detail on South Africa, since you are likely to have more information here than elsewhere: don't forget that not a lot of detail will be required for 4 marks, and you must take care not to over-develop the last part of your answer at the expense of the earlier parts.

# A TUTOR'S ANSWER TO Q.3

**3** BRITAIN AND AFRICA, 1870–1913

1 a) Kruger was President of the Transvaal in 1891. In 1896 Joseph Chamberlain was British Colonial Secretary in Salisbury's government.

b) *Franchise* means the right to vote, and this is one of the things the Uitlanders were asking for in 1899. The reference to *Justice for Uitlanders* indicated that they were also asking for improvements in other respects: they wanted better living and working conditions, fairer taxes, a better deal in the courts and more equality of social status. The word *Uitlander* itself is an Afrikaans word for outsider i.e. immigrant.

2 Chamberlain's words were a prediction of uncanny accuracy. The South African war was indeed serious, and may be said to have altered Britain's entire attitude towards the phenomenon of an overseas colonial empire, especially in the light of the excesses to which the British claimed to have been driven. It was also a civil war, in that it was fought between two white communities, the Bantu people playing little or no part in it. It was longer than expected, especially in its concluding guerrilla stages. The peace treaty at Vereeniging, furthermore, in failing to deal with the underlying question of black/white relations, allowed the embers of the racial question to smoulder on, as to a large extent they still do.

3 Rhodes's astonishing assertion in Source A would certainly have alarmed Kruger if he had ever heard it mentioned; there could have been relatively few who shared his extreme viewpoint even in 1877. Source B provides an indication of Kruger's ambitions for his country – a seaport, a small navy and an independent trade policy,

all of which would detract from Rhodes's dream and which he would therefore not have been willing to accept. Source E shows that the Uitlander question in the Transvaal was a bone of contention between Britons and Boers, involving both Kruger and Rhodes, especially in the matters of *franchise* and *justice.*

4   a) Source A gives us a clear indication of Rhodes's thinking on the subject of imperialism; what is less clear is how widely such views were shared. Source B is perhaps a better indication of British aims, since in order to find it necessary to talk in this fashion, Kruger must have been experiencing difficulties in pursuing independent policies respecting his navy and his trade, and must have felt that Britain was hedging him in by adjacent territories. Chamberlain in Source C shows that he knows the price of future conflict, but this in no way seems to weaken his imperial ambitions. Source D (like Source A) is a very individual point of view and is not typical of British opinion in 1898. Finally, Source E is intended for popular press consumption: the best that can be said of it is that it typifies the stereotyped thinking going on in Britain e.g. by portraying Kruger as an indignant garden gnome. All in all the evidence is very brief and selective, and cannot be expected to say much about British aims.

   b) Their *reliability* is acceptable enough, since the four extracts, though short, and the cartoon, all appear to be authentic. But how *accurate* an indication they provide of British aims in Africa is more open to question. The evidence is short, selected from sources which are sometimes rather eccentric and untypical, and in the last case giving unwitting evidence that is much more important than its witting evidence. All in all, they provide insufficient evidence of the true aims of British policy in Africa in the late nineteenth century.

5   The question creates a problem where none exists. Chamberlain is reluctant to go to war only in the sense that everyone should be; for though his observation is expressed 'more in sorrow than in anger', there is every indication that he does intend to go to war. He would have profoundly disagreed with Blunt, whom he would have considered a feeble 'wet'. It should be added, however, that Blunt's view was not typical of his time, and to suggest that his view reveals that 'most English people did not agree with Chamberlain' is a fatuous observation unsupported by any facts.

# A STUDENT'S ANSWER TO Q.4 WITH EXAMINER'S COMMENTS

> Should also mention that he is a South African of Dutch descent.

> There are no reasons here: the answer says that the British were victorious because the Boers were defeated.

> This, however, is a very good point. Note that you do not have to accept all the implications of the question.

a) Boer means farmer

b) British and Empire forces were successful in a series of battles against the Boers at Colesberg, Paardeberg and Diamond Hill and by the autumn of 1900 had captured the two Boer capitals. Soon Boer resistance was at an end, although even now they would not give way, but resorted to guerrilla warfare. It is wrong, however, to suggest that the British lost the First Boer War. They were defeated at Majuba Hill, but reinforcements were already on their way to South Africa when the war ended, and Gladstone did not yield any more after that defeat than he was prepared to yield before. To say that Britain lost the war is to fall into the same error as the Boers, who also believed this.

c) The Boers had more influence after 1910 because they were more

> **Succinct and well worth saying. More specific reference to 'Prime Ministers', however, would have helped.**

> **Excellent: again the candidate does not accept the implications of the question.**

> **This is a very uneven answer: having answered d) excellently, the candidate makes a poor attempt at e). The answer is not even divided into i)/ii). Perhaps the question goes outside the period studied – in which case the student should think twice before attempting it.**

numerous. It also proved to be a mistake to think that the Boers would model themselves on Britain's good example by gradually extending the vote to the natives, as in Cape Colony. Milner believed this but he was wrong. This was a clear case of bad driving out good, and not good driving out bad. There appeared to be almost no bad Boer example that British South Africans were not ready to follow.

d) Anyone who thinks that the British South Africans for the most part were not largely in favour of 'apartheid' is deluding himself. Apart from a handful of British South African Liberals there was wide backing for the policy amongst both communities, for English-speaking South Africans have their roots as deeply in Africa as Australians do in their country. One of the Dutch-descended Presidents said 'South Africa – the land opened to us by Afrikaaner Voor-trekkers and British settlers – is our own country, our one and only homeland.' The myth that the English are 'different' comes from snobbish exclusiveness of an unrepresentative minority in parts of Natal and the eastern Cape.

e) South Africa's racial policies are unpopular amongst the mass of the African people and this can be seen in the way O.A.U opposes 'apartheid'. It is also unpopular amongst the nations of U.N.O. The effect of this has been to make South Africa isolated from the rest of world opinion.

# SUGGESTIONS FOR FURTHER WORK

1. Collect photographs of the Imperial Durbar in Delhi in 1911. What do pictures such as these tell us about British India before the First World War?
2. Write a letter home to your parents in England describing your early experiences as a free settler in Tasmania in the 1840s.
3. Take *three* or *four* British colonial settlements in the nineteenth century and build up a dossier on each to improve your knowledge and understanding of the conditions in, and the development of, these colonies. This may be used as part of your coursework, and could be useful in answering an examination question such as Question 2 in this chapter.

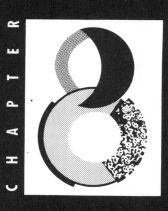

# BRITISH FOREIGN POLICY, 1890–1914

## GETTING STARTED

Palmerston's defeat over the Schleswig-Holstein question in 1864 began a period when Britain was not diplomatically linked with the continent of Europe, a period of isolation which lasted nearly half a century. This was partly due to the beliefs of British political leaders, since Gladstone was inclined to be a 'little Englander' and put Britain first, whilst Disraeli was by preference an imperialist and interpreted his European attitudes in the light of his ideas on empire. It was also partly due to considerations of commerce, because Britain, a leading industrial and mercantile power, believed that a more secure future was to be found in a peaceful free-trading world in which Britain avoided becoming entangled in the quarrels of European states.

The Conservatives were in power almost continuously for twenty years after 1886, mainly under the Marquess of Salisbury, who did not retire from politics until 1902. Aloof and aristocratic, he did not believe in democracy, and disdained what he called the *aura popularis* (personal charisma). For much of the period he combined the two offices of Prime Minister and Foreign Secretary, and carried out much of his diplomatic business through private correspondence rather than through official channels. He did not always take the trouble to explain himself fully: nevertheless it is possible to make an accurate estimate of his importance.

# HISTORICAL DEVELOPMENTS

**SPLENDID ISOLATION**

The phrase *Splendid Isolation* was invented by a Canadian journalist, and was not one that Salisbury would himself have used. It meant that Britain used its superior world position to avoid diplomatic entanglements which would involve it in European quarrels where it had no real concern. Britain concentrated instead on winning a worldwide colonial empire. How far such a policy may be truthfully said to be 'isolation', however, is doubtful.

From cultural and financial standpoints, Britain was never isolated from Europe. Also, from the point of view of commercial markets as well as for much of its foodstuffs and raw materials, it depended on its outside contacts. If Britain was isolated at all, it was purely a diplomatic matter. Certainly, Salisbury was no believer in formal alliances. He took the view that if there was an identity of interest between two powers they would act together; if there was not, then no amount of effort could keep them in alliance with each other. All the same, Britain had continued diplomatic relations with European powers throughout these years.

Salisbury accepted the traditional view that France and Russia were the two chief dangers, and he approved of Bismarck's alliance system as a means of restraining them, even though he did not formally join it. In 1887, for instance, he allowed himself to be drawn into a *Mediterranean Pact*, much of which was unpublished, to secure peace by defending the existing territorial settlement in the Mediterranean area. Though he did not officially ally himself with Bismarck when invited to in 1889 (his refusal is a masterpiece of sounding as if he is saying 'yes' when in fact he is saying 'no'), he struck a useful bargain with Bismarck the following year, when he agreed a colonial pact whereby Britain gave up Heligoland in return for Zanzibar on the east coast of Africa, an exchange declared to be like 'getting a whole suit of clothes in exchange for a trouser button.'

**66 How Splendid was Isolation? 99**

But after 1890 the situation changed. In Germany, Bismarck was forced to resign and his successors embarked on ambitious commercial and naval projects. France and Russia, after some hesitation, entered into a Dual Alliance with each other, which seemed to threaten Britain's world position. A series of episodes soon showed that isolation was not as 'splendid' as might have been supposed.

## 1894: THE ARMENIAN MASSACRES

A series of atrocities against Turkey's Armenian subjects, both in Armenia on the Russian frontier, where about 100,000 were butchered in about eighteen months, and in Constantinople (the Ottoman Bank outrage in 1896), led to British protests. However, only the Tsar was willing to intervene, and Salisbury certainly did not wish to encourage that. The Germans had less doubt; they were anxious to establish themselves as Turkey's protectors, to secure for themselves, if possible, concessions for a Berlin-Baghdad railway.

## 1895: VENEZUELA BOUNDARY DISPUTE

Venezuela had for some time been claiming land also claimed by British Guiana, and had taken the thoughtful precaution of granting concessions there to a U.S. oil corporation. President Cleveland, hoping to improve his chances of winning the 1896 Presidential election, came out in favour of Venezuela (as well as of Esso) and, invoking the Monroe Doctrine, condemned British policy. Salisbury had to agree to allow the dispute to go to international arbitration – though in 1899 he was thankful to see the British position sustained.

## 1896: THE KRUGER TELEGRAM

When a force from British Bechuanaland under Dr. Jameson invaded the Transvaal in order to help the Uitlanders overthrow the Boer government (see Chapter 7), the Kaiser sent a telegram of congratulation on the success in dealing with the rebels. His comment

> I sincerely congratulate you that, without appealing for the help of friendly powers, you with your people, by your own energy against the armed hordes which as disturbers of the peace broke into your country, have succeeded in re-establishing peace and maintaining the independence of your country against attacks from without.

showed how hostile was Europe's view of Britain's part in the exploit. The British newspaper *The Morning Post* was not slow to grasp this point:

> To speak quite plainly, it is impossible to survey the world at the present moment without seeing that Great Britain stands alone, and that the attitude or the policy of four of the great powers are such that each or all of them may at any moment become her enemies.

### 1898: PORT ARTHUR

Russia, aiming to provide a warm-water port as the eastern terminus of the Trans-Siberian Railway via the proposed South Manchurian Railway, secured a lease of Port Arthur on the Liaotung Peninsula. Britain, which had extensive commercial interests in China (nearly 80% of Chinese trade and almost all Chinese rails were British-owned) was extremely alarmed by this new development. Shortly afterwards the British government copied Russia, and obtained a lease for Wei-hai-wei. They also began an active search for a Far Eastern ally to counter Russian expansion in Manchuria.

### 1898: THE FASHODA INCIDENT

The Fashoda crisis.

The encounter between Marchand and Kitchener where the 'Cape-to-Cairo' line crossed with the 'Dakar-to-Djibouti' line, would have thrust Britain into war with France, had not Delcassé (French Foreign Minister in the new Dupuy government in Paris) sensibly given way. Britain's victory in the affair made French feeling intensely anti-British. It was only with the appointment of Paul Cambon as French Ambassador to London that the Anglophile Delcassé was able to bring about an improvement.

### 1899–1902: THE BOER WAR

This war, which many foreigners saw as a small power being bullied by a large one, produced a solidly hostile reception from the European powers. Many were extremely pleased when the British received a severe mauling during 'Black Week.' A telegram from the Kaiser, this time to his grandmother, suggested that she should accept defeat by the Boers in the same spirit of fortitude as she had accepted defeat in the recent Test Match against Australia. It provided another opportunity for Queen Victoria 'not to be amused.' The Boer Republics were eventually defeated, but the coldness of Britain's treatment helped to reinforce the dawning realization that isolation had its price, as well as its advantages.

## 2 > CHAMBERLAIN AND GERMANY

Joe Chamberlain's views on Germany.

Although, as Colonial Secretary, Chamberlain's main interest was in the Empire and not in the Foreign Office, he believed there was room in the world both for Britain and Germany, and that their rivalry might develop into co-operation. Several leading figures in Britain, such as the Duke of Devonshire, agreed with him, and the view found favour also on the German side with Baron Eckhardstein and Count Hatzfeldt. Even the Kaiser professed to have an affection for Britain. Salisbury allowed Chamberlain to make the necessary overtures to Germany, though he was never convinced that they would succeed. As things turned out, he was right.

The first attempt was in 1898. The talks lasted for about two months, but probably failed because at the time the Navy Bill was going through the Reichstag. If the Kaiser loved anything more than the British, it was his Navy, and since there was no point in challenging Britain's maritime strength if the two powers were to be allies, he made his excuses to Chamberlain. The Kaiser not only snubbed the British government, but betrayed it as well. Although the talks had been secret, he mentioned the matter in a letter to the Tsar, and this heightened continental feeling about Britain's dangerous unpredictability.

In November 1899, just as the Boer War was starting, the Kaiser visited Windsor on his grandmother's eightieth birthday. Chamberlain put forward his idea of an alliance for a second time. Wilhelm and the German Chancellor Bülow seemed to receive it favourably, and suggested the idea be widened into an *Anglo-Saxon Pact* to include Britain, Germany and the United States. With the U.S.A. deeply attached to its ideas of isolationism, there was very little chance that this extravagant plan would succeed. None the less, Chamberlain announced it in a speech in Leicester which produced a painful silence. When the Kaiser arrived back home in Germany he promptly disowned the whole idea.

Chamberlain's third proposal was in 1901, but had no better success. Two drafts were made of a treaty, and even a memorandum of Salisbury criticising them. But again it was Germany who was the stumbling-block, and as British victories in South Africa began to mount, so German hostility to the alliance increased.

<table>
<tr><td>**3 > THE ANGLO-JAPANESE TREATY, 1902**</td></tr>
</table>

By 1902 it had become clear that Britain and Japan needed each other's diplomatic support. Britain was very conscious of Russia's expansion in northern China, and looked for support against Russia. For a while they thought they had a friend in Germany, grateful for the protection given to German nationals when they took refuge in the British Legation in Peking on the occasion of the Boxer Rising in 1900. However, Germany was unwilling to provide active support. At the same time Russian encroachment in Manchuria, their leasing of Port Arthur and their supposed designs on Korea all seemed very threatening to Japan, which believed it had certain claims on these same areas of Chinese land. The path lay open to an understanding between London and Tokyo.

In Britain, public opinion greeted the suggestion with ribaldry, but the new Foreign Secretary, Lord Lansdowne, seemed set on it, and Salisbury, ageing very rapidly in his last year as Premier, did not seem much disposed to divert him. To begin with, Japan approached both Britain and Russia. The Japanese statesman Ito was sent to St. Petersburg to discuss an arrangement with the Tsar, and Baron Hyashi came to London to suggest that Russia should be restrained. He was against any further Russian expansion, he said:

> My government will certainly fight to prevent it; and it must be the object of their diplomacy to isolate Russia, with which power, if it stands alone, they are prepared to deal.

In the end it was with Britain that the bargain was struck.

**"The Japanese Alliance."**

The alliance provided for much closer relations in future. If one of the allies was at war with *one* other power, the other should remain neutral, but if the war was joined by a *second* attacker then the ally should come to the aid of the victim. Thus if Japan were attacked by Russia, Britain promised no more than benevolent neutrality, but if France joined Russia in the attack, Britain bound itself to go to Japan's assistance. The converse, incidentally, was also true. When Britain was at war with Germany in 1914, Japan was neutral, but when Austria came in on Germany's side, Japan declared war on the Central Powers. This alliance was to last for five years, and be renewable. It was, in fact, renewed in 1907, 1912 and 1917, though it was replaced by a looser arrangement in 1922.

An alliance with the so-called 'little yellow gentlemen' was something of a novelty in this country, but it served useful functions. First, it gave Britain the co-operation of the expanding Japanese fleet in the Pacific, conserving Britain's own naval strength and allowing the withdrawal of more ships from Far Eastern stations to confront the Germans more effectively in home waters. Second, it meant that the Japanese would monitor not only their own interests in China, but also Britain's. The only snag came when Japan tried to check the growth of Russian influence during the subsequent Russo-Japanese War. It took the form of the *Dogger Bank Incident* in October 1904, when the Russian Baltic Fleet, en route for the Far East, fired on British trawlers in the North Sea, apparently under the misapprehension that they were Japanese torpedo boats. The newly-signed Anglo-French Entente was tested almost to breaking-point when the Russians looked to Paris for support against Britain, which had demanded reparations and an apology. The Kaiser displayed mischievous enjoyment at the powers' confusion, but the Entente survived and Anglo-French relations were actually improved as a result.

<table>
<tr><td>**4 > THE ANGLO-FRENCH ENTENTE, 1904**</td></tr>
</table>

Meantime, relations between Britain and Germany had declined further since Chamberlain made his offers of alliance to the Kaiser. German commercial competition had intensified, and in mocking reference to the British *Merchandise Markings Act* a Hamburg-Amerika liner sailed up Southampton Water, its bows bedecked with a streamer boasting 'Made in Germany.' The German desire for colonies and 'a place in the sun' brought the two countries into conflict in other parts of the world. The two countries clashed in the Pacific islands; the Germans were a thorn in Britain's flesh in Egypt, where they always demanded a price for their support against the French. After 1902, when they began to build the Berlin-Baghdad railway, they seemed to be a menace to British middle-eastern interests. At the same time there was a challenge from Germany over naval building. Admiral Sir John Fisher maintained the Malta and the Channel fleets and created a new fleet, the Atlantic fleet, based on Gibraltar. He also embarked on the creation of a new naval base in 1903 at Rosyth. After 1906, too, there was a drive to replace the ageing ships of the British navy by 'all-big-gun' ships, or *Dreadnoughts*.

These events forced Britain and France closer together whether they liked it or not. Delcassé and the French Ambassador in London were already trying to improve relationships. Queen Victoria had always favoured Germany, but her son Edward VII was pro-French. He spent many summer holidays in France, liked the women, and also horse-racing. In March 1903 the official suggestion was made that he should pay a state visit to Paris. He charmed all who met him with his well-turned compliments, and a few months later President Loubet paid a return visit to London, the first since the days of Napoleon III. Shortly afterwards, negotiations began to remove various causes of dispute between the two countries, and in April 1904 the *Entente Cordiale*, or Cordial Understanding, was finally agreed.

The agreements fell into two broad classes. First, there were fairly minor colonial disputes, none of much significance, but which had irritated the two countries for some time. For instance, agreement was reached over the Gambia, over the boundary between Nigeria and Chad, between Siam and Indochina, and the future government of Madagascar and the New Hebrides. France surrendered its claim over Newfoundland fishing rights, whilst the British monarch finally discontinued his annoying practice of calling himself 'Roi de France.'

Fig 8.1  Entente Cordiale From Purnell's *History of the Twentieth Century*, (Purnell, 1968), Vol. 1, pp. 11 & 85 (Copyright given alongside)

*a)*

*b)*

*a) Watched by Germany's Kaiser Wilhelm and Russia's Tsar Nicholas (dancing with the French Republican maid), Britannia murmurs reassuringly to Colonia: 'After all, my dear, we needn't trouble ourselves about the others.' Colonia replies: 'No, we can always dance together, you and I.' When this cartoon appeared in* Punch *on Christmas Day 1901, the isolation of Great Britain and her empire might have been a little tarnished – but it remained splendid all the same.*

*b) British cartoon of the* entente cordiale. *Caption was 'Let Germany be careful now'.*

More importantly, there were two matters of high strategical importance. Britain recognized France's rights in Algeria and Morocco, where it was agreed that in future France should have a 'free hand' to take over the decadent sultanate and restore order there. For their part, the French recognized Britain's rights in Egypt and the Sudan, and gave Britain a similar 'free hand' in these areas.

At first, one believed in the solidity of the Entente, and it was soon subjected to severe tests. In its first year, the Dogger Bank Incident nearly involved Britain and France on opposite sides in the Russo-Japanese War. In 1905, the Kaiser tested it further while on a yachting holiday in the Mediterranean. He landed at Tangier to assure the Sultan of Morocco of his unswerving support, showing his opinion of the Anglo-French arrangements for that country. The visit was a failure; not only did the German official sent to greet the Kaiser fall into the sea, but the Sultan sent his uncle instead. But the challenge was clear, and caused panic in Paris, where in the absence of a formal alliance it was assumed that Britain would let France down. This conviction grew when the Conservatives fell from office and the Liberals won an overwhelming victory at the election early in

**The French Entente.**

**The First Morocco Crisis.**

1906. Delcassé was driven from office for having bungled things. Nevertheless, at the Algeciras Conference in January 1906, Grey, the new Foreign Secretary, came down firmly on France's side, reaffirming British support and denying Germany any compensation for the loss of her supposed 'rights' in Morocco. France promised not to annex Morocco formally – and indeed for five years did not. Soon, the bonds of the Entente drew closer, with top-level military conversations in 1907 between the two general staffs, co-ordinating their plans in case they should be involved in a war as allies. That year, Haldane, as part of his army reforms, introduced the B.E.F. – an army of about 160,000 men which proved to be a decisive weapon in 1914 (though the Kaiser referred to it as 'this contemptible little army').

*❝ ... and the Second Morocco Crisis. ❞*

In 1911 there was a second Morocco Crisis, when France, pleading violent disorders in Fez and Rabat, finally annexed the country. The Germans were furious, and once more demanded compensation. France accepted some of the German claims, but haggled over the details. It was to influence this decision and to threaten Britain with a nearby German naval base that the German gunboat *Panther* and its smaller sister ship *Berlin* were sent to Agadir in western Morocco in July. Once again the Germans were testing the Entente, and once again the British came to France's support. Lloyd George, a man not usually given to aggressive statements, made a stirring speech at the Mansion House in London making it clear to the Germans that Britain would not be trifled with. Eventually the *Panther* slipped quietly away and Germany retreated, accepting in compensation a large area of scrubland adjoining Kamerun on the borders of French Equatorial Africa.

Shortly afterwards, Winston Churchill became First Lord of the Admiralty and opened secret naval conversations with France. These left France to concentrate her forces in the Mediterranean, whilst Britain guarded the Channel and the Western Approaches. The arrangements meant that, though Britain was not officially committed to an alliance with France, it would be difficult for British ships to stand by whilst the German Fleet sailed down the Channel to invade northern France. Thus, by 1912, Britain and France were bound much more closely together than most people knew and many politicians were prepared to admit.

## 5 ▷ THE ANGLO-RUSSIAN CONVENTION, 1907

Another sign of worsening relations between Britain and Germany was the signing of an Anglo-Russian Entente in August 1907. Britain had been on poor terms with Russia for most of the century, and had consistently mistrusted the Tsar's intentions in the Balkans and the Middle East since Palmerston's days. Disraeli and Salisbury had taken the lead in opposing Russia at the time of the Congress of Berlin (1878), and Salisbury saw Russia as Britain's principal enemy for as long as he lived. By 1907, the German threat was intensifying after the country's rebuff at Algeciras, whilst that from Russia seemed to be fading.

*❝ The Russian Treaty. ❞*

The Anglo-Russian Convention was designed on the same principles as the Entente between Britain and France. The basic assumption was that relations could be improved if sources of diplomatic friction between the two countries were resolved. After the Russo-Japanese War, Far Eastern difficulties had resolved themselves after Russia's expulsion from Manchuria, but other areas of conflict remained. One area was *Tibet*, where there had been some danger of an Anglo-Russian conflict since 1903. In this instance, both countries bound themselves not to have dealings with that country except through the Chinese, who were suzerain over it. Another area was *Afghanistan*, where there had been repeated conflict for many years. Here, the Russians promised to keep out, and Britain undertook not to make any moves which might be thought hostile to Russia. *Persia* was a more difficult case. The country was in an advanced state of decay. Russia was developing its strategic interests in the north, where roads and railways had been built, while Britain was very concerned with the south, an area thought vital for excluding Russia from a warm-water port on the Persian Gulf, and one which was rich in oil. Eventually, the powers split the country between them. The North came under Russian influence, and the South under British influence. In between, around Tehran, there was a neutral zone as a 'buffer' between the two. By far the major difficulty between the two countries lay in the eastern *Mediterranean*. Russia was determined to acquire Constantinople and open the Straits, whilst Britain was equally determined to prevent this. No agreement could be reached – indeed in the following year, 1908, Britain went to some lengths to check such a scheme (see Chapter 14). Only after the outbreak of the First World War, when Britain and Russia were allies, did the British government concede that Russia had a special claim on this area, and even then Grey's pledge, given in 1915, was not honoured. As a result, the whole question of the Straits was omitted from the Entente, and, like Tweedledum and Tweedledee, the two powers agreed to differ.

The Convention had the effect of combining the Franco-Russian Dual Alliance of 1894 with the Anglo-French entente of 1904 in a powerful *Triple Entente*. Though it was not at first seen as a weapon against Germany, it came to be used in such a way as to give some justification to the Kaiser's complaints of diplomatic *encirclement*.

## 6 > THE BALKAN QUESTION BEFORE 1914

### 66 The Bosnian Crisis. 99

### 66 The Balkan Wars. 99

### 66 The Murder at Sarajevo. 99

The Balkans were an area about which most western politicians had little knowledge or understanding. Yet the problems the area posed were of decisive importance (see Chapter 14), and the French Foreign Secretary is said to have predicted 'When war comes, it will be caused by some damned thing out of the Balkans.'

In 1908 the Austrians annexed Bosnia-Herzegovina, an area wanted by Russia's Balkan *protégé*, Serbia. There was an acute crisis, with Austria stating its intention to persist, and Russia threatening war if it did. The problem was resolved when Germany declared an intention to side with Austria (the Kaiser said rather grandly that he had 'stood by his ally in shining armour'). With ill-grace the Russians gave way and accepted diplomatic defeat at the hands of the Central Powers. The annexation, however, showed the weakness of Turkey, in whose territories the two provinces lay; shortly afterwards Italy attacked Tripoli and conquered Turkey's last remaining north African province. These hints were not lost on the smaller Balkan powers. Under Greek leadership, a *Balkan League* of Greece, Bulgaria, Montenegro and Serbia was set up which in 1912 launched a united attack against the Turks.

Within a year, Turkish resistance was ended, and in 1913 Serbia and Greece took ample reward for their efforts. As far as Austria was concerned, however, an enlarged Serbia was a danger, especially since it was supported by Russia. Grey sensed the danger, and presided over a Conference of Ambassadors of the European powers in London in 1913 to try to arrange an amicable settlement. The minor powers were stubborn; the major powers unco-operative. The Conference broke down and Bulgaria, which had received only meagre reward for all its efforts, suddenly attacked its allies in the summer of 1913. A second Balkan War followed. In a month Bulgaria was crushed, and Greece and Serbia emerged stronger than ever.

Austria had already decided that the Serbian menace had to be tackled. It was clear to the military clique which dominated Austrian policies that war must come, probably in 1914, before Serbia and the Triple Entente became too strong. They believed that Germany would stand by them again, and that in view of Britain and France's indifference to Balkan affairs, Russia would also give way under pressure. It was a perilous policy of brinkmanship, but the Austrians thought that in view of the rewards, the risks were worth taking.

The affair which actually began the war was the assassination of the heir to the Habsburg throne, Franz Ferdinand, at Sarajevo in June 1914. Having secured assurances of German support by the end of July, the Austrians sent an unacceptable ultimatum to Belgrade, allowing only 48 hours for a reply. Grey called it

the most formidable document I have ever seen addressed by one state to another.

Soon Austria and Serbia were at war. Grey tried to revive his Ambassadors' Conference, but to no avail. The situation was out of control, and by early August the First World War had begun.

## 7 > THE BELGIAN QUESTION IN 1914

### 66 Belgian neutrality. 99

Under Palmerston's settlement of 1839, the major powers had agreed to preserve the independence and the permanent neutrality of Belgium. Meanwhile, Graf von Schlieffen had worked out a meticulous plan to invade France through the Belgian plain, avoiding the heavily defended area of the Ardennes and further south. The whole success of the German war strategy hinged on this plan. These facts perhaps explain why the Kaiser referred to the Treaty of London as 'this scrap of paper'; perhaps the Germans were right to regard the treaty as out-of-date, but irrelevant it certainly was not.

For a long time, Sir Edward Grey tried to maintain communication between the powers. He thought that if he hesitated in taking France's side they would behave with more caution; if the Germans thought that Britain might be neutral, they might also be prepared to act more moderately. But instead of encouraging Britain's allies and deterring its enemies, it had the opposite effect of deterring the allies and encouraging the enemies. The Germans thought that Britain would stay out of the conflict; the French thought that the British would let them down. On the eve of the war, Cambon asked if the word 'honour' had been removed from the English dictionary, and his country steeled itself for the possibility that it might be fighting alone.

Having been so unhelpful in promoting a peaceful settlement, Bethmann-Hollweg, the German Chancellor, lost confidence at the last moment. He hastily telegraphed Vienna that Grey's proposal deserved serious consideration. He also sought to assure Britain that the territories of Holland would be respected, that the inevitable invasion of Belgium would be only temporary, and that Belgian independence would be restored quickly on the conclusion of the campaign, provided the Belgians did not resist. Britain found these assurances impossible to accept, much to the Kaiser's annoyance. A rapid general mobilization in most of the European capitals continued, and on 3 August German troops entered Belgium. That afternoon Grey announced in the House of Commons that war would result unless Germany agreed to respect Belgian neutrality. An ultimatum was dispatched to Berlin with the demand for a reply by midnight. As Grey waited at the Foreign Office, lamps were lit in his room and in the street outside. He said to his companion the prophetic words:

**The Ultimatum to Germany.**

> The lamps are going out all over Europe. We shall not see them lit again in our lifetime.

Germany's actions made sure that the country entered the war a united nation.

## 8 ▷ SIR EDWARD GREY

Grey had the instincts of an upper-class English gentleman, earnest and upright. He had little ambition for office, and often longed to be back in his Northumberland home with his books and his field-glasses, looking at birds. He took his responsibilities very seriously and never stopped asking himself whether there was anything more he could have done to avert the outbreak of war.

 **Role of Grey.**

Critics of his actions and policies before 1914 accused him of ensnaring Britain in the alliance net without most of the British, and many of his cabinet colleagues, being aware of how deeply Britain was committed to France's support. The influence which senior servicemen had over policy decisions, and the shroud of secrecy which they drew over their actions in the name of national security, meant that few politicians *were* fully aware of what was going on. The effect of this was that, in order to avoid a cabinet split on the issue of the war, he had to use the German invasion of Belgium to drum up support for his government. His critics also said that he should have acted more decisively. They believed he spent too much time calling conferences and trying to negotiate when he should have been taking action. If he had not sat on the fence and had warned Germany earlier that Britain would give unhesitating support to France, the Germans might have been deterred.

These criticisms may have been valid, but the answers to the last criticism are plain. For one thing, Grey *did* make the British position abundantly clear in a series of warnings all duly passed on to Berlin by the German ambassador in London, Count Lichnowsky. For another, it made little difference whether he made himself clear or not, since by 1914 the German General Staff had decided that war was inevitable and that the Schlieffen Plan was the only way to wage it. A more damaging criticism may have been that he had not the total grasp of the diplomacy of the time to avoid the catastrophe, but that, for all his care and conscientious attention to detail, he lacked the wisdom and the knowledge to find the solution. This may have been true; but, if it is, it is true for everybody at that time. There was no superman who knew how to avert the collapse of the old order.

# IDEAS AND PRINCIPLES

**Brinkmanship**

The art of going as close to war as possible, without actually starting it. Thus a national leader may take his demands to the brink of conflict but then withdraw, or compel his opponent to withdraw. A game of 'diplomatic chicken' in which the boldest wins and the defeated suffers considerable humiliation.

| | |
|---|---|
| **Buffer state** | A neutral state created in order to separate two possibly opposing areas, thus preventing conflict between them. |
| **Entente** | An Entente (the French word meaning *understanding*) is a diplomatic arrangement looser than an *alliance*. An alliance commits a power to an agreed line of policy when the circumstances covered by the treaty are operative, but an entente does not. It merely sorts out the details of problem situations between the two parties, e.g. in the 1904 and 1907 cases, colonial and overseas situations. |
| **Jingoism** | An extreme form of patriotism, from a mild nineteenth-century oath 'By jingo!' The phrase occurred in a popular music-hall refrain aimed at Russia in 1878. |
| **-phile** | A suffix signifying 'love of' attached to words in ordinary use. Thus an *Anglophile* loves England and a *Francophile* loves France. |
| **-phobe** | A suffix signifying 'hate of' attached to words in ordinary use. Thus a *Russophobe* hates Russia and a *xenophobe* hates all foreigners (the Greek word *xenos* means a stranger). |
| **Sphere of influence** | When a powerful state exercises considerable influence over another weaker state, without actually ruling it, the weaker state is said to be in the sphere of influence of the more powerful one. The weaker state is sometimes said to be a *satellite* of the stronger, presumably because, politically speaking, it revolves around it in orbit. |
| **Warm-water port** | Some northern ports such as Murmansk and Vladivostok are ice-bound for a number of months in the year because of their latitude. It is obviously convenient for a power to have access to a port where the water does not freeze, in order that it may be used all year round. |

# APPLIED MATERIALS

## BOOKS

CASE, S. L. & HALL, D. J., (1967). *World History from 1783 to the Present Day*. Arnold. Chapter 13.
HILL, C. P. & WRIGHT, J. C., (1981). British History, 1815–1914. Oxford. Chapter 16.
LINDSAY, D. & WASHINGTON, E. S., (1960). *Portrait of Britain between the Exhibitions, 1851–1951*. Oxford. Chapter 15.
MACPHAIL, I. M. M., (1962). *Modern Times, 1880–1945*. Arnold. Chapter 7.
RICHARDS, D. & HUNT, J. W., (1987). *Illustrated History of Modern Britain, 1783–1980*. Longman. Chapter 19.
UNSTEAD, R. J., *Britain in the Twentieth Century*. A & C Black. Chapter 3.

## MORE DETAILED BOOKS

FOOT, M. R. D., (1956). *British Foreign Policy Since 1898*. Hutchinson.
TELFORD, Judith, (1986). *British Foreign Policy, 1870–1914*. Blackie.

## DOCUMENTARY SOURCES

BETTEY J. H. (Ed.), (1967). *English Historical Documents 1906–1939*. Routledge PB. pp. 48–52.
PARKINSON, Roger, (1970). *Origins of World War One*. Wayland Documentary.
TEED, P. & CLARK, M., (Eds.), (1969). *Portraits and Documents: Later Nineteenth Century, 1868–1914*. Hutchinson, pp. 109–117, 156–169.

## AUDIO-VISUAL

Attitudes to War in England Before 1914　　Audio Learning HEA 043

# EXAMINATION QUESTIONS

**1**   Show why Britain abandoned 'splendid isolation' after 1902. How was Britain drawn into war against Germany in 1914?       (London)

**2**   What were the reasons for, and what were the terms of, the agreements made between Britain and a) Japan in 1902, b) France in 1904 and c) Russia in 1907? In what ways did Britain show increasing solidarity with France in the years 1905 to 1914?       (London)

**3**   With reference to the twenty years before the outbreak of the First World War, describe and explain a) Britain's deteriorating relations with Germany and b) Britain's improving relations with France and Russia.       (London)

**4**   Study the cartoon below (Punch; August 1911).

SOLID

GERMANY. "DONNERWETTER! IT'S ROCK SOLID. I THOUGHT IT WAS GOING TO BE PAPER."

Now using the cartoon and your own knowledge, answer the following questions:
a) Was the conflict between Germany on one side and Britain and France on the other the main quarrel between the countries in 1911?
b) Did Britain's foreign policy change much between 1890 and 1914?
c) The cartoon gives the impression that Germany was the country causing the problem in these years. Do you agree with this? Give reasons for your answer.

*(30 marks)* (SEG)

**5**   Write a brief editorial for the August 5th 1914 edition of a British newspaper, explaining your country's attitudes towards the outbreak of war overnight between Britain and Germany.

# O U T L I N E   A N S W E R S

1   The first question demands a two-part answer, and will be marked out of a flexible 10/10 (probably 12/8 *either way*). The first part relates to reasons, since it asks *why* Britain abandoned 'splendid isolation' after 1902. Material relevant to your needs may be found early in this chapter under the appropriate heading. Descriptive material is eligible for credit if it goes towards illustrating the reasons for British dissatisfaction with this policy. You should note that the question does *not* ask for the terms of any of the treaties of 1902, 1904 or 1907.

The second part asks *how*, and here profitable use may be made of narrative material, relating to Britain's entry into the war. The phrase 'drawn into' the war shows you the kind of focus that is desirable in your answer. It appears that the relevant area for discussion here ought to be the concluding stages of the 1900–14 period, beginning with the Anglo-French Military and Naval Conversations, and going on to deal with the Sarajevo and Belgian crises. Again, there is a good deal of material in this chapter which could well be incorporated into your answer.

2   This is a more complex question, and the answer should fall into four parts, marked out of a flexible 5/5/5/5. Note also that the first three parts all have two components, dealing with the *reasons* for and the terms of the three agreements which Britain signed. In your answer, you should try to deal with all these aspects if you wish to score high marks. The concluding part of the question seems to be more straightforward, but you should note that the required focus here is 'increasing solidarity with France', and should therefore place less emphasis on British relations with other powers: the dates selected are also a useful guide, since you are clearly expected to begin with the First Morocco Crisis in 1905, and then to proceed forward in an orderly chronological manner.

3   This is another two-part question, marked out of 10/10 (or a flexible 12/8 *either way*), but like question 2, the sub-sections are themselves divided into *description* and *explanation*. There are one or two tricky elements in this question. For one thing, there are the dates: remember that 'the twenty years before the outbreak of the First World War' goes back as far as 1894, and as far as a) is concerned includes the Jameson Raid and the Kruger Telegram – and, as far as b) goes includes Fashoda and the Russian leasing of Port Arthur. Another factor that should be noted is that b) deals with *two* powers – France *and* Russia – and not just one. It would be quite proper to write rather more on this half of the question than on the other – even to tackle it as if it were a 7/7/6 question, with three parts.

It is worth observing that all these questions use very similar material, and may include points taken from this chapter; what is also worth noting is that the answers you give should not be interchangeable, for the questions are phrased very differently, and the various focuses in the answers must be clear in order to score high marks. Nevertheless, once you have mastered the relevant factual material, your *skills* in history ought to enable you to write answers of a suitable design.

# A   T U T O R' S   A N S W E R   T O   Q . 4

4   a) The cartoon shows the Kaiser nursing his foot after kicking against the immovable rock of the Entente Cordiale. Judging by the date of the cartoon, its appearance may have been linked with the Agadir Crisis and the bellicose speech given at the Mansion House on that occasion by Lloyd George. The cartoon shows that it was the cartoonist's view that the conflict between the Anglo-French combination and Germany was the main cause of the problems of the pre-1914 period. Supporting such a view it would be possible to find joint evidence relating to the First and Second Morocco crises, as well as separate evidence such as Franco-German

conflict over Alsace-Lorraine, and Anglo-German conflict in the course of the naval race. But the cartoon, like most cartoons, is a one-dimensional explanation of the conflict, portraying Wilhelm as a blundering nincompoop speaking comic-strip *Deutsch*. It is important also to take into account, as basic ingredients in the war situation before 1914, conflicts such as the long-term clash between Teuton and Slav in eastern Europe, the strategic clash between Russia and Austria over the control of the Balkans, and the Austro-Serbian quarrel over Bosnia-Herzegovina. To represent the Anglo-French agreement as being in the nature of an immovable rock is in itself an indication of the cartoonist's lack of objectivity.

b) There may have been an underlying consistency in Britain's foreign policy *aims* in the period 1890–1914, but the *methods* of this policy are seen to evolve continuously. At the beginning of this period Britain was broadly isolated from long-term obligations on the international scene, seeing its security as being best served by preserving freedom of action to deal with whatever situations arose. Britain still felt strong enough to resolve its difficulties unilaterally, and thought that foreign entanglements would generally prove to be more trouble than they were worth. A series of problems, like those which occurred in the Far East with the Russian leasing of Port Arthur from the Chinese, or with the conflict between British and French forces in the Sudan at Fashoda, persuaded the Foreign Office (though not the Prime Minister, Lord Salisbury) that co-operation with foreign powers was better than attempting to 'go it alone.' After 1902, therefore, Britain came into closer contact with these powers: an alliance was signed with Japan in 1902; and ententes to resolve outstanding disputes with France and with Russia were agreed in 1904 and 1907. After these dates Britain moved closer to its European partners. By 1914, in spite of the lack of a specific commitment to them it had become almost an impossibility for Britain to remain neutral.

c) The view that it was Germany which was the source of all the trouble in Europe before 1914 was naturally the view that a British cartoonist would take, and in the light of episodes such as the Kruger Telegram (1896) and the Kaiser's *Daily Telegraph* interview (1908), this seemed to most people not an unreasonable view to take. The Kaiser's actions always achieved a high profile in the international press, and to some extent may have been designed to achieve this. There are indications, too, that he was behind the proposed visit to Tangier in 1905, though he later made a half-hearted effort to pretend that it was all Bülow's idea; the same may be said of the Agadir Incident of 1911. Both may be seen as challenges to the Entente – and clearly the cartoon sees at least the latter in this light. To some extent, too, the episodes reveal the increasing influence of Germany's 'top brass' of the Army and Navy over decision-making, but it is not possible for Wilhelm to avoid the ultimate responsibility for their actions – after all, it was he who was Kaiser and not they. He was also inclined to meddle and to be indiscreet with secrets, as is revealed in the *Willy-Nicky correspondence*, the letters that were exchanged between the Kaiser and the Tsar; he also undertook irresponsible, and to his government terrifying, initiatives in policy, such as that of the *Björkö Agreement* with Russia in 1905. All of these episodes indicated the Kaiser's limited intelligence and understanding. Nevertheless the historian should try to avoid the well-established, but stereotyped, view of Wilhelm as a swaggering bully and cheat: this was simply the First World War's propaganda portrait of him. In any case – even if the Kaiser was as black as he was painted – there were many other wider factors leading to problems in the years before 1914, such as French resentment over the loss of Alsace-Lorraine in 1871, Austrian expansionism in the Balkans at the time of the annexation of Bosnia-Herzegovina, the Russian-backed pan-Slav movement in the Balkans, and so on; to put the whole blame on the Kaiser personally, as the cartoonist seems to be trying to do, is a distortion.

# A STUDENT'S ANSWER TO Q.5 WITH EXAMINER'S COMMENTS

5  So it is to be war at last! We'll teach these foreign fellows a thing or two! In the words of the song:

We don't want to fight, but by jingo if we do
We've got the men, we've got the ships, we've got the money, too!

That frightful Kaiser, with his handlebar moustache and his withered arm  must be taught to mind his p's and q's. His soldiers, too, rightly called Huns, are guilty of the most inhuman excesses in their invasion of Belgium. There are well authenticated reports of premises being looted, women being raped and these fearful Huns dressed in the religious garb of nuns swarming over the countryside and seizing key strategical positions. How can civilized nations have confidence in any nation which regards an international treaty as a mere 'scrap of paper' and attacks a defenceless neighbour with all its armed might?

This war is the climax of many years of German provocation. They have dared to challenge the sacred right of Britain to be the world's premier power, builder and owner of a vast empire, 'on which the sun never sets', a great Britannia who truly rules the waves. Our policies have been beyond reproach, our allies have been proud of us and we have the confident knowledge of our own moral rightness in the great and glorious struggle that is to come.

When peace comes, after the brutal and senseless carnage of the trenches, this country will build a world fit for heroes to live in, a world where there will be no more war. We will restore liberty to all those who have lost it the millions of Serbs and Belgians presently groaning under the heel of a foreign conqueror, and liberate the down-trodden peoples of the colonies, leading them forward to a brighter future where they will have governments of their own choosing. So onwards, British men and women, and forwards! God save the king!

> 66 This combination of tub-thumping 'jingoism' and cruel personal comment is a good imitation of the current style of popular journalism in 1914. 99

> 66 There were plenty of rumours of this sort in 1914, though perhaps August 5th is a bit early for them to be circulating. 99

> 66 This again is a very good imitation of the popular journalism of the time. 99

> 66 Can you pick out the anachronisms here? Such a passage as this might have been written in 1919, but it is of doubtful 1914 origin. 99

# SUGGESTIONS FOR FURTHER WORK

1  Mark in, and number, on a map of Europe those areas where there was international tension or conflict in the ten years before 1914, and write notes to be attached to the map under each of the numbers marked on it.

2  To what extent do you believe that colonial problems were a main underlying cause of the First World War? Find out the details of these problems, and discover the extent to which they had been resolved before the outbreak of war. This information might be used in a coursework project, or could be useful in answering an examination question if there was one set on this subject.

3  If you had to speak in a debate on the motion that service officers in many of the European capitals had too much influence in the political decisions that were made by governments, what would be the points that you would wish to make?

# THE LIBERALS IN POWER, 1906–14

## THE LIBERAL 'LANDSLIDE' OF 1906

## DOMESTIC REFORMS

## THE PEOPLE'S BUDGET (1909)

## THE PARLIAMENT ACT (1911)

## FURTHER LIBERAL REFORMS

## LIBERAL FOREIGN POLICY BEFORE THE FIRST WORLD WAR

## THE END OF AN ERA

# GETTING STARTED

In many ways the years between the death of Queen Victoria in 1901 and the outbreak of the First World War in 1914 were years of great affluence. A writer, Violet Markham, looking back, says:

> It was an age of boisterous wealth and prosperity for the upper and middle classes. Life was incredibly free and comfortable for the well-to-do, untroubled by passports, forms and regulations. The postman delivered letters on a Sunday morning; and if you had money in your pocket to pay the fare, you took a cab to Victoria and boarded the continental train without any tedious preliminaries.

The Edwardian Age is sometimes called a Golden Age. This is partly because the golden sovereign was still in general use instead of paper money, but more probably because, after the First World War, people tended to look back on these years in a rosy glow, forgetting the less pleasant features. World trade was flourishing, British output and exports were high, and overseas investments greater than ever. Standards of living, and the levels of wages and industrial profits had also risen. The population of the United Kingdom, now passing 45 million, was mostly better housed, better fed and better cared for than ever before.

But there were serious warning signs. Much of Britain's prosperity stemmed from the old staple trades – textiles, coal, iron and steel, ship-building. These industries were beginning to decline, as competition from powerful new world rivals such as Japan, Germany and the U.S.A. challenged Britain's monopoly position in world markets. Even the fact that there were such enormous surpluses to invest overseas was itself an indication that income was badly distributed. The poor were *too* poor, as well as the rich *too* rich. The growth of the trade unions and the spread of labour discontent was a sure sign that under the surface all was not well. There was still a great deal of room for social improvement in areas like health, education and welfare; still room for modernization and greater investment in industry; much too much concentration on conspicuous consumption by those who were better-off, instead of prudent efforts to strengthen the nation's industrial performance.

# HISTORICAL DEVELOPMENTS

Figures produced by such men as Charles Booth, whose *Life and Labour of the People of London* was completed in 1903, and Seebohm Rowntree, who studied people living 'below the poverty line' in York and published in 1911 a book called *Unemployment*, showed that high rents, inadequate wages, excessive drinking but above all joblessness produced much suffering. These findings were seized on by a young Liberal, William Beveridge, whose book *Unemployment: A Problem for Industry* turned the thoughts of many in his party towards the problem of social reform.

## 1 > THE LIBERAL 'LANDSLIDE' OF 1906

**Reasons for the Liberal Landslide.**

By the end of 1905 the Conservatives had been in office almost continuously for over twenty years. They had seen the country through a period when the British colonial empire had enormously grown and in which the country had emerged in its foreign policy from a period sometimes known as *Splendid Isolation*. There had been, too, especially in later years, some concentration on the problems of domestic reform, with new laws relating to licensing hours, unemployment and education. The Liberals, on the other hand, had been out of office for a long time, and lacked government experience. They seemed to have little to offer but criticism. Yet, with the support of the newly-created Labour Party, they were able to win a sweeping victory at the polls in the general election of January 1906. Why was this?

Recent Conservative involvement in overseas ventures had been heavily criticised. Though the Boer War in South Africa was conducted with considerable enthusiasm at the time, attitudes towards colonialism were beginning to shift. There was criticism of the *methods* employed by the British forces in suppressing South Africa, in particular of the use of concentration camps. Alarm was felt at recent policies which allowed the importation of cheap Asian labour on the Rand – a move which some saw as the 'Yellow peril'. The Liberal party was split by the war into two groups, the anti-Boer Liberal Imperialists and the pro-Boer sympathizers, but was now united in its criticisms. The Conservatives, who had patriotically supported the war, were now divided in their attitude to it.

Recent Conservative policies also came under fire. Liberal Non-conformists resented the terms of the Education Act of 1902, which many of them believed gave unfair advantages to Anglicans. Others quarrelled with the Licensing Act of 1904, and the Aliens Act and the Unemployed Workmen's Acts of 1905. In particular, there was resentment at the recent role of the House of Lords, whose members were seen as enemies of social change and an obstacle in the way of reform. A special anger was directed against the Law Lords of the Upper Chamber for the vindictive limitations placed on the trade union movement by the Taff Vale Judgment of 1901. The feeling that things would never change as long as the Conservatives were in office steadily grew. In this, Liberals were supported by the members of the fledgling Labour Party, which began to contest parliamentary seats in some numbers. Labour and Liberal candidates worked out a *Lib-Lab Pact*, which meant that in a number of agreed constituencies the two would not fight against each other.

The most devastating weakness in the Conservative Party arose from the growth within it of protectionist sentiment. Joseph Chamberlain, who in the 1880s had split the Liberal Party over the Irish Question, now threatened to split the Conservatives over a proposal to abandon that sacred dogma of British nineteenth-century policy, free trade. In the last years of the century, in response to the great depression and the rise of foreign competition, a movement had developed in favour of 'fair trade'. This coincided with a move towards 'imperial federation', a scheme to bind the colonies and the mother country more closely together. Chamberlain was deeply involved in both. As an industrialist and a keen imperialist, he felt that the country was getting a raw deal from the continuance of free trade. In 1903 he founded the *Tariff Reform League*, which proposed the idea of a protective tariff on foreign imports, combined with a scheme for *imperial preference*. This would permit imports from the Empire to enter the country at lower rates of duty. Free traders sprang to the attack at once, arguing that tariffs would make goods dearer. Even preferential tariffs would raise prices somewhat, unless they were at zero level, in which case they would give no protection. Chamberlain made the damaging admission:

**The Tariff Reform League.**

If you are going to give a preference to the colonies . . . you must put a tax on food.

The issue deeply divided the Conservative Party. Orthodox free-traders thought that the principle was too fundamental to abandon, and that policies which put up food-prices would be unpopular with the voters. The protectionists argued that though prices might go up, there would be greater job security if people were buying British, and this would improve the prospects of British industry. The Prime Minister, Balfour, failed to give a strong lead. In 1905 he declared in favour of closer ties with the Empire, and in favour of tariffs – but only for the purpose of raising revenue, not for general protection. This half-and-half attitude satisfied nobody, and even the cabinet divided on the issue. By December 1905, Balfour was forced to resign, and the incoming Liberal, Campbell-Bannerman, called an election in January.

The Liberals swept the board. With Labour support, they secured 377 seats, a majority of 84 over all the other parties combined. Labour got 53 – about half of them elected with Liberal support as 'Lib-Labs'. The Irish Party returned 83. The Conservatives secured only 157, and 109 of these were Chamberlainites. This result gave the new government an overwhelming mandate to put through an ambitious programme of social reform. It also, incidentally, increased the determination of the Conservatives in the Lords to use their strength there to block it – a decision which focused the resentment of the Commons on an unelected Upper Chamber.

## 2 ▷ DOMESTIC REFORMS

**Results of the Liberal Landslide.**

Campbell-Bannerman remained Prime Minister until 1908, and was succeeded by Asquith, who was previously Chancellor of the Exchequer. Asquith's Chancellor was Lloyd George, previously President of the Board of Trade under Campbell-Bannerman. Between them, the strong new Liberal team put through a big programme of domestic reforms. Of these, the *military* reforms were perhaps the least controversial, but the *economic* and *social* reforms dealt with difficult and delicate matters that were close to the hearts and consciences of a great number of thinking people.

### MILITARY REFORMS

The Secretary for War, R. B. Haldane was conscious of the fact that the army was not strong enough to sustain the burden of Britain's world role. Many recruits at the time of the Boer War were very poor physical specimens, and he set about modernizing the armed forces. He reorganized the regular army, and combined the Militia, the Yeomanry and the Volunteers into a new Territorial Army as a reserve. He also set up an Officers' Training Corps to ensure a supply of recruits. Most importantly, he set up an Army General Staff, and created a B.E.F. (British Expeditionary Force) in case Britain became involved in a European War, complete with plans for its speedy transportation to the continent.

Naval preparations went on simultaneously. Though the Admiralty still liked to think that Britannia ruled the waves, they were aware that British ships might one day be out-gunned by the German fleet. British ships were still regarded as the best, but many were very old, and some still made of wood. The German High Seas Fleet, on the other hand, was the product of that country's best scientific and technical brains. Its armour-plating and accurate, long-range gunnery were of enviable quality. In response, the British Admiralty launched the first of a new generation of powerful warships, the *Dreadnought* class in 1906; and Britain reaffirmed its intention to maintain what was often known as the *two-power standard* over its rivals. Sir John Fisher at the Admiralty, pressed ahead vigorously with building many more ships.

### POLITICAL REFORMS

There was still great prejudice, even in the Liberal Party, against giving women the vote in national elections, although there was some progress towards enfranchizing them locally. The 1907 *Qualification of Women Act* entitled them to be candidates, as well as voters, in local government elections; they could also become J. P.s. There was also a *Plural Voting Bill*, based on the principle of 'one man, one vote', to prohibit an elector from voting in more than one constituency, but this was thrown out by the Lords.

### TRADE UNION REFORMS

In 1906, under the terms of the *Trade Disputes Act*, the decision like the one in the Taff Vale Case was outlawed. Members of trade unions could now strike without civil proceedings being taken against them, either for breach of contract or for damages for losses suffered. Since criminal proceedings were not allowed either, this act meant in effect that trade unions had become corporations almost above the law. Though several Liberals were not keen on this proposal, they passed it in the Commons, secure in the knowledge that the Lords would reject it. But the Lords backed away from giving the working-classes further offence, and let the bill pass. Not only now were the industrial powers of the unions secure, but they were becoming politically more ambitious. They began sponsoring Labour candidates for parliament, and also collected from their members a political levy to pay salaries and other expenses (See Chapter 2). This continued until it was challenged in the courts in 1909.

## LABOUR AND INDUSTRIAL REFORMS

Working people had several grievances outside their trade unions, and it was to remedy these that the Liberals passed a number of reforms after they came to power. In 1906, the *Workmen's Compensation Act* provided compensation for accidents arising in the course of employment (provided they were not due to the worker's own negligence), and for what were called 'industrial diseases', like lead poisoning or silicosis. Those earning more than £250 per year were excluded from the scheme. In 1909, the *Trade Boards Act* set up wage and arbitration machinery in the so-called *sweated industries*, i.e. those industries not protected by Factory Acts, and where conditions were appalling and wages miserably inadequate. Such trades as net-mending and paper-box making were often conducted in the labourers' own homes in indescribable filth and squalor. The workers – often women – were desperately in need of protection. This act was the first step to make their lives tolerable. In 1909, too, there was the *Labour Exchanges Act* to help the out-of-work to find employment. The country was divided into ten districts, with Labour Exchanges set up out of the public funds, where employers looking for labour were put in touch with workers seeking jobs.

There were also laws relating to particular industries. In 1906 there was a *Merchant Shipping Act*, designed to improve conditions aboard ship for British crews. The act also compelled foreign users of British ports to conform to the same standards. In 1908 the *Port of London Act*, largely the brain-child of the President of the Board of Trade, Lloyd George, set up a single Port of London Authority to replace or to amalgamate the many conflicting private companies competing for work there. Whether or not this measure was constructed on liberal or on socialist principles, it enormously speeded the development of Britain's greatest port. Whilst at the Board of Trade, Lloyd George was also responsible for a *Patents Act*, and for introducing the first *Census of Production*, in order to provide authorities with up-to-date information on which to base their actions. In 1908, the Liberals also brought in a *Coal Mines Act*, introducing the eight-hour day – the first time that British governments had ever regulated the hours of adult male labourers.

The Liberals also tackled the land question, but without much success. In 1907 a bill passed the Commons but was mutilated by the House of Lords. In the same year, two Scottish bills were rejected by the Lords altogether. The Upper House seemed to insist on the preservation of the rights of land-owners, whatever Liberals might have wished.

## CHILDREN'S REFORMS

Concern was also shown for the welfare of young children, and in 1906 a law was passed enabling local authorities to provide school meals for needy school-children. In 1907 an act was passed making it the duty of education authorities to arrange for the medical inspection of younger pupils. Further measures followed in 1908, together making up what was sometimes referred to as a 'Children's Charter'. There was a *Prevention of Crimes Act* intending to protect the interests of young offenders. It set up the Borstal system instead of putting young people into ordinary jails, and special juvenile courts with suitable anonymity for youthful wrong-doers. It also introduced the probation system. There was also a *Children's Act*, forbidding children to beg in the streets, or to purchase liquor or tobacco, or to go into the bars of public houses.

The Liberals also made repeated efforts to remedy Non-conformist grievances by modifying the Education Act of 1902. The first, in 1906, passed the Commons but failed in the Lords. Two others, in 1907 and 1908, were withdrawn before they had got through the Commons. A fourth, in many ways the best, was introduced later in 1908, but various denominations of the church declared against it, and the attempt was finally abandoned.

## SOCIAL REFORMS

Lloyd George took this aspect of the government's work very seriously, deploring the need to spend £60m a year on defence when, as he said

> we have other enemies to fight: intemperance, ignorance, crime, vice, and that most dreaded of all invasions that sooner or later enters every home. Are the dominions of death not wide enough that the nations should spend four hundred millions a year on extending them?

The social aspect of the government's policies was impressive, though its general spirit was interventionist rather than liberal. In 1907 a *Deceased Wife's Sister's Act* allowed a widower to marry his dead wife's sister, rather than bring her to the house to look after the children and be compelled to cohabit illegally with her. In 1909 a *Housing and Town Planning Act* empowered the Local Government Board to order local authorities which neglected their duty to carry out their obligations. It also required them to ban back-to-back housing, and allowed corporations to buy land for future building and to restrict the development of their areas in the interests of amenity. The government had less success with its *Licensing Bill*, which like so many others, was rejected by the House of Lords.

One major measure was the *Old Age Pensions Act*, which came into force at the start of 1909. In scope it was quite modest. It gave only 5 shillings (25p) a week to old people over 70, and even this had attached conditions. The old people should not have been a burden on the system of public relief previously; they should not have a criminal record, and they should not have income from savings of more than about £30 a year if they were to qualify. There was outcry from comfortable folk about the cost of such a scheme, but Lloyd George defended it. At least it kept a large number of old folk out of the workhouse.

Conditions in workhouses had improved a lot since they were brought under strict central control in 1834, but even after 1900, there was still a great degradation involved in entering a workhouse. In 1905, Balfour had set up a Royal Commission on the poor law, which produced its report in 1909. In fact, there were two reports: a majority report proposed the abolition of the poor law guardians, and a more ambitious minority report suggested the complete abolition of 'poor relief' which was substituted with adequate welfare services to provide a minimum standard, below which no one should be permitted to fall. This idea was received by a young Liberal called William Beveridge, but the implementation of such a wide-ranging plan for a welfare state had to wait for nearly half a century.

These social measures aroused great controversy, and added to the financial problems involved in providing the cash for the old-age pension proposals. It was these which touched off the next great struggle – that between the House of Commons and the House of Lords. (N.B. The programme of Liberal reform was not totally aborted by this crisis – you will see that it continued after 1910.)

## 3 ▷ THE PEOPLE'S BUDGET (1909)

The conflict between the Lords and the Commons had been building since 1906, and with it the resentment of the Liberal majority in the lower house. Lloyd George, in a vigorous public speech asked whether

> Five hundred men, ordinary men, chosen accidentally from the unemployed, shall override the judgment of millions of people who are engaged in the industry which makes the wealth of the country.

 Conflict with the Lords.

He ridiculed the pretensions of the upper house by presenting them as the idle rich, using all their ingenuity to preserve their privilege. He made fun of the hereditary principle of the title going to the first-born, saying that they were merely 'the first in the litter'. He welcomed the coming fight. He knew that if the Lords gave way, well and good, and many would feel the benefit. If they stood out against the democratic will, he would do away with them altogether.

The result of the challenge was that Lloyd George brought forward the *People's Budget* in 1909. It was the result of massive spending increases. There had been pressure for more battleships, and also the need to finance old-age pensions. The Exchequer had to find about £16 million extra in the next financial year – a task which the Chancellor willingly embraced.

The budget cast a wide net, and many of its proposals were quite revolutionary. The government proposed to provide about £600,000 a year for a road fund to finance the modernization of roads. The money was to be raised by a special tax on petrol and motor licences. There was also to be an allocation of about £100,000 a year for the new Labour Exchanges. A further sum was to go towards financing a Development Commission to preserve the environment and natural resources. Another necessary reform was the introduction of tax allowances, in respect of children, for those who paid income tax. The sum was not large; only £10 per child under 16 was deducted from the taxes levied, and only for those with incomes of less than £500 per year – but at least it conceded the new principle.

The raising of large new sums of money proved more controversial. Some was done by raising indirect taxes on items such as liquor and tobacco. More was aimed at the well-to-do, such as increases in stamp duty and death duties on estates over £5000 (those over £1 million were to be taxed at the rate of 25%). Direct taxes were also increased: income tax went up from 1s (5p) to 1s 2d (6p) in the £, and for those with incomes over £5000 per year there was a 'super-tax' of a further 6d (2½p) in the £ levied on the amount by which these incomes exceeded £3000. This was directly aimed at the better-off. So also were the new *land value duties* – an annual charge on the capital value of undeveloped land and minerals, and, most controversial, a 20% duty on increases in land values levied each time the site was sold. The landed class naturally objected strongly to these last items; and the more they did so the more the Commons were determined to force them through.

The unwritten custom of the British constitution was that the House of Lords did not interfere with money bills. 'Taxation by consent' meant that those who mostly paid such taxes should have the final say as to what these taxes were. But Lloyd George had now manoeuvred the Lords into a position where they seemed to be an irresponsible group of rich men trying to dodge their share of the burden. In rejecting the budget, as they did when it was presented to them, they protested in vain that they were only exercising the same rights as the Commons claimed for themselves. How could it be fair for taxes to be imposed by one section of the community and paid by another? The Conservatives formed the *Budget Protest League*, arguing that the Liberals had no electoral mandate for this policy, and Lloyd George took up their challenge in speeches in which, in his favourite role of playing to the gallery, he said of the titled gentry:

> A fully-equipped Duke costs as much to keep up as two Dreadnoughts; and Dukes are just as great a terror and last longer.

**4 ▸ THE PARLIAMENT ACT (1911)**

In December 1909, Asquith carried a resolution that the action of the Lords was

> a breach of the constitution and a usurpation of the rights of the Commons

He informed the King, Edward VII, that he could not continue as Prime Minister if the Upper House continued to deny him the funds to meet the government's expenses. He even asked the King to create enough peers to force the budget through. Edward gave this pledge, but refused to create peers until after a *second* general election. Asquith said nothing about this at the time, but ordered a dissolution and called a general election for January 1910.

The Liberals had no mandate to challenge the powers of the Lords before the election, and arguably had no mandate after the election. The Irish Party now held 82 seats, and the Labour Party, suffering from a shortage of funds in the wake of the Osborne Judgment, went down to 40 seats. The Liberals and Conservatives were evenly balanced; the Liberals had 275 and the Conservatives 273. With the support of both smaller groups the overall majority of the Liberals was 124. This was enough to press ahead with their plan for bringing in a *Parliament Act* to limit the powers of the Lords, an intention which, for reasons of their own, the Labour Party and the Irish both supported. The Liberals pressed on, bringing in and handsomely passing the three parliamentary resolutions on which the Parliament Act was finally based. Simultaneously, they passed the People's Budget a second time, and once more sent it up to the Lords.

This time the Lords passed it without even a division, concentrating all their energy on the coming struggle over the Parliament Act. After another general election in December 1910, with almost identical results to the earlier one in January, the Liberals succeeded in passing the Act into law, together with a resolution to award parliamentary salaries to Members of Parliament. These two Acts brought about a big shift in the balance of political power in Britain for the future (see Chapter 1).

The People's Budget went into operation immediately. Most of the new ideas it contained proved to be lasting, and began a significant redistribution of wealth. The Land Value duties, however, were never successful, and were allowed to lapse in the post-war years. Only after the Second World War was any attempt made to revive them.

## 5

**FURTHER LIBERAL REFORMS**

❝Reforms, 1911–14.❞

The period after 1910 did not produce the same flood of reforming legislation as there had been before. In part this was due to a wave of apathy which overtook the country after its exertions during the constitutional crisis, punctuated only by furious ill-feeling between the two major parties. It was partly due also to the necessity of passing the same bill in identical forms in successive sessions, as the Parliament Act obliged them to do if the Commons were to circumvent the Lords' veto. This gave their business a repetitive tedium, which lessened public interest in proceedings. None the less, there were a number of important measures.

## POLITICAL REFORMS

In 1913 the *Plural Voting Act* put on the statute book the ideas first put forward in 1907. Apart from university seats, where members continued to be elected by the graduates of the university concerned, people were now prohibited from voting in more than one constituency. At the same time, the residence qualification for voting was reduced. No steps, however, were taken in the direction of a female franchise; this had to wait until 1918 before advance was made.

## INDUSTRIAL AND LABOUR REFORMS

Between 1911 and 1913 a number of laws began to regulate conditions in a variety of industries. A *Shops Act* avoided the question of regulating the hours of shop assistants, but awarded them a weekly half-day holiday. Another *Coal Mines Act* was passed to improve working conditions; travelling time underground was counted as part of the eight-hour day. Arbitration machinery was set up to arrange a minimum wage, which was brought into force the following year by the *Minimum Wage Act*. There were also several general measures: an *Official Secrets Act*, the first of a series of increasingly restrictive measures against espionage; an *Aerial Navigation Act* designed to prevent aircraft from flying too low over heavily-populated areas, and a *Copyright Act*, harmonizing British law with continental law on this subject and stopping overseas pirating of copyright material.

The main labour reform was the *Trade Union Act* of 1913. Since the Osborne Judgment of 1909, unions had found it hard to collect political levies from their members, and this was one reason why they performed poorly in the two elections of 1910. The problem was partly solved by the *Payment of Members* resolution in 1911, but the years were ones of increasing industrial unrest and Liberal politicians found it necessary to appease Labour discontent. This act was the result. In future the creation of a political levy was to be within the powers of trade unions, provided that it was approved by a majority of the membership, incorporated as part of the rules, and provided that any member who objected to paying was allowed to 'contract out' by informing the union's officials of their decision. Even then they were not to be penalized by the loss of any union privileges; and not to be named publicly.

A land measure earlier proposed by the Liberals was now enacted. A *Smallholders (Scotland) Act* gave security to tenants of holdings of a limited size and created a Scottish Board of Agriculture, on the pattern of the English one. Whether they liked it or not, the Lords had to accept the passing of the act.

## SOCIAL REFORMS

The most ambitious of these was the *National Insurance Act* of 1911. The act was in two parts: Part I established a system of national health insurance and Part II dealt with the relief of unemployment. *Unemployed workers*, except in seven industries named as 'precarious' (including building and engineering, where there were frequent fluctuations), were entitled to benefits of 7s a week (35p) for the first thirteen weeks of unemployment, paid from a fund to which the worker, the state and the employer each contributed 2½d (1p) per week during normal times. Benefits would then cease until the worker in his new job had contributed a further 13 weeks contributions, when he would become eligible again if he lost his job in future. The benefit was intended only to be a transitional one, helping men to transfer from one job to another. The idea that they should be unemployed over a long term was not a problem to which the act addressed itself. *Sickness* was also dealt with by the act. All workers between the ages of 16 and 70, if they earned less than £160 per year, should be entitled to a scheme of medical benefits covering illness, disablement, hospital benefits and maternity grants for female workers. This scheme was also contributory: the worker paid 4d (2p) a week, the employer 3d (1½p) and the state 2d (1p) (thus giving rise to Lloyd George's observation that the worker was getting 'ninepence for fourpence'). The scheme operated largely through the existing Friendly Societies, which achieved the status of 'approved' societies for the purpose. Workers enrolled in a system of 'panels', set up by the doctors, under which most of the patients had a choice of doctor, and their panel doctor provided them with the treatment to which they were entitled during the period of their disability.

The act aroused furious opposition. There was a meeting in the Albert Hall, where duchesses urged servant girls to preserve their independence and not allow Britain to become a nation of stamp-lickers. The Harmsworth press weighed in to keep the country free from the monster of 'bureaucracy'. The British Medical Association declared against it. The trade unions were opposed to the idea of a compulsory insurance scheme – if there had to be one, they believed that it should be non-contributory. The Friendly Societies, fearing loss of business, were distinctly unfriendly to it. Employers disliked having to contribute toward its cost.

It was exactly the challenge that Lloyd George enjoyed, and a number of skilful concessions silenced the critics. The Friendly Societies became one of the lynchpins of the new system, and even trade unions were more important as a result of it. Although the doctors had objected to possible 'state control', many of them did very well out of the panel system, as did chemists. Fears of advancing bureaucracy proved unfounded. Even the workers accepted the system as being in their interests. The state was soon handing out over £6½ million per year in panel payments to doctors and about £1¼ million per year to chemists for prescriptions they made up. By 1920, 12 million of the 14 million working population were enrolled in panels, and annually about 60% of insured persons, or 20% of the total population, was receiving some form of treatment.

## WELSH DISESTABLISHMENT

For years there had been a strong move against the Anglican establishment on the part of the mass of Welsh Non-conformists, and this produced a bill to disestablish and partially disendow the official church. Passed by the Commons, the bill was rejected by the House of Lords in 1913, but allowed to pass at its second presentation in 1914, despite stout Anglican resistance.

## THIRD IRISH HOME RULE BILL

One reason why the Irish Party was keen to limit the powers of the House of Lords in 1911 was to frustrate the Lords in their self-appointed role as champions of the Ulstermen, long the enemies of the Home Rule movement. As a result of the 1911 Act, a third Home Rule Bill had been introduced in 1912 to create a separate Irish Parliament in Dublin for the whole of the country, with just a small representation continuing at Westminster in the U.K. Parliament. Ulstermen, fearing domination by the mass of southern Irish Catholics, were prepared to resist this measure, if needs be by force. They began to enrol paramilitary forces and import arms to equip themselves for the coming struggle. In the south, the forces of the Irish separatist party, Sinn Fein, and their military wing, the Irish Republican Army (I.R.A.), embarked on a similar course. Ireland seemed to be poised on the brink of civil war. The continuing resistance of the House of Lords, which rejected the bill in 1912 and in 1913, did nothing to improve the situation. In 1914 the bill was about to be passed for the third time, and would become law in spite of the Lords' veto. This situation prompted both sides to sit down to negotiate a compromise whereby those in the north wishing to opt out of Home Rule should be allowed to do so. Partition, however, was welcome to nobody. Even if the principle were accepted, the size of the area to be exempted from the Home Rule arrangements was going to be hard to agree. Should it be the three counties immediately adjacent to Belfast, or six counties, or nine? The two sides were still far from agreement when the First World War broke out and the problem of Ireland was shelved for the duration (See Chapter 6).

**6  LIBERAL FOREIGN POLICY BEFORE THE FIRST WORLD WAR**

Conservative governments before 1906 had already begun the process of bringing Britain out of its former condition of isolation by reaching agreements with two major foreign powers, Japan in 1902 and France in 1904. Foreign policy proved to be a matter where there was general agreement between the parties, for the Liberals continued along the same lines. Haldane undertook military discussions with the French after 1907 in case Britain and France should become allies in a continental war, and the Admiralty took part in

similar naval discussions with the French following the Agadir crisis of 1911. In 1907 also, Grey, the British Foreign Secretary, signed the Anglo-Russian Convention whereby Britain solved many of the outstanding problems separating the two countries. The effects of all these steps was to draw Britain ever closer to the powers of the Continent (See Chapter 8).

The Liberal leadership was acquainted with these arrangements but there were some in Parliament, and even in the cabinet, who knew nothing about them and would have disapproved if they had. Lloyd George, for one, and several Liberal radicals, were unwilling to see Britain dragged by Europe into foreign entanglements which were none of its concern. Some politicians, like the Labour Party's Ramsay MacDonald, went even further in denouncing what they called the 'capitalists' war', and refused to serve in it. Hence there was a potential crisis in 1914. Many believed that Britain had no firm commitment to either side when war began, and there would have been some danger of a disastrous national split had Grey not used the German invasion of Belgium as an excuse to whip up feeling against the 'Huns' for their faithlessness and their brutality. Thus Asquith carried behind him in August 1914 a nation that was not only politically united, but actually enthusiastic to take part in the ghastly carnage which was to follow.

## 7 ▶ THE END OF AN ERA

To astute observers, the peaceful and orderly Britain that most people took for granted in Edwardian times was already beginning to break up in the last few years before the war. George Dangerfield, in his book *The Strange Death of Liberal England* says:

> It was in 1910 that fires long smouldering in the English spirit suddenly flared up, so that by the end of 1913 Liberal England was reduced to ashes.

But certainly it was not at all fanciful to see the beginnings of a decay in public order at this time.

### FEMALE SUFFRAGE

By 1900, the cry of 'Votes for Women' was increasingly heard. In 1903 Mrs Emmeline Pankhurst founded the *Women's Social and Political Union* to press for changes in the electoral law. They seemed to have little chance of success with the Conservatives, but had hopes of faring better with the Liberals. They were, however, disappointed, and soon the *suffragettes*, as they became known, felt obliged to resort to direct action. They interrupted public meetings, chained themselves to railings, slashed pictures in public art galleries, dug holes in golf courses, smashed shop windows and even burned down a railway station in Leicester. Half-hearted attempts were made to introduce bills in parliament to remedy the women's grievances, but it was all to no avail. The Liberal government was firmly against it. In 1913, one suffragette, Emily Davidson, attempted to stop the King's horse from winning the Derby by grabbing at its bridle at Tattenham Corner. She was trampled under the hooves of the horses, and later died in hospital. Such extreme actions were impossible to ignore. Many suffragettes were arrested, tried and imprisoned. Whilst in prison, many went on hunger strike and were forcibly fed, or were released rather than allowed to die. The government reacted with the *Cat and Mouse Act* of 1913. This allowed a prison governor to release a hunger-striking woman, but to re-arrest her again when she had recovered her strength so that she could complete her sentence. The only gleam of hope came in the government's promise in that year to accept any feminist amendment which the Commons might make to the proposed Reform Bill. Although three amendments were tabled, the Speaker unexpectedly ruled them all out of order and the House had to be content with a ban on plural voting instead.

### IRELAND

Ulster resistance to the Third Home Rule Bill began to develop as soon as the Protestants of Northern Ireland realized they could no longer count on the House of Lords to protect them with its veto on Commons' legislation. Ulstermen were led by Sir Edward Carson, a man of inflexible purpose who addressed his supporters as if they were a prayer meeting. Most Conservatives thought he was right. Both sides were already enrolling volunteers. In the North there were the Ulster Unionist Volunteers (U.U.V.) who were prepared to fight for the maintenance of the 'union' with Britain. In the South, the Irish Volunteers, many of whose members were also supporters of the I.R.A. Both sides began military training, sometimes pooling their resources to hire shooting ranges, so that their rifle practice would make them more skilful for the future in shooting at each other.

In March 1914, on the eve of the final enactment of the Third Home Rule Bill, a sinister development took place in County Kildare. Officers at the Curragh Army Camp were advised by their Commander either to resign or to 'disappear' (i.e. desert) if their orders to enforce the law in Ulster offended them. The army seemed to be in revolt against the government. Brigadier Gough from the Curragh was summoned to London, where he obtained a promise from the government that objecting officers would not be asked 'to enforce the present Home Rule Bill on Ulster.' Asquith felt compelled to ask the War Minister, Col. Seely, to resign, but preferred to turn a blind eye to the real culprits behind what became known as the Curragh 'Mutiny'.

Later in 1914 both sides began to arm themselves. In April, at Larne, officers of the U.U.V. landed 30,000 rifles and about 3 million rounds of ammunition purchased in Germany, and distributed them amongst their supporters. This was a treasonable act, but the government did nothing about it. Shortly afterwards the Irish Volunteers did the same thing. To counter the Ulstermen and ensure that Home Rule went into effect, they landed 25,000 German rifles in broad daylight at the port of Howth close to Dublin. Units of the regular army intervened, some of the guns were recovered and the Volunteers were put to flight. It appeared that the British government would allow people to defy the law, but would not support it.

## LABOUR MILITANCY

Some of the Irish leaders were labour leaders and were as much socialists as nationalists. Men like the seamen's leader, James Larkin, and James Connolly, wanted a violent revolution to free the Irish worker at a single blow from the yoke of capitalism and of Britain. Connolly had connections with the American movement known as the Industrial Workers of the World and with the French Syndicalists, and supported strikes and other forms of direct action to overthrow the system and liberate the toiling masses.

There were syndicalist tendencies in Britain, too. Sorel's book *Reflections on Violence*, written in 1908, was the 'bible' of the movement. Syndicalists believed that capitalism could be brought to its knees by a general strike of all workers and by a persistent refusal to play the capitalists' game. Afterwards, democratic control of industry would usher in a working-class utopia and banish exploitation for ever. The years before 1914 were indeed troubled. There were numerous strikes, in one of which, at Tonypandy in 1911, the government felt obliged to use military force against the strikers. There was even a strike by the police in Liverpool in 1911. A syndicalist Education League was set up to enlighten the workers, and in 1912 there was established a revolutionary workers' newspaper, known as the *Daily Herald*.

In three major industries trouble threatened. On the *railways* there was a series of strikes, culminating in a national rail strike in 1911. In the *coalmines* there was a similar threat in 1911 and 1912. Conditions amongst the *dockers* were worse still. The shipping interests, headed by the Chairman of the Port of London Authority, Lord Devonport, would yield nothing. He demanded the unconditional surrender of dockers who struck in 1912, and got it. Powerless before such unfeeling harshness, their leader, Ben Tillett prayed at a strikers' meeting for God to strike Lord Devonport dead. In 1914 there was a new and ominous development. This was the *Triple Alliance* of miners, dockers and railwaymen, whose object was to threaten the government with what amounted to a general strike by the three unions concerned if any one of them was involved in a further industrial dispute. Such a strike seemed to be a virtual certainty before the end of 1914.

The old world ended, however, before that happened. Whilst the cabinet met to discuss its failure to ward off impending civil war in Ireland, ministers learnt of the Austrian ultimatum to Serbia. Within a week, the Germans had invaded Belgium and the war had begun.

# IDEAS AND PRINCIPLES

**The Doctrine of Mandate**

Political leaders had always explained their views to voters at election times, but with the formation of nationally-organized parties in the 1870s, the need for common agreement on policy programmes became evident. Joseph Chamberlain, in fact, in 1885 produced considerable misgiving amongst the Liberal leadership by issuing an *Unauthorized Programme*, thus high-lighting the need for an official party manifesto. The Liberal *Newcastle Programme* in 1891, was one example of such a manifesto.

The notion that a party returned to office by a general election should be bound by the promises it had made in its manifesto, and should refrain from introducing policies which it had not previously mentioned, was something which the Conservatives seem to have thought of after 1906. The doctrine was used by them in order to deny the legitimacy of the Liberal attack on the House of Lords. Of course, the Liberals could reply that when there are new developments ruling parties are compelled to bring in policies on which they have not consulted the voters: but this did not stop the idea of an *electoral mandate*, in which the electors bound the government to certain lines of policy, from gaining wide acceptance in the twentieth century.

**Civil and Criminal Law**

Crimes are offences against society, where a prosecution is brought against the offender in the name of the Crown by the police force. *Civil offences* are offences against individual people or groups, where the onus of prosecution rests with the parties concerned. The former are often punished by imprisonment; the latter usually by fines and damages.

**Imperial Preference**

Where tariffs or duties are imposed on foreign imports, governments may choose to prefer imports coming from certain favoured countries, such as their own colonies.

**Protection**

This is the economic policy of imposing tariffs on imported goods with a view to protecting the interests of the home producer of similar goods. The farmer is thus said to be *protected* by tariffs on farm produce, or the manufacturer by tariffs on manufactures.

**'Two-power' standard**

A phrase used before the First World War to describe British naval policy i.e. the strength of the British Navy should be as great as that of its two most powerful neighbours combined. Since British resources were incapable of keeping pace with German or U.S. resources, let alone a combination of the two, the importance of the concept was largely propagandist.

# APPLIED MATERIALS

## BOOKS

HILL, C. P. & WRIGHT, J. C., (1981). *British History, 1815–1914*. Oxford. Chapters 14 & 15.
REYNOLDSON, Fiona, (1987). *Twentieth-century British History, Book 1, 1900–1914*. Heinemann.

RICHARDS, D. & HUNT, J. W., (1987). *Illustrated History of Modern Britain, 1783–1980*. Third Edition, Longman. Chapter 18.

TEED, Peter, (1964). *Britain, 1906–51.* Hutchinson. Chapters 2 & 3.

UNSTEAD, R. J., (1966). *Britain in the Twentieth Century.* A. & C. Black. Chapters 1 & 2.

### MORE DETAILED BOOKS

BENNING, Keith, (1986). *Edwardian Britain: Society in Transition.* Blackie.

COOTES, R. J., (1966). *The Making of the Welfare State.* Longman: Modern Times series. Chapters 4 & 5.

McKELLAR, Ian, (1986). *The Edwardian Age: Complacency and Concern.* Blackie.

### DOCUMENTARY SOURCES

BETTEY, J. H., (Ed.), (1967). *English Historical Documents, 1906–39.* Routledge & Kegan Paul. pp. 1–47.

PEARCE, M. L., (1987). *Sources in History: The Twentieth Century.* Bell & Hyman, Section 2.

TEED, P. & CLARK, M., (Eds.), (1969). *Portraits and Documents: Later Nineteenth Century, 1868–1919.* Hutchinson. pp. 81–108, 149–155, 201–247.

### AUDIO-VISUAL

Asquith: Pre-1914                 Audio Learning    HEA 006    (Track A)

Lloyd George: the Making of a Prime Minister    Audio Learning    HEA 035    (Track A)

The Changing Role of Women, 1870–1970      A.V.P.    1507

# EXAMINATION QUESTIONS

**1**   Read the source material below carefully, and then answer the questions which follow.

### Source A

This is the crux of the whole problem . . . The truth is that in practice the House of Lords gives effect to the will of the House of Commons when you have a Tory majority; the House of Lords frustrates the will of the Commons when you have a Liberal majority; and in neither the one case nor the other does it consider – what indeed it has no means of ascertaining – the will of the people.

(H.H. Asquith in a speech in the House of Commons, 1907)

### Source B

The House of Lords has long ceased to be the watchdog of the Constitution. It has become Mr. Balfour's poodle. It barks for him. It fetches and carries for him. It bites anyone that he sets it on to. (1908)

This is a war budget. It is for raising money to wage implacable war against poverty and squalidness. (1909)

A fully-equipped Duke costs as much to keep up as two Dreadnoughts, and they are just as great a terror, and they last longer. As long as they were contented to be mere idols on their pedestals, preserving that stately silence which became their rank and intelligence, all went well, and the average British citizen rather looked up to them.

But then came the budget. The Dukes stepped off their perch. They have been scolding like omnibus drivers purely because the budget cart has knocked a little of the gilt off their old stage coach. Well, we cannot put them back again.

The question will be asked whether five hundred men, chosen accidentally from among the unemployed, should override the judgment – the deliberate judgment – of millions of people who are engaged in the industry which makes the wealth of the country. (October 1909)

(Lloyd George, excerpts from speeches, 1908–9)

**Source C**

Today will be signalled by an event of the highest constitutional and historical importance – the exercise by the House of Lords of an unquestionable and indispensable right which it has not been necessary to use for a very long time thanks to the wise moderation with which, upon the whole, our Constitution has been worked by statesmen of all parties. That traditional moderation has been abandoned by the present government.

(*The Times*, November 30th 1909)

**Source D**

RICH FARE
THE GIANT LLOYD-GORGIBUSTER:

Fee, Fi, Fo, Fat,
I smell the blood of a plutocrat;
Be he alive or be he dead,
I'll grind his bones to make my bread.'

a) What was the important event which, according to Source C, was about to happen in the House of Lords on November 30th 1909?

(1)

Explain what *The Times* meant by the Lords' 'unquestionable and indispensable right'.

(2)

What evidence is there in any of the other sources which agrees or disagrees with *The Times'* view of the behaviour of the House of Lords?

(2)

b) What image of the Chancellor of the Exchequer is portrayed by the *Punch* cartoon?

(3)

c) What were the 'Dreadnoughts'?

(1)

What was Lloyd George's purpose in comparing the cost of them with the cost of a 'fully-equipped Duke'?

(2)

Explain the phrase '. . . the budget cart has knocked a little of the gilt off their old stage coach.'

(2)

d) What kind of evidence is Source A? How reliable is this comment by H. Asquith on the conduct of the House of Lords at this time?

(5)

e) What do you think Lloyd George's intentions were in delivering the speeches quoted in Source B?
Do they give a different image of the Chancellor and his budget plans from the one given in Source D? Account for any difference you find.

(7)

(WJEC)

2   The Development of the Welfare State.
    The National Insurance Act of 1911 was one of the most important reforms passed by
    Asquith's Liberal Government.

# THE DAWN OF HOPE.

Mr. LLOYD GEORGE'S National Health Insurance Bill provides for the insurance
of the Worker in case of Sickness.

## Support the Liberal Government
in their policy of
## SOCIAL REFORM.

a) i) Identify the politician, shown in the cartoon sitting on the chair, who was
responsible for introducing the National Insurance Scheme.

*(1)*

ii) Explain how the scheme was paid for.

*(3)*

b) Explain why the Liberal Government introduced a system of National Insurance.

*(6)*

c) Which of the following governments contributed more to the improvement of the
living conditions of the British people: the Liberal governments of 1905–14, or the
Labour governments of 1945–51? Explain your answer thoroughly.

*(15)*

# A   T U T O R ' S   A N S W E R   T O   Q . 1

**1**  a)  The event implied by Source C is the exercise of the House of Lords' veto, all the more important because it so seldom occurs.

The right of veto had been exercised in the past, even in matter relating to finance (the most recent as late as 1860), and hence could be said to be 'unquestionable'. *The Times* referred to it also as 'indispensable' because it accepted the need for the Lords to be able to act in their own defence in financial matters.

Neither Asquith nor Lloyd George (Sources A & B) can be expected for a moment to agree with *The Times*. Source A says 'the House of Lord frustrates the will of the Commons' in a tone of disapproval, and Source B says that far from being the watchdog of the constitution, the House of Lords is 'Mr. Balfour's poodle'. The tone of the *Punch* cartoon is one of playful and affectionate approval of the Chancellor rather than the opposite. None of the other sources, therefore, show any support for the right-wing *Times*.

b)  The cartoon shows Lloyd George as a bloodthirsty orgre intent on bludgeoning the cowering aristocracy with his club. This fairytale presentation of the Chancellor as the giant in 'Jack and the Beanstalk' is not entirely intended seriously, as is evident from the whimsical tone of the caption. The phrase 'I'll grind his bones to make my bread' does, however, accurately represent the popular view of the intentions of the Liberals at the time of the People's Budget.

c)  Dreadnoughts were heavily-armed battleships, reputedly unsinkable.

Lloyd George's vivid imagery and his mocking sarcasm as demonstrated here are a good example of his great delight at 'playing to the gallery'. They always went down well with the crowds, whose mentality he instinctively understood. His comparison of a Duke with a Dreadnought suggests that the apparently cheap process of giving out titles in fact has heavy social costs, whilst the damage likely to be inflicted by a battleship is no more hurtful than those resulting from peerages.

'Cart' is a homely image, appropriate for describing the budget, whilst the phrase 'stage coach' is historic, and intended to be rather classy. At the same time, Lloyd George goes rather over the top with his banter – an omnibus driver was not likely to be in charge of a stage coach.

d)  Primary evidence. It is reliable in that coming from accepted sources it accurately represents Asquith's opinion, but this does not in itself make his opinion a reliable one. As Prime Minister and leader of one of the two sides in the dispute he is clearly less than impartial. Those wishing to discover the reasons why the Liberals thought as they did can usefully study an extract such as this; but opponents would clearly have looked at the whole matter far differently.

e)  He is whipping up political support for Liberal policies by presenting them to the mass of the voters in a simplified and amusing style, a task at which Lloyd George, a skilled demagogue, was extremely proficient.

The image presented by the cartoon is not markedly different from the tone of Lloyd George's own speeches, since both present him rather indulgently. It seems quite likely that *Punch*, a popular and rather superficial magazine, is taking the Chancellor at his own valuation. But underlying the speeches there is a note of seriousness missing from the cartoon, which is purely playful.

*(Please note that if you are presented with a question of this kind, where the sub-sections of the question are themselves sub-divided, though without any i)/ii)/iii), it is desirable to start each sub-division on a new line. Otherwise the examiner may not be able to disentangle the various parts of your answer.)*

# A STUDENT'S ANSWER TO Q.2 WITH EXAMINER'S COMMENTS

> This is much too long for 1 mark; the name alone is enough.

> This is quite succinct, accurate and about the right length for 3 marks.

> A good start, but should be developed more in order to get the 6 marks on offer.

> A crude over-simplification, and in any case not relevant.

> Rowntree has been misspelt here, and the name of William Booth, the founder of the Salvation Army, confused with the social pioneer, Charles Booth.

> A full, if rather muddled summary of the work of the Liberals, deserving about a third of the marks. There is however, no comparison with the work of Attlee, and no indication that the candidate has read the question properly.

a) i) Lloyd George. He was born in 1863, in Manchester, the son of a Welsh schoolmaster. He was brought up by his uncle in North Wales near Pwllheli and entered Parliament for Caernarfon Boroughs as a liberal in 1890. He was President of the Board of Trade under Campbell Bannerman and succeded Asquith as Chancellor of the Exchequer in 1908 when Asquith became Prime Minister. He was Prime Minister himself from 1916 to 1922. He died in 1945.

ii) The scheme was paid for partly by contributions from the insured workforce, partly by contributions from the employers and partly by the state. It covered unemployment and sickness. The notion that the unemployment contribution amounted to '9d for 4d', however, was quite wrong; both the employer's and the state's contribution came indirectly from the taxpayer's own pocket, so that he was really getting '9d for 9d!

b) Wages were low, living conditions were poor and many labourers were simply too poor to be able to take out insurance policies privately to protect them against misfortunes such as unemployment. The Conservatives did nothing about it anyway because they didn't care whether the poor perished or not.

c) The Liberal Government of 1905-14 contributed a lot to the improvement of the living conditions of the British people. They were very concerned with the poor standard of housing they lived in, slums such as had been described by Seebohm Roundtree and William Booth. They passed laws about housing and town planning, and would not allow houses to be built back-to-back with tanneries and other smelly places. They also aided the underprivilaged by helping those who had no trade unions to support them, such as in the 'sweated industries', and helped old people by old-age pensions and the unemployed by setting up Labour Exchanges. They also helped the trade unions by outlawing for the future the Taff Vale Judgment and allowing unions to strike without having to pay damages. There was the Workmen's Compensation Act in 1906 and various acts to help children like the Children's Charter. The most famous was the National Insurance Act in 1911 which laid the foundation stones of the welfare state by bringing in insurance for unemployment and for sickness and bad health. Women were allowed maternity benefit. There were other acts to do with the coalmines and with shops. All these helped to improve the living conditions of the British people.

# SUGGESTIONS FOR FURTHER WORK

1  Use some contemporary writings to find out more about the living conditions of the British people at this time. Tip: Try C.F.G. Masterman, *The Condition of England* (1909, reprinted Methuen, 1960).

2  Use the two cartoons in this chapter, and other cartoons, to write about the usefulness of political cartoons for the historian.

3  Produce *two* brief biographies of Asquith and Lloyd George in the years down to 1914, making use of an encyclopedia. What light do these throw on the later quarrel between the two men in 1916?

# THE CONGRESS 'SYSTEM'

## GETTING STARTED

Napoleon's defeat at Waterloo brought to an end twenty-five years of almost continuous war. During its last stages the victorious allies had been meeting at Vienna to discuss the terms of peace, and even Napoleon's 'Hundred Days' adventure had hardly disturbed their discussions. Not that these were without incident. The great powers who had contributed so largely to winning the war, Russia, Austria, Prussia and Great Britain, were by no means unanimous in their decisions about the disposal of territories, and there was much argument and compromise.

# HISTORICAL DEVELOPMENTS

**1** ▷ **THE CONGRESS OF VIENNA 1815**

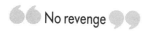
No revenge

France, the defeated power, was treated leniently, being reduced to its pre-war frontiers and having to pay a small indemnity (or fine) of £28,000,000. This was to cover the cost of Napoleon's return from exile in 1815, and no-one seriously suggested making France pay the cost of the whole war from 1792. But Prussia was bitterly disappointed that France was allowed to keep Alsace and Lorraine, and was not pacified by being awarded a considerable area of the Rhineland, and being allowed to join in a victory parade through Paris. Prussia had also hoped to swallow up the whole of Saxony, whose king, unlike other German princes, abandoned Napoleon too late. Britain and Austria managed to prevent the disappearance of Saxony – Prussia gained only two fifths of it. But Prussia had to pay a price: some of her Polish territory, including the Polish capital Warsaw, was joined to Russian Poland to create a revived Kingdom of Poland, which was virtually under Russian control despite the granting of a constitution. Russia also acquired Finland from Sweden, and Sweden was compensated by receiving Norway from defeated Denmark. Austrian power was strengthened by losing the burdensome Austrian Netherlands, and acquiring compensation in Italy: Austria regained Lombardy, kept Venetia to which it had little or no claim, and Austrian Dukes were installed in Italy's central Duchies. Britain appeared to be generous in renouncing any territorial ambitions, so Britain's 'modest' gains included Heligoland, Malta and the Ionian Islands in Europe, several remote islands in the South Atlantic including Napoleon's exile of St. Helena, several valuable islands in the West Indies including Tobago, and in the Indian Ocean the islands of the Seychelles, Mauritius and Ceylon. The Dutch province of the Cape of Southern Africa was also retained by Britain, so that Britain had secured a firm grip on most of the world's major sea routes, and incidentally gained more square miles of territory than either Austria or Prussia.

As the Allies had been largely fighting for twenty-five years to prevent the Europe of 1789 from being thrown into confusion and turmoil by the French Revolution, it is not surprising that where possible they restored the rulers and boundaries of 1789, even if some of the rulers turned out to be unsuitable to rule. They did not restore the Holy Roman Empire, but set up in its place the German Confederation, whose 39 princes were supposed to meet occasionally under the presidency of the Emperor of Austria to discuss matters of common German interest. It was not the Allies' fault if the Confederation became more concerned with strengthening the independence of the German princes than with the furthering of aims and policies common to all Germany. But the Allies were more concerned with France than with Germany. Lenient treatment it was hoped would make France less likely to seek a war of revenge. To diminish this possibility the Allies ringed France with buffer states which enjoyed Allied guarantees and protection. The union of the former Austrian Netherlands and the United Provinces was a sensible idea to create a strong Northern neighbour for France; Prussia was given Rhine territory and thus a commitment to prevent France from expanding eastwards; the independence and neutrality of Switzerland was guaranteed by the Allies; Piedmont acquired a coastline in Genoa, and France thus had a more powerful neighbour to her south-east. It was not, of course, expected that France would try to upset these arrangements in the immediate future, but it was the best the Allies could do to try to prevent a renewal of war. Few previous international treaties had lasted unchanged for long, and even fewer had done anything positive to preserve peace for the future other than to make a few pious and hopeful pronouncements. The Allies wanted this peace to last, so by the Quadruple Alliance they bound themselves to maintain the terms of the treaty by armed force for twenty years, and by Article VI of this alliance they declared:

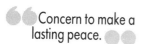
Concern to make a lasting peace.

> To assure and facilitate the execution of the present Treaty, and to consolidate the intimate relations which to-day unite the Four sovereigns for the good of the world, the High Contracting Parties have agreed to renew, at fixed periods, whether under the immediate auspices of the Sovereigns, or by their respective Ministers, reunions devoted to the great common interests and to the examination of the measures which, at any of these periods, shall be judged most salutary for the repose and prosperity of the peoples, and for the maintenance of the peace of the State.

Thus the Allies were to hold 'fixed period reunions' to discuss 'common interests' and to decide on 'appropriate measures'. The peace conference at Vienna had been called a

'Congress', a lofty word for a meeting of delegates, so the reunions too, were given the high-sounding name of Congress. And as the Allies were to be responsible for the measures to maintain peace, only the Allies were to join in the 'reunions'. Later historians criticized the peacemakers for not creating an early nineteenth-century League of Nations; but the Allies were realists, not idealists, and had no intention of cluttering up their deliberations with many small powers who could provide much talk but little muscle. The Congress 'System' was also much criticised for not being a 'system', something it never set out to be. The 'fixed period' was not adhered to. There was no provision for regular Congress meetings; there were no headquarters, Secretariat or agenda. All the Allies agreed to do was to meet to consider what to do whenever the peace of Europe was threatened. At least this was better than the Holy Alliance dreamed up by Tsar Alexander of Russia: this provided for a Christian brotherhood of princes who were to rule their peoples in accordance with Christian brotherly love, and were to guarantee to each other their thrones and territories. It is not surprising that Britain's Foreign Secretary Lord Castlereagh advised the Prince Regent against joining the Holy Alliance, and pinned Britain's hopes of maintaining European peace on the success of the Congress System.

> **An attempt to mix politics and Christianity.**

## 2 > THE CONGRESS OF AIX-LA-CHAPELLE 1818

The Holy Alliance highlighted the differences of emphasis among the Allies. Russia, together with Austria and Prussia, were concerned about thrones and territories. Britain was concerned about peace. They would intervene in a country's internal affairs to save a throne, even if there was no threat to peace. Britain would allow thrones to topple and territories to change hands without intervention unless there *was* a threat to international peace. At first there was no major issue to show up the Allied differences. For three years France enjoyed respectable government under the restored Bourbon monarchy. Louis XVIII was not as absolute a monarch as were his Bourbon predecessors, but he allowed the illusion of a little power-sharing only to the privileged few. His concern was to pay off the indemnity as quickly as possible, remove the Allied army of occupation, and restore France's self-respect as a great power. This, he hoped, would mean France being regarded as a Congress power on equal terms with the Congress System's founders. So when in 1818 France had paid off the £28 million fine, it requested the removal of the army of occupation, and a Congress was held at Aix-la-Chapelle to discuss the matter. France's good behaviour since 1815 made it easy for the Allies to agree, but a secret resolution, committing the Allies to intervene in France to suppress any revolutionary movement which might threaten European peace, caused major division among the Allies. Castlereagh and the Austrian Chancellor Prince Metternich feared that Russian intervention in the internal affairs of countries such as France could lead to an extension of Russian influence. They therefore undermined the secret resolution by extending the Quadruple Alliance into a Quintuple Alliance by allowing France to become a member, thus making France in effect one of the five Congress powers, and they all joined in a declaration against unilateral intervention in the internal affairs of states. Thus should it become necessary joint intervention might take place, but not an attack by one power on another on the pretext of maintaining European peace. Even on matters which involved joint intervention there was disagreement. Castlereagh opposed joint intervention against the Barbary pirates because he did not wish to see a contingent of the Russian navy in the Mediterranean; the other powers would not take joint action against the slave trade because such action would be dominated by the British fleet.

## 3 > THE CONGRESS OF TROPPAU 1820

Metternich's opposition to intervention was soon to falter. The disturbances in Germany in 1817 he tackled without foreign assistance, but the growing agitation in some of the Italian states threatened the stability of Italy and Austrian domination of it, and troubles in Spain provoked sympathetic reactions in Italy. In 1820 the agitation led to full-scale revolution in both countries and Tsar Alexander I of Russia demanded a Congress in which the revolutions should be discussed and intervention considered. Castlereagh did not even think the revolutions justified a Congress and Britain and France only sent observers to the Congress which met at Troppau. It was not that Castlereagh was a friend to revolutions – he detested them as much as Metternich and Alexander. Britain had a constitutional system of government with parliamentary institutions, and Castlereagh would have to defend in the House of Commons any commitment to intervene in the internal affairs of other countries. Moreover such a commitment might well be unacceptable to future British governments, and if the intervention principle became established, what was there to prevent the Congress powers deciding that the change of British government was a threat to peace and taking action accordingly? In his State Paper of May 1820 Castlereagh made Britain's position clear:

> We shall be found in our place when actual danger menaces the system of Europe; but this country cannot and will not act upon abstract and speculative principles of precaution. The Alliance which exists had no such purpose in view in its original formation. It was never so explained to parliament: if it had, most assuredly the sanction of parliament would never have been given to it.

Metternich was frightened by the revolutions in Spain and Italy and by the recent unrest in Germany. He joined with Alexander and Frederick William of Prussia in issuing the *Troppau Protocol*, a public statement of their position on intervention – a statement which it would be impossible for the British government to accept and embarrassing for it to refuse. Both Metternich and Alexander reckoned that Britain could not openly oppose the Protocol without wrecking the Congress System, and Castlereagh was known to be profoundly committed to the Congress System. The three powers declared themselves against any change of government arising from revolution, and went on to state rather menacingly:

66 Britain isolated. 99

> If, owing to such alterations, immediate danger threatens other states, the Powers bind themselves by peaceful means, or, if need be by arms, to bring back the guilty state into the bosom of the Great Alliance.

If the three powers were expecting Britain to accept quietly, they were mistaken. Castlereagh would not shift from the views expressed in the State Paper. The Congress was moved from Troppau to Laibach after a brief adjournment.

## 4 THE CONGRESS OF LAIBACH 1821

The British lack of commitment seemed confirmed when the British observer, Stewart, found his wife's giving birth more important than the diplomatic deliberations and absented himself from the Congress for three weeks. Castlereagh modified Britain's public distaste for intervention to agree, in private, that Austria's interests in Italy justified intervention there. He could not do much else, because Austrian preparations to suppress the Italian revolutions were far advanced, and British disapproval would have made no difference. Ferdinand of Naples, who had been invited to the Congress, had promised a Constitution to his rebels, but denounced it once he reached the safety of neutral territory. An Austrian army marched into Naples, restored Ferdinand with full tyrannical powers, and enabled him to deal with his liberals by imprisonment and execution. The liberal revolution in Piedmont was similarly suppressed by Austrian troops, with the so-called liberal Alexander of Russia ready to pour in another 100,000 troops should they be needed. Castlereagh made no protest to these events.

But Castlereagh's flexibility on Italy was matched by his inflexibility on Spain. He was determined to oppose any intervention there. His motives were clear enough; any intervention in Spain could only come from France, and while Castlereagh was prepared to accept France as an equal partner in the Congress System, he certainly was not prepared to sanction French intervention in Spain, a territory in which the Peninsular War had been fought from 1808–14 at enormous cost and where Wellington had acquired his international military reputation. Moreover, Wellington was now becoming an important Tory politician with something of a reactionary reputation. If Wellington was opposed to French intervention in Spain, then *who* in Britain could possibly be in favour of it? The British parliament did not want Wellington's Peninsular victories thrown away by allowing the French into Spain and also remembered that the Spanish rebels were demanding the Constitution promised, with Britain's blessing, by the Spanish monarchy in 1812. It would be something of a breach of faith for Britain, who had once intervened in Spain on behalf of Liberalism and a constitution, to stand aside when another attempt to achieve the same aims was being threatened.

## 5 THE CONGRESS OF VERONA 1822

It could be argued that Castlereagh's differences from Austria, Prussia and Russia were so great that the Congress System was no longer in effective operation. Because of overwork, Castlereagh committed suicide in 1822, but only after he had sent Wellington to the new Congress proposed for Verona. The choice of Wellington was significant.

Congress System already effectively at an end.

Castlereagh suspected that Alexander would propose direct military intervention in Spain, and Wellington could be expected to resist this proposal strenuously. Canning, Castlereagh's successor, confirmed Wellington's appointment, and sent him to Verona with virtually the same instructions as Castlereagh. For a long time historians supposed that Castlereagh created the Congress System and tried desperately to keep it going, while Canning had little interest in it and allowed it to break up. This is unfair to Canning. The Congress System was on the verge of collapse in 1820–21. It was Castlereagh, not Canning, who proposed to send observers rather than representatives to the Congresses of 1820–22. It was also Castlereagh who found himself opposed to the policies of his European Allies. Canning made no significant change of policy; his aims at Verona were those of Castlereagh. Wellington protested vigorously at Alexander's proposal to send 150,000 Russian troops into Spain. He also protested at the French offer to intervene there. So far, Canning was following in Castlereagh's footsteps, but now there was a new factor in the international situation – a revolution in Greece. This had begun in 1821 in the Danube provinces where the Greeks were very much a minority race. But by 1822 the revolt had spread to the main Greek-speaking areas of the Southern Balkans and threatened the Turkish domination of the area. Alexander was expected to oppose the Greek revolt, in the way he opposed that in Spain. But the Greeks belonged to the same Greek Orthodox Christianity as did the Russians, and, more importantly, Alexander saw the Greek revolt as the opportunity to weaken the Turkish Empire that the Russians had long wanted to occupy. Thus Alexander proposed to help the Greeks as a prelude to helping himself. Wellington protested at proposals to intervene in both Spain and Greece, and having made Britain's position clear, withdrew from the Congress. With Britain's withdrawal the Congress System was in effect at an end.

Once the delegates returned empty-handed from Verona, events moved fast. French troops invaded Spain within a month. Alarmed that French forces might be used to reconquer Spain's revolted colonies in the New World and interrupt Britain's growing trade with them, Canning recognized the independence of Spain's former colonies and was sympathetic when President Monroe of the USA declared the Americas a forbidden area for European colonization.

Follow this argument carefully.

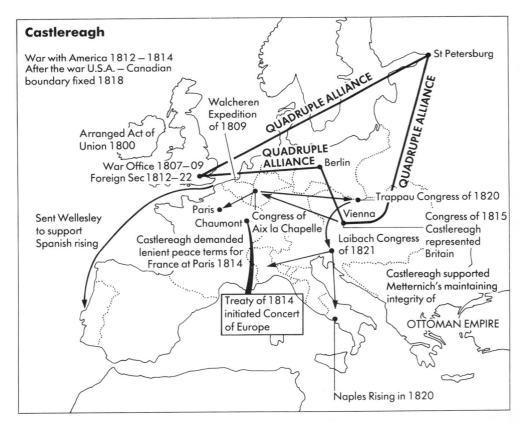

Fig 10.1

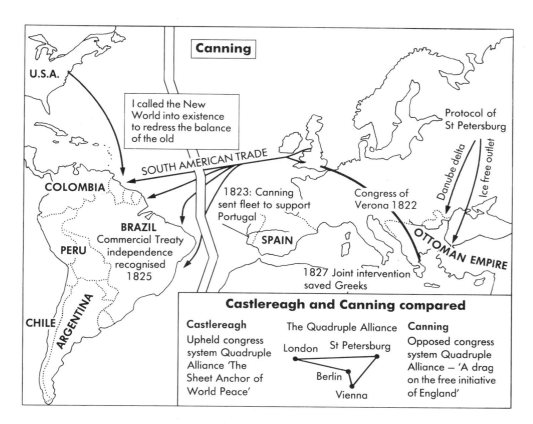

Fig 10.2

## 6

## THE END OF THE CONGRESS SYSTEM

Although Alexander had tried to settle the Greek Question in his own favour, Britain's protests and the persuasion of Metternich made him hesitate. After all, the Greeks were sweeping all before them, had cleared the Morea and other parts of Southern Greece, and captured a number of Aegean islands, massacring several Turkish island communities. Greek success could only be to the advantage of the Russians and it calmed the Russian clamour for revenge for the Greek patriarch of Constantinople, hanged by the Turks from the balcony of his palace on Easter Day 1822. Oddly enough, while Greek success pacified the Russians, it alarmed Metternich, who feared that unrest in the Balkans could spread into the Austrian Empire from the South.

But in 1825 the situation changed. Unable to defeat the Greeks, the Sultan of Turkey looked about him for allies. The extent of his desperation is clear from his choice: Mehemet Ali, Albanian adventurer and Governor of Egypt, admittedly possessed of a powerful fleet, but also of unlimited ambition. Promises of governorships in Crete and Syria, and private ambitions of his own, led Mehemet Ali to put the services of himself and his fleet at the disposal of his nominal superior, the Sultan. In the summer and autumn of 1825 the route of his fleet and armies along the Greek coast could be traced by the fires and devastation they left behind. The Greeks were no match for Mehemet Ali, neither on land nor at sea. The new Tsar Nicholas I (1825–55) made it clear that he would not tolerate the destruction of the Greeks and public opinion in Britain and France agreed. When it became clear that the Russians were determined to intervene to save the Greeks, Canning decided that it would be too great a risk to peace to allow the Russians to intervene alone. At St. Petersburg in 1826 Britain and Russia committed themselves to securing Greek independence, and when the Turks failed to respond, followed this with the Treaty of London, 1827, agreeing to put an immediate end to the fighting in Greece. France was a party to the treaty, but Austria refused. The jealousy which had prevented a joint naval expedition to the Mediterranean in 1818 was forgotten as a combined Allied fleet was assembled. It followed the Egyptian-Turkish forces along the Greek coast and caught up with their fleet in Navarino Bay. The Egyptian commander refused to stop landing troops, but the battle was provoked when the Turks opened fire. The Allies did not cease firing until they had destroyed the only navy the Turks and Egyptians possessed.

Unable to supply his forces by sea, Mehemet Ali had to abandon his campaign, and the Sultan really had to agree to Greek independence. But he tried war against Russia first. This proved to be a disaster and when Russian armies were within a hundred miles of his capital, Constantinople, he gave way, and signed the Treaty of Adrianople, 1829, by which the great powers were to decide the fate of Greece. Britain's new Foreign Secretary

Wellington (Canning had died two months before Navarino) had become Prime Minister in 1828 and tried to limit Russian influence and the Turkish decline by proposing to keep Greece as small as possible, and to divide it into separate, tiny states. Wellington fell from power in 1830 and Palmerston, the new Foreign Secretary proposed a larger, unified Greece, although most Greeks were still to remain under Turkish rule. He gave the Greeks respectability by providing them with a monarchical constitution and a German king. These proposals were agreed by treaty in 1832.

In some ways, the Greek problem showed the complete collapse of the Congress System. Russia wanted intervention; Austria opposed it. Britain and France liked the Greeks, but disliked intervention. Prussia lacked a will of its own and supported Austria. When the Greeks were successful the Russians were less inclined to take action, the Austrians more so, and when the Greeks were being defeated after 1825 the Russians committed themselves to intervention, with or without the support of other powers, and Austria became more firm than ever in its opposition to intervention. Thus the two great powers of the Troppau Protocol were on opposite sides, and their collaboration in the Congress System had crumbled away. But co-operation was not dead. Britain and France joined Russia at St. Petersburg and London, 1826–27, to tackle the Greek problem even though Austria and Prussia refused to take part. Wellington wished that Britain had also refused, but he took part in the discussions in 1829 and 1830, and paved the way for the final agreement. So international decisions solved the Greek problem for the moment, but the statesmen were careful not to call their meetings Congresses. How could they, when two of the major powers were missing? Formal Congresses had died in 1822, and no-one for the moment seemed willing to try them again.

---

**7 > ASSESSMENT**

*❝Analysis of this kind is vital in developing historical skills. ❞*

It may seem that the Congresses were a failure. They bred argument and disagreement. After the first two they produced no worthwhile joint decisions, and they seemed to exist only to publicise the policy differences between the Allies. Yet the purpose of the Congresses had been to solve international disputes by negotiation and to maintain European peace. While the Allies seemed ready to abandon the formality of set-piece congresses they were not ready to abandon the habit of international co-operation and negotiation, that was acquired through the Congress System. Thus the Greek Question was tackled in 1827 by a conference held in London, and the problem of Mehemet Ali was solved, also in London, in 1840. The word Congress was even revived for the peace conference at Paris which ended the Crimean war in 1856. And the Eastern Question which threatened a general European war in 1878 was settled at a Congress held in Berlin. The statesmen of 1815 could not have foreseen that although Europe would see some savage wars in the nineteenth century, there would be no *general* European war until 1914.

# IDEAS AND PRINCIPLES

| | |
|---|---|
| **Absolutist government** | Government is controlled by one ruler, usually a king or dictator. Power is not shared with any other person, or any other organization such as a parliament. |
| **Congress** | An important political meeting. In the context of the early nineteenth century it refers specifically to international meetings of the representatives of heads of states. |
| **Constitutional government** | Here government is determined by a set of rules, written or otherwise, which specify how government is to be shared. In the early nineteenth century monarchs who allowed some power, however limited, to an elected parliament, were regarded as constitutional monarchs. (See liberalism below). |
| **Holy Alliance** | The alliance of Austria, Prussia and Russia in 1815, ostensibly to ensure that Europe was governed according to Christian principles, but in fact intended to guarantee the thrones and territories of the members and to suppress revolutions. |

**Indemnity**

In the international sense a payment by one country to another to cover the cost of a war or part of a war.

**Liberalism**

A belief, the main aim of which was to secure some form of constitutional government. European liberals of the early nineteenth century were not necessarily democrats as the Liberals were in nineteenth-century Britain (see chapter 2); their main concern was to oppose absolutism and to establish parliamentary government – not necessarily the same thing as democratic government. A criticism often levelled by historians against the peacemakers at Vienna was that they ignored liberalism in their decisions. Yet constitutions with some form of parliament were approved for France, Switzerland, Poland, Norway, the United Netherlands, and Finland, and Britain at least was committed to a constitution in Spain. Even if the new German Diet could hardly be called parliamentary, constitutional governments were the rule rather than the exception in Western Europe in 1815.

**Nationalism**

The wish of a people with a number of things in common (i.e. one or more of language, religion, history, economic interest, geography, heritage) to become a state. For the Germans and Italians nationalism would mean the creation of a unified Germany and unified Italy; for other nations such as the Czechs and the Hungarians they could only become states if the Austrian Empire fell apart, and the Polish nation could only become a state if three Continental winners of the Napoleonic Wars, Austria, Prussia and Russia, were each to give up substantial territories. Nationalism is sometimes confused with patriotism: during the Napoleonic Wars the Germans who fought for Prussia were Prussian patriots rather than German nationalists, and those who fought for their beloved Austria whether they were Czechs, Germans or Slavs could hardly be described as nationalists. Even in Italy hatred of the foreigner and demands for constitutional government dominated the disturbances of 1820; only a few idealists dreamed of Italian unity, and those historians who write of Italian and German nationalism in this early period often exaggerate its importance.

**Protocol**

In its diplomatic sense this is an important international agreement on policy, usually brief and often tacked on to another agreement.

**Quadruple Alliance**

The alliance of 1815 whose main function was to preserve the arrangements made at the Congress of Vienna for the next twenty years. Its members were soon to differ on the extent of their roles as international policemen. The addition of France in 1818 turned it into the Quintuple alliance.

**Reactionary**

Opposed to all change. The absolutist powers of Europe, Austria and Prussia and eventually Russia, set themselves against all changes such as liberalism, which could threaten their absolutism. Thus by definition absolute governments were reactionary governments.

**State Paper**

A government document, usually confidential, which sets out government policy on some major issue.

# APPLIED MATERIALS

### TEXT-BOOKS

LANE, P., (1978). *Success in British History 1760–1914.* Unit 9, Murray.
PEACOCK, H. L., (1982). *A History of Modern Britain 1815–1981.* Heinemann. Chapter 4.
PEACOCK, H. L., (1982). *A History of Modern Europe 1789–1984.* Heinemann. Chapter 4.
WATSON, J. B., (1981). *Success in European History 1815–1941.* Units 2 and 3, Murray.

### DOCUMENTARY

*English Historical Documents 1815–1870.* Methuen (1964).
ALBRECHT-CARRIE, René, *The Concert of Europe 1815–1914.* Harper and Row (1968).

### MAPS

*The Penguin Atlas of World History, Vol. II.* Penguin (1978).

# EXAMINATION QUESTIONS

**1** a) What were the attitudes of each of the following statesmen towards the European Congresses which met in the course of the seven years after 1815?
   i) Castlereagh,
   ii) Metternich,
   iii) Tsar Alexander I.
   b) Write a paragraph to explain the Troppau Protocol, 1820.
   c) Why did the European Congresses not continue after 1822?

(LEAG)

**2** Study the Source below:

> At the Congress of Vienna, resumed after Waterloo, the allies claimed the rewards of victory . . . Amongst those who had helped to defeat Napoleon and preserve Europe from domination by one man, none had borne a stouter or more successful part than Britain . . . She had subsidised the allied armies, mastered the enemy fleets, swept up enemy colonies, and finally, by the deeds of her troops in the Peninsula and at Waterloo, had made a powerful military contribution by land. For all these reasons, when victors fell to dividing the spoils, she did not feel herself unjustified in retaining the Cape of Good Hope, Mauritius, Ceylon, Heligoland, Malta, the Ionian Islands, Trinidad, St. Lucia and Tobago.

(from *Britain 1714–1851* Richards and Quick (1961))

Now, using the Source and your own knowledge, answer the following questions:
   a) Was keeping the colonies won during the wars Britain's only aim at the Congress of Vienna? Explain your answer.
   b) How were Britain's aims at the Congress of Vienna similar to, or different from, the aims of the other powers?
   c) Do you agree with the Source that Britain had made such a large contribution to winning the war against Napoleon?

(SEG)

# OUTLINE ANSWERS

1   It is important to notice in a) that the seven year period is 1816–22 inclusive, and that detailed treatment of the Congress of Vienna would be unnecessary; the question does say *after* 1815. You should also notice that your answer to a) should be constructed with care in order to avoid undue overlap with b) and c). A comparison would help, and this is a skill specifically required in assessment objective 2. It should not be too difficult to point out the contrast between Castlereagh, a minister in a constitutional government, unable to commit his country to preventing the growth of constitutional movements elsewhere, and Metternich and Alexander whose policies were less subject to scrutiny by colleagues and not subject at all to scrutiny by an elected parliament. Castlereagh wished to preserve European peace by international diplomacy, Metternich wished to use the Congress system as an international policing agency to curb the growth of liberalism. The attitude of Alexander was uncertain in the early years as he was posing as a liberal. But his Holy Alliance showed him to be more concerned with security than freedom, and his attitude towards European revolutions in 1820 brought him into temporary agreement with Metternich, while Castlereagh had good strategic and trading reasons as well as constitutional ones for taking an opposite view. Some knowledge of the contents of the Troppau Protocol is needed in b), but it is more important to show that the Protocol represented the views of the absolutist powers on the situation in Europe, and that its contents were unacceptable to Castlereagh. In c) you should not only point out the differences between Britain and her allies on the subject of Spain and Greece and explain the reasons for these differences, but you should make it clear that the Congresses had been breaking down as early as 1820.

2   Obviously a) would not be asked if keeping colonies was Britain's only aim. Nevertheless you should devote some time to discussing the colonial aim before you move on to a list of other reasons. It would be good to show the unified nature of Castlereagh's aims: he was concerned for Britain's security and prosperity, so the safeguarding of trade routes by the acquisition of bases, the safeguarding of peace by preventing the return of Napoleon and by maintaining the balance of power, and support for the Congress System to ensure no threat to peace were all part of Castlereagh's overall strategy. In b) you should point out the similarities: all the powers were concerned to prevent the return of Napoleon, to maintain peace and to prevent an upset in the balance of power. The differences arise from the different interests of the major powers. France as the defeated nation was obviously concerned to recover respectability as a great power and to avoid isolation. The other three Continental powers were concerned about Continental issues, the disposal of territories and the restoration of legitimate rulers, while Britain was more interested in colonies and trade routes and thought of the maintenance of peace in Europe in general rather than specific terms. c) seems to require knowledge of the period before 1815, but there is the source to help you. Basically while Russia made the biggest single contribution to Napoleon's defeat in the campaign of 1812, it is possible to argue that without Britain's formation of coalitions and continued defiance of Napoleon the war would have been over in 1805, and the Russian defiance of Napoleon would never have occurred. And if Britain's contribution is to be evaluated then the contributions of not only Russia but also of such powers as Austria need to be dealt with.

# SUGGESTIONS FOR FURTHER WORK

1   Using a good historical map of Europe in 1815 and the text of the Treaty of Vienna (e.g. as in Methuen's English Historical Documents), identify the main places where territorial changes took place in 1815.

2   Study the work of the British Foreign Secretary Canning (1822–27) and show how far Canning's work was a continuation of that of Castlereagh.

# 11

# ALEXANDER II

**RUSSIA IN NEED OF REFORM**

**EMANCIPATION, 1861**

**THE REFORMS OF THE 1860s AND 1870s**

**FOREIGN POLICY**

**REACTION, REPRESSION AND TERRORISM**

# GETTING STARTED

Nicholas I was not widely loved in Russia. When he insisted on reviewing his troops in the middle of the Russian winter, his bad cold turned to the pneumonia from which he died. News of his death was concealed for several days while gloomy medical bulletins were issued; it seems likely that the authorities were afraid of popular disturbances which might break out when people knew that the old tyrant was dying or even dead. His successor Alexander became Tsar in February 1855 in the middle of the Crimean War which Russia was losing. His first aim was to extricate Russia from the war which it now appeared to have little chance of winning, with as little permanent damage as possible. In general, Alexander was well satisfied with the Treaty of Paris in which Russian territorial losses were kept to a minimum, and whose most punishing clauses – those concerning the Black Sea – were destined to be short-lived.

Many who analysed the reasons for the defeat of Russia's vastly superior armies by a poorly led and poorly equipped enemy, blamed Russia's backward economy and outmoded social system. Some said that serfdom, which kept most of the peasants as virtual slaves, obstructed economic progress and hindered the growth of an urban working-class and middle-class. Others saw in defeat in war the danger of revolution, with the frequent peasant uprisings merging into a great social upheaval which would destroy autocracy and Russian society. So while some wanted reform to accelerate progress, others wanted it to prevent revolution.

# HISTORICAL DEVELOPMENTS

## RUSSIA IN NEED OF REFORM

Alexander wanted to prevent revolution. His title of 'Tsar-Liberator', given to him by later admirers, flatters him. His reputation during his father's reign had been that of a reactionary who supported absolute monarchy and who was a resolute ally of the nobility and their interests. But he had gained considerable administrative experience during his father's reign, and was aware that if reform did not come from above, it would be extorted from below. He made a good beginning by releasing the survivors of the Decembrist movement from their thirty years of exile. Even so, it surprised his nobility when in 1856 he accompanied his announcement of the conclusion of peace with these words:

> May Russia's internal welfare be established and perfected; may justice and mercy reign in her law-courts; may the desire for instruction and all useful work grow everywhere with new strength; and may everyone enjoy in peace the fruits of honest labour under the shelter of laws equally just to all, equally protecting all.

Alarmed conservative gentry tried to put pressure on the Tsar to declare that he had no intention of taking away their serfs, even though the Tsar's phrase about equally just laws seemed to imply just that. Alexander replied to criticism with a clear statement of intent when he addressed the nobility of Moscow:

> It has been rumoured that I want to give liberty to the peasants. This rumour is unjust and you can say so to everyone, on all sides. But a hostile feeling between peasants and their masters does, unfortunately, exist and this has already led to several cases of insubordination. I am convinced that sooner or later we must come to emancipation. I think that you agree with me consequently that it is better that it should come from above, rather than from below. I request you, gentlemen, to reflect on how this may be achieved.

**His intention seems to be Emancipation without liberty.**

He proceeded to set up committees of noblemen to decide how this could best be done. The task facing them was formidable. Serfdom was a comparatively new phenomenon. Wars, economic decline and seventeenth-century legislation had turned a nation of peasant land-owning proprietors into a nation of serfs, tied to the land, paying dues and labour-services to a lord, who could have them sold, flogged or sent to Siberia. A serf could be sent to a factory or regiment without his own consent, while his property (if he had any) was deemed to be the property of his lord. He had no redress against his lord's ill-treatment. The land he worked barely provided the basic needs of his family, and the survival of the strip system combined with the innate conservatism of the Russian peasant made the introduction of new farming methods almost impossible. In areas where strips were rotated amongst the peasant families the land became increasingly unproductive. No peasant would carry out improvements on strips which in a year or two's time would pass into the hands of a neighbour. It is not surprising that facing grinding poverty and lacking personal freedom, the peasants in their despair resorted to violence, and local disturbances often took on the characteristic of a full-scale rebellion. When these occurred, the local nobility who had been slow to get away were often massacred, and the arrival of the troops led to slaughter and savage reprisal. Yet the days of serfdom were surely numbered. It was an antiquated medieval institution which had long since disappeared from western Europe. Humanitarians and liberals condemned it, and it was not capable of an effective defence. The so-called 'liberal' Alexander I had vigorously supported anti-slavery measures proposed during the Congresses, but he did little to help his serfs. Nicholas I, surprisingly, tried to do more but his decrees were mostly ineffective. Even so, by the 1850s educated liberals in Russia were concluding, as American liberals had concluded before them, that serfdom or slavery were not only indefensible, but must be brought to an end. In the USA, slavery's defenders were about to fight a rearguard action in the shape of a bloody civil war. In Russia, the decision to end serfdom was made by the Tsar himself, and the defenders of serfdom were thrown into disarray.

**A comparison with the U.S.A.**

Technically the serfs were in a minority in Russia. But this is partly because Russia extended well into Asia. There was no serfdom outside European Russia; Siberia had plenty of political exiles but no serfs. And in the non-Russian areas of the Baltic and Finland the vast majority of peasants were free, either working their own small plots or hiring themselves out as labourers. It is also because the state peasants, whose only difference from serfs was that they were owned by various state and local authorities and not by private landowners, were not always technically counted as serfs. Their status was regarded as marginally superior to that of private serfs, but they, too, had no rights, and on many estates were treated no better than animals. Marginal differences in customs and title persisted in the various provinces, but these should not obscure the fact that in most parts of European Russia 80% of peasants were in effect, if not in name, serfs.

While Russia's agriculture languished and her industry had progressed only slowly since the time of Peter the Great, Europe generally, and Britain in particular, was moving into the industrial age. If Russia was to be industrialised there must be plenty of cheap labour. As the serfs were forbidden to leave their villages, factories could not recruit volunteers from the countryside. The practice of some landlords in hiring out their serfs to industrial enterprises, particularly to mine-owners, was unpopular and degrading to the serfs and not particularly profitable to the industrialists who were saddled with a resentful and untrained labour force. But if the serfs were freed, and their ties with the land loosened, there should be a ready pool of labour available for hire, and industry could begin to advance.

## 2 ▷ EMANCIPATION, 1861

The committees who debated the problem of serfdom during the late 1850s were concerned not so much with the interests of the serfs – these they assumed to be taken care of by emancipation itself – but with protecting the interests of the landowners. Some noblemen saw the chance to liberate *themselves* from the land. If they could ensure that adequate compensation was paid for the land allotted to the serfs, and if this could include compensation also for the loss of serf labour, then enterprising landowners could take their compensation, sell the land that was left, and live in the cities on the proceeds. So it was in their interest to secure as much as possible. Virtually all the pressure groups who influenced the Tsar in drawing up the Edict of 1861 were on the side of the landowners. Even before the Edict was issued, the case for the serfs seems to have been lost by default. To most reasonable people it seemed that personal freedom would be a revolutionary advance in the status of the peasants. But peasants were as much concerned with land as with status. What was the point of a peasant having freedom if he ended up with little land and a huge burden of debt?

> **66** Make sure that you are familiar with, and understand the terms of the Emancipation Edict. **99**

So from the start, the great reform pleased the educated people who were not directly affected by it, but displeased the peasants, who were. The Emancipating Edict was issued in March 1861. It gave the peasants their immediate personal freedom, and approximately half of the cultivated land. The landowners were to be given compensation, payable at once in new issues of government bonds. The peasants were to pay the state for land they had always regarded as their own by redemption payments, spread over a period of forty-nine years. The allocation of land between gentry and peasants was to be made by special Arbitrators of the Peace, who were expected to deal sympathetically with the peasants' interests. This they found difficult to do. The allocation of land in strict proportion to the size of the pre-1861 holdings left the peasants with plots too tiny to provide a living. As the peasant population grew and the plots were further sub-divided, the late nineteenth century and early twentieth century saw growing land hunger. Sometimes the larger area provided for the landowner gave him a valuable monopoly of scarce water and forest. The peasant, in order to survive, often had to rent land from the gentry at rents which, added to his redemption payments, kept him virtually destitute. And even when the land was finally paid for, in forty-nine years, it was not to be the peasant's personal property, but to be the property of the village commune, the *mir*, which controlled peasant affairs throughout all except the extreme west of Russia and Russian Poland. True, the mir was expected to hand over the plot to the peasant when the redemption payments were completed, but in the meantime, the mir determined agricultural methods on a communal basis, and denied peasants passports for travel outside their area (usually twenty miles), especially if the peasant was in arrears with his redemption payments. These payments considerably exceeded the value of the land allocated to the peasants. This was because the landowners were compensated for the loss of the free labour of their serfs, as well as the value of the land. The peasants therefore had gained personal freedom in return for a huge burden of debt, and even the personal freedom was in doubt when the mir could control peasant migration, and inflict corporal punishment if its orders were not obeyed. Widespread peasant dissatisfaction led to peasant disorders during the late nineteenth century. Redemption payments were often in arrears and were eventually cancelled altogether in 1906. The land problem was, if anything, made more acute by emancipation. Richer peasants bought out the less fortunate, and a growing class of landless peasants began to emerge. However, two years in advance of the USA, and without a civil war, the personal servitude of vast numbers of Russian peasants had been swept away. The opposition of the landowners to social change had been overcome by the autocracy of the Tsar, and the way was now open to further reform.

<table>
<tr><td>**3**</td><td>**THE REFORMS OF THE 1860s AND 1870s**</td></tr>
</table>

## LOCAL GOVERNMENT – THE ZEMSTVA

The end of both serfdom and the direct personal link between landowner and peasant meant that certain aspects of local government would break down if not replaced. The serfs had been responsible for the repair of roads and bridges. Who was to repair them now? The mir dealt with village relationships and the agricultural calendar. It had no responsibility for local taxation or local administration, so by decree in 1864 the Tsar established local councils, the *Zemstva*. These were at two levels, the district zemstva and the provincial zemstva. In the councils representatives of the nobility, townsmen and peasants, were separately elected. At district level, representatives of the nobility slightly outnumbered those of the peasants; at provincial level the electoral advantage of the nobility was even greater. These councils were created to supplement the work of central government; they were not allowed to take over any of the *functions* of central government, thus they could levy local taxes for the repair of roads and bridges, but were not allowed to assume responsibility for local policing. No sooner had the zemstva been established than the government began to restrict their power. From 1866 their right to levy local taxation was cut back, and they even had to use their limited funds for services previously provided by the central government. The zemstva met for only ten days each year and the committee which carried out the zemstvo's functions when the zemstvo was not in session was invariably presided over by one of the nobility. Although the system of zemstva was extended to the cities in 1870, it remained restricted to European Russia, and overzealous zemstva were always likely to fall foul of the authorities and risk having their powers transferred to a state official. The success of the zemstva, therefore, might well seem surprising. Yet the very fact that they had no responsibility for the police and were, in fact, sometimes hounded by them, helped to give them popularity. They tended to attract as members or employees liberals and revolutionaries who were not keen to enter government service, but who could see in the zemstva the opportunity to be of service to the people of Russia. The failure of the government to provide elementary health and education services created a gap which the zemstva was willing to fill. The peasant demand for education proved insatiable and in many areas, especially round Moscow, the zemstva brought elementary education within reach of all. Hospitals began to bring the benefits of the developments in medicine in the mid and late nineteenth-century to provincial Russia, and in at least one area a zemstvo was active in railway building. Thus in Alexander's time the zemstva performed the dual function of a vehicle for reform and a breeding-ground for revolutionaries.

## FREEDOM OF SPEECH AND FREEDOM OF THE PRESS

It is never very wise for the subjects of autocrats to express themselves freely, and during the reign of Nicholas I those who had dared to criticize the government, no matter how indirectly, were in grave danger from the Tsar's police. Newspapers were closed down or heavily fined, and universities were forbidden to employ non-Russian staff or to teach controversial subjects such as Philosophy and History. Alexander did not abolish censorship, but he did relax it. In the new liberal spirit which prevailed, at least temporarily in the early 1860s, newspapers enjoyed a new-found freedom to print largely what they pleased, and the number of new newspapers and journals increased enormously. A new Statute for secondary education was introduced in 1864, regulating what was to be taught in Russian secondary schools. The classics were strong, but some schools concentrated on science and drawing. Another statute of the same year shared responsibility for elementary education between the Ministry for Education, the zemstva and the church. This joint effort to make Russia literate saw an increase in the number of elementary schools from 8,000 in 1856 to 23,000 by 1880. Universities, too, enjoyed great expansion during the same period. The universities became largely self-governing, administering their own censorship internally and restoring the study of philosophy and constitutional law, which had been banned in the previous reign. Later attempts to curb the new freedoms were not entirely successful, and it is no coincidence that the reign of Alexander II coincided with a flourishing of Russian art, music and literature. This was the age of Tolstoy, Dostoevsky and Tchaikovsky.

## MILITARY REFORM

Russian failure in the Crimean War had placed grave doubts on the quality of the Russian army. Large numbers of conscripts, recruited mainly from the serfs, had fought ineffectively under the leadership of officers recruited exclusively from the nobility. The reforms of 1863–75 extended liability to military service to all classes, of whom one quarter would actually be called upon to serve. The twenty-five year service was reduced to fifteen, and considerably less if the recruit was educated. Officers were increasingly recruited from outside the nobility, although the nobility tended to dominate the officer class until the Revolution. Once in the army, the recruit was found to be of better use if he was literate. More Russian men learnt to read and write in the army than in all the schools set up by the zemstva. General Miliutin, who had the main responsibility for these reforms, was aware that the ending of serfdom required more than a reduction in long years of service. Free men would not tolerate military conditions resembling those of a penal colony. So education was accompanied by a sharp reduction in brutal punishments, the provision of better food and living conditions, and better prospects of promotion. Now there was less emphasis on endless drilling, and more on training with new equipment. The new Russian army became more professional and better able to meet the modern demands made of it. Although the army did badly against Japan in 1905 it would have fared far worse had it not been for Alexander and Miliutin.

## LEGAL REFORM

Until 1861 the peasants were at the mercy of their lords who acted as magistrates and punished their alleged crimes with great severity. The personal freedom given to the peasants by Emancipation meant that they were freed from the jurisdiction of their lords, and a new system of lower courts had to be created to fill the gap. As the higher courts were notorious for their incompetence and injustice it seemed a good opportunity to tackle these too. There was no clearcut hierarchy of courts before 1864. The Senate was the highest court of appeal, but the other courts were often overlapping, and cases could be moved from one court to another, prolonging the legal process and delaying legal decisions, sometimes for a lifetime. There were no juries, the judges were sometimes illiterate and usually untrained, and indeed it was laid down by Edict that where *all* the judges were illiterate, the clerk of the court would be responsible for recording the decision in writing. Accused persons did not meet their judges. Cases were decided upon the weight of written evidence, and the rank of the witnesses determined the credibility of the evidence which could not be challenged for its accuracy. Decisions depended often not on the skill of the lawyers, but upon the ability of the accused to bribe the judges. Preliminary investigation in criminal cases was done by the police, whose methods often led to accusations of brutality – a point of considerable significance when confessions were regarded as the weightiest evidence of all. Punishments in criminal cases were usually savage and excessive, often involving corporal punishment. Costs in civil cases were such as to make contesting a case out of reach of all but the very rich.

The reforms initiated in 1864 were remarkably far-reaching. Lower courts were established to deal with minor offences. These were to be presided over by magistrates appointed by the local zemstva. A proper hierarchy of courts was set up and appeals from the magistrate's courts could proceed all the way up to the Senate, which retained its function as the highest court of appeal. Properly trained judges were to be appointed, highly paid so as to reduce the temptation to accept bribes, and they were to be appointed for life in order to make them independent of government influence. Accused persons would now meet their accusers and judges face to face, evidence could be challenged, and equality before the law meant that witnesses would be judged on the merits of their evidence and not on their personal status while the accused would be guaranteed a fair trial regardless of rank. Trial by jury, widespread in western and central Europe, was introduced, although with the innovation that majority, rather than unanimous, verdicts were required. Although the voting of the juries was to be secret the proceedings of the courts were to be public for the first time, and it was hoped that if the new Russian justice was *seen* to be done, it would gain public respect. Some of the savagery, too, was taken out of the law. Corporal punishment was mostly swept away, and the transfer of preliminary investigations from police to magistrates reduced, but did not remove, the risk of brutality and forced confessions.

It is easy to belittle these reforms by pointing out their limitations. Church courts, military courts and peasants' courts were outside the new system, and the military courts

66 Reform of the law possibly more revolutionary than serf Emancipation. 99

were soon increasingly used to try political offenders. The independence of the judges was undermined to the extent that they relied on government patronage for promotion, but this is an unavoidable characteristic of most judicial systems. Jury verdicts by majority are, within limits, now acceptable. Flogging was still retained in the army, in the Siberian penal colonies, and in some peasants' courts. But these limitations should not detract from the great success of the new system. The Russian Bar was established with Alexander's consent, and this provided skilled lawyers for prosecution and defence and for promotion to judge's rank. Public interest in court proceedings and attendance at them grew rapidly. Court cases were widely reported in the Russian press, and insofar as many of the cases were political, defence lawyers' criticisms of the régime secured widespread publicity. Alexander himself, and his successors, were to pursue reactionary policies which undermined the new system. Except in the handling of political offences, the inroads they made were small and often marginal, and the high reputation of Russia's judicial system was to continue until 1917. It even secured the grudging admiration of Lenin, himself a lawyer.

## INDUSTRIAL PROGRESS

One of the main aims behind the emancipation of serfs had been to create a free labour force for employment in the cities. Not that there was a great deal of native industry to make use of such a force, but during Alexander's reign, large spinning mills grew up in the Moscow and St. Petersburg areas, using cotton from Turkestan and benefiting from Britain's difficulties during the American Civil War to establish effective competition with the British. Many of the mills were actually British owned, and British capital and enterprise began to exploit the coal and iron from the Donets region, and to turn the oil production of the Baku area from the primitive production of hand-digging to the more lucrative returns from mechanical oil-wells. Railway expansion using foreign capital and expertise saw an expansion during the reign from about 1,000 miles of track to about 14,000 miles of track – even so a small mileage for so vast a country so late in the century.

## POLAND

When, during the years 1772–1795, the kingdom of Poland had been destroyed, Russia had been the chief, but not the only, beneficiary. Possession of much of Poland gave Russia military security in the west, and gave Russia lands which had never been Polish in character – the Western Ukraine, and much of White Russia and Lithuania. Polish patriotism had not died in 1795, and concessions made to it by Napoleon in 1807 and by Alexander I in 1815 had not satisfied those of the old Polish nobility who dreamed of restoring to independence not just the areas of Polish nationality, but the vast Empire Poland had possessed before 1772. For them, the measure of self-government Alexander gave to the Grand Duchy of Poland was not enough. In 1830–31 they had challenged Russia with a major rebellion, fought with great bravery, but lacking adequate armies and foreign assistance they were inevitably beaten. Poland's punishment was the attempt by Nicholas I to extinguish Polish nationalism. The University of Warsaw was closed and Russian was declared the official language. The cause of Poland went underground, but it was always a minority cause. The Polish peasants hated their grasping and repressive Polish landlords as much as they hated their Russian conquerors, and their support for independence was lukewarm at most.

The Emperor Alexander's message to the Poles at his accession had been a bitter disappointment:

The happiness of Poland is to be found in complete fusion with the peoples of my Empire.

And twice he repeated the phrase *No dreams*. It is not surprising that Polish patriots thought the time right for another attempt to break away from Russia. Alexander was a reformer, but he offered little hope to Poland. Yet the Crimean War had weakened Russia, and the Italian patriots were already showing what could be done in liberating their country from an oppressor. Protests and processions by Polish patriots were met by Russian troops armed with bayonet and rifle, weapons the troops were quite prepared to use. Rebellion became widespread in January 1863, but lacking the army they had possessed in 1830 the Poles were forced to resort to guerrilla warfare, and the peasants generally did not take part. Hopes of foreign intervention proved optimistic, and Prussia signed a Convention with Russia which in effect closed the Prussian frontier to Polish refugees.

**Polish and Russian liberals unable to co-operate.**

Hopes of support from Russian liberals were not justified; nearly all the leading liberal groups rallied to the Emperor – the Polish Revolution turned them all into patriotic Russians! It took 80,000 Russian troops eighteen months to completely crush the revolt, but the Poles had never really had much chance. To make matters worse their divisions between the *Whites* and the *Reds* had weakened them even further. The Whites had the support of the liberal nobility and wanted to restore the Poland of 1772; the Reds wanted Polish independence secured by radical social change. The only thing the two groups had in common was hatred of the Russians.

The gradual collapse of Polish resistance gave the Russian government an opportunity to end the tentative reforms in Poland, to Russianize the Warsaw Medical school, to restore Russian as the official language and to ban the use of Polish in secondary schools. They also divided Poland into provinces of Russia, subject to the direct rule of St. Petersburg. But the Polish peasants benefited too; their allotment of land under the Edict of Emancipation was increased and the compensation paid to the gentry kept small, so that in effect the Polish peasantry gained freedom from serfdom – except in the Grand Duchy of Poland where serfdom had not been restored in 1815 – with much more generous terms than the peasants of Russia. It was a reward for their indifference during the rebellion, but freed from the oppressions of their nobility the Polish peasant, too, would soon begin to play a more active role in Polish nationalism.

**4 ▷ FOREIGN POLICY**

## THE CRIMEA AND AFTER

Apart from minor territorial losses in the Caucasus, the main punishment inflicted by the Allies upon Russia for losing the Crimean War was to demilitarise the Black Sea. This meant that Russia was forbidden to maintain fortifications on the Black Sea coasts, or to have a Black Sea fleet. It was Alexander's intention to reverse this humiliation at the earliest opportunity and when in 1870 France and Prussia engaged in the Franco-Prussian War, Bismarck bought Russian neutrality by encouraging Russia to repudiate the Black Sea clauses. France was in no position to protest, Prussia was sympathetic, and it was left to Prime Minister Gladstone of Britain to complain that if the Russians wanted to modify the terms of the Treaty of Paris they should have done it by going through the proper channels i.e. a conference of all the Treaty of Paris signatories. Britain's protest was ignored and Russia's restored strength in the Black Sea meant that Russia was once again in a position to play a vital role in the Eastern Question.

## TERRITORIAL EXPANSION

The check administered to Russia's westward ambitions by defeat in the Crimean War caused Russia to adopt her usual policy of turning to the East. During Alexander's reign the Russian frontier was extended southwards to the borders of Persia, Afghanistan and Chinese Turkestan. Russian settlement had reached the Pacific in the seventeenth century, but in Alexander's reign Amur and Ussuri province on the borders of Manchuria were taken and confirmed to Russia by treaty with China in 1860, and in the same year the port of Vladivostok was founded. This, together with the taking of Southern Sakhalin in 1875, was to sow the seed of the future quarrel with Japan. Only in America did Russia draw back. The promise of future profits to the Russian American Company was set against the need for immediate capital for railway development and the Russians sold Alaska to the USA in 1867 for a mere $7,200,000. Money may not have been the only reason for this. Alexander was not keen to see the new Dominion of Canada (1867) succeed, and the sale of Alaska to the USA would help to hem it in. A direct conflict with Britain's interests also occurred in Afghanistan; the Russian attempt to take Afghanistan under its protection in 1878 led directly to British intervention there (see Chapter 5) from which neither the British nor the Russians eventually emerged with much credit.

## THE EASTERN QUESTION, 1875–78

While Russia turned its attention eastward after 1856, major changes were taking place in Europe. The emergence of a united Italy and a united Germany reduced the need for Russia's participation in the 'Concert of Europe', and prepared the way for a new system of alliances. Bismarck, the political leader of the new Germany, had used the friendship of Russia as a stepping-stone to German unification, and hoped to retain this friendship after 1871. In 1872 the Emperors of Germany, Austria-Hungary and Russia signed the

*Dreikaiserbund*, the League of the Three Emperors, an informal verbal agreement to keep socialism in check and to act in concert on major international issues, particularly the Eastern Question. The League was of five years' duration and was renewed in 1877. But Bismarck had ended Austria-Hungary's role in Germany by war, and if throwing the Habsburgs out of Germany was to be regarded by Austria-Hungary as the lenient treatment historians have always claimed it to be, then Bismarck would have to give active encouragement to Habsburg ambitions elsewhere. This could only mean the Balkans, where Alexander II was by no means ready to give up Russia's role of protector of the Slav peoples of the Balkans, nor to abandon Russia's territorial ambitions there, with the ultimate prize of Constantinople and access to the trade routes of the Mediterranean.

" Familiarity with a map of the Balkans is essential here – see page 196 "

In 1875 a revolt broke out in Bosnia. The Austrians were alarmed at disturbances so close to their frontier, especially as the Slavs of Bosnia were being assisted unofficially by Serbia. If a much enlarged Serbia were to result, Habsburg territorial ambitions in the Balkans would be effectively blocked. Attempts by Germany, Austria and Russia to contain the revolt by demanding from the Turks concessions to the revolutionaries proved ineffective. The revolt spread to other areas of the Balkans, including Bulgaria. Here the Turks tried to re-establish control by a policy of massacre. Alexander had no desire for war, but when the Serbs and the Montenegrins went to war with Turkey, ostensibly on behalf of the Bulgarians, public opinion in Russia was universal in its support. Thousands of Russians joined the Serbian army as volunteers, while Alexander met the Austrian Emperor and agreed not to intervene unless it became absolutely necessary. Further pressure was put on the Sultan to make concessions, while the Great Powers including Russia disclaimed any territorial ambitions against Turkey. The Turks even introduced a parliamentary constitution in order to play for time, but Russian patience became exhausted and Alexander declared war on Turkey in April 1877.

The Russian army entered Turkey at the end of June. The army reforms of Alexander had not yet taken effect and the Russian advance was slow. The Turks defended the vital fortress of Plevna with great skill and tenacity, but its capture, with the aid of a major contingent of Romanians, allowed the Russians to by-pass the Turkish defensive lines. The Russians had already captured Adrianople when the Turks asked for an armistice in January 1878. Rumours that the Russians intended to advance on Constantinople caused the British to send a fleet there *to protect British citizens*, even though the Russians declared that they were quite capable of protecting all Christians in Constantinople should the need arise. British suspicion of Russian ambitions was intensified when details became known of the treaty signed at San Stefano in March between Turkey and Russia. Increases in territory for Serbia and Montenegro, and independence for Romania had been widely expected. But the huge Bulgaria, although agreed in the armistice, was unacceptable to both Britain and Austria-Hungary. Such a state, with huge national minorities, would be so dependent upon Russia as to make it almost a Russian dependency. The Russian army of 50,000 men could well need to stay in Bulgaria to protect the infant state for more than the stipulated two years, and the continued presence of a Russian army so close to Constantinople would pose a threat to peace.

The Russians had often announced their willingness to submit the Eastern Question to a conference of the Great Powers, and the understanding between the members of the Dreikaiserbund gave them a moral obligation to do so. Pressure from Britain, in the form of warlike speeches and the sending of troops to Malta, angered the Russians, but it was Bismarck's insistence that the Treaty of San Stefano should be revised, while Russia was sorting out the essentials of the settlement with Austria, which persuaded Alexander to agree. If the Tsar hoped for any support from Bismarck as payment from Russia's pro-Prussian policy in the 1860s, he was to be disappointed. In the real negotiations before the Congress of Berlin, Bismarck sided with Britain and Austria. Austria emerged in permanent occupation of Bosnia and Herzegovina, Britain acquired Cyprus, Bulgaria was broken up and partly restored to Turkey. Although Russia regained most of her territorial losses of 1856, including Bessarabia and Batum, Russian policy had suffered a major setback. Russia had received a diplomatic humiliation, and Alexander was furious with Germany and regarded the Dreikaiserbund as having collapsed, especially when Germany signed a formal alliance with Austria in 1879. Bismarck could not repair the damage with Alexander, although he had some temporary success with Alexander III in 1881. In Russia, the foreign policy failure could not have come at a worse time. Patriotic and Pan-Slav sentiment united the country in 1877–78 and isolated the Nihilists, but after the Congress of Berlin the widespread sense of failure helped further to estrange Alexander from his people and to encourage the resort to terrorism.

## 5 ❯ REACTION, REPRESSION AND TERRORISM

Alexander was not an enthusiastic reformer. His reform programme seemed to him to be a necessary step towards the revival of Russia after defeat in war. But he was quite unwilling to do anything to compromise his own authority, and it is not surprising that Russian liberals were disappointed in his failure to introduce parliamentary institutions and to place a limit on his own autocracy. No sooner were the reforms begun, when attempts were made by the government to curb extravagant hopes of further change by weakening the reforms themselves. The Polish revolt seemed to Alexander to have been largely brought about by those who believed that reform was a sign of weakness. He felt obliged to continue his reform of local government and the army, but from the mid–1860s Alexander became increasingly reactionary.

As the government tightened its grip, the opposition was undergoing a profound change. Russian liberals no longer dominated it. As the reforms ground to a halt the liberals seemed to have no programme of action which could force the Tsar into further concessions. So other groups came to the fore. The *narodniks* claimed to speak for the *narod* – the people. The peasants, who were the vast majority of Russians, were to be the spearhead of a spontaneous revolution in which full personal liberty and freedom of speech and press would lead to a kind of optimistic socialist Utopia. Narodnik propaganda flooded the country from secret presses, and the government felt obliged to take action. Press censorship was tightened, and demonstrations and meetings were increasingly interfered with or forbidden. When a student attempted to assassinate the Tsar in 1866 the universities were placed under close government supervision. Staff and students became liable to instant dismissal and teaching was scrutinised in order to detect subversive propaganda. Persecution led many of the narodniks to adopt *Nihilism*, the belief that in the new society *nothing* should be allowed to survive from the past, and that nothing should be created in its place which was not based on science and reason. This meant that the Nihilists were absolutely opposed to Tsardom and religion, that they expected their new society to be born out of violent upheaval, and they were prepared to resort to violent methods to achieve it.

To these new revolutionaries the peasants were a disappointment. Although they sometimes expressed their grievances in spasmodic rioting, especially as disillusionment with Emancipation became widespread, the peasants were too illiterate to respond to the intellectual appeal of Anarchism and Nihilism. And if they had good reason for hating the landowners they had an almost touching respect and reverence for their 'Father', the Tsar. He naturally regarded terrorism as a crime rather than a 'legitimate' political activity. He punished political murder with hanging, and subversive political activity with exile to Siberia, where he sent almost a quarter of a million of his subjects during the course of his reign. The terrorists responded with attacks upon his life. They attempted to justify such action in their underground literature.

 **Terrorists or liberators?**

> Political murder is primarily an act of vengeance . . . under existing conditions political murder is the only means of self-defence and one of the most effective methods of propaganda. By striking at the very centre of the government it shatters with terrible force the entire system.

The secret society known as *The People's Will* passed sentence of death upon the Tsar in 1879 and set out to put the sentence into effect. Some attempts were farcical; others costly in human life. An attempt to blow up the royal train led to the destruction of the wrong train with many innocent victims. Alexander was unable to win the support of the zemstva against terrorism because he was unwilling to establish an elected parliament. But in 1881, Alexander agreed to a national conference of zemstva whom he could consult on a purely advisory basis. He seemed to be looking for active co-operation with the zemstva, and a move towards some form of constitutional government without in fact giving up any of his autocratic power. Whether it would have achieved anything if it had ever met remains doubtful, but a few days after he signed the decree establishing it his carriage was blown up in a bomb attack, and he died a few hours later.

# I D E A S   A N D   P R I N C I P L E S

| | |
|---|---|
| **Anarchists** | Those who believe in the overthrow of all existing forms of government, and look to an ideal form of society in which government is unnecessary. Violence may be necessary to eliminate the existing forms of government, which are in themselves coercive and therefore violent, but in the new society violence will cease to exist. |
| **Autocracy** | Government by one person whose power is unlimited. The term usually applies to an absolute monarchy, but can also refer to a dictatorship. |
| **Concert of Europe** | The informal links between the rulers of the major states to try to maintain the peace of Europe by consultation and agreement. This particularly applies to the period after the collapse of the Congress System and up to the development of the major alliance systems of the late nineteenth century. |
| **Emancipation** | The freeing of slaves or serfs, by which they acquire personal freedom and legal rights. In a wider sense, of course, it means the freeing of anyone, e.g. the emancipation of women. |
| **Mir** | The long-established village commune or co-operative system whereby heads of households among the Russian peasantry decide on and allocate what work is to be done and when it is to be done. In 1863 the mirs became responsible for the collection of redemption payments. They could often be very effective as a focus of resistance to agricultural change. The word *mir* means 'world' – some indication that the Russian peasant regarded the *mir* as a virtually universal system. |
| **Nihilists** | Similar to anarchists, but basing their new society on reason and science rather than vague idealism, and particularly committed to terrorist methods to destroy the evils of existing society. |
| **Serfdom** | A system of personal slavery in which the serfs had no personal or legal rights and in which they were usually, although not always, tied to the land by labour services. |
| **Zemstva (singular zemstvo)** | Local councils, created by Alexander II by decree in 1864. The zemstva covered all the rural areas of European Russia. The municipal councils which were set up in the major towns in 1870 had similar powers to the zemstva. |

# A P P L I E D   M A T E R I A L S

## BOOKS

PEACOCK, H. L., (1971). *A History of Modern Europe, 1789–1970*. Heinemann. Chapter 14.
ROBERTS, M., (1986). *Britain and Europe, 1848–1980*. Longman. Chapter 3.
STOKES, J. & G., (1973). *Europe and the Modern World, 1870–1970*. Longman. Chapters 4 and 7.
WATSON, J. B., (1981). *European History, 1815–1941*. Murray 1981. Unit 14.2.

## DOCUMENTARY SOURCES

BREACH, R. W., (Ed), (1964). *Documents and Descriptions in European History, 1815–1939*. Oxford.

**AUDIO-VISUAL**

Alexander II        Audio Learning HUA045 (advanced).

# E X A M I N A T I O N   Q U E S T I O N S

**1**  a)  Why did Alexander II undertake a programme of reforms?
   b)  How far were the people of Russia satisfied with these reforms?

**2**  a)  What is meant by referring to Tsar Alexander II as the 'Tsar Liberator'? How fully
       did he deserve this title for his work?
   b)  Give an account of his other domestic reforms up to 1870.
   c)  In what major European war did he find himself at the beginning of his reign? How
       did he bring this war to an end?                                         (LEAG)

# O U T L I N E   A N S W E R S

**1**  a)  The two parts of the question will carry approximately equal marks. Note that a) is
       asking for *reasons* and not a reform narrative. It would not be easy to suggest that
       Alexander was a reformer by conviction, especially in view of his reactionary
       background, but it could be argued that he was by inclination less repressive than
       Nicholas I, and only adopted full-scale repression later in his reign out of necessity.
       So it would be better to look for the reasons as arising out of a response to Russia's
       needs. Alexander in emancipating the peasants may well have been influenced by
       peasant disturbances and Russia's economic needs, but he was aware that slavery
       lacked moral justification, that liberal opinion condemned it and that the peasants
       themselves had for a long time regarded emancipation as inevitable and imminent.
       The other reforms were in part a consequence of the impetus of Emancipation, but
       they each had their own justification e.g. army reform necessary after the Crimean
       War failures, judicial reform because of the universal lack of confidence in the
       existing system. Each major area of reform will therefore require separate
       treatment.
   b)  This is not asking whether they were satisfied, but *how far* they were satisfied.
       Peasant grievances about the emancipation land settlement should be developed.
       Apart from this it is worth pointing out that dissatisfaction was expressed only by an
       activist minority. In particular they resented the Tsar's failure to follow up his
       reforms with the introduction of parliamentary institutions, and his unwillingness in
       any way to compromise his autocracy. In so far as their disillusionment with the
       Tsar resulted in agitation and violence, so the Tsar responded with whittling away at
       the reforms already granted and becoming more repressive, thus adding a new
       cause of dissatisfaction, and alienating more of his subjects. The failure of the
       Zemstva to condemn terrorism, despite the Tsar's express request, is a useful
       yardstick in measuring the extent of hostility towards the Tsar. The famous
       acquittal of Vera Zasulich in 1878 was greeted with enthusiasm by enormous
       crowds and even some senior officials, even though she had undoubtedly seriously
       wounded the military governor of St. Petersburg. Terrorism was for a minority of
       activists, but sympathy with it was certainly becoming widespread in the major
       towns, if not in the countryside.
**2**  a)  Basically his reputation as Liberator rests on his Emancipation of the serfs, but you
       will need to explain the change in the personal status of the former serf, and more
       particularly you will need to elaborate on details such as the redemption payments
       and arrangements for allocation of peasant plots in order to assess the Tsar's title.
       In return for personal freedom the peasant was burdened with enormous debt and

allocated inadequate land. Your assessment of the Tsar's merit to the title is therefore likely to be a qualified one. *(maximum 7 marks)*

b) The narrative request here is likely to be rare in GCSE. You should cover as wide a range of reforms as possible, and make some attempt to assess their effectiveness if you are to attain the highest level. The limiting date of 1870 is a consequence of the sectionalisation of the LEAG Syllabus, but virtually all Alexander's worthwhile reform was completed by 1870. *(maximum 8 marks)*

c) The limiting date of 1870 prevents a question on the whole of Alexander's foreign policy, so the Crimean War only is asked for. Alexander's recognition of the need for peace and his willingness to enter into negotiations will be needed as well as a discussion of the main terms of the Treaty of Paris. Note that this sub-question does *not* ask for the fate of the Black Sea clauses in 1870. *(maximum 5 marks)*

# A STUDENT'S ANSWER WITH EXAMINER'S COMMENTS

'Alexander II was a failure both at home and abroad.' How far would you agree?

> The biographical background of his early life is not very relevant. No failure or success is high lighted although there is some implication of success in family life and in Siberia.

> Here the technique is not very good although there is useful knowledge. The judgment of the first line should come at the end, not at the beginning, and a catalogue of reforms should indicate success/failure by how effective they were or how long lasting. It is not true to say that he abolished conscription. It was in fact extended, although the ballot system meant that only one in four would have to serve.

> The comment required in the previous paragraph has been presented separately here. It would have been better to have put the evidence and comment together, but this is quite useful although a little thin on the peasant question.

Alexander was born in 1818, and the poet Zhukovsky took charge of his academic education; he is believed to have given Alexander his concern for the common people, and to have made sure that he learned foreign languages and history. As a young man Alexander visited Siberia and was so shocked by the conditions of prisoners and exiles there that he did something to improve them when he became Tsar. He married for love and had eight children, but later he took a mistress. Like his father he was fond of military uniform and display.

At home it would be untrue to say he was a failure. He liberated the peasants and made sure they were given allocations of land. He introduced local councils called zemstva and these achieved a great deal in setting up hospitals and schools and in keeping the roads in repair. He abolished conscription and allowed peasants to become officers in the army, and he reformed the judicial system, introducing trial by jury and equality before the law, and making sure that the judges were worthy to hold office. He so reduced censorship of the press that newspapers were able to print virtually what they liked, and he encouraged the development of universities and allowed them to teach subjects which had previously been forbidden.

Some of these reforms were very successful. The peasants were grateful for their freedom, and although they often rioted against the local landowners, they were always loyal to the Tsar and a great disappointment to the extremist agitators who tried but failed to recruit them. The zemstva survived until the revolution and did a great deal to improve the condition of the people, and the law courts achieved under Alexander and his successors a respect which they previously had lacked. Army reform went part of the way towards providing Russia with an army that was modern and efficient.

In foreign affairs Alexander had his disappointments, but it is not a story of continuous failure. The terms of the

Treaty of Paris which ended the Crimean War in 1856 deprived Russia of territory in Bessarabia and the Caucasus which Russia was to recover in 1878. The Black Sea clauses of the Treaty were cancelled by Alexander in 1870, largely as a result of the friendship between Prussia and Russia, a friendship that had helped to isolate the Poles in 1863, making their rebellion a nuisance rather than a danger. Alexander's greatest humiliation came with the Congress of Berlin in 1878. But Alexander could hardly have expected the great powers to allow Russia to dominate the Balkans: Russia did emerge with increased territory, a further weakening of Turkey and a grateful Bulgaria. While this was going on Russia was advancing virtually unchecked southwards through Asia. If Russian ambition was temporarily halted in Afghanistan Russia had the satisfaction of knowing that Britain had been unable to establish permanent influence there either.

So Alexander was not a complete failure. He has gone down in History as the 'Liberator'. Reform movements and terrorism were very much the work of a minority. Alexander might have done better to encourage reform and suppress terrorism, instead of trying to stamp out both. But I suppose a man who gets himself assassinated after trying to do so much for his people cannot really expect to be remembered as a success.

> This is better. Here the evidence and comment are offered together, and the judgment that Alexander failed abroad is effectively qualified. The section is, however, a little brief.

> There is certainly an attempt to put forward a point of view. More could be offered on terrorism and reform movements. Avoid the first person (I) in history essays.

# SUGGESTIONS FOR FURTHER WORK

1  Write a) an obituary for Alexander in 1881 as it might have appeared in a widely circulating Russian newspaper of the time, and b) another obituary as it might have appeared in one of the revolutionary underground newspapers of the period.
2  Find as many reasons as you can to explain why the vast majority of Russians were so poor during Alexander's reign.
3  Explain the main aims of Russian foreign policy during the Years 1855–81. To what extent were these aims achieved? In so far as Russia failed to achieve some of these aims, why was this?
4  Some historians think that Alexander's failure to continue with his policy of reform made revolution inevitable. Do you agree? Give reasons for your answer. (Tip: to answer this you will need to look at the whole of Russian history from 1855–1917, and not just confine yourself to Alexander's reign.)

# ITALIAN UNIFICATION

# GETTING STARTED

Italy had been a geographical area rather than a nation ever since the Middle Ages. For long periods it was subjected to foreign rule by France, Spain and Austria in turn, and then most recently France again, with Napoleon I cast in the role of liberator. As 'liberator' of Italy, Napoleon is often credited with being the creator of modern Italian nationalism, and if intensifying patriotic hatred of the foreigner is nationalism, then Napoleon does deserve some credit for it. His welcome as a liberator was shortlived. He exiled Italy's spiritual leader, the Pope, and although he created the first kingdom of Italy in modern times, he took care to annex substantial areas to France. What was left became a kingdom for one of his former marshals, Murat, whose portion of Italy called itself the Kingdom of Naples, but was in fact little more than one of France's vassal states. Murat's effort to restore Napoleonic Italy during the Hundred Days led to his own execution, but probably created very few nationalists.

Although Napoleon's Italy was a nation-state only in name, the Congress of Vienna, by attempting in part to put the clock back to 1789, seemed even more insensitive to Italy's needs and hopes. Strengthening Italy's only Italian monarchy, Piedmont, by adding the decaying Republic of Genoa to it, made sense. But Austria was given a stranglehold on Italy, not only by the restoration of Lombardy but by keeping Napoleon's gift (1797) of the Republic of Venice and by installing the Austrian Emperor's relatives in the central Italian Duchies of Parma, Modena and Tuscany. Thus Italy was restored to Austrian influence, with that influence strengthened. Moreover, the restoration of the reactionary Ferdinand to the backward Kingdom of Naples gave Austria an important ally in keeping Italy weak and divided, and the Pope's return as temporal ruler of a large area of Central Italy merely emphasised that weakness.

# HISTORICAL DEVELOPMENTS

**1** **THE
BEGINNINGS OF
ITALIAN
NATIONALISM**

66 Political activists had
local rather than national
aims. 99

At first, Italians reacted to their condition after 1815 by adopting liberalism and demanding constitutional government. Those actively engaged in political activity soon found themselves harassed and persecuted, and took to the hills. They kept warm at nights by burning charcoal fires, and so became known as 'Carbonari' (Italian for charcoal-burners). Their common name did not give them a common aim or a common organization; each state and province had its own Carbonarist bands who had few links with Carbonari of other areas. Some were political idealists, others were little more than outlaws and criminals. In the Kingdom of the Two Sicilies (Naples) those not engaged in full-time banditry demanded a parliamentary constitution from Ferdinand. Similar constitutional demands were made in Rome and in Piedmont. In the central Duchies and in Venetia and Lombardy the main aim was to get rid of the foreigner, i.e. Austria. Despite their internal divisions and their frequent inability to separate political from criminal activity, the Carbonari did rather well. In Naples in 1820, Ferdinand was forced to make concessions which he could only cancel by calling upon Austrian military assistance on a large scale. In Piedmont, the Carbonari forced King Victor Emanuel I to abdicate before they were suppressed by his successor, again with Austrian help. In 1830, however Carbonarist division and weakness speedily led to the collapse of their revolts in the Papal States and central Duchies, and convinced Giuseppe Mazzini that the aims and methods of the Carbonari were inadequate for Italy's needs.

## MAZZINI AND YOUNG ITALY

Mazzini founded his 'Young Italy' movement in 1831. Unlike most of the Carbonari, members of Young Italy aimed to create a unified Italian state. Thus Mazzini, rather than Napoleon, was the founder of Italian nationalism. The very name Young Italy showed that the movement was aimed at Italian youth and within a few months its followers numbered tens of thousands. Mazzini was not too worried about the obstacles in the way of unity. The Pope was spiritual leader of the Roman Catholic church, but was also the temporal ruler of the Papal States, and Mazzini assumed that his territories would be swallowed up by the new Italy. When Mazzini failed to persuade Charles Albert, King of Piedmont, to head the movement for unity, Young Italy attempted to overthrow Charles Albert, and its failure led to savage reprisals and Mazzini's enforced exile from Italy. From that moment, in 1833, Mazzini had become a convinced republican, committed not only to the expulsion of Austria from Italy, but also to the removal of all Italian princes, including the Pope and Charles Albert, from their thrones.

66 Similar aims, but
differing methods. 99

Mazzini's adoption of republicanism proved to be unfortunate. Conservative and monarchist elements in Italy, although supporting unification, hated the thought of republicanism and its companion socialism. They thought that Italy needed a *respectable* leader. If Charles Albert was not ready to lead his country, then who could be more respectable than the Pope? He was Italian, and had the spiritual allegiance of all Roman Catholics, whether Italian or not. Moreover, any attempt by nationalists to deprive the Pope of his territories in Italy might lead to intervention on his behalf by foreign Catholic powers. Any attack on him would give them a marvellous excuse for it, whereas the Pope as head of a united Italy might well be the best solution. There was, of course, the snag that the Papal States were very backward and reactionary, and so were the Popes. They might be ready to defend the Church against such vandals as Napoleon, but they were not prepared to embark on a dangerous struggle for Italy. Even when the writer and philosopher Gioberti appealed directly to the Pope in 1843, Gregory XVI ignored his plea. His successor, Pius IX (1846–78), seemed more promising. He was reputed to be a liberal. He began his reign by releasing political prisoners, announcing judicial and economic reforms, and ignoring Austrian protests. Upon him seemed to rest the hopes of Italy during the crisis years of 1848–49.

**2** **THE FAILURE
OF 1848–49**

If the Italians were to achieve unity, they were divided on *how* to achieve it. Liberals were suspicious of Mazzini; conservatives detested him. Royalists pinned their hopes on Charles Albert, devout Catholics looked to Pius IX. But too much was expected of the Pope. He enjoyed the public admiration that his reform plans had earned him, but he shrank from the vigorous action necessary to expel the Austrians from Italy. Events moved too fast for him. Tobacco tax riots in Milan were followed a week later by a successful rebellion in Naples which forced a constitution on the reluctant Ferdinand II. Renewed rebellion in Lombardy forced the Austrian General Radetzky to retreat behind the fortifications of the Quadrilateral. At this point, prompt action was essential, as Austria was paralysed by the fall of Metternich and riots in Vienna. The Pope did nothing, but Charles Albert, having granted his people a liberal constitution, placed himself at the head of the Italian movement and after a few crucial days of delay, declared war upon Austria. The Pope agreed to allow Papal troops and volunteer civilians to join Piedmont, but would not, as spiritual leader of the Catholics, declare war – especially on Austria, regarded by Pius as one of the main bulwarks of the Faith. Charles Albert entered Milan amid scenes of wild enthusiasm, but when he attacked the Quadrilateral in July, Radetzky defeated him at Custozza and forced him to sue for an armistice. Excited mobs in Rome, angered by the Pope's unwillingness to commit himself and his recall of the Papal forces who were on their way to the front, murdered the Pope's Prime Minister, Count Rossi, and established a Roman Republic. In March 1849 the Romans welcomed Mazzini as their leader. But it was too late. Charles Albert made one final effort in the same month but was beaten at Novara. After a spirited resistance, the Republican leader of Venice, Daniel Manin, was driven out in July 1849, and although Mazzini was strengthened by the help of the adventurer Garibaldi and his men, his overthrow was not long delayed. Ferdinand of Naples, who had regained his own throne with Austrian help, tried unsuccessfully to take Rome, but the forces of General Oudinot of France proved too powerful, and the Pope was restored to Rome by French troops in June 1849. To the bitter disappointment of most Italians 1848–49 had seen the strengthening rather than the weakening of the foreign hold on Italy. Only a minority concerned themselves with the fact that Italy had failed to achieve unity.

Although the military skill of Radetzky and the intervention of the French had been vital in this disaster to Italian hopes, much of it was of Italy's own making. Pius IX had failed Italy at the crucial moment, and through the rest of his long reign he remained a political reactionary, horrified and frightened by the events of 1848–49. Devout Catholics could no longer look to the Pope for political leadership. Neither could they look to Young Italy. Mazzini's Roman Republic was to them the worst kind of blasphemy and they equated Republicanism with bloodshed, extremism and atheism. Only Charles Albert had emerged with any credit, even though his initial hesitation in March 1848 had been crucial. Not only had he fought for Italy, he had refused to buy better terms for Piedmont by abandoning the constitution, and he had shown his willingness to accept the blame for failure by his abdication. To the small but growing group of nationalists the new King of Piedmont, Victor Emanuel II, seemed to be Italy's best hope, but he could hardly be called a nationalist. He aimed at strengthening Piedmont and removing Austria from Northern Italy, but he did not wish Piedmont to be saddled with the poverty and lawlessness of the Italian South, and neither could he see any way to remove the Pope from Rome without provoking French and possibly international intervention. And here Victor Emanuel's views were little different from those of his rapidly rising minister, Count Camillo Cavour.

 Distinguish between unification and the ending of foreign domination.

### 3 CAVOUR AND THE STRENGTHENING OF PIEDMONT

Despite his aristocratic background, Count Camillo Cavour had strong liberal sympathies, which he had demonstrated in the newspaper he founded in 1847. His newspaper, *Il Risorgimento* (meaning the resurgence or revival), was concerned with the revival and strengthening of Piedmont and the removal of foreign influence from Italy. It soon gave its name to the whole movement for Italian unification, thus crediting Cavour with ambitions for Italy in excess of his hopes and plans.

The first step towards strengthening Piedmont had been legislation to curb the power of the church. Cavour's reward for his support of this legislation was to be given his first government post as Minister of Agriculture in 1850. From here he had secured rapid promotion to the Prime Ministership in 1852, and it is not surprising that the Pope viewed his appointment with some concern. Cavour continued to reduce the power of the Church, but he was also involved with the economy, introducing Free Trade, building a railway network, and establishing banks to promote industry and agriculture through investment. His interest in trade led him to encourage the development of a merchant navy, making the establishment of a royal navy necessary for its protection. But above all he strengthened Piedmont militarily by the expansion and modernization of the Piedmontese army. It was left to Piedmont's neighbours to speculate whether Piedmont's enormously increased military expenditure was intended purely for defence.

## PIEDMONT AND THE CRIMEAN WAR

The Piedmontese army was certainly the envy of the British and French governments, whose own armies were bogged down in the Crimea. Both Britain and France tried to persuade Piedmont to join them in a war against Russia in which Piedmont had no direct interest. Victor Emanuel was flattered by so much attention from the great powers and was prepared to demonstrate Piedmont's growing power and self-confidence by taking part. Cavour was not so sure. But Austria, at whose expense Piedmont hoped to dominate Northern Italy, had carefully kept out of the war, and Cavour hoped that Piedmontese participation would win the gratitude of Britain and France while they were still irritated by Austria's neutrality. Cavour's willingness to buy a diplomatic advantage with the lives of Piedmontese troops aroused much opposition in the Piedmontese parliament, and although Cavour was able to use Piedmont's right as a belligerent to speak out at the peace conference against the Austrian presence in Italy while the Austrian delegates as horrified observers had no right of reply, Cavour came away from the Paris peace conference in 1856 with no more than expressions of sympathy from Britain and France.

**4 > ORSINI AND PLOMBIÈRES**

Eighteen months passed, during which time it seemed that the Piedmontese soldiers were sacrificed in vain in the mud and snow of the Crimea. Felice Orsini, Italian patriot and revolutionary, shared Italian disappointment, and showed it by his decision to assassinate the French Emperor Napoleon III. Orsini's bomb killed several in the crowd near the Paris Opera, but Napoleon was unhurt. Not surprisingly, the outrage concentrated Napoleon's mind on the Italian Question. He had already conducted secret negotiations with Cavour, and perhaps fear of another attempt on his life urged him on. After all he had once been a member of a Carbonarist group, and had a genuine interest in the Italian cause especially if it could be made to serve the purposes of France.

> **Note the limited nature of Cavour's aims.**

Napoleon and Cavour held a secret meeting at Plombières in the summer of 1858. Cavour aimed to secure French help in expelling the Austrians from Northern Italy, and possibly as far south as the Duchies. Napoleon aimed to please the French liberals by helping the Italian cause, and to please the French conservatives by winning a successful military operation in Northern Italy in imitation of Napoleon I and against the old enemy Austria, and by continuing to give public support for the Papacy. It was agreed that France should help expel the Austrians, provided Austria could be tempted to go to war against Piedmont. In return for helping Piedmont secure Northern Italy, Piedmont should give up to France the predominantly French-speaking areas of Nice and Savoy. No change was to take place in Southern or Central Italy, although the Pope might be compensated for losing some of the most northern parts of the Papal states by becoming President of a loose federation of the enlarged Piedmont, the Papal States and the Kingdom of Naples. This concession to Italian unity was marred by the fact that both Cavour and Napoleon knew that the Pope was most unlikely to accept the role thus cast for him.

**5 > THE WAR OF 1859**

In the event it did not prove too difficult for Cavour to provoke a war with Austria. The Austrian armies were slower to mobilise than those of Piedmont, and once Cavour had managed to engineer some frontier incidents the Austrians began to put their armies on a war footing. Britain suggested a general European Congress to discuss the Italian Question to which France agreed with alacrity and Piedmont with reluctance. Austria suspected such a congress would have as its main purpose the dismemberment of Austria, and refused to agree to such a meeting unless all sides agreed to disarm. This was Cavour's opportunity; in his reply to the Austrian ultimatum of April 1859 requiring Piedmont to disarm within three days he linked the proposed European congress with the question of disarmament, and concluded:

> The conduct of Sardinia on this occasion has been appreciated by Europe. Whatever may be the consequences that it may produce, the King, my august Master, is convinced that the responsibility will rest with those who were the first to arm (i.e. the Austrians), and who have rejected the propositions formally drawn up by one great Power (i.e. Great Britain), and recognized as just and reasonable by others, and who now substitute for it a threatening summons (i.e. the ultimatum).

> **Cavour makes the best of a shaky case.**

So Cavour placed the blame upon Austria. Austria declared war, and even managed to win a few of the early skirmishes. But with the aid of Piedmont's excellent railway network

200,000 French troops soon drove the Austrians back into Lombardy, and Napoleon achieved his desired military glory in the bloody battles of Magenta and Solferino in June 1859. However these victories liberated only Lombardy. If the Austrians were to be expelled from Venetia, the main Austrian defences of the Quadrilateral would have to be tackled. Napoleon had been appalled at the bloodshed of Solferino, yet an attack on the Quadrilateral would be even more costly. Moreover the Italian campaign had not united his people behind him. Catholics were worried about the threat Napoleon's Italian policy posed to the Pope, conservatives had reservations about the wisdom of a war against Austria. Prussia, too, was a problem. Although Prussia had no intention of joining the war, Napoleon could not be absolutely certain of Prussia's neutrality, and some innocent Prussian troop movements near the French frontier kept him guessing. Whatever the reasons, Napoleon seemed to have had enough of the war. He contacted the Austrians without Cavour's knowledge and signed a truce at Villafranca in July 1859. The Austrian Emperor handed over Lombardy to France, and Napoleon promised to transfer it to Piedmont.

Before the terms were made permanent in the Treaty of Zurich, November 1859, Cavour resigned in disgust, his plans for Northern Italy in apparent ruins. Although the Zurich Treaty revived the idea of a Papal Federation of all Italy, the Pope refused to take part, especially when he found out that France proposed to reduce substantially the size of the Papal States. Neither were the Duchies of Tuscany, Parma and Modena keen to continue under the rule of their Habsburg princes. Amid popular excitement the princes were overthrown and the Duchies demanded union with Piedmont. There is no doubt that Cavour's agents had helped to stir up the trouble in the Duchies; their union with Piedmont would help to compensate for the failure to acquire Venetia. But the situation required skilled diplomatic handling. There was a danger that Austria would consider any change in the status of the Duchies a breach of the Treaty of Zurich, and a renewal of the war might undo what had already been achieved. But Napoleon III did not want war; he wanted territory, and his failure to complete his promise of Lombardy and Venetia meant that he could not justifiably claim Nice and Savoy. He now expressed a willingness to see the Duchies incorporated into Piedmont after the population had expressed their approval by a plebiscite. Austria could not very well resume the war if France was backing Piedmont and Britain was giving Piedmont diplomatic support. Cavour quickly reclaimed office, agreed to surrender Nice and Savoy to France, and confidently awaited the results of the plebiscites. These provided huge majorities for union with Piedmont. Italian nationalists were not very pleased with either Napoleon or Cavour: Napoleon they regarded as cynically taking advantage of Italy's problems to gain Nice and Savoy, and Cavour's exchange of Nice and Savoy for the Duchies they regarded as unforgiveable. For the moment, however, Cavour was able to meet the new parliament of the enlarged Piedmont in April 1860 in a much happier mood than when Piedmont had been deserted by France eight months before.

## 6 ▷ THE KINGDOM OF NAPLES AND THE PAPAL STATES

Cavour had always kept in touch with the main nationalist groups, either directly or through his agents. But this did not mean that he was committed to the principle of unification. His first loyalty was to Piedmont and King Victor Emanuel, and he did not wish to see a unification in which Piedmont would be absorbed by Italy, or an attempt made on the Papal States or Naples which would lead to the intervention of the Catholic powers and a reversal of the progress made in 1859–60. So it was with mixed feelings that Cavour heard of the attempts of Garibaldi to raise volunteers to fight against the King of Naples. Garibaldi was an adventurer, reputedly with Republican leanings, who was certainly not concerned to protect the interests of Piedmont. But he had many connections and was widely admired, both in Italy and abroad. Cavour was under pressure from Nationalists both in Piedmont and elsewhere. As Garibaldi's planned expedition began to gather in the Piedmontese port of Genoa, Cavour was all things to all men. Publicly he denounced Garibaldi – this would please Austria and Naples and was in diplomacy strictly correct. But secretly he gave the expedition his approval – this would please the Nationalists and their foreign sympathizers such as the British. Deep down, he wondered how damaging an attack on Sicily and Naples would be – if Austria intervened then Piedmont's cause as well as that of Italy could well be lost. At least if Garibaldi failed, as Cavour half expected him to, and half hoped he would, no blame could be attached to Cavour. It would mean that Cavour would be rid of Garibaldi for ever, and that he would no longer have to pander to Italian nationalist sentiment, most features of which he despised. If on the other hand Garibaldi

**❝❝Cavour's deviousness.❞❞**

succeeded, then Cavour would have to see what benefits could accrue to Piedmont from the new situation.

Garibaldi's expedition sailed in May 1860 and was an unexpected success. The incompetence of the Neapolitan troops, their alleged confusion of the Redshirts with British troops, and the curious proximity of two British warships paralysed the defence. As fresh volunteers flocked to join him, Garibaldi defeated the defenders at Calatafimi and Sicily was his in less than two months. He prepared to cross the Straits of Messina to attack the Italian mainland. Cavour was alarmed, both at Garibaldi's unprecedented popularity and his ambitious plans. Was Garibaldi intending to challenge Piedmontese leadership in Italy by setting up a Southern Italian Republic? And what was to happen to the Papal States? Cavour confided in a letter:

> On the one hand, we must at all costs prevent Garibaldi from passing on to the mainland, and on the other we must provoke a revolution in Naples. If this succeeds, the government of Victor Emanuel would be proclaimed without delay.

In August 1860 Garibaldi crossed the Straits and was in Naples within a month. By now, Mazzini had joined him and Garibaldi's refusal to hand over his conquests to Victor Emanuel could mean to Cavour only one thing – that the two leaders intended to create a Republic in southern Italy. In such circumstances, Austrian intervention seemed inevitable, especially if there was any threat to the Papal States, and Garibaldi was only a few miles from the Papal frontier. To do nothing was certain to lead to disaster, so Cavour decided to take action. He sent the Piedmontese army into the Marches and Umbria – the eastern provinces of the Papal States – promising to steer well clear of Rome. This promise satisfied Napoleon and made isolated action by Austria unlikely. The Piedmontese forces easily defeated the Papal army at the battle of Castelfidardo, and swept round to the south-west of Rome, reaching the sea north of Naples and blocking Garibaldi's route to Rome. He had been held up by Neapolitan resistance on the Volturno river.

> **" Cavour's most difficult problem yet. "**

The Piedmontese parliament declared the union of Garibaldi's conquests to the Piedmontese kingdom and ordered immediate plebiscites which confirmed this to be the wish of the inhabitants. Garibaldi had been outmanoeuvred. He had no choice but to accept the situation gracefully. Five days after the plebiscites in Southern Italy (October 1860), he met Victor Emanuel near the front line, and a few days later joined him in a triumphant victory parade through Naples. Afterwards, Garibaldi retired to the island of Caprera, although the world had not yet heard the last of him. The first parliament of the newly united Italy met in Turin in February 1861, and the Kingdom of Italy was proclaimed in the following month. Now, even Cavour publicly admitted that Italy was incomplete without Rome, but his sudden death in June 1861 deprived Italy of its greatest statesman while he was still desperately needed.

## 7 > VENETIA AND ROME

> **" It is important not to credit Cavour with any of this. "**

While the eyes of all Italian Nationalists were fixed on Rome, Cavour's successors showed how out of tune they were with Italian sentiment by imprisoning Garibaldi for an attack on Rome in 1862, and by transferring the capital from Turin to Florence in 1864. In 1866, Italy offered Austria neutrality in the coming war with Prussia in return for Venetia. Austria refused, and changed its mind too late when it discovered that Italy had signed an alliance with Prussia. Italy kept its part of the bargain and launched its troops into Venetia when war broke out between Prussia and Austria, but Italian forces were heavily defeated. Nevertheless Italy's participation forced Austria to defend on two fronts and Austria was defeated by Prussia in six weeks. Italy received the promised reward of Venetia, but as a gift from Prussia, and not as Italy would have wished it, as a conquest from Austria.

Now only Rome remained. Once again Garibaldi, in 1867, attempted to take it by force. He failed to dislodge the French troops who were protecting Rome, and Napoleon III remained resolute in his commitment to prevent Rome from falling into Italian hands. But France went foolishly to war with Prussia in 1870. Soon Napoleon needed his Rome garrison urgently at home, and in September 1870, General Cadorna moved his Italian troops into Rome as the French moved out. Italian unification was virtually complete, even though there were Italian populations still under Austrian rule in the Tyrol and in Istria.

## 8 > POSTSCRIPT

Italy was not united in the way the ardent Nationalists had planned. Mazzini had not got his republic; Garibaldi had not become Italy's political leader. Piedmont, which wanted to dominate the North, had ended by absorbing the South and Centre, and Cavour had

❝❝ You need to develop the ideas in this paragraph in depth, if you are studying Italy after 1871. ❞❞

achieved by 1861 what he had never dreamed of in 1859. After the achievements of Cavour and Garibaldi, the solution to the problem of Venetia and Rome was merely a matter of time.

But unification brought as many problems as it solved. The seizure of Rome caused the Pope to retire into his palace in the Vatican and to refuse all co-operation between Church and State. He forbade Roman Catholics to take part in politics in the new kingdom, and although the conflict between Church and State was more muted than their public attitudes would lead one to suppose, relations between the two remained strained until 1929. Cavour had doubted the desirability of prosperous Piedmont being saddled with the poverty-stricken South, and the contrast between North and South was no less marked, now that the two were united in one kingdom. Italian politicians tried to tackle the problem of Southern poverty, but could make little impression on it. Moreover Italian politics exhibited more corruption than was good in a country aiming at democracy. The corruption in politics seemed an additional justification of the aloof attitude of the Church, and helped to prevent a democratic tradition from taking root. The greatness of Italy was held back by political incompetence, economic weakness, and the fact that Italy had arrived late as a newcomer to the ranks of the great powers. Many Italians equated lack of greatness with lack of colonies. Italy resented its exclusion from Africa, expecially when France took the coveted Tunisia in 1881. Failure in Abyssinia in 1896 was partly balanced by success against the Turks in 1911, but Italy pinned her expansionist hopes both in Europe and elsewhere on the First World War. Italy's war-time sacrifices were severe and rewards at the peace conference were meagre. It is not surprising that Italian disappointment helped to pave the way for the rise of Mussolini.

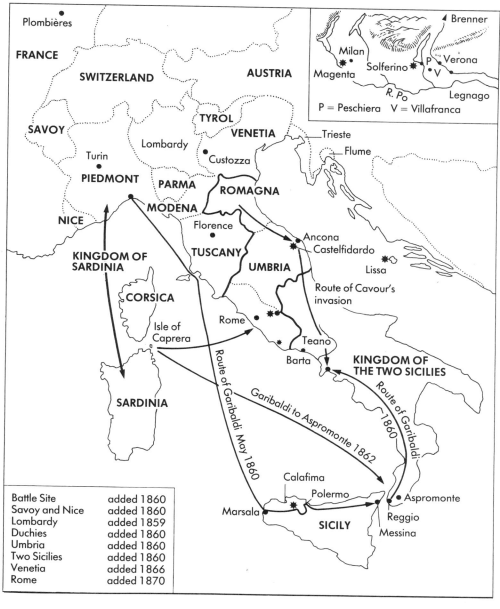

| | |
|---|---|
| Battle Site | added 1860 |
| Savoy and Nice | added 1860 |
| Lombardy | added 1859 |
| Duchies | added 1860 |
| Umbria | added 1860 |
| Two Sicilies | added 1860 |
| Venetia | added 1866 |
| Rome | added 1870 |

Fig. 12.1 Union of Italy 1859–70

# IDEAS AND PRINCIPLES

**Abdication** — The action of a hereditary ruler in giving up or renouncing his throne.

**Constitutional government** — See Chapter 10

**Federation** — A union of several states, with each state retaining important powers of self-government.

**Liberalism** — See Chapter 10.

**Nationalism** — See Chapter 10.

**Neutrality** — The policy of keeping out of a war.

**Patriotism** — Love of one's country, i.e. state.

**Plebiscite** — A vote by the electorate on a specific issue put to it.

**Temporal and spiritual** — Temporal refers to matters relating to *this* world, spiritual refers to matters of the *next* world (i.e. the life hereafter). These terms, in the context of Italy, almost invariably refer to the Papacy. The Pope was temporal ruler (i.e. political ruler) of the Papal States, and spiritual ruler and leader of the Roman Catholic Church.

**Ultimatum** — A demand from one state to another, usually backed by threat of war.

# APPLIED MATERIALS

## BOOKS

PEACOCK, H.L., (1971). *A History of Modern Europe.* Heinemann. Chapter 10.
ROBERTS, M., (1986). *Britain and Europe 1848–1980.* Longman. Chapter 4.
WATSON, J.B., (1981). *European History 1815–1941.* Murray. Unit 7.

## DOCUMENTARY SOURCES

ALBRECHT-CARRIE, R., *The Concert of Europe.* Harper and Row (1968), Topic VI.
Wallet, Jackdaw, *Garibaldi and the Risorgimento.* Cape.
LEEDS, C., *The Unification of Italy.* Wayland.
ROBERTS, M. *The Unification of Italy.* Wayland.

## AUDIO-VISUAL

Italian Unification     Audio Learning HMO.

# EXAMINATION QUESTIONS

1  a) Explain how i) Mazzini ii) Garibaldi and iii) Cavour helped to bring about the unification of Italy.
   b) Which of these men made the most important contribution to the unification? Give reasons for your answer.

2  Account for the failure of the Italian revolutions of 1848–49.

# OUTLINE ANSWERS

**1**   The question is not asking for a simple *description* but for an *explanation*. Thus while it may well gain useful credit to offer a narrative of the work of each of them, higher marks (i.e. a higher Level) can only be achieved by a more discriminating approach.

   i)   Mazzini was an idealist. His practical ventures were all failures: he met disaster in Piedmont in 1831, his Roman Republic was overthrown in 1849. Yet it was he who created the first truly nationalist and nationwide organization in 1831, and once Italian nationalism had been awakened there was very little chance of it being put to sleep again.

   ii)   Garibaldi was Italy's hero. He was the successful adventurer who took the path politicians were too cautious to tread. His liberation of Sicily and Naples forced Cavour to abandon the rather restricted aim of a Piedmontese dominated North, with possibly a Papal federation of the whole country, and to replace it with a Piedmontese absorption of Central and Southern Italy. But Garibaldi was no politician. His expertise was in the military not the diplomatic field. His plans for Naples seemed more likely to create disunity than to promote unity, and his later attempts to conquer Rome were embarrassing failures.

   iii)   Of the three, Cavour was the professional. He was a shrewd politician and statesman. He was single-minded in his determination to promote the interests of Piedmont and to harness the forces of nationalism for that purpose. He was less enthusiastic about a united Italy. Thus he *initiated* the policy of strengthening Piedmont and expelling the Austrians from Italy, while the acquisition of the Centre and the South resulted from policies he did *not* specifically initiate. His tight-rope diplomatic skill saw him in 1860 fending off foreign intervention with honeyed words on the one hand, while fuelling with feigned encouragement the hopes of the nationalists on the other. Good statesmen are usually good opportunists. Cavour certainly was.

   b)   Here comparative assessment is required. You have to make a *balanced* judgment as to which of these men made the most important contribution to Italian unity. You might think that without Mazzini nationalism would have been a far less powerful force, or that without Garibaldi the Centre and South would never have united with the North. But without Mazzini nationalism might have been held back temporarily but not stifled for ever, and before Garibaldi even thought of an expedition to Sicily in 1860 there was much talk of unity or federation, and there was a certain ring of inevitability about it. So you might conclude that it was Cavour who made it all possible. He bundled the Austrians out of Italy with the aid of the French; he prevented Italian hopes being wrecked by foreign intervention; he, willingly or not, determined the *course* of the unification. You might like to argue it differently. Any attempt to argue it will gain good credit, and the examiner will not penalise you if his views differ from yours provided that you make your points effectively.

**2**   This is a *reasons* question, and those aiming at high marks should be prepared to offer a number of reasons for the failures of 1848–49. It is vital that you do not offer a narrative answer to this sort of question. It may well be that your narrative contains hints of relevant reasons within it, but it is not the examiner's responsibility to sort out and focus your material for you, and such an answer no matter how well informed could at best achieve only one of the lower grades.

   Note that the question is asking for failures, and here lies much of the clue to the answer. The crisis of 1848–49 was not, except for the few committed nationalists, an attempt to bring about Italian unity. In each part of Italy the aim was different, and the result was a number of failures, rather than a failure for Italy as a whole. Piedmont wanted Lombardy and Venetia, but both these provinces were more concerned to get rid of the Austrians rather than become part of some enlarged Piedmont or federation. Lombardy was very late in looking for union with Piedmont; the Republican leader of Venice, Manin, never did. Mazzini's Roman Republic seemed to have achieved its main object in removing the Pope, and in Naples the aim was to remove tyrannical government rather than fight for a united Italy. Thus disunity was an important but not the only reason for failure. You will be able to develop a number of points: the lack of foreign assistance, the dangerous early delays by Charles Albert, the unwillingness of the Pope to commit himself, the defensive strength of the Quadrilateral, the military competence of the Austrians, especially Radetzky. The divisive nature of Mazzini's Roman Republic, and French intervention there will help to show that for the Italians there were still several roads to unity, and this constituted a major weakness.

# A  TUTOR'S  ANSWER

Read this French document of April 1859, and then answer questions a) to e) which follow:

Piedmont occupies an important position in the European system, and Piedmont has shown herself worthy of this position by the care which she has always taken to improve her internal condition. The British Cabinet should remember this, in our joint efforts to persuade the other states of Italy to consider the wants and wishes of the populations, the progress made by Piedmont is much to be admired. England and France cannot forget . . . the support which Piedmont has given to our policy in the recent war against Russia. From all these considerations the support of England would seem to be due to Piedmont in the struggle which is about to commence.

a) How does this French document attempt to persuade the British Cabinet to join France in support of Piedmont?
b) What phrase in the text refers to Italian nationalism?
c) 'The struggle which is about to commence' was the Franco-Austrian War which occurred in 1859. How did this struggle increase the hopes of Italian nationalists for unity?
d) Show how, from 1860–70, Italy continued to advance towards unity.
e) How far in the 30 years after 1870 did Italy become a truly united country?      (SEG)

a) The French comments on Piedmont's 'internal condition' are a reminder to Britain that Piedmont was the most progressive of the states of Italy at this time, that Piedmont had a constitutional form of government unique in Italy, and that the British government and people were admirers both of Piedmont's political and also her economic progress. Moreover Piedmont's assistance in the Crimean War was invaluable, and Britain owed a debt of gratitude to Piedmont which now Britain was in a position to repay.

*(4 marks)*

b) 'The wants and wishes of the populations'.

*(1 mark)*

c) The taking of Lombardy from Austria was one step towards the removal of the foreigner from Italy and thus a step towards unity, but more importantly the defeat of Austria was a successful blow against one of the main obstacles to unification, and Austria would be less willing and less able to defend the existing division of Italy if it should be again challenged.

*(4 marks)*

d) The defeat of Austria removed the restraining hand from Italy. The Duchies of Central Italy refused to return to their own allegiance, and Cavour, by buying French support with Nice and Savoy, was able to acquire the Duchies in 1860 without fear of Austrian intervention. The Kingdom of Naples, too, always seething with revolt, took the opportunity to break out into open rebellion, even though Francis who succeeded 'Bomba' in 1859 had none of the sadistic taste for punishing rebels that had given his predecessor his reputation. The Neapolitan monarchy had outlived its usefulness, it could no longer rely on Austrian protection and its people preferred to be part of an Italian constitutional state, rather than remain sufferers under a Bourbon despotism. The international climate was thus favourable for Garibaldi's expedition; even Cavour dared not openly oppose it, and British sympathy for the Italian cause was such that no-one knew whether the British warships that appeared at crucial moments were merely chance observers or possible belligerents. Cavour viewed Garibaldi's success with mixed feelings, but he could not allow the establishment of a separate Italian republic in the South. He gambled on Austrian weakness, British sympathy and French uncertainty when he by-passed Rome in his bid to acquire Garibaldi's conquests for Piedmont.

When this succeeded without foreign intervention (except for the French occupation of Rome itself) the acquisition of Venetia and Rome was merely a question of the right opportunity. Austria had her hands full defending her position in Germany in 1866, and this was much more important than defending her position in Italy where Austrian influence had been shattered in 1859. So Venetia became Italian while Austria grappled with the consequences of defeat both in Germany and Italy. Now only France was willing to take on the international duty of defending the Pope's temporal possessions in Italy. But France, too, had at a time of crisis to defend Paris rather than Rome, and so in 1870 Rome at last became Italian, and unification was almost complete.

*(8 marks)*

e) In September 1870 Italy seized Rome and Italy's capital was transferred there in 1871. Unification was almost complete; the incorporation of the Italians of Istria and the Tyrol into the new kingdom remained a hope and aim for the future. Italy at least had geographical unity, a unified system of government, with a king to focus Italian allegiance and a parliament of all Italy to conduct national policies. But while Italy gave the outward appearance of unity there was much internal division. Politically the Neapolitans objected to the introduction of Piedmontese law, taxation, administration and justice. Many of them looked upon Piedmont almost as a foreign state. They wanted to keep their own way of doing things, and strenuously objected to centralisation. Economically the North was much richer than the South, and efforts to expand the economy of the South had met with little success by 1900. The cultural differences between North and South reflected not only the economic differences but also several hundred years of separate development, and many regarded the South as more Spanish than Italian, a consequence of centuries of Spanish rule. Differences in dialect became less important with the development of widespread education, but cultural differences remained. The greatest apparent evidence of disunity was the refusal of the Church to recognize the new Italian state and the Papal injunction on the faithful to refuse to take part in Italy's political life. Fortunately for Italy most Catholics found it possible to disobey the Pope and live with their consciences, and particularly after the death of Pius IX in 1878 the next Pope was willing to take a much more relaxed attitude towards the new state unofficially than he was prepared to do officially. So Italy's internal weakness and division should not be overstressed; the religious problem was a nuisance rather than a handicap, and the North/South divide is not unique to Italy. In view of the weakness and corruption of Italian governments after 1870 it is surprising that the Italian state held together at all, unless the internal divisions were not really as serious as they have sometimes been painted. The growth of trade unions and the rise of socialism cut across provincial separatism. Certainly in Italy as in other countries social divisions rather than geographical ones seemed the greater threat as the twentieth century approached.

*(8 marks)*

# SUGGESTIONS FOR FURTHER WORK

1 Give the sort of advice you think Cavour would have received from various sources when he was considering
   a) what attitude to take to the request of the Duchies to join Piedmont;
   b) what attitude to take to Garibaldi's planned expedition to Sicily;
   c) what attitude to take to Garibaldi's refusal to hand over his conquests to King Victor Emanuel.
2 Write *brief* biographies of Mazzini and Garibaldi. Encyclopedias will give you the best help. List the main similarities and the main differences between the character and aims of the two men.
3 On a map of Italy number in sequence the territories acquired by Piedmont during unification, and put in the appropriate dates. Write a brief note on the acquisition of each to attach to the map. Mark in the Quadrilateral, and name and date the major battles occurring during the years 1848–70.

## GETTING STARTED

A sense of German unity went back to Napoleon's days. German national sentiment did not die after 1815 even though, under the influence of Metternich, tyrannical government became the norm there. Because of Metternich, the movement was largely frustrated before 1848, but after that time it began once again to gather momentum.

Early in 1848 revolutions broke out in Italy and France, and soon spread to Germany and the Habsburg Empire. The Empire's laboriously-constructed but fragile framework carefully preserved by Metternich was destroyed almost overnight, and the effects spread rapidly to central Europe. In Vienna, Metternich abandoned his desk when the Viennese populace hammered at his doors. He escaped with false papers to grateful anonymity in England, while revolution spread through the entire area.

# HISTORICAL DEVELOPMENTS

1 › **THE 1848 REVOLUTIONS IN GERMANY**

**❝❝Austria after Metternich. ❞❞**

## THE AUSTRIAN EMPIRE

The lands ruled by the Emperor Ferdinand suffered six almost simultaneous revolutions, in Vienna, Milan, Venice, Budapest, Zagreb and Prague. The Hungarian revolution posed the most serious threat. The Magyar aristocracy demanded a separate constitution and equality with Austria. This claim would not have been so bad if Hungary had been peopled entirely by Magyars, but they were in a minority in their part of the empire, and were unwilling to grant to their subject peoples the rights that they claimed for themselves. Nonetheless, they enacted the *March Laws*, giving their legislative assembly a semi-sovereign status, and forced Ferdinand to agree to their terms. Vienna was paralysed by revolutionary disturbances. Its government was in the hands of a succession of ramshackle cabinets, and its streets in the hands of the mob. The Emperor was in no position to argue with Hungarian leaders, and was expelled from the capital and forced to take refuge in Innsbruck, surrounded by courtiers, but powerless to do much more than observe the course of events.

Meantime, trouble was brewing in Prague, where a Pan-Slav Congress representing several Slavonic nations met in the summer of 1848, but the Congress broke down with bitter infighting between the groups of delegates. There was fighting, too, in the Hungarian provinces, where the Magyars were engaged in suppressing other nationalities, apart from their own. In the Carpathians, the Magyar national leader, Louis Kossuth, himself of Slovak extraction, was sending Slovak leaders to the gallows to be hanged by what they called 'Kossuth's neck-tie'. In the south, the Slavs of Croatia, and the Romanians of Transylvania were also demanding their rights. Around Zagreb the trouble flared most seriously. The Governor of Croatia, Count Jellacic, himself a Croat, took control of the national movement to fight the Magyars. He summoned a Croatian Diet and enrolled troops to fight for the province's freedom. The Hungarian government suspended him from office, but the Emperor gave him his backing and he returned in triumph to Zagreb. He was given the command of all imperial forces in Hungary, and at the head of an Austrian and Croatian army he moved towards Budapest. By the end of the year, the Habsburg Empire had disintegrated completely under the various nationalist pressures.

**❝❝A Liberal episode.❞❞**

In Vienna, a Constituent Assembly, elected for the first time by universal suffrage, tried to create a parliamentary system under radical leadership. The Assembly was largely German in composition; the Czechs elected were more interested in national independence than in making the system work. They did not enjoy the confidence either of the ruling classes, or of the imperial army, and were often at the mercy of extremists, who established (on the French revolutionary pattern) a 'Committee of Public Safety' and an Academic Legion, a sort of National Guard, largely composed of students. Many Viennese Germans were more interested in supporting the Frankfurt Liberal Parliament, called in May 1848 to express the country's wishes for a unified and strengthened national parliament.

## GERMANY

**❝❝Prussia. ❞❞**

In 1847, a Prussian United Diet had met in Berlin, but was soon suspended by the King, Frederick William IV. But since then German liberals had not been idle; in September they held a conference in Heppenheim, and in Heidelberg the following March demands were renewed for the calling of a German National Parliament to speak for the whole nation. Frederick William IV yielded to popular pressure by abolishing press censorship and calling the United Diet together again, promising a constitution. Disturbances in Berlin, however, continued. The barricades were erected in the streets and the king withdrew to Charlottenburg, removing his troops from Berlin. His younger brother, the future William I, known as the 'Cartridge Prince' because of his fondness for the use of bullets, was all in favour of a show-down, but the king cherished a sentimental regard for the national cause and wished to profit from it as much as he could. He even agreed to the formation of a popular National Guard in Berlin, and appeared on horseback in the streets, wearing the red, black and gold sash of the Holy Roman Empire in his pose as *Deutscher Kaiser*. He claimed:

I have assumed today the old German colours, and have placed my people under the revered banner of the German Empire. Prussia's interests shall henceforth be those of Germany.

Perhaps unsurprisingly, German liberals regarded his conversion with suspicion.

**The German Liberal Parliament.**

Meantime, in response to the Heidelberg demands, steps were taken to ensure the summoning of a *Vorparlament*, popularly elected to consider the best way of creating a united Germany. This body met in April and arranged for the election of a National Parliament, whose function was to draw up a constitution for the whole country. This National Parliament met in May in Frankfurt, taking up its premises in the Pauluskirche close to the building where the Diet of the 1815 Bund held its meetings. Consisting at first of about 300 members, its numbers eventually swelled to about 550, and debates were launched as to the future form of Germany.

The discussions achieved little. Most Germans regarded it with suspicion, believing that it was an opinionated and self-elected body without proper legal foundations. It was natural that its membership consisted largely of professional doctrinaires, journalists and lawyers, all anxious to make their mark on the proceedings. The result was that much time was wasted on an elaborate declaration of rights, with the trivial and the grave being discussed at equal lengths; discussions were not completed until Christmas. The only useful thing accomplished was the appointment of a Habsburg prince, Archduke John, to be *Imperial Vicar*, a sort of Regent or Provisional President until the Constitution was finalized. But the weaknesses of the Liberal Parliament were never overcome.

There were serious divisions over the future form of the government, and these proved hard to resolve. What were to be the future limits of Germany? Was it to include non-German peoples as well as Germans, or was it to be racially 'pure'? Was it to include the lands of the Habsburg Empire, many of which were not German at all, or only the German parts of this Empire? Was it, in other words, to be a *Big Germany* or a *Little Germany*? Who was to be its new leader, Austria or Prussia? Was it to be a Republic, as many radicals desired, or a Reich, the form favoured by sentimentalists and conservatives? Furthermore, because of its uneasy legal status, it lacked any very real powers. Though it had a Habsburg Prince as its Head of State, and a vocal middle-class backing, it had no armed forces to enforce its will and hesitated to tax the German nation in case they refused to pay. Besides, the two great German powers Austria and Prussia staged a miraculous recovery in 1849 and put paid to Liberal hopes. But the immediate cause of the decline of the Frankfurt Parliament was the Schleswig-Holstein question of 1848–49.

**The Schleswig-Holstein Question.**

Danish kings for some time had been trying to incorporate the Duchies of Schleswig and Holstein into the Kingdom of Denmark, and this attempt was renewed by Christian VIII just before his death in 1848. The Diet of Holstein, however, appealed to the Frankfurt Parliament, the self-appointed guardian of German national feeling. German liberals found this plea difficult to ignore. Unfortunately they lacked an army, but Frederick William IV of Prussia took up their cause and ordered his troops into the Duchies. Threatened by a European coalition he drew back, ordering his troops to withdraw. The Frankfurt Parliament foolishly tried to countermand his orders, but proved unable to deflect Prussia from agreeing with the Danes the Convention of Malmoe, whereby the King withdrew his forces from Denmark in return for a promise from the Danes not to press ahead with their amalgamation plans. The signature of this agreement produced furious reactions in Frankfurt. Liberal politicians protested, and nationalist mobs rioted in the streets. By the end of 1848 public confidence in the liberal Parliament, already undermined by this episode, was beginning to ebb away.

**2 ▸ THE COLLAPSE OF THE REVOLUTIONS**

**The revival of Austria . . . .**

Though the military might of the two great German powers Austria and Prussia had been temporarily disabled by the events of these revolutions, neither was really smashed, and both showed remarkable powers of recuperation. In Italy, Marshal Radetsky had defeated Piedmont at Custozza and had gone on to crush the rebels in Lombardy, recapturing Milan and re-establishing Imperial authority throughout the area. The Austrian general Windisch-grätz meantime crushed Prague, then turned south against the capital, Vienna. When Jellacic moved into Hungary and war broke out between Austria and Hungary there was a new rising of the radical populace of the capital, who, showing support for the national claims of the Hungarians, sided with them against their own royal family, recently returned from exile in Innsbruck. The Minister of War, Latour, was murdered, and the Emperor once more forced to flee, this time to Olmütz in Moravia. The veteran Napoleonic hero Josef Bem was given command of the city's forces and fortified the city against the Imperial army, with help from the Hungarian forces advancing on Vienna. But Jellacic from Hungary, and Windischgrätz from Bohemia, converged on the city, defeated the relieving Hungarians, and forced Vienna to surrender.

Politically, too, the German Empire began to revive. Late in November, Prince Felix Schwarzenberg was appointed as Imperial Minister. Though he had the broad support of the reactionary party, Schwarzenberg was something of a radical, with little respect for tradition or the aristocracy. His main objective was to restore Austria's greatness by defeating the Hungarians. In December he persuaded the incompetent Ferdinand to abdicate and to hand the throne to his eighteen-year-old nephew Franz Josef. He promptly refused to accept the Hungarian Constitution, and declared the Austrian Empire indivisible. Windischgrätz invaded Hungary, occupied Budapest and defeated the Hungarians at Kapolna. However, their forces rallied and under the rebel general Görgei, won a series of victories against the Austrians, declaring themselves independent, with Kossuth as Governor. This was a serious error; Tsar Nicholas I, who feared the effects of a declaration of independence on the turbulent Poles, declared against it and in May moved his troops into Hungary, smashing Hungarian independence at Vilagos. Kossuth fled into exile in Turkey; Görgei and twelve other rebel generals were hanged, and Austrian control was restored. Austria was now well on the road to a complete recovery. Charles Albert of Piedmont was defeated at Novara by Radetsky in March 1849, and was forced to abdicate in favour of his son Victor Emanuel II. Only Venice held out. Attacked by land and by sea, and with cholera raging in the city, the Venetian Republic collapsed and at the end of August 1849 the Austrians celebrated their triumph with a solemn *Te Deum* in St Mark's Cathedral.

The revolution in Germany fared little better. Already, the appointment of Count Brandenburg at the head of a reactionary ministry in Berlin in November 1848 had shown where Frederick William IV's true sympathies lay. Shortly after, the decision of the Frankfurt Parliament to confine the lands of the new Germany to those which were ethnically German produced protests from the Austrians, who wished to preserve the integrity of Habsburg territory. The Frankfurt Assembly then excluded Austria altogether, which pleased them even less. Austrian participation in the discussions at Frankfurt ceased, and the Austrian delegation was withdrawn. The Assembly therefore turned to Frederick William IV, who was offered the title of Kaiser in March 1849, and the crown of a United Germany. Frederick William was naturally timid and conservative; to accept the throne of a Germany which deliberately excluded Austria would almost certainly produce a war with the Habsburgs. But more importantly, he believed in the divine right of kings, and was reluctant to accept a throne given by the hand of the people. In April, he spoke of 'picking up the crown out of the mud' and would 'wear no crown of shame'. The Frankfurt Assembly regretfully agreed that its constitution for Germany was not acceptable, and, accepting the inevitable as gracefully as it could, in June declared itself dissolved.

With the liberal parliament out of the way, Frederick William could pursue his conservative ideas of German unification. He called a conference to discuss a new constitution based on the idea of a 'College of Kings', but found Schwarzenberg, who was concentrating on fostering the suspicions of other German rulers of Hohenzollern ambitions, unwilling to support it. So, the king formed with Saxony and Hanover the League of the Three Kings (Dreikönigsbund) for an alternative union under Prussian leadership. It was not suggested that this Union be compulsory; like the Zollverein, it was hoped that states would want to join. Many of the smaller states would have joined, but Frederick William's main allies discovered he was trying to fool them. He recently had suggested a share-out of power in Germany to Austria along the lines of the old Federal Bund; the powers surrendered by Archduke John when he resigned the regency were to be divided between Prussia and Austria according to what became known as the 'Compact of the Interim'. Saxony and Hanover objected to this inconsistency, and withdrew from the Dreikönigsbund, forming instead a Vierkönigsbund (League of the Four Kings) with Würtemberg and Bavaria. Frederick William now had the support only of the minor states, and although he called them together in a new German Parliament at Erfurt in March 1850, they could not give him sufficient backing. The other German states, distrusting Prussia, were turning to the traditional leadership of the Austrians, and Schwarzenberg, now with many of his domestic troubles happily behind him, was able to provide the lead they needed. A crisis in Hesse-Cassel gave him his opportunity. Its ruler had recently annulled the constitution given to his people in 1848, and his subjects appealed to the Prussian League to prevent this. Frederick William was in a cleft stick; if he rejected their appeal, his League would collapse; if he took up their cause, there would be a war with Austria and

**...and Prussia.**

**The end of the German Liberal Parliament.**

Prussia might be defeated. Not for the first time he baulked at the challenge. Austrian and Bavarian troops intervened in Hesse and subjugated it. The King of Prussia was forced in October 1850 to accept the *Convention of Olmütz* (sometimes for obvious reasons called the *Submission* of Olmütz) by which the 1815 Confederation under its traditional Austrian leadership was to be restored, and the German Union of Erfurt, under Prussian leadership, was to be dissolved. The Prussian initiative collapsed.

**66 The Humiliation of Olmütz. 99**

The reasons for the failure of the 1848 revolutions are easy to identify. They were supported by a fairly limited portion of the population, the bourgeois. The bulk of the nobility opposed them, and the vast mass of the ordinary peasantry remained resolutely conservative. Karl Marx sized the opportunity to issue his famous appeal to the German proletariat in his *Communist Manifesto,* but in a largely pre-industrial era there was little backing for it. The liberal movements in the various state capitals were not co-ordinated, and were often at odds with one another. The central organ, the liberal parliament in Frankfurt, wasted many months in constitution-mongering and when tested was found to lack political muscle. It had no armed forces, and it lacked financial resources and the determination to impose taxes. Germany's powerful neighbours, like Russia, proved to be hostile to the movement. Finally, the two great military powers – Austria and Prussia – though temporarily eclipsed by the events of 1848 showed remarkable powers of recovery. Their ruling classes stuck together, and the discipline of their armed forces proved tough and durable. The utter collapse of the revolutions seemed to vindicate conservative thinking; it also went a long way towards discrediting popular liberalism in the second half of the nineteenth century.

**3 > PRUSSIAN POLICIES, 1850–62**

After Olmütz, Schwarzenberg aimed to use Austrian ascendancy in the Federal Bund to transform it into a real instrument to rule Germany. The Head of the Prussian delegation to the Diet, Count Bismarck, resisted this, and claimed for Prussia a veto over proposals which his government disliked. For instance, he refused to accept an Austrian plan to maintain a federal navy, and forced the Diet to auction it off. He also repeatedly claimed a veto over many other kinds of federal legislation, even though, as in the case of proposals extending press censorship, he might have approved of the laws themselves. The German federal assembly in the 1850s has generally been considered to have been hopelessly inefficient over matters relating to trade, coinage, insurance, weights and measures, and a host of others. But if this accusation were true, it was almost entirely because of Bismarck's policies of blocking the way to reform through an extension of the powers of the old Bund. Prussia preferred to use special agreements between states i.e. treating the states as sovereign instead of as federal members.

**66 Bids for leadership. 99**

In the later 1850s German national sentiment approved of Prussia's efforts to keep their country out of Austrian control. By 1859 there was a *National Society* and a liberal *Coburg-Gotha Party* amongst the princes, to further the *Kleindeutsch* ideal. (This was the one favoured by Prussia.) At the same time, almost by chance, Prussia was going through a liberal phase. In 1857 Frederick William IV finally went insane and his brother William was appointed Regent (the 'Cartridge-Prince' of 1848). In Berlin a moderate liberal ministry was given office, owing some of its influence to the Princess-Regent Augusta, and soon began to put through a series of liberal measures which gave heart to other liberal-nationalists.

But Prussian conservatism was not dead; it was only sleeping. Prince William was a soldier, and put his trust in the 'God of battles', believing that Prussia's main strength was in its army. He appointed von Moltke Chief of the Prussian Staff, and von Roon his Minister of War. When his brother died in 1861, Prince William became King William I. He immediately came into conflict with his liberal government. He aimed to reorganize and strengthen the army, enrolling 39 new regiments of infantry and 10 of cavalry. The liberals, however, resisted such ambitious plans because they wanted parliamentary control over the armed forces.

Meanwhile, in Austria, Franz Josef, after a brief flirtation with aristocratic federal conservatism under Prince Goluchowski, turned in the *February Patent* of 1860 to a nominated Central Council for the whole Empire as the first instalment in a programme of reform. Austrian liberals, not perhaps aware of the dead weight of provincial resistance, favoured the idea of a centralized and efficient Empire as a vehicle for modernization, and in the end democracy. Under their leader Schmerling they were firmly in power for the next decade.

The difference was that in 1859, Prussia was liberal and progressive, whilst Austria was autocratic. In 1862, Austria was liberal and progressive, whilst Prussia was autocratic. The rise of Bismarck emphasized this transformation.

**THE RISE
OF BISMARCK**

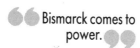

Bismarck's
background.

Bismarck was born in 1815 and saw as a youth the ambitions and the limitations of the liberal movement. Hence his life was marked by a strong political conservatism. Though much of his background was bourgeois, he liked to pose as a *Junker*, a member of the 'landed aristocracy', and aped their mannerisms and even their vocabulary. His primary loyalty lay to the Hohenzollern family whom he served, his second to the Kingdom of Prussia. At the time of the 1848 revolutions he could not conceal his contempt for German liberalism, which he dismissed as 'whimpering sentimentality'; nor did he approve of the idea of submerging Prussia in Germany. He said:

> The Frankfurt crown may be very brilliant, but the gold which provides the substance of that brilliance must first be won by melting down the gold of the Prussian crown, and I have no confidence that the recasting of it will fit the form of our Prussian constitution.

He served in both the Prussian United Diet and in the Federal Diet in Frankfurt, and gained valuable experience in politics in both. At Frankfurt, from 1850 to 1859 he observed the Austrians at work at close quarters. He soon saw that Austria and Prussia were rivals for supremacy in Germany and that the Habsburgs had no intention of treating the Hohenzollerns as equals. They preferred to regard them as minor fry, like all the other petty ruling families of Germany. He resisted all attempts by the Austrians to transform the Federal Bund into a genuine instrument of government under their own control. Though he approved of many of the reforms discussed in the Diet, such as the citizenship law, he wished to see them enacted by the separate sovereign states, so buttressing royal authority. By the same token, he refused to let the Austrians put him down in day-to-day business. It is said that when the Austrian delegate was so impolite as to smoke during a committee meeting, Bismarck lit an even bigger cigar. On another occasion, when the Austrian spokesman was in his shirt-sleeves, Bismarck threw off his own jacket saying 'Yes, it is rather hot, isn't it?'

Bismarck widened his experience after 1859 by acting for a time as Prussian Ambassador to Russia, where he saw at first hand the Tsar's policies working – it is from this time that we may date his later determination to 'keep open the wire to St. Petersburg'. He was then promoted briefly to Prussia's most prestigious embassy, in Paris, where he again profited by getting the measure of the Emperor Napoleon III. It was whilst he was serving here that he was abruptly recalled to Berlin in September 1862 to become Minister-President.

The situation between William I and the Prussian Diet by this time had reached crisis point. The king started to enrol the additional regiments he had been requesting even though the Diet forbade it. This met furious resistance both inside the chamber and on the streets. William was on the point of abdicating when Roon persuaded him to send for Bismarck and put him in charge. Bismarck found himself intensely unpopular and was even challenged to a duel by one of his opponents. With royal backing he ignored parliament, which he called the 'House of Phrases', and went on enrolling troops. When the Diet refused to pass a budget, he carried on without one, and threatened to collect taxes at the point of the bayonet. His ruthless realism soon won him the reputation of 'a bully and an absolutist', but for nearly thirty years he was one of the dominant figures on the European scene. For morality, unless it served the national interest, he showed a calculated indifference: his view quite simply was:

Bismarck comes to
power.

> Germany is looking not to Prussia's liberalism, but to its power . . . The great questions of the day will not be decided by speeches and parliamentary decrees – that was our mistake in 1848 and 1849 – but by blood and iron.

It has been said that the phrase 'blood and iron', often used to describe Bismarck's policies, does him an injustice: that by 'blood' he merely meant 'kinship', and by 'iron' he meant 'the metal industry'. But these were excuses offered for him by German nationalists and liberals, who liked to think he was really on their side. Bismarck was quite content to let them think so, as long as they did not get in his way.

Bismarck is often credited with a far-sighted, ingenious plan for political unification, continually out-witting his opponents by revealing details of his strategy little by little, while single-mindedly devoting himself to the ideal of a Greater Germany. This was the version he produced for himself after his dismissal in 1890, when he had eight years left in which to justify himself in his memoirs. In fact he was a gifted opportunist who turned the events of the 1860s to his own advantage. He did not so much unite Germany, as conquer it.

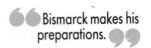
**Bismarck makes his preparations.**

It took about four years for his political opponents to accept him, part of which time some of them spent in jail. When they were released they found the apparatus of an authoritarian state much strengthened. The press was censored, meetings restricted and police powers extended. Bismarck had no theory of the Prussian state; he worked with the Diet where its members would co-operate, and ignored them where they would not. It was his view that the Prussian constitution had a 'hole'. It was supposed to work through the co-operation of the crown and the legislature, but where they did not agree, he believed the king had the right to fill the 'hole' until a solution was found. Since he had a strong army behind him this meant that the king could do whatever he liked. Some historians take the view that far from seeking to resolve this tension, Bismarck actually fostered it, since it was the one thing which bound together the ruling elements in the state – the monarchy, the upper classes, the army and the bureaucracy. Certainly he made sure that there was no serious challenge to his power for many years.

## 5 THREE GERMAN WARS, 1864–70

**The German Civil Wars of the 1860s.**

The struggles which divided Germany during the 1860s are often seen as episodes in a German civil war, much like the struggle in the U.S.A. between the North and the South. There may be some truth in this; it was certainly a struggle between the new and the old, the industrial and the rural, between two sides which spoke nearly the same language but whose outlooks were totally different. But there is some danger in pressing the analogy too far. The main objective of the 'Union' in the North was to compel the Southern states to remain within the confederation. Bismarck's main objective was to *expel* the Austrians, and substitute Hohenzollern for Habsburg domination. He said as much on a visit to Britain just before he became Minister-President:

> As soon as the army is strong enough, I shall take the first opportunity of settling accounts with Austria, dissolving the German Federation . . . and setting up a United Germany under Prussian leadership.

This was his underlying aim, though the tactics he improvized as he went along.

When the Poles revolted against Tsar Alexander II in 1863 Bismarck saw where his advantage lay. There was widespread support for the rebels amongst European liberals, and this in itself was almost enough to turn Bismarck against them. But his chief reason for refusing to support them, and even for closing the frontier to prevent refugees from seeking asylum in Prussia, was his fear of how his own Polish provinces might be stirred up by a successful revolution in Warsaw. Accordingly, Prussia and Russia signed a treaty pledging mutual support against the rebels, and rejected an offer from Britain, France and Austria to mediate. The Polish leader Langiewicz was defeated and fled into Austria, Warsaw was occupied and the revolution was stamped out. Bismarck's attitude towards his Russian neighbour and towards threatened revolution was not forgotten later in St. Petersburg.

At this point the Austrian government renewed its efforts to uncloak the selfish and reactionary stance of Prussia in Germany by once more proposing a reform of the German Federation, and calling a Congress of Princes in Frankfurt to back it. The Austrian Emperor personally invited William I to attend, and Bismarck found it difficult to dissuade him from going. Bismarck saw in the plan a manoeuvre to buttress Austrian leadership in a united Germany, and hence opposed it. Later he said:

> In the sweat of my brow I persuaded him to refuse the offer . . . When I had succeeded I was so exhausted I could hardly stand. When I left the room I was staggering and in such a nervous condition that as I shut the door from the outside I actually broke off the handle.

For though Bismarck liked to pose as the champion of German rights against the Habsburgs, he had little real sympathy with liberal-national aspirations, but – like Cavour in Italy – wished merely to use them to further his own schemes. In fact his attitude blocked the drive towards federal reform, emphasizing the division in Germany between the Austrian and Prussian spheres of influence. The showdown between them was not long delayed.

### THE DANISH WAR, 1864

**. . . in the North.**

Since the Protocol of 1852 between the Danes and their German neighbours over the Duchies of Schleswig and Holstein there had been an uneasy peace in the area. Frederick

VII had come to the throne promising not to incorporate the Duchies into Denmark; but the likelihood that he might die without a male heir made him renew his efforts in the early 1860s, for fear that his lands should be broken up. He therefore aimed to annex the Duchies and set about fostering a pro-Danish party there, and imposed on them in 1863 a reformed constitution making them part of his kingdom. When Frederick died in late 1863, he was succeeded by Christian IX (known as the 'Protocol King' because of his acceptance of the conditions laid down in 1852). Christian faced a difficult choice of presiding over the break-up of his lands, or incurring the wrath of Germany and possibly a war with the Confederation. In the end, he decided to confirm the 1863 Constitution. However, in the meantime the German claimant to the Duchies, the Duke of Augustenburg, son of the Augustenburg who was deemed to have surrendered his rights by the earlier agreement, renewed his claims, appealing to the Federal Diet to support him. They did so, sending a federal army of Saxon and Hanoverian contingents to occupy Holstein. But Bismarck had no wish to see the old Federation becoming a political and a military reality, and refused to co-operate. Instead he invited Austria, as a co-signatory, to intervene with Prussia to enforce the 1852 Protocol. Austria could not afford to stand by and let Prussia settle the matter by itself, so rather reluctantly, decided to go along with Prussia.

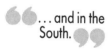 **The Convention of Gastein.**

Early in 1864 Austria and Prussia declared war on Denmark, and after an easy victory, compelled the Danes to give up the two Duchies. Austria was now in favour of installing the Duke of Augustenburg there, but Bismarck, although previously agreeing, now raised objections, insisting on such conditions for his support that eventually Augustenburg gave up his claim. At first, the Duchies were jointly occupied by Austrian and Prussian troops, but by the *Convention of Gastein* in 1865, they were shared between the two, Prussia occupying Schleswig and Austria Holstein. The Austrians were now in severe difficulties. With discontent in the provinces, their treasury empty, and a large portion of their army two hundred miles to the north and flanked north and south by numerous Prussian forces, they were trapped. Bismarck, who had already earned the Tsar's gratitude, had Russian support, and reached an agreement with Napoleon III at Biarritz in 1865 whereby the Emperor, seeing Prussia as a useful ally against Austrian domination in Germany, promised to be neutral in any conflict between them. Bismarck also secured in 1866 an alliance with the Italians, which meant that the Austrians were going to have to fight on two fronts if there was a war. In a short space of time the Austrian government had been militarily and diplomatically outmanoeuvred by the Prussians.

## THE AUSTRO-PRUSSIAN WAR, 1866

**...and in the South.**

William I drew back from a conflict with Austria, acknowledging that Prussia had no rights in Schleswig-Holstein. But Bismarck responded robustly. He reminded William of Olmütz, and told him of Moltke's and Roon's assurances of Prussian military readiness. So, ignoring criticism in Germany, the king ordered Prussian mobilization. Austria meantime had referred the question of the Duchies to the Diet. Bismarck denounced his manoeuvre, claiming that the Diet was simply an Austrian tool, and surprised Austria by proposing a scheme of federal reform. Whether he seriously meant this, or whether it was another manoeuvre to satisfy his liberal critics in Prussia and to reassure Napoleon III of the purity of his nationalist intentions it is hard to say. He certainly proposed a novel idea that the reconstructed Germany should have a national parliament based on the principle of universal manhood suffrage – a proposal that certainly far outbid any plans outlined by the Austrians. When Austria rejected it, Prussian troops marched into Holstein. Austria denounced this in the Diet, and Bismarck, stating that every vote against Prussia in that assembly would be counted as a declaration of war on them, withdrew from the Diet and declared the German Confederation at an end. War began in June 1866.

The two sides appeared very unevenly matched. Prussia had a population of only 18 million, with long frontiers broken by enemy territory. Its only allies were Mecklenburg and a few minor states. The Prussian armies numbered only 350,000, with many part-time soldiers without proper training. The Austrians had over 750,000 men who were generally considered superior. Appearances, however, were deceptive. Austrian troops were weak, and their generals mediocre. Though Austria had some allies, the south German states gave only mild support. Neither Russia nor France helped at all. Above all, Prussian artillery and small arms were better; although not always more accurate, they were more manageable, with many field guns and breech-loading rifles. Europe was surprised by the speed and completeness of Prussia's victory. Within three days Prussia had occupied Hanover, Cassel and Dresden, and in a fortnight the whole of northern Germany was under Prussian control. The Austrian commander Count Benedek, implored Franz Josef for immediate reinforcements, hoping to beat the Prussian armies which had crossed from Saxony into Bohemia before they could be joined by another under Crown Prince Frederick, advancing from Silesia. The two sides met at Sadowa in eastern Bohemia in early July. It is said that Bismarck watched the battle from the top of a large tree, with a revolver in his pocket, in case the Prussians were beaten.

King William began the battle while the Crown Prince's army was still ten miles off. The Bavarian army failed to reinforce the Austrian left wing and William held the Austrians until the Crown Prince arrived. The Prince stormed the enemy's central defence and won not only the battle but the campaign. The Austrians fell back on the nearby village of Königgrätz, took refuge on the other side of the Elbe, and shortly afterwards, with the Prussians advancing on Vienna, sued for peace. Meanwhile, the Italians declared war and invaded Venetia. Unhappily they had little success: their land forces were defeated at Custozza, and their Adriatic navy was smashed by the Austrians near Lissa. Nevertheless by this time the foundations of the Prussian victory had been laid.

**The Treaty of Prague.**

Having humiliated the Austrians in war, Bismarck had no intention of doing it again in the peace settlement. Perhaps he feared that the astonishing success of his *blitzkrieg* would alarm Napoleon and lead to French intervention. More likely he recognized his good fortune and knew when to stop. The preliminaries of peace were agreed in July, and the Treaty of Prague signed in August, only seven weeks after the war had begun. Venetia was surrendered to Italy, but Bismarck claimed no Austrian territory for Prussia and gracefully gave up any idea of a military entry into the enemy's capital. Nonetheless, the German Confederation was not restored; it was replaced by a smaller confederation, the North German Confederation to the north of the River Main, consolidating Prussia's territories and excluding Austria. The south German states were left alone, although within the year they came into close treaty relationships with Prussia. In Prussia, Bismarck was criticized for letting the Austrians off lightly, but, having angled for French neutrality during the war with Austria, he now had it in mind to secure Austrian neutrality in case he had to deal with France.

## THE FRANCO-PRUSSIAN WAR, 1870–71

Having hoped to create a subservient Prussia as his ally in Germany against the Habsburgs, Napoleon III found out that he had created a dangerous monster – a 'great grey Prussian wolf' which at first disguised itself in the harmless sheep's clothing of German nationalism. Even before signing the treaty of Prague the Emperor was looking for some reward for his support: 'a little tip', as Bismarck contemptuously called it. 'Oh, if Germany only had a Savoy', Napoleon is supposed to have sighed. Lacking this, Napoleon asked for a part of the Rhineland. Bismarck pretended to consider it, asked for a note of it in writing, and locked it away in his desk for future use. After Prague, French indignation began to mount, asking for 'Revenge for Sadowa'. Napoleon, sensing that some of the anger was directed against himself, was forced to strike ever more aggressive attitudes. Later in 1866, when the renewed French demands alarmed German feelings, Bismarck used Napoleon's memorandum to frighten Würtemberg, Baden and Bavaria into close alliance with his new Confederation in the *August Conventions*. In 1867 Napoleon turned to Belgium, suggesting that Prussia should support France if their troops entered Belgium and made appropriate frontier adjustments. When this fell through, the French Emperor made a bid for Luxemburg, suggesting the withdrawal of the Prussian garrison, the ending of the Duchy's connection with the Zollverein and purchase of the territory from the Dutch ruling house, to which it belonged. This suggestion produced an even bigger outcry, and Napoleon had to abandon it. His last effort was a rather feeble proposal in 1868 to extend special running rights to French rail traffic over the Belgian network, but this was defeated by the hostility of the incoming Gladstone government. European opinion was thus hostile to the French Emperor.

Bismarck had so little difficulty in averting French threats that by 1870 it looked as though a war with France might be avoided after all. But a sudden and unexpected storm blew up. In 1868 a revolution in Spain had deposed the former Queen Isabella, and the Spanish government eventually offered the throne to Prince Leopold of Hohenzollern-Sigmaringen, a distant relative of the King of Prussia. He hesitated to accept it without King William's approval as head of the family, but eventually decided to do so. The French Ambassador, Benedetti, met the King and informed him that his government could not accept Leopold's becoming King of Spain. William replied that the matter was out of his

The Ems
Telegram.

hands, but promised to discuss it with Leopold. He telegraphed Leopold to advise withdrawal of his candidature. Leopold obeyed, but Benedetti, on the instructions of his government, later stopped William on the riverside promenade at Ems, and pressed him for a pledge that the candidature would never be renewed. William was unaware that Leopold had withdrawn, but was irritated by the demand, and did not wish to make such a promise 'for ever and ever', as he put it. He firmly ended the interview and declined to discuss the matter further, although he did send a message to Benedetti the following day, when he found out about Leopold's withdrawal, saying that he hoped that would be the end of the affair. He subsequently telegraphed his government from Ems to tell them what had transpired. This was the famous *Ems telegram*.

Before sending the telegram to the press, Bismarck deliberately abbreviated it to make the interview appear much more curt and ill-tempered than in fact it had been, and a crisis appeared out of nowhere. The crowds in Paris roared 'A Berlin!', and those in the Prussian capital clamoured 'Nach Paris!' Bismarck, reassured by Moltke and Roon, was not upset by this, but the bombastic announcement of the French Minister of War, that his army was ready 'down to the last gaiter button', was all too soon disproved.

The fall of the Second
Empire.

Three German armies invaded France. The first, under the Crown Prince, attacked the French army in Lorraine at the point where it hinged against the army in Alsace, and defeated it at Worth. Marshal MacMahon, its commander, was forced to fall back on Châlons and leave those in Alsace to their fate. Another, under Prince Frederick Charles, inflicted a series of defeats on Marshal Bazaine and forced him to take refuge in Metz. The Emperor in person tried to relieve him, but he was outflanked and driven back against the Belgian border at Sedan. In early September he was defeated and forced to surrender with over 100,000 of his troops. It was whilst on his way to captivity at Wilhelmshohe that he was told that the Second Empire had been overthrown. Some time afterwards, the French army in Alsace surrendered at Strasburg, as did Bazaine with 180,000 men at Metz. A Government of National Defence was formed in Paris, but the Germans pressed on relentlessly against the city. Efforts were made to raise fresh troops in the provinces, whilst the Parisians defended themselves against the besieging force. All their efforts were in vain. After a four-month siege, during which the defenders suffered terribly from bombardment, cold and famine, Paris capitulated, and the war came to an end at the Treaty of Frankfurt in May 1871.

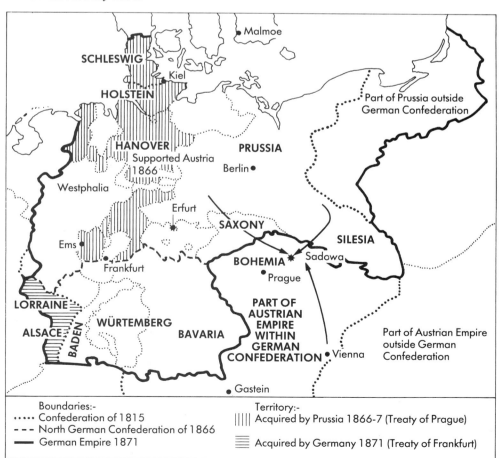

Fig 13.1  Union of Germany

Boundaries:-
•••• Confederation of 1815
- - - North German Confederation of 1866
—— German Empire 1871

Territory:-
||||| Acquired by Prussia 1866-7 (Treaty of Prague)
☰ Acquired by Germany 1871 (Treaty of Frankfurt)

**The Treaty of Frankfurt.**

By this treaty France agreed to surrender Alsace and Lorraine to Germany, to pay a war indemnity of 5,000 million francs (£200 million) in gold, and to support a German army of occupation until the treaty had been fully carried out. Privately, Bismarck suspected that these terms were too harsh and would only store up resentment for the future, but pressure from the King and from the army overruled him and he was obliged to accept.

Even before the surrender of Paris, the last scene in the story of German unification had taken place in the Hall of Mirrors at Versailles. Here, to the cheers of the assembled multitudes, William was acclaimed as German Kaiser with shouts of 'Long Live Emperor William!' He embraced his son, shook hands with his generals and strode from the Hall to the strains of the Hohenfriedeberg March. Bismarck, briefly out of favour and disapproving of developments, stood aloof, uncomfortably fiddling with a pair of white gloves.

## 6  PRUSSIA AND THE NEW GERMANY

Having succeeded in achieving a more united Germany under Prussian influence, Bismarck set about consolidating what he had won. The *external* dangers he faced – the resentment of France, the rancour of Austria and the rivalry of Russia – were grave. But the *internal* perils were almost as threatening. The supremacy of the ruling classes in Prussia and the supremacy of the Prussians in Germany were above all to be preserved.

One way to do this was through the constitution of the new Empire. This was based on that of the Norddeutsche Bund, already in existence for four years and therefore settled except on points of trifling detail. The new Reich – the first since the days of the Holy Roman Empire – was a confederation of 26 states, with Prussia the largest and most important at its head. Each state retained full sovereignty in some matters, preserving its own rulers – kings, princes etc. – its own governments and law courts, but surrendered it in others. At the centre was a federal government now in Berlin and not in Frankfurt, consisting of a legislature of two Houses, a federal executive and a supreme court: it was this central government which Bismarck had to control.

Within the Federal government, the Lower House (the *Reichstag*) represented the people of the Reich according to the population of each state, and was elected by manhood suffrage for a period of five years. The Upper House (the *Bundesrat*) represented the states as separate units, not on the basis of equality, but according to a quota agreed by the governments. This quota gave Prussia 17 seats and votes (later increased to 20 when a Prussian regent became ruler of Brunswick and controlled its 2 votes, and when the Hohenzollerns purchased the vote of the Prince of Waldeck), and all the others a much smaller number. In the Reichstag, Prussia held 235 seats out of a total of 397, and in effect, therefore, controlled the federation. Not only did it contain two-thirds of the total territory of the Reich and three-fifths of its population, but it enjoyed a built-in majority of seats in the Reichstag, and a holding of twenty votes out of 57 in the Bundesrat – enough to enable it to abort constitutional amendments, where 14 negativee votes would block the necessary three-quarters majority. Furthermore, at the head of the federal executive was the King of Prussia in his role as Emperor (*Deutscher Kaiser*). The Imperial Chancellor (the

**The Iron Chancellor.**

*Reichskanzler*) was Prussia's chief minister, Bismarck. He was much more than Prime Minister: he was above all the other ministers on the civil side, and could control all their actions, dismissing them if he chose. His counter-signature was required on all imperial decrees to validate them, and in the absence of a parliamentary tradition in the British sense, his government could not be dismissed nor his policies amended (though they could be vetoed) by a hostile vote in the Reichstag. The Kaiser said that the office was specially designed 'to fit the big cuirassier boots of Bismarck'. Nevertheless it would not be true to say that he was all-powerful. Much of his power derived from Prussia and not from the Confederation at all. Furthermore, the Reichstag in practice sometimes modified his policies, and under the constitution their approval was certainly needed for the new taxes. At the same time he had no influence over military matters, where the General Staff and the War Ministry formed an autocracy within an autocracy. Always above him there was the Kaiser. With a committee of the Bundesrat he was in charge of foreign policy and policy towards the other states; they made alliances and made war and peace. In the last analysis the Kaiser could (and in 1890 did) dismiss the Chancellor altogether in favour of another.

**The New German Order.**

The other states did not always take kindly to Prussian ascendancy in the Reich. Those in the south, more closely akin to Austria, tried to preserve their own nationalities. The Bavarians, for example, regarded themselves as Bavarians rather than as Germans, and resented the dominance of the Prussians. There were areas, too, where people of Danish, French or of Polish origin lived, and these sometimes thought of themselves as being under foreign rule. Above all, the country was divided by religion. The Rhineland, and areas of south of the River Main were Roman Catholic; those to the north were largely Protestant. This presented Bismarck with a problem. German states were given concessions to keep them sweet. They continued, for instance, to issue their own postage stamps after 1871, even though the management of the post office was a federal affair. Their princes were accorded a dignity beyond their real importance and the self-esteem of little states was fostered in a variety of ways. Non-German peoples were variously treated: the French in Alsace and Lorraine kept their own language and customs, and were assured of good employment prospects by being integrated into the industrial fabric of the Rhineland and the Ruhr. On the other hand Poles, who were more numerous and lived closer to Berlin had a much tougher time. Polish schoolchildren were flogged if they could not recite the Lord's Prayer in German. Religious strife was avoided by laws strictly limiting the powers of the Catholic Church in the Reich, whilst assuring Catholics of their liberty to worship according to their own rites. In the end Bismarck won over the Catholic Centre Party to his side, and they were numbered amongst his most loyal supporters.

Politically, too, he dealt with dangers from the Socialists and from the Liberals. The Socialists – 'these fellows without a Fatherland' as they were sometimes called – suffered persecution. Their meetings were banned, their press censored, their supporters arrested and detained. From time to time, they found themselves accused of conspiracy and even of treason. Even so, their numbers grew and by 1890 they had 12 members in the Reichstag. The Liberals were split by the government's decision to introduce a protective tariff in 1879. The National Liberals, as they called themselves, abandoned their free trade beliefs to accept it, and also became supporters of Bismarck's new order.

Perhaps Bismarck's most significant contribution to German greatness came from his industrial and economic policies. In carefully prepared stages he reversed the liberal economic policy of the mid-century until he brought in protection in 1879. Though in form it was a federation, in fact the new Reich was centralized under Prussia, and economic centralization followed the same pattern. The impetus was already provided by the Zollverein. There were other interests that were well-served by centralization. The money market benefited from a single currency and a national system of weights and measures. Capital became easier to raise for investment in growing industry. The policy had its agrarian side; not only did it help the land-owning aristocracy – the class whose interests Bismarck always fostered – but it also helped to make the country self-sufficient and to lessen the need for agricultural imports. Finally it led to the rapid industrialization of Germany, with a national, and later an international market for its produce. The German steel industry, helped by a technology which made possible the use of the limestone of Lorraine, led to the growth of railways, armaments and ship-building, and later to the secondary industries of chemicals – invaluable for explosives – electrical appliances, scientific equipment, and so on. With their monopolies of the home market secured by tariffs and pegged to a high level of prices, German industrial cartels came into being, and promoted the country's entry into the international market on very favourable terms. By 1890, German coal and steel output were rapidly closing on Britain's. The ship-building industry was nearing 100,000 tons of new output per year, and exports at £250 million a year ranked Germany third in the world league. It was only a question of time before it began to demand a powerful merchant marine, a colonial empire and a share in world power.

# IDEAS AND PRINCIPLES

**The Zollverein:** Prussia introduced a free trade area in 1818 with the intention of transforming the scattered territories of Prussia into a viable industrial and commercial unit. The first non-Prussian state to join was Schwarzburg-Sonderhausen in 1819, and by 1822 there were a number of others, including Gotha and Weimar. The success of the Zollverein led to attempts to imitate it. In 1828 there was a League of the South launched by Bavaria and Würtemberg, and shortly afterwards there was a third Union in which Saxony and Hanover played a major part. By 1833 these alternative unions had broken up and their main members had become linked with Prussia, now at the head of a true Zollverein comprising 17 states and a total population of nearly 30 million people. With an elaborate constitution and a comprehensive table of dutiable commodities it had important economic effects on Germany, promoting industrial output, the growth of imports and exports and encouraging the improvements of communications (especially railways). The Zollverein continued to grow in the 1840s with the addition of places like Frankfurt and Baden, and soon was concluding commercial treaties with foreign states such as Britain and France.

At first Metternich showed calculated indifference towards the Zollverein, but as its importance came to be recognized, attempts were made to secure Austria's admission. Negotiations in 1841 failed, chiefly because of the difficulties of either including or excluding Italy and Hungary. After the fall of Metternich, Schwarzenberg renewed Austria's efforts to gain admission; but a conference at Dresden in 1851 rejected the idea. Austria's application for membership was also rejected in 1863 and 1864. A commercial treaty was arranged between Austria and the Zollverein in 1853, and this was renewed in 1860 and 1866, but at the latter date it became terminable at only six months' notice. A year later a reform of the Tariff Parliament (in which member states were represented) made it clear that Austria was not to be allowed to take part. The tariff arrangements of the Zollverein after 1871 became part of the economic structure of the First Reich.

**Bureaucracy**    A *bureaucrat* is an office-holder, a civil or a public servant carrying out a professional function in the administration for which he draws a salary; bureaucracy is a system of government by such officials, generally reckoned to be responsible to their superiors rather than to the general public.

**Cartel**    A combination of industrial or commercial firms to prevent competition between them and to ease their operation, sometimes with a view to streamlining their activity and reducing costs, and quite often to create an artificial market monopoly at the expense of the consumer by keeping up prices. Such cartels can become very rich and powerful and (as in Germany's case) provide a powerful lobby to influence the government.

**Junker**    A member of a group of Prussian landowners with estates beyond the Elbe e.g. in Pomerania, providing the government with its leading administrators and the bulk of its officer corps for the army. The term derives from the word *Jungherr* and was first applied to sons of the nobility serving as officer cadets.

# A P P L I E D   M A T E R I A L S

## BOOKS

DICKINSON, Martin, (1986). *History in the Making: Vol. 4, Britain, Europe and Beyond, 1700–1900.* Macmillan.
RICHARDS, Denis, (1986). *Illustrated History of Modern Europe 1789–1984.* Longman, 7th Edition. Chapters 10 & 12.
WALLER, Bruce, (1986). *Bismarck.* Blackwell.
WATSON, J. B., (1981). *Success in European History: 1815–1941.* Murray. Units 5 & 7.
WILLIAMSON, D. G., (1986). *Bismarck and Germany, 1862–90.* Longman.

## MORE DETAILED BOOKS

CARR, William, (1986). *History of Germany, 1815–1985.* Arnold. Chapters 1–4.

## DOCUMENTARY SOURCES

PFLANZE, Otto, (Ed), (1968). *Unification of Germany, 1848–71.* European Problem Studies, Holt, Rinehart and Winston.
ROHL, J. C. G., (1970). *From Bismarck to Hitler (Problems and Perspectives in History).* Longman.

### AUDIO-VISUAL

Nationalism, 1850–1914                    Audio Learning   MJ/1165/12
Bismarck and the German Problem           Audio Learning   HUA 028   (More advanced)
Bismarck                                  Audio Learning   HM 0004
The Making of the German Nation           E.A.V.   N 1026   (Second Edition)

# EXAMINATION QUESTIONS

**1**   GERMANY, 1862–1949
Study the map below of Germany and her neighbouring territories, and then answer
questions a) to c) which follow.

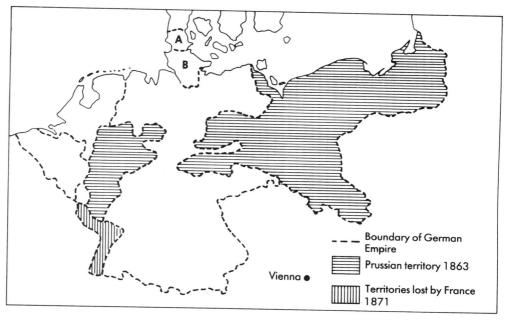

Vienna ●

- - -  Boundary of German Empire

▦  Prussian territory 1863

▥  Territories lost by France 1871

a) The territories marked A and B on the map are Schleswig and Holstein, lost by
   Denmark after a war in 1864.
   i) Why did Schleswig and Holstein become important again in 1866?
   ii) Under what circumstances was part of these territories later regained by
       Denmark.
b) What for Germany were the consequences of the Franco-Prussian War?
c) The map shows that Prussia formed a large part of the German Empire
   i) In what ways did Prussia dominate the German Empire?
   ii) How far did the other German states continue to have a place in the German
       Empire?

*(25 marks)* (SEG)

**2**   'Before 1870, Bismarck defeated France in diplomacy; in 1870–71, he defeated France
in war; after 1871 he organized Europe to isolate France.' Illustrate the truth of this
statement, *in each case* explaining Bismarck's motives.

(London)

# OUTLINE ANSWER TO Q.1

**1**   Whilst the use of the map is not strictly prescribed for the purposes of the questions
below it, candidates are clearly expected to refer in their answers to the map. For
example, in b), one of the consequences of the Franco-Prussian War is clearly the

exclusion of Vienna, the Austrian capital, from the Reich; whilst in c) i) it is obviously relevant to say that territorially Prussia dominated the new Confederation, and to use the information contained in the map to support this assertion.

In your answer to a) i), you should refer to events after the Convention of Gastein divided the administration of the two Duchies between Austria and Prussia in 1865. Failure to arrange a permanent settlement for the Duchies led to accusations from Prussia that Austria was encouraging an agitation there in favour Augustenburg; these in turn led to Austria's threat to bring the matter before the Federal Diet, and to Prussia's military occupation of Holstein and its withdrawal from the Bund. This brought the outbreak of the Austro-Prussian War in June 1866. Note that no reference is required by the question to the events of the 1864 war. The answer to ii) goes beyond the subject-matter of this chapter, though not beyond the scope of the question-heading. It involves a reference to the circumstances at the end of the First World War when plebiscites were held in Schleswig, as a result of which the northern part of the province voted to unite once more with Denmark, though the southern area, together with the whole of Holstein, was allowed to remain with Germany.

The consequences specified in b) are limited to *Germany*: you should resist the temptation to observe that the war brought the end of the Second Empire in France, or helped the Kingdom of United Italy to acquire Rome. A number of points could be made here. It established Berlin instead of Vienna as the focus of German political life; it resulted in the expulsion of Austria from German affairs; it extended the dominions of Prussia and secured Prussian control over Germany for the future; and it led to the rapid development of the country in economic, political and diplomatic matters over the next four years. Some development of detail would help the mark scored here.

Mention should be made in c) i) to the terms of the 1871 constitution, as well as to the policies of Bismarck in harmonizing the policies of the federated states and subjugating the foreign nationalities. Anti-socialist policies and the *Kulturkampf* are also relevant. Stress should be laid on the military domination of Germany by Prussia, and the subordination of German to Prussian interests in international matters. ii) requires some authentic detail to produce a convincing answer. The preamble to the constitution took the form of an international treaty, and thus depended on the consent of the various states; the executives of these states, even after 1871, continued their existence under their respective heads of government, and remained the responsibility of the separate governments, managing local matters and carrying out their share of federal decisions; the states retained their own law-courts and their own sets of laws; customs duties were collected by state officials; state mints coined the requisite money; the states issued their own postage stamps. There was no federal army in peacetime, but four separate armies belonging to Prussia, Saxony, Bavaria and Würtemberg, over which in a large number of matters these states retained control. The Navy, on the other hand, was under Imperial control, and even the merchant fleets of the states were federalized.

# A STUDENT'S ANSWER TO Q.2 WITH EXAMINER'S COMMENTS

> Before students try to write about Bismarck they ought at least to be able to spell his name correctly.

> Contains some useful detail, though perhaps a little over-simplified.

Bismark secured the diplomatic isolation of France in the later 1860s in a number of ways. He reminded the Italians how deeply they were in his debt as the result of a treaty he had brought about to give them Venetia, and pointed out that he could offer them Rome when French troops withdrew from it during the Franco-Prussian War; he also played on British fears of French designs against Belgium and suggested to the Austrians that since the French had left them in the lurch when they needed help in 1866, their neutrality would be a good way of paying the French back in 1870. Bismarck also

The student makes a useful point and comments fairly on the question. But note the misspelling of 'contemporaries'.

Quite picturesque, but deals with the *causes* of the French defeat rather than with the facts. Note also the wrong spelling of 'breech-loading'.

This appears to relate to Bismarck's domestic policies, and is not made directly relevant to this question.

Disappointing. This answer does little more than repeat the question, and is very weak on the period after 1870. The question also asks the candidate to explain *in each case* Bismarck's motives, but this answer fails to do so sufficiently clearly.

secured Russian neutrality by playing on their gratitude for Prussian support at the time of the Polish Rising in 1863, suggesting too that he had no very great reason for objecting to Russia's repudiation of the Black Sea clauses of the Treaty of Paris imposed on the Tsar at the end of the Crimean War. The result was that when war broke out Napoleon III found himself entirely without support in Europe. All the same, to give all the credit for these events to Bismarck is to fall into the trap of thinking of him as a one-man band who manipulated all his contemparies without needing anybody else's help. The credit is largely his but we must not exaggerate.

As a result of the Franco-Prussian War the French army was defeated. Its recent manoeuvres in Algeria and in Mexico did little to prepare it for the rigours of a campaign in Europe, and its morale had been rotted by long idle hours of garrison service in provincial France with plenty of girls and wine but little military duty to do except spit and polish. Though their chassepots were superior in quality to the Prussian breach-loading rifle, they were slow in being posted to their wartime stations, and many had been issued with quite irrelevant maps of Bavaria rather than of Alsace-Lorraine where they were really fighting. Many were suprised at France's defeat but it was not really suprising.

After the war, Bismarck reorganised Germany and introduced a constitution which guaranteed Prussian domination in the new Reich. He encouraged the development of German industry and trade and used economic policy to consolidate the country further. Soon Germany was very rich and had one of the biggest and best equipped armies in the world, though there was little of a navy so far. He was not really interested in overseas colonies and did not wish to upset Britain by seeming to challenge its world power. But in diplomacy he certainly organised Europe to isolate France, playing on European fears of French republicanism in order to prevent them getting allies.

# SUGGESTIONS FOR FURTHER WORK

1 Construct a map of German unification, shading and naming the main states and giving the dates at which they became linked with Prussia.
2 Write a biographical outline of the life and career of Bismarck, comparing his role in the unification of Germany with the role of Cavour in Italian unification.
3 Use brief biographies of *each* of the following to work out what his attitude was towards German unification: Tsar Alexander II of Russia; Napoleon III; William Gladstone. If you had been a political critic or opponent of any *one* of these figures, in what ways and for what reasons would you have criticized this attitude?
4 Find out in as much detail as you can what arrangements were made under the Constitution of the First Reich of 1871 for the future government of Germany. (Tip: a fairly detailed account of the provisions and working of this Constitution is given in Chapter 2 of *Germany, 1866–1945* by Gordon Craig (O.U.P., 1981).) How far would you say that it was true that the constitution was designed to fit the 'big cuirassier boots of Bismarck'?

# THE EASTERN QUESTION AND THE ALLIANCE SYSTEM

## GETTING STARTED

After the Crimean War the decay of Turkey, plagued by domestic difficulties, accelerated. In the later nineteenth century, the Balkan Question turned out to be the most complex problem confronting Europe. Reference to the physical and racial map of Europe (Fig 14.1) will reveal its main features.

The mountain and river systems divide the area up into desolate upland areas and fertile river valleys. The weaker and less organized Slavonic peoples were driven into these upland areas by the more powerful lowland peoples like the Magyars, and the whole region in the fifteenth century passed into the control of the Turks. Though they were Moslems, they made little effort to stamp out Christianity. Some of these Christian peoples were Catholics, but most were Orthodox Christians, using the Greek language for the celebration of their faith. The Patriarch of the Orthodox Church had fled to Russia at an early date, and this fact reinforced the claim of the Russians to be protectors of the Balkan Christians. In the nineteenth century the Turks permitted a national, cultural and political revival, and this led directly to the disintegration of their Empire.

# HISTORICAL DEVELOPMENTS

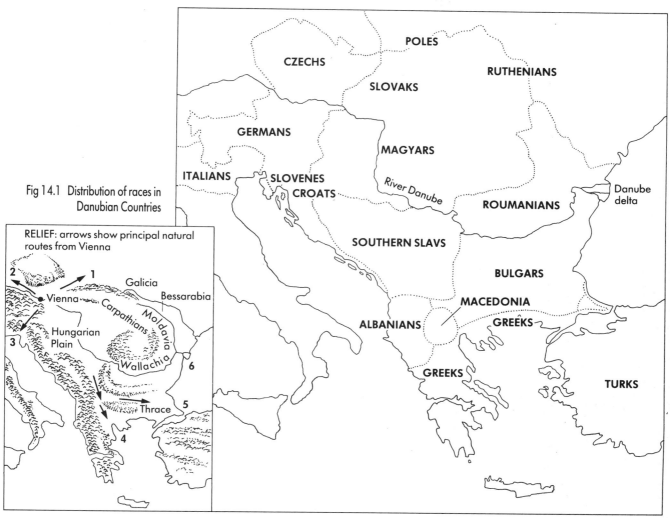

Fig 14.1  Distribution of races in Danubian Countries

RELIEF: arrows show principal natural routes from Vienna

1 > **THE BALKANS AFTER THE CRIMEAN WAR**

**The Sultan's Dilemma.**

**The Balkan Revolts.**

One requirement of the Treaty of Paris at the end of the Crimean War in 1856 was that the Turkish Sultan should improve the treatment of his subjects in order to avoid any future interference in his country's affairs by neighbouring powers. Sultan Abdul Aziz, who ascended the Turkish throne in 1861, appears to have wished to do this. He wanted to introduce widespread reforms into his empire; to improve communications and undertake public works; to improve education; to reorganize finance; and to modernize and secularize the state. Much of this effort was to no avail. Part of the failure was due to the inertia of the Turkish system, but most was due to the whims of a half-crazy monarch. The Turkish Empire, in which he carried on the dual roles of Sultan and Kaliph, remained a theocracy. Even the reforms which he started were later abandoned, usually because of lack of money. Abdul Aziz found himself in a dilemma. If he introduced reforms he had to put up taxes, yet many of his subjects refused to pay more taxes until he delivered his reforms. In particular, the north-western provinces of Bosnia and Herzegovina gave him special trouble (the Montenegrins never paid any taxes anyway). They were desperately poor, and had been in the past depopulated by frontier wars. They were encouraged in their defiance by the neighbouring Serbs, who had been semi-independent since 1829. In 1875 the inhabitants of these two provinces came out in revolt.

The Bosnians refused to pay any further taxes until their demands had been conceded, and called for help from neighbouring Montenegro and Serbia. Supported by volunteers from these countries, Bosnia defeated a Turkish army in July. Local consular officials helped the rebels to formulate their demands, which revealed for the first time the appalling conditions under which they had been living. The Porte (Turkish government) published the suggested reforms during the autumn, but the rebels were not impressed. Eventually the Austrian Chancellor drafted what came to be known as the *Andrassy Note*, which drew attention in December 1875 to the shortcomings of the Turkish government and urging immediate reform. The Note had general support, but Disraeli for Britain, who harboured dark suspicions of Russia, hesitated to approve it for fear that it should weaken the Turkish Empire, the maintenance of which was one of the prime aims of his policy. Abdul Aziz accepted the Note, promising widespread reforms as soon as the rebels laid down their arms. The rebels promised to lay down their arms just as soon as the reforms were made. So deadlock persisted and the situation steadily got worse.

**The Berlin Memorandum.**

Meeting under the chairmanship of Bismarck in May 1876, the powers now drafted the *Berlin Memorandum*, threatening action against the Sultan if he did not comply immediately with the powers' requests. The abrupt tone of this document upset Disraeli: he was prepared to let the Turkish government take its own time, and mistrusted the Russians, whom he suspected of harbouring private ambitions in the Balkans. The Turks, who had enjoyed the support of Britain on more than one occasion, noted Britain's reservations and grew less co-operative. Thus, during summer 1876, the disruption in the Balkans increased. The Turks became tired of rebuffs from foreigners, and launched a nationalist revival in the form of a *Young Turkey* movement. Its supporters deposed Abdul Aziz, replaced him by the half-witted Murad V, whom they also deposed after a few weeks, and finally settled for the stronger rule of Abdul Hamid II (affectionately known to his people as Abdul the Damned). Serbia, and then Montenegro saw their chance and declared war on Turkey. They seized control of Bosnia and locked out the Turks by shutting the Sanjak of Novibazar, the corridor through which Turkish troops had to pass in order to reach their distant province. The presence of masses of ill-disciplined Turkish irregulars in Bulgaria caused disorder in that province too. Some years earlier the Turks had been persuaded to restore the independence of the Bulgarian Church in the form of an *Exarchate* separate from the control of the Patriarch of Constantinople. Now, in summer 1876, the Bulgarians tried to speed that aim by refusing to obey Turkish officials and insisting on having governors of their own. The Turks panicked, and ordered a savage repression of the rising. A large number of troops, about 20,000 semi-savage Bashi-Bazouks from Asia Minor, were turned loose on the Bulgarians. What followed became known as the *Bulgarian Massacres*. Some Bulgarian villages were destroyed completely; in others, numbers of people locked themselves in churches, which the troops then burnt down. As many as 30,000 perished in three or four weeks.

Gladstone in Britain denounced what he called the *Bulgarian Horrors* in a pamphlet in which he demanded that the Turks

> carry away their abuses in the only possible manner – namely by carrying off themselves . . . one and all, bag and baggage . . . from the province they have desolated and profaned.

The dreadful reports of the slaughter, which Disraeli at first dismissed as 'coffee-house tattle', made it difficult for Britain to support the Turks further. Russia renewed its pressure, the Porte gave way and in December a *Conference of Ambassadors* met in Constantinople to present their demands for reform. The day before the Conference met, Abdul Hamid unexpectedly announced the granting of a parliamentary constitution which in his view made the conference quite unnecessary. The powers were amazed by this development – except the Russian representative, Count Ignatiev, who was clearly unimpressed. When, in April 1877, the Sultan revoked the constitution, removed the minister whom he had chosen to operate it, arrested him and subsequently had him murdered, Russian patience ran out altogether, and, having first secured Austrian neutrality and Romanian co-operation, the Russian government declared war on Turkey.

## 2 ▷ THE RUSSO-TURKISH WAR, 1877–78

European powers like Austria and especially Britain were, at the time, obsessed by what they saw as a grave danger from Russia, which was supposedly contemplating expansion in the Balkans, reaching out towards Constantinople as the first step towards the Middle East and India. These countries always put the worst construction on Russia's actions, however disinterestedly the Russians may have meant them. This war provided a case in point.

**The Defeat of Turkey.**

In early summer 1877 there was a renewal of the war by Montenegro and Serbia against Turkey, and the launching of a Russian offensive across the Danube into Bulgaria. At Plevna the Russian advance was halted by Turkish troops under Osman Pasha, who withstood a five-month siege until, in December, he was forced to surrender. Having broken the back of the Turkish resistance, the Russians advanced rapidly towards Sofia and Adrianople, taking both before the end of January 1878. In the Caucasus they were equally successful, capturing Kars and advancing on Erzerum. Turkey requested an armistice, and a peace treaty was signed at San Stefano, just short of Constantinople, in March 1878.

**The Treaty of San Stefano.**

By this treaty Russia was to gain Kars, Ardahan, Batum and other territories in Asia, whilst in Europe they took Southern Bessarabia from their Romanian allies, who were compensated by a useless stretch of the Dobrudja around the delta of the Danube. Serbia and Montenegro were to be enlarged, and Turkey was to recognize the independence of Romania. The Turks also undertook to demolish their fortresses on the Danube, to introduce reforms into Armenia and Bulgaria, and to allow Russia and Austria jointly to supervise Bosnia-Herzegovina. The Turkish Empire in Europe was split into four disconnected fragments, three of them out of reach from Constantinople except by sea. The most striking feature of the treaty was its proposals for Bulgaria, which in future was to be a self-governing principality of Turkey, under its own Christian government and with a national army of its own. It was to stretch from the Danube south to the Aegean, and from Albania in the west to the Black Sea. Whilst not officially a dependency of Russia, it was clear that the new state, which covered a much larger area than that occupied by the Bulgarian nation, would be heavily dependent on Moscow for money, military support and administrative expertise – a useful stepping-stone on the way to Constantinople.

Europe was aghast at the treaty. Greece, which had laid claim to Thessaly in the later stages of the war, was alarmed at the lavish extension of Bulgaria's frontiers. Romania, a loyal and useful ally of Russia was angry to have been excluded from the negotiations and to have received only the Lower Dobrudja. Austria looked with dismay on the extension of Russian influence in Bulgaria and the rest of the Balkans, Germany, which had tried to avert a split between its allies Austria and Russia over the Balkan question, now saw that it was going to have to choose between them. The British Prime Minister Disraeli was the most alarmed of all. He sent the Tsar a stern warning about the likely cost of his aggression. To back up his warning the British fleet, which had been sent to Besika Bay off the Turkish coast not far from the Straits, was ordered to pass through the Dardanelles, and Disraeli ordered 7,000 Indian troops to embark for Malta to reinforce British strength in the Mediterranean.

Russia found itself faced by a European coalition if it did not agree to resubmit the treaty to a congress for revision. Bismarck, offering his services as an 'honest broker', called a congress in Berlin in June 1878, where the arrangements made at San Stefano were extensively revised.

## 3 > THE CONGRESS OF BERLIN

The dominant figure at the Congress of Berlin turned out to be Disraeli. Even Bismarck, not easily given to compliments, said of him 'That old Jew – he is the man.' Between them, Bismarck and Disraeli largely redrew the European map and reduced the advantages which the Tsar had gained at the Treaty of San Stefano.

**The Treaty of Berlin.**

Russia was allowed to retain its conquests in Southern Bessarabia and on the eastern side of the Black Sea. But though it had been the chief victor in the war, it was not the only gainer by it. Austria was allowed to police Bosnia-Herzegovina and to garrison the Sanjak, whilst Britain was to occupy and administer Cyprus for as long as Russia held Kars and Batum. The smaller Balkan states, Serbia and Montenegro, did not get as much territory as before, and the Sanjak was opened up as the corridor to Bosnia. Romania still had to give up Southern Bessarabia in exchange for the Dobrudja. Greece got nothing at all – Disraeli said rather unkindly that Greece was 'a country with a future which could afford to wait.'

The biggest change took place in Bulgaria. The 'Big' Bulgaria was divided into three: the northern part became a self-governing state subordinate to Turkey (capital, Sofia), the middle part was restored to the Sultan who placed it under a Christian governor as an Exarchate approved by the powers (capital Philippopolis, and known as Eastern Rumelia though there was no Western Rumelia) and the southern third, Macedonia, was returned unconditionally to Turkey. The four scattered fragments of the Turkish Empire were now re-integrated to form a solid block of land from Albania eastwards to Constantinople.

The Turkish Empire had once again been saved from collapse by the intervention of the powers. But the Balkan question was postponed rather than solved, for it was not long before Turkish disintegration began again. In 1881 Greece gained Thessaly, and Turkey was powerless to prevent it. In 1885, Eastern Rumelia and Bulgaria (known as the 'Two Bulgarias') were united together, and to all intents and purposes became independent. In the early 1890s Turkish cruelty and incompetence was further revealed during the

Armenian Massacres, episodes which moved the Balkan peoples even more rapidly in the direction of independence. In 1896 there was a national uprising in Crete, and a Graeco-Turkish War, as a result of which the island achieved autonomy in 1897. The most serious situation occurred in Macedonia, an area of no clear national character and one where Serbia, Bulgaria and Greece all had natural ambitions. There had been a series of disturbances there in the 1890s, and eventually a *Macedonia Committee* was set up in Sofia in 1899 to make plans for the ending of Turkish rule in the province. In 1903 Macedonia rose in open revolt, and only international intervention at the time of the *Mürzteg Programme* laid down by the emperors of Austria and Russia averted disaster. For a few years, by general European consent, the Balkan question was 'put on ice'.

## 4   THE AUSTRO-GERMAN ALLIANCE

The decline of Turkey had an important impact on the policies of the three eastern empires of Germany, Russia and Austria after 1870. Germany had been united by Bismarck, 1862–70, and for twenty years after this was preserved by him against attack from the outside. He safeguarded the infant Reich by three main policies: keeping the friendship of Britain for as long as he could by seeming not to challenge its colonial and naval power; maintaining France in isolation, so as to prevent any attempt at a war of revenge in which the French would try to recover Alsace and Lorraine; and seeking to preserve the *status quo* in central Europe by fending off a quarrel between Austria and Russia. To this end he was successful in creating in 1872 what become known as the *Dreikaiserbund*, or League of the Three Emperors, an informal understanding between the three rulers to safeguard their interests against the kind of revolutionary republicanism manifest in France at that time. The agreement had a five-year term, and was renewed in 1877. Almost immediately afterwards came the Russo-Turkish War, the Treaty of San Stefano and the Congress of Berlin. The Tsar, who rather imagined that the Kaiser owed him a debt of gratitude for services he had rendered to Germany in 1863 and 1870, found to his dismay that Bismarck, when faced with a straight choice between Russia and Austria, chose Austria. Their *Dual Alliance* was signed in 1879, and took the form of a defensive treaty – one which gave rather more to Austria than it did to Germany. If Russia attacked Austria, Germany promised to go to Austria's assistance, but if France attacked Germany, Austria promised no more than to be neutral. It was this Austro-German Dual Alliance which turned out to be the kingpin of Bismarck's foreign policies.

 The Austro-German Alliance.

Tsar Alexander II never forgave Germany for its deceit, but after his murder in 1881, his son Alexander III vowed to repair the damage. He patched up the quarrel by producing a renewal of the Dreikaiserbund on much the same terms as before – except that this time Bismarck made it clear that he expected to be called on to mediate in any Austro-Russian quarrels in the Balkans in future. It was also to be renewed at three-year intervals, and was so renewed in 1884. Bismarck was always keen, however, to elaborate his defensive structures, and the Dual Alliance did not remain dual for very long. In 1882 Italy, upset by France's seizure of Tunis in north Africa, joined in the Alliance to make it *Triple*, and in 1883 Romania, with a Hohenzollern sovereign on the throne, became a Balkan ally and made the alliance *Quadruple*.

In 1887 the new Dreikaiserbund came up for renewal for a second time. Bismarck was still as anxious as ever to preserve a balance between the Austrians and the Russians in the Balkans and to avoid a public quarrel between them: hence he strained the resources of his diplomacy to the utmost to find a negotiated solution.

## 5   THE REINSURANCE TREATY

The terms of the *Reinsurance Treaty* between Germany and Russia in 1887 showed that the diplomatic hand of Bismarck even in his old age had lost none of its cunning. The treaty laid down the following arrangements. If Austria attacked Russia, Germany would promise to be benevolently neutral and localize the conflict, but if Russia attacked Austria, Germany threatened to 'consult her own interests' (a polite way of saying that the Russians should watch out for hostile reactions). On the other hand, if France attacked Germany, Russia would be benevolently neutral, but if Germany attacked France, Russia would likewise 'consult her own interests'. Bismarck took the view that he got all that he needed from the treaty, since he could now feel sure that in the event of a French invasion, Russia would be neutral – an assurance purchased at a small price, since he was well aware that there was little chance that Austria would ever attack Russia. There was some evidence that Russia took the same view, for the Tsar's government at first believed that there was little in the treaty for them – not even an expression of disapproval against Bulgaria, whose government the Tsar had not yet forgiven for instigating the union of the 'Two Bulgarias' in 1885–86. Bismarck secured a Russian signature only by partly disclosing details of the Dual Alliance of 1879, which had the desired sobering effect on the Russians. They signed with rather ill-grace, and Bismarck thought it best to strengthen his position by arranging the *Mediterranean Pact* to preserve the situation in the Mediterranean area and to protect Turkey in the Balkans. He also hastened to renew the *Triple Alliance* with Italy and Austria when this fell due for renewal in the same year. None of this deterred the Tsar from continuing to meddle in Bulgarian affairs, and there was a new Austro-Russian crisis. Bismarck now published the Dual Alliance with Austria to show where he stood. In the Reichstag he also made it clear:

> Bulgaria is not an object of sufficient magnitude to set Europe aflame in a war whose outcome no one can foretell. I do not expect an early breach of the peace. But I advise other countries to discontinue their menaces. We fear God and nothing else in this world.

The Russians accepted the situation in Bulgaria, and contented themselves with the thought that they had accepted the mediation of the German government in the Balkans earlier, and the new arrangement was not much different.

The old Kaiser, Wilhelm I, thought that the Reinsurance Treaty was a masterpiece. He told Bismarck he was like a juggler on horseback, who tossed five balls in the air and caught and threw them up again as they fell. He was a man of about Bismarck's own age, with a sympathetic understanding of what the Chancellor was doing, but died in 1888, as did his successor, Frederick III, shortly after. His grandson Wilhelm II, – the 'young' Kaiser, as he was called – took a different view. He regarded any secret agreement with Russia as contrary to the spirit of the existing Dual Alliance with Austria. He was probably right, for certainly the Austrian government would have been upset by its terms if they had fully been aware of them. But such moral scruples did not trouble Bismarck, who believed that what he was proposing was in Germany's best interests. When he fell from office in 1890, it is significant that the Kaiser's new Chancellor made no effort to renew the treaty, even though by this time the Russian government would have been willing.

| 6 | **THE FRANCO-RUSSIAN ALLIANCE** |

Bismarck had retired to write his memoirs in 1890, and was not surprised at what he saw as the Kaiser's lack of flexibility. Russia and France, whatever their antipathy for each other, found themselves thrust more closely together. The process had begun before Bismarck was forced out of office. Alexander III, trying to show his sympathy for the Poles, in 1888 had signed an imperial *ukase* against the further purchasing of Polish estates by German landlords. In retaliation, the German government closed the Berlin Bourse to Russian loans, cutting off much-needed foreign capital from that country. In the course of the next few years, however, Russia was able to raise the money without too much trouble in Paris, and Alexander was persuaded to swallow his dislikes of French republicanism when it was sweetened by a few hundred million francs. In 1891 the French fleet paid a ceremonial visit to Kronstadt, where the Tsar stood to the strains of the *Marseillaise*, the marching tune to which the Napoleonic armies had advanced to Moscow in 1812. In 1893, the Russian Baltic squadron returned the compliment (the Black Sea fleet, of course, was not permitted to pass the Straits) by visiting Toulon. The same year saw the signing of a Military Convention between them according to which the French were to put 1,300,000 men in the field and the Russians 800,000. Their defensive Franco-Russian Alliance was signed in 1894, though it was not announced until January 1895, after the death of the Tsar. By this treaty, France promised to help the Russians if they were attacked by Germany, or by Austria supported by Germany, and Russia promised to help the French if they were attacked by Germany or by Italy supported by Germany.

**The 'Armed Camps'.**

Thus the foundations of the two *armed camps* in Europe, the mutually-hostile groupings of the Triple Alliance (of Germany, Austria and Italy, originally with the adhesion of Romania) and the Dual Alliance (of France and Russia) were laid. As yet, Britain belonged to neither grouping, though many in Britain, like Joseph Chamberlain would have preferred the German side. Even so, by the middle 1890s, Bismarck's policy of 'keeping open the wire to St. Petersburg' had failed, and the spectre of the 'war on two fronts', which Germans so dreaded, was beginning to materialize.

## 7 > THE RISE OF SERBIA, 1903–14

Serbia had by 1900 begun to establish itself as a power to be reckoned with in the Balkans. First recognized in 1812, it achieved autonomy at the time of the Treaty of Adrianople in 1829, and its independence was confirmed at the Congress of Berlin 1878, though it did not gain all the lands it had been promised at the Treaty of San Stefano. In 1885, jealous of the power which Bulgaria achieved when Eastern Rumelia joined with the independent part of Bulgaria, Serbia launched what turned out to be a disastrous attack against its neighbour. Serbia was repeatedly defeated, and it was only the friendly intervention of Austria which saved it from complete humiliation. The country also played an important part in the Macedonian dispute at the end of the century.

To begin with, relations with Austria were fairly cordial. Though Serbia had a representative parliament, the country was governed by the semi-authoritarian dynasty of the Obrenovic, under Milan until 1889, and then under this son Alexander. Both spent a good deal of time out of country, often in Vienna, and Serbia depended fairly heavily on Austria for finance and trade. Until 1900, Serbia's policies enjoyed the benevolent patronage of the Habsburg Empire.

**The Macedonian Question.**

The Macedonian question became more acute in 1900. Greece claimed the area on historic grounds combining religion and language, and pointed out that the population of the coastal towns, including the important seaport of Salonika, were ethnically Greek. Bulgaria also claimed it, pointing out the considerable number of Bulgarians resident in the hinterland, and reminding the world that the area had been allotted to Bulgaria under the terms of the San Stefano treaty. The Serbs were also quite determined to acquire it, partly for ethnic reasons, since some of the Macedonians were racially akin to the Serbs, and partly because, in the absence of an Adriatic port, it seemed the easier way to the sea. Meantime, amongst the Turks themselves, a nationalist revival was under way, one which chafed at foreign interference in their affairs and threatened the turbulent nationalities with reprisals. Widespread disorders in the province led to its being placed under a loose sort of foreign supervision by the *Mürzteg Programme* in 1903. This irritated the Young Turks all the more.

Meanwhile, in Serbia, there had been a change of dynasty. Alexander, who had forfeited some of Austria's support because of his headstrong disregard of their advice, had married a divorcee incapable of having children, and had quarrelled with his army leaders, many of whom objected to the new Queen. In June 1903 both King Alexander and Queen Draga were brutally murdered by a crowd of drunken officers. The new king was Peter, founder of the Karageorgeovic dynasty. The family was descended from Kara George ('Black' George), a former brigand, and their behaviour was often thought to be thuggish. Peter broke with Austria and turned to Russia for support, which was finally given. Secret societies like the notorious 'Black Hand Gang', which carried out quite uncivilized acts in the name of Serb nationalism, were formed, and shocked the Austrians into deeper hostility. The antagonism between the two countries soon became evident.

**The Growth of Serbia.**

The Serbs quickly laid claim to surrounding territories. Adopting the ideas of the Bishop of Djakova, who had virtually invented South Slav nationalism single-handed, the Serbs' aim was to build a united South Slav state, to be called Yugoslavia. They began to claim Central Macedonia as rightfully theirs. They also claimed Bosnia-Herzegovina, policed by Austria since 1878, on the grounds that several million of their compatriots lived there. In 1906 there was a tariff war between Austria and Serbia known as the 'Pig War', when the Austrians increased tariffs on its chief imports from Serbia, bacon and other pig-meat. As Serbian relations with Russia improved, so those with Austria gradually grew frostier.

## 8 > THE BOSNIAN CRISIS, 1908

The Balkan problem came to life again in 1908. Early in the year the Austrian Foreign Minister Baron Aehrenthal declared the Mürzteg arrangements at an end, and announced his plans to build a railway (a branch of the Berlin-Baghdad line) down the Vardar Valley to Salonika. It became clear that Austria, tiring of co-operation, had decided to go it alone in the Balkans. At once the *Committee of Union and Progress,* a revolutionary body of Young Turks from Salonika, effected a coup in Constantinople. They forced Abdul Hamid II to programme an extensive series of reforms, and when this broke down they deposed him, and replaced him with Mohammed V, in the control of a military junta aiming at re-asserting Turkey's position in Europe. The result was rather different from the one expected. Crete broke away from Turkey and voted for a union with Greece. The Prince of Bulgaria, Ferdinand, repudiated Turkish overlordship and declared himself 'Tsar of the Bulgarians'; and Franz Josef of Austria annexed Bosnia-Herzegovina outright.

**The seizure of Bosnia-Herzegovina.**

This last coup was prepared with care and cunning. Aehrenthal had been negotiating with his opposite number in Russia, Izvolski, on a resolution of their difficulties, and had come up with the *Buchlau Bargain*. The Russians were to ditch their Serbian allies and accept the Austrian annexation of Bosnia. The Austrians were to withdraw their opposition to the opening of the Straits, provided that Russia secured the consent of its partners Britain and France. Izvolski came to London, but found neither Britain nor France willing to help. Since Austria occupied and policed Bosnia already, annexation was purely a formality; an agreement was signed and Izvolski found himself 'high and dry'. He could not complain to the Serbs without revealing that he had been willing to sell out the Bosnians in return for an Austrian treaty. Naturally he was furious, and threatened war against the Austrians.

According to the terms of their alliance with Germany, the Austrians were supposed to inform the Germans in advance of any changes proposed in the Balkan situation. The Austrian Foreign Minister did this in a curious way. At a drunken dinner-party with the German Ambassador, he whispered information into Chancellor Bülow's ear. Bülow kept the knowledge to himself, but when the Kaiser found out that he had to give the Austrians full support, he gave Bülow a private roasting, although in public declaring his intention of 'standing by his ally in shining armour' – at the same time making it clear that it had better not happen again!

The 'Knight in Shining Armour'.

Germany thus came out strongly in support of Austria, whilst both Britain and France, who found the Balkan tangle very confusing, were not at all enthusiastic on Russia's side. Izvolski swallowed his humiliation as best he could, and knuckled under to the pressure of the Central Powers. But it is significant that when war came, in 1914, he is reported to have said 'It's my war!'

## 9 THE BALKAN WARS, 1912–13

After 1908 it was clear that the Young Turks were soldiers first and reformers afterwards. Massacres of disaffected minorities began again, and the instigators went unpunished. The keynote of nationalist policies was *Turkification*. Everywhere discipline was tightened, more money spent on arms and military training (often under the guidance of German officers appointed for the task), and non-Turkish minorities suppressed. There was a Moslem religious revival too. The Greek Patriarch observed:

> We are treated like dogs. Never under Abdul Hamid or any Sultan have my people suffered as they are suffering now.

The result was a mounting tide of resentment against the continued Turkish presence in Europe, coupled with increasing evidence that reactionary policies were failing in their first aim – to strengthen Turkey. In 1911 Italy, which had long been watching the sole remaining north African possession of the Sultan, Tripoli, declared war and invaded it. The struggle was more difficult than they thought, but they eventually won. By a peace treaty signed in 1912, the Italians received the province, and shortly afterwards the Dodecanese Islands, off the mainland of Turkey itself. This was the signal for Venezelos, Foreign Minister of Greece, to organize a *Balkan League* composed of Greece, Bulgaria, Montenegro and Serbia. The League declared war on Turkey in October 1912.

The Balkan League.

The Bulgarians bore the brunt of the war, fighting on two fronts. In Macedonia they grabbed as much territory as they could get their hands on, while in Thrace they defeated the Turks in the hard-fought battles of Kirk Kilisse and Lule Burgas and moved in to besiege Adrianople. In the meantime, their allies seized most of the spoils. Serbia defeated weaker Turkish forces at Kumanov, occupied Uskub and went on to win again at Prilep. Greece invaded Macedonia from the south and threatened Salonika. By the end of the year Turkish forces had been confined to four fortresses of Scutari, Janina, Adrianople and Constantinople, and the four victorious allies had split up the Balkans between them. An armistice was arranged in December and negotiations began between Turkey and the League powers. In Constantinople, Enver Pasha changed the government, shot the War Minister and announced he would not yield another inch of Turkish territory. But when the war was renewed in February 1913, after the expiry of the armistice, his assurances proved unavailing. Turkish resistance collapsed altogether, and all the strongpoints except Constantinople fell to the League powers. Nothing remained but to yield to the inevitable.

The First War.

Grey's efforts to arrange peace terms at the Conference he called in London in the spring of 1913 were unavailing. The small powers were incapable of deciding how to divide the spoils, and hung on to what they had secured, leaving Bulgaria very dissatisfied. The large powers, too, were unable to agree. The Russians feared that Bulgaria might win what they themselves wanted and secure Constantinople. At the same time, they favoured

The Conference of London.

Serbia's claim for an Adriatic port. Austria resisted this, and Italy, with its eye on Albania, agreed. The best the powers could do was to accept the idea of an independent Albania so as to keep out its ambitious neighbours. Nobody liked this, and the Montenegrins had to be forcibly expelled from Scutari, which was then added to the new state. The worst effect was that Serbia, denied an outlet elsewhere, became all the more determined to control the Vardar Valley, and, as Germany had predicted, refused to surrender anything the Serbs had occupied during the late war.

When the Treaty of London was signed, therefore, at the end of May 1913, it failed to make any agreed arrangements. The smaller powers were simply left in control of what they had captured. So the quarrel over Macedonia and Salonika was rekindled. At the end of June, the Bulgarian army suddenly attacked the Greeks and the Serbs in their trenches in Macedonia in order to increase the size of their share of conquered Turkish lands, and the Second Balkan war began. The Serbian army defeated the Bulgarians at Bregalnica, fighting them up the Struma Valley and back into Bulgaria itself, laying waste the provinces they captured. Then the Romanians joined in, seizing the Upper (i.e. Southern) Dobrudja. Finally, the Turks seized their chance to renew the first war, and took back areas of Thrace, including Adrianople, from the Bulgarians. All in all, it was not a happy time for Bulgaria, and within four weeks their armies were completely smashed. Only the intervention of Austria prevented them from being overrun.

By the Treaty of Bucharest, August 1913, the Balkan Wars came to an end. The main loser was Turkey, now almost expelled from Europe. It had lost all its European territories apart from the small region of Eastern Thrace and the two cities of Adrianople and Constantinople. Bulgaria did not fare much better, losing most of Macedonia to the Serbs and the Greeks. They did not gain Salonika; they did not even get the second port of this coastline, Kavala. Their only 'window' on the Aegean was a short stretch of barren coast and the open roadstead of Dedeagatch. Their small gains were little compensation for their tremendous efforts, and there were now over a million Bulgarian inhabitants of Macedonia living under Serbian or Greek government. These humiliations increasingly forced the Bulgarian government to the side of the Central Powers, if only to find some way of revenging themselves on their former allies.

The Greeks did very well out of the two wars. They gained Salonika, the principal port of the Aegean, and Janina, the principal fortress of Albania. They even secured the lesser port of Kavala. But the Serbs came out of the war with an enormous increase in territories and influence. They took the whole of Central Macedonia, and acquired the two cities of

**"The Second War."**

**"The Treaty of Bucharest."**

**"Assessment."**

Fig 14.2 Balkan States 1878–1914

Uskub and Monastir. By doubling the area of their territories, they were now clearly a major threat to Austria. Indeed, it was only Austrian pressure that forced the Serbs out of part of Albania – pressure in which they obtained the full support of the Kaiser, who gave a thundering assurance of support for his ally:

> If the Emperor Franz Josef demands something, then the Serbian government must yield: if it does not, then Belgrade will be bombarded, and occupied until the Emperor's will is carried out. Of this you can be sure, that I stand behind you, and am ready to draw the sword if it is ever necessary.

The Serbs might have seen in this the shape of things to come.

## 10 > THE SARAJEVO ASSASSINATION, JUNE 1914

**❝A preventive war?❞**

By 1914 the Austrians had realized that Serbia had to be dealt with. The Chief of the Austrian General Staff, Count Conrad, believed a preventive war must be fought without delay. If it were delayed, even until 1915, there was a chance that Austria would not be strong enough to overthrow its foe. If it were left until 1917, the Serbs would be strong enough to win. Hence his advice was that no opportunity should be lost in picking a quarrel with Belgrade.

The occasion arose in June 1914, when the heir apparent to the Austrian throne, Franz Ferdinand, was to make a royal visit to Bosnia. South Slav nationalists considered him the mortal enemy of their movement because of his support for the idea of awarding the Slavs a place within the Habsburg system, possibly even an equal say with the Germans and the Magyars who controlled it after 1867. Serbian national guerrillas (such as the Black Hand Gang) seized on this as an excuse to assassinate the Archduke. The Serbian government was alarmed, and tried to warn the Austrians, but the visit went ahead in late June 1914.

An attempt was made to kill the Archduke as he arrived in Sarajevo by bombing his car. The attempt failed, but injured some of his entourage. Franz Ferdinand was angry but he nevertheless stayed to the ceremonial lunch. He decided to visit his wounded fellow-officers in hospital, but because there was no police protection along the route, followed the official route. Unfortunately his chauffeur took a wrong turning and while struggling to reverse the car Gavrilo Princip, who had been sitting on the terrace of a corner cafe, saw the car stationary in front of him. He walked over, stood on the running-board and shot both the Archduke and his wife with a revolver. He was grabbed by the crowd, and later beaten by the police. He was too young for the death penalty, but died a few years after in an Austrian jail.

Austria claimed on rather slender evidence that the plot was hatched in Belgrade, and wished to make an issue out of it. Before this could be done, however, the Austrian government, recalling the Kaiser's dire warning of 1908, first had to secure the agreement of Germany. This took longer than the Austrians had imagined, and might not have been obtained at all had it not been for Wilhelm II's morbid fear of being left without allies. Eventually he gave the support asked for, and at the end of July, a whole month after the assassination, Austria sent a fearsome ultimatum to Belgrade. Even so, the Serbian government returned a humble and accommodating reply. They accepted the ten points the document contained except two – those demanding the admission of Austrian officials to help suppress anti-Habsburg propaganda, and to take part in the trials of the accused persons – and even these they were prepared to refer to international arbitration. Austria none-the-less treated this reply as a rejection and on 28 July declared war.

**❝The Austrian Ultimatum.❞**

In the later stages of the crisis, impressed by Serbia's unexpected submissiveness, the Kaiser had urged moderation on the Austrians, but they were determined not to let their opportunity slip. They mobilized part of the army, and as Austrian guns began to bombard Belgrade, the Russians ordered mobilization. Austria and Germany followed suit, the Germans demanding that Russia demobilize, and declaring war when they failed to do so. Then Germany declared war on France as well. Italy took the opportunity to announce its neutrality. Even so, a full-scale European war was now breaking out.

At first, Britain was not involved, though the Admiralty took the precaution of preventing the disbandment of the battle fleet concentrated at Portland after finishing its naval manoeuvres. The British Foreign Secretary, Grey, asked both France and Germany whether they would respect Belgian neutrality. The French agreed at once, but the Germans made an evasive reply. The Germans made other efforts to detach Britain from France by promising to restore Belgium after the war, but in fact their troops were already on Belgian soil and were not withdrawn even when Britain sent its ultimatum. When this expired at midnight on 4 August, Britain came into the war.

# IDEAS AND PRINCIPLES

**Union of the Two
Bulgarias, 1885**

When it was set up in 1878, Bulgaria was saddled with an unworkable constitution and an unpopular Prince. He was Alexander of Battenberg, the nephew of Tsar Alexander II, and his nominee. Though he proved to be a competent ruler and quite capable of acting independently of Russia, he was hampered by resistance from within the Bulgarian Parliament (the *Sobranje*).

In 1885 the Turkish Governor at Philippopolis was thrown out of Eastern Rumelia and Prince Alexander was invited to become ruler of a United Bulgaria. Russia, however, already irritated by his lack of subservience, objected, and the new Tsar Alexander III arranged for his cousin's kidnapping and his eventual abdication. The new ruler was Ferdinand of Saxe-Coburg, an able but unscrupulous man who first exploited the talents and the loyalties of the capable Stefan Stambulov, one of the leading members of the Regency Committee chosen after the fall of Alexander of Battenberg, and when he had profited from his ideas, arranged his removal from office and his later assassination.

It was a paradox that Russia, which had been the power chiefly interested in creating Bulgaria and at first its chief patron, should now have turned against it to oppose the union with Rumelia; whilst Austria and Britain, both most alarmed by the Big Bulgaria, should now have come to regard it not so much as a stepping-stone to Constantinople as a bulwark to protect it. These facts explain why Russia in the later 1880s made several efforts to unseat Ferdinand.

**Dualism v Trialism**

Under the terms of the *Ausgleich,* signed in 1867, the Austrians, who had single-handedly wielded power in the Habsburg Empire for centuries, agreed to a share-out of power with the Magyars, the dominant nation in the eastern half of the Empire. A kind of federal arrangement was accepted, with the Austrian State government dominant in the western half of the Empire, and the Hungarian State government dominant in the east – an arrangement pithily expressed by the Hungarian leader who suggested to Franz Josef: 'You rule your barbarians, and we'll rule ours.' The Imperial Government still handled matters to do with finance, war and foreign policy, but other matters were now decided separately.

By the beginning of the twentieth century, however, of the 51 million subjects of Franz Josef, about 10 million were Magyars, 11 million were Germans, and the largest single national minority – about 26 million – were Slavs. The excellent work performed by the Austrian government in Croatia and Slovenia, and since 1878 in Bosnia-Herzegovina, in reforming and modernizing these areas, had given substantial benefits to the people and had done much towards winning over the hearts and minds of the Slav people, some of whom groaned under less satisfactory Magjar administration. To some leaders the best thing to do was to broaden the basis of the *Dual* Monarchy of Austria-Hungary, by making it instead a *Trial* Monarchy by admitting the Slavs as equal partners. This was a solution much favoured by Franz Ferdinand, and perhaps explains why the Serbian nationalists were so anxious to kill him; for if the Slavs received a useful place within the

Habsburg Monarchy, they would not be so keen to leave it, and Serbia's hopes of a take-over might be dashed.

One of the factors preventing the emergence of a unified Southern Slav state was the continuing friction between the Croats and the Serbs, a source of conflict which has never been fully overcome. Trialism would have linked the Croats with Austria, and would have divided present-day Yugoslavia into two.

| | |
|---|---|
| **Autonomy** | Self-rule; political independence. |
| **Exarch; exarchate** | An official in the Orthodox Church ranking between a Patriarch and a metropolitan bishop, exercising the functions of a legate and acting as a provincial governor; an Exarchate is the area ruled by him. |
| **Magyar** | As the name suggests, the Huns first occupied Hungary, but they were replaced about 900 A.D. by the Magyars, who dominated the area thereafter. Pronounced: *Modger.* |
| **Orthodox Church; Greek Church; Eastern Church** | After the Roman Empire was divided into two, the Western Church began to call itself 'Catholic' (i.e. universal), whilst the Eastern Church claimed to be 'Orthodox' (i.e. doctrinally correct) – both claims being rather exaggerated. For centuries the Latin language was used in the Catholic Church and even today the Greek language is used in the Orthodox Church. |
| **Patriarch** | The Catholic Church is headed by the Pope (the Archbishop of Rome), as *Father,* or *Papa* of the Church; the Orthodox Church is headed by a Patriarch, or *Chief Father.* |
| **Porte** | The name given to the Turkish Imperial government before the abolition of the Sultanate in 1922. The *Sublime Porte* appears to have been a reference to a *high gate* in the wall of the main government building. |
| **Secular; secularize** | *Spiritual* power is the type of power exercised by the church; *secular* power is temporal or civil power as exercised by the state. To *secularize,* therefore, means to reinterpret laws, morals, education etc., independently of the teachings of the church, or to replace church values by the values of the state. |
| **Status Quo** | From the Latin *Status quo ante* – the situation as it existed before. A government that is likely to lose by an alteration of the existing state of things will object to changes in the status quo: it will advance the argument that the present state of affairs is the correct one, and changes to it will have to be justified. |
| **Theocracy** | A state in which God is regarded as the sole sovereign authority, in whose name government is carried on; one where the laws are seen as divine commands rather than as human ordinances. In such a state, spiritual and temporal power coincide, and *sins* are often confused with *crimes.* |
| **Ukase** | An edict with the force of law in Imperial Russia. |

# A P P L I E D   M A T E R I A L S

## BOOKS

CASE, S.L. & HALL, D. J., (1967). *World History from 1783 to the Present Day.* Arnold. Chapter 13.

ISAAC, M.L.R., (1963). *History of Europe, 1870–1950*. Arnold. Chapters 6, 7 & 8.
LINDSAY, Donald, (1979). *Europe and the World, 1870 to the Present Day*. Oxford. Chapters 4, 5, 8 & 9.
RUNDLE, R.N., (1979). *International Affairs, Vol. I 1890–1939*. Hodder & Stoughton. Chapters 1, 2 & 3
SNELLGROVE, L.E., (1972). *The Modern World since 1870*. Longman Secondary Histories. Chapters 6 & 7.
STOKES, John & Gwynneth, (1973). *Europe and the Modern World, 1870–1970*. Longman. Chapters 4 & 11.

### DOCUMENTARY SOURCES

BREACH, R.W., (Ed.), (1964). *Documents and Descriptions in European History, 1815–1939*. Oxford. pp. 74–86, 157–162.
HURST, Michael, (Ed.), (1972). *Key Treaties for the Great Powers. Vol. 2*. David and Charles. Documents no. 108 (Treaty of San Stefano) & no. 113 (Treaty of Berlin).
PARKINSON, R., (1970). *Origins of World War One*. Wayland Documentary.

### AUDIO-VISUAL

| | |
|---|---|
| Causes of the First World War | Audio Learning HM 0016 |
| Sarajevo, 1914 | Audio Learning DM 01 |
| The Eastern Question, 1856–1923 | Audio Learning HUA 017 Track B (More advanced) |
| Origins of the First World War | Audio Learning HUA 005 & 071 (More advanced) |
| Origins of the First World War | Audio Learning EM/1250/12 (More advanced) |
| Causes of World War I | E.A.V. N 3450 |

# EXAMINATION QUESTIONS

### 1   Origins of the First World War

#### Source A

Note to the Cabinet from the Prime Minister Lord Salisbury in May 1901:
> The British government cannot undertake to declare war, for any purpose, unless it is a purpose of which the people of this country would approve . . . I do not see how we could invite nations to rely upon our help in a struggle which must be formidable, where we have no means whatever of knowing what may be the attitude of our people in circumstances which cannot be foreseen.

#### Source B

Extract from an interview with Kaiser Wilhelm II published in the *Daily Telegraph*, 28 October 1908:
> You English are like mad bulls; you see red everywhere! What on earth has come over you, that you should heap on us such suspicion? What can I do more? I have always stood forth as the friend of England.

#### Source C

From a speech made in the German Reichstag, November 1911:
> Now we know where the enemy stands. Like a flash of lightning in the night, these events have shown the German people where its enemy is . . . When the hour of decision comes we are prepared for sacrifices, both of blood and treasure.

**Source D**

Lenin in 1911:

A war with Austria would be a splendid thing for the revolution. But the chances are small that Franz Josef and Nicholas would give us such a treat.

British diplomat in July 1914:

I have my doubts as to whether Austria will take any action of a serious character and I expect the storm will blow over.

Franz Josef in July 1914:

How can we wage war if they all jump on us, especially Russia?

**Source E**

Cartoon, *A Chain of Friendship,* published in the *Brooklyn Eagle*, July 1914:

**Source F**

Telegram from Nicholas II of Russia to George V of England, sent on 2 August 1914:
Ever since the presentation of the Austrian ultimatum at Belgrade, Russia has devoted all her efforts to some peaceful solution of the questions raised by Austria's action. The effect of this action would have been to upset the balance of power in the Balkans which is of such vital interest to my Empire. Every proposal put forward was rejected by Germany and Austria.

1　a)　Which event had brought about the 'Austrian ultimatum at Belgrade' referred to in Source F?

　　b)　Explain *briefly* how the situation shown in Source E had come about in the twenty years before 1914.

2　a)　Explain why Russia was so concerned about 'Austria's action' (Source F).

　　b)　What caused the German outbursts in Sources B and C?

3　Sources A and E show that a considerable change took place in British foreign policy between 1901 and 1914.

　　a)　Using Sources A and E explain what this change in policy was.

　　b)　Using any of these sources, and your own knowledge, explain why this change in policy took place.

4　How do Sources D, E and F help to explain Austria's part in the coming of European war in 1914?

5　'Nobody really wanted war in 1914.' How useful are these sources in helping you to decide whether this statement is true or not? *(30 marks)* (MEG)

2　　a)　Why was there so much unrest and rivalry among the nations and empires of south-east Europe in the early years of the twentieth century?

　　b)　Why did Gavrilo Princip assassinate the Archduke Franz Ferdinand on 28 June 1914?

　　c)　Why were the great powers able to contain the Balkan crises of 1908 and 1911–12, but unable to prevent the Balkan crisis of 1914 from developing into a widespread European War? *(30 marks)* (SEG)

# OUTLINE ANSWERS TO Q.1 AND Q.2

1   It is not unusual in this examination to have a number of short extracts and other sources used as the basis for a question: in this case, it takes up to about 45 minutes and comprises half the examination paper. It is essential, therefore, to study the sources closely before embarking on your answers. You will observe that only 1 mark is awarded for the answer to 1) a), and that a very brief answer will suffice – though you are obviously expected to know that Belgrade is the capital of Serbia, if you are to make any sense out of the question. 1) b) is given a rather greater weighting. When you examine the cartoon, you will see that it refers to the various links in the alliance system, and asks for an explanation of how these links came about in the twenty years before 1914. Some knowledge of the Franco-Russian Alliance and the two Ententes will be expected, but detailed information of developments before 1894 will not be required.

Question 2) a) enquires into Russia's reasons for supporting Serbia in the Balkans and for being concerned about Austria's ambitions in this area. You will note that the document refers to a 'peaceful solution', suggesting either that Russia's intentions were less warlike than has frequently been supposed, or else that the Tsar was a consummate liar. 2) b) refers to two documents, B and C, and asks for explanations of German indignation. N.B. both relate to earlier crises – the first the Austrian annexation of Bosnia in 1908, and the second the Agadir crisis of 1911; furthermore, both of them are very public pronouncements, the first in a newspaper, the second in the German parliament, and have more than half an eye on propaganda impact: hence they may be expected to lack some of the cool logic of more official diplomatic documents.

Question 3) seeks to contrast the situation of Britain in 1901, the last year of its 'splendid isolation', with 1914, when it was a member of the Triple Entente, and on the brink of war. Part a) asks for an indication of the *nature* of this change from isolation to involvement, and scores 2 marks; whilst b) invites an *explanation* of the change for 4 marks. You should note that any of the sources may be employed to give this explanation, and that answers are not limited to the sources, but may contain information recalled from your own knowledge.

Question 4), for 5 marks, requires reference to each of sources D, E and F. The extracts from Lenin, the Emperor Franz Josef and the British diplomat in D show that Austria and Russia are on opposite sides, and that the Austrians have a sense of being the victims of an international conspiracy; and that at least one responsible British figure at the time of the final crisis did not take the effects of the archduke's assassination too seriously. The cartoon 'A Chain of Friendship' in E illustrates Austria's position in the alliance system, threatening Serbia and in turn being threatened by Russia. Source F presupposes a more detailed knowledge of the Austrian ultimatum, and some knowledge of Austria's (and Germany's) rejection of the Serbian response. If your answer does not refer to all these sources, you cannot expect to get the full mark.

All six sources should be used in Question 5) in your attempt to show whether the quotation – 'Nobody really wanted war in 1914' – is true or not. There seems to be little evidence that anyone except possibly Lenin actually wanted war, though no one except the British diplomat seems to have been taken by surprise by its outbreak. Far from wanting a war, both the Austrian Emperor and the Russian Tsar try to give the impression that they are against it – though there is a hint in Tsar Nicholas's words that he will fight if he has to. It must be remembered, however, that this evidence is extremely limited, and that there may be masses of other evidence much more conclusive than this seems to be.

2   a) The question here is asking for *reasons*, and to offer a *description* of the rivalry will not suffice as an answer. The underlying factors explaining the decline of Turkey and the rise of Balkan nationalism, or the issues at stake in the strategical struggle in the Balkan area between Russia and the Dual Monarchy, should be clearly spelt out. You should note the limit imposed by the question to 'south-east Europe', and avoid being tempted into discussing the conflicts, for example, between France and Germany.

b)  Some acquaintance should be shown here with the details of nationalist societies in the Balkans such as the Black Hand Gang, on whose behalf Princip was operating. This question also deals with the realm of *reasons*, and is seeking to probe what lay behind nationalist claims on Austria in 1914. You must assume that Princip was fully acquainted with these issues; it would not do to say that Princip committed the murder because he was young or because he was deluded.

c)  This is not an easy question to answer. Certainly it would not do simply to give a descriptive account of these crises and their outcome, although clearly you will have to be acquainted with this material if you are to give an answer at all. The simple answer is that in the crises of 1908 and 1911–12, the powers were anxious to seek a peaceful solution to their problems; this can be seen in the fact that Russia gave way in 1908 and accepted humiliation at the hands of Germany rather than risk a war where its government could not be sure of its allies' support, whilst in 1914 no nation appeared to be willing to counsel moderation, except possibly Britain, and Germany in the last stages, when the die was cast. A likely explanation would seem to be that each subsequent crisis reduced individual power's freedom of man-oeuvre, producing a situation in which no power dare give way. As late as the Balkan wars, however, when the minor powers, sensing that the major states feared to intervene lest they should unleash an uncontrollable catastrophe, impudently tweaked their whiskers, peaceful counsels prevailed; but no one seemed capable of checking the chain reaction of 1914.

# SUGGESTIONS FOR FURTHER WORK

1  On a map of Europe as it was in 1914, indicate the alliances which linked, and the quarrels which separated, the powers you have marked and named.

2  Construct a table of the main international crises after 1900, attaching brief notes to each to outline the main facts, and to suggest the motives of the powers involved.

3  What arguments would have been advanced by a German and an Englishman in August 1914 to justify their countries' attitudes towards the First World War? What arguments would you have used in relation to one or the other of these two to persuade them that they were wrong?

# INDEX